THE IDEA OF USURY

THE IDEA OF
USURY

From Tribal Brotherhood to
Universal Otherhood

Second Edition, Enlarged

BENJAMIN NELSON

THE UNIVERSITY OF CHICAGO PRESS
CHICAGO AND LONDON

The original edition of this volume was published by Princeton University Press as No. 3 in the "History of Ideas Series" under the editorial sponsorship and direction of the Editorial Committee, *The Journal of the History of Ideas:* John Herman Randall, Jr. (chairman), Gilbert Chinard, Arthur O. Lovejoy, Marjorie H. Nicolson (*ex-officio*), Philip P. Wiener, Paul O. Kristeller, George Boas.

Standard Book Number: 226-57160-2 (clothbound);
226-57161-0 (paperback)
Library of Congress Catalog Card Number 71-76205

THE UNIVERSITY OF CHICAGO PRESS, CHICAGO 60637
THE UNIVERSITY OF CHICAGO PRESS, LTD., LONDON W.C.1

*To My Parents, Brothers, and Friends
—And in Memory of
Max Weber and Sir Henry Maine*

CONTENTS

CONTENTS

the Ingolstadt Jesuits in support of a new extrinsic title in justification of interest on loans—J. H. Boehmer on Deuteronomy—Blackstone and Calvin

The wanderings of the ghost of Deuteronomy in the modern world—France: Turgot, Napoleon's pressure on the Assembly of Jewish Notables—England: the anonymous *Letters on Usury,* Archdeacon Paley, Bentham—Father Jeremiah O'Callaghan as quixotic champion of the Deuteronomic tradition—Father O'Callaghan's odyssey, Ireland, Rome, the United States—Summary

A. Antonio's Friendship in the Light of the Prudential Morality of Elizabethan Capitalists and Courtiers
B. Luther and Shakespeare: *Agape* and *Eros*
C. The Devaluation of "Ideal Friendships" and "Christian Charity" in International Law and Moral Philosophy (16th-18th Centuries)

CONTENTS

PROLOGUE

T HIS volume is a somewhat augmented edition of *The Idea of Usury,* which appeared in 1949 as No. 3 in "The History of Ideas Series" under the imprint of the Princeton University Press.

The enlargements comprise: this Prologue; a Notice to Readers, presented below under the title "After Two Decades"; a New Postscript, aiming to clarify a number of points which have been under discussion since 1949; lists of selected New References published since 1949, arranged in a dozen titled sections for the convenience of readers wishing to follow their own lines of interest; and, lastly, New Acknowledgments, which include some comments on the responses of readers and reviewers on the occasion of the first appearance of this book two decades ago. I have also added some formal expressions of gratitude to those who have afforded me aid, counsel, and spiritual sustenance in recent years. Apart from these amplifications, the text of the original book has been allowed to stand unchanged.

Let me quickly make a personal admission: The new pages tell a story which has its prelude here, acquires added momentum in the Notice to Readers, continues at length in the New Postscript, and comes to an end only with the last paragraph of the New Acknowledgments.

And now I turn abruptly to a few points which address themselves directly to those wishing to be informed at once concerning the book's current relevance:

One: A literary conceit of mine in the ensuing Foreword to the first edition (p. xvi) has misled excessively literal readers and reviewers into supposing that I wrote *The Idea of Usury* "as a footnote" to Max Weber. My book was fully formed before I stumbled across the passage from his posthumously published lectures that I cited in my original Foreword.

Yet it is true that once I discovered the work of Weber I found myself possessed of an anchor I had hitherto lacked.

My continuing commitment to the *spirit* of Weber's effort helps to explain why I have championed his cause against successive recent attacks on him by a number of writers, notably Kurt Samuelsson, Herbert Luethy, and H. Trevor-Roper.

The present relation of my work to Weber is more complex than one would guess from my repeated marks of readiness to enter the lists on his behalf. The New Postscript and the recent articles listed under my name in section 11 of the New References will reveal that for many years now I have been driven to go beyond Weber's *Protestant Ethic* in the direction he seemed to me to be pursuing at the very end of his career. I was doing this under the spell of the magisterial essay which he wrote as an author's general introduction to the posthumously published *Collected Essays in the Sociology of Religion,* which many scholars have mistakenly identified as an introduction to Weber's *Protestant Ethic.* This change of my outlook is already implied in my eleventh-hour footnote reference (pp. 137n-138n) to Sir Henry Sumner Maine, whose name also recalls another motif of which I must take notice next in this already lengthy Prologue.

Two: Scholars and students of the current generation seem to be finding increased meaning in my odd story of the Deuteronomic commandment on usury in the Western world. I can hardly believe that the explanation of this expanded interest is a growing taste for legendary traditions.

Every day that passes, the problems of the brother and the other, tribal brotherhood and universal otherhood, general and special friendship, and so on achieve increasing actuality on the state of world politics. Whoever doubts this has only to ponder headlines we read about Africa, Southeast Asia, and Latin America. Those who are not blinded by the blinkers of literalism will surely recognize that, in one sense at least, the episodes reported here have the ring of a parable too long lost to memory. Is it any surprise that it has occurred to one incredulous critic to wonder whether I have not spun the tale out of whole cloth? Once again I must invite each reader to make his own tests.

Lastly, a word on a situation that has greatly improved since 1949. When my work appeared two decades ago, a purist historian had only to call me a sociologist and a defensive sociologist to say that I was a historian to end the interest in my book among their respective sets of colleagues. The last two decades have seen a great move forward on this front. Throughout the world now, younger historians and sociologists, humanists and social scientists are making increasing numbers of expeditions together without mishap or remorse.

Understandably, the issue of an Italian translation of this work in the distinguished "Biblioteca Sansoni" and the current notices in the Italian press seem to me especially encouraging signs of this welcome change.

BENJAMIN NELSON

FOREWORD

MAX WEBER's account of the relation between the Protestant ethic and the spirit of capitalism has been hailed the world over. It has not, however, customarily been emphasized that to him the Reformation's denial of the supremacy of the monastic vocation was but one episode in a larger development, the permeation of Western culture by a universalist morality conducive to systematic capitalist enterprise.

In the Middle Ages, Weber noted, different standards of conduct prevailed, one for the monks and another for the world. This invidious code was outlawed by Luther and Calvin. Everyone was put under the same obligation to labor his life long in his allotted calling. To desert the world in response to Christ's counsel of perfection and to espouse the ascetic life under a formal rule no longer conferred peculiar prestige or certitude of salvation. The world itself became a kind of cloister, wherein all men, whatever their status, were declared subject to the same norms and eligible for the same rewards.

As Weber's career approached its summit, his writings came to have a new accent. He insisted that the singular triumph of methodical bourgeois capitalism in the West was exceptionally favored by Occidental priority in completing another and even more impressive advance toward the adoption of a single moral standard for all society—the transcendence of the traditionalist and tribalistic ethic of the Gentile era. In the Orient, he observed, the crystallization of a strictly competitive calculus had been checked by the persistence of clannish and communalistic associations, which bound their membership in sacred fraternal union and treated aliens as enemies, morally out of bounds. In the West, the axe had been laid both to the taboo against commercialism among the insiders and to the toleration of unlimited expropriation from the outsiders. The ground was thus cleared for the establishment of a new sort of "brotherhood," universal rather than tribal, competitive rather than cooperative, which we have here been led to call the "Universal Otherhood," a distinctive society, wherein—if we may anticipate—all men are "brothers" in being equally "others."

Was Max Weber preparing to chart the course of this evolution at the time of his premature death? Although he turned repeatedly to the problem of the destruction of the clan ethic, he never so vigorously insisted on its significance for the emergence of the Occidental capitalist spirit and society as in his last completed course of lectures in the winter semester of 1919-1920. In a sense, the present essay is a footnote to his almost concluding declaration:

"Originally, two opposite attitudes toward the pursuit of gain exist in combination. Internally, there is attachment to tradition and to the pietistic relations of fellow members of tribe, clan, and house-community, with the exclusion of the unrestricted quest of gain within the circle of those bound together by religious ties; externally, there is absolutely unrestricted play of the gain spirit in economic relations, every foreigner being originally an enemy in relation to whom no ethical restrictions apply; that is, the ethics of internal and external relations are categorically distinct. The course of development involves on the one hand the bringing in of calculation into the traditional brotherhood, displacing the old religious relationship. As soon as accountability is established within the family community, and economic relations are no longer strictly communistic, there is an end of the naive piety and its repression of the economic impulse. This side of the development is especially characteristic in the West. At the same time there is a tempering of the unrestricted quest of gain with the adoption of the economic principle into the internal economy. The result is a regulated life with the economic impulse functioning within bounds."

Weber knew—and had reminded Sombart—that modern capitalism rises upon the ruins of the tribalistic communalism of the Hebrew brotherhood. He may even have anticipated that the pursuit of this theme would lead him through the dense underbrush of exegesis on the ambivalent Deuteronomic law of usury, whose curious turnings are herein surveyed. Would he have blinked, however, at the suggestion that the road to capitalism was paved with the best intentions of Christian universalism?

B.N.

INTRODUCTION

THE Deuteronomic commandment on usury, xxiii:20-21 (19-20) has had a fateful career. Its checkered fortunes over a twenty-five-hundred-year span in Orient and Occident disclose an unexplored episode in the tangled history of "transvaluations of values" which culminated in the spirit of capitalism. To follow its meanderings from the Jerusalem of the Prophets and Priests to mid-nineteenth century Europe is to survey the major phases of the ethical evolution of the West: first, the kinship morality of the tribal society; then the universal brotherhood of medieval Christianity; and finally the utilitarian liberalism of modern times.

The story falls readily into five parts. In the following pages, however, the venerable text, which will be discovered to have served as prime protagonist of the piece, at once its hero and its villain, is introduced only by way of prologue. The proper theme of the four chapters of this essay will be a chronicle of the vicissitudes of the wandering Hebrew commandment in the Western Christian world.

Prologue—Deuteronomy formed a cornerstone of the blood brotherhood morality of the Hebrew tribesmen. It assumed the solidarity of the *mishpaha* (clan) and the exclusion of the *nokri* (the foreigner, as contrasted with the *ger*, the protected sojourner, or the *toshab*, the resident stranger) from the privileges and obligations of the fraternity.[1] It for-

[1] W. Robertson Smith, *Lectures on the Religion of the Semites*, ch. ii, and 75-78; Max Weber, *Das antike Judentum*, 357; A. C. Welch, *The Code of Deuteronomy*, 214-15; A. R. Siebens, *L'origine du code deutéronomique*; A. Causse, *Du groupe ethnique à la communauté religieuse*, esp. at 123; 125, n. 5; 151, 161, n. 3; 175; A. S. Peake, *Brotherhood in the Old Testament*, esp. 75-78. The hostility to the *nokri*, it is generally agreed, is especially intense in Deuteronomy. L. G. Lévy, *La famille dans l'antiquité israélite, passim*, esp. 86-89; A. Bertholet, *Die Stellung der Israeliten und der Juden zu den Fremden*; J. A. Selbie, *s.v.* "Foreigner," *in Dictionary of the Bible*, ed. J. Hastings, II, 49-51. A systematic review of Hebraic concepts of social relationships will now be found in H. A. Wolfson, *Philo*, II, 352-64, esp. at 363-64.

bade the Hebrew to take *neshek* (usury, interest) from his brother (*aḥ*),[2] but permitted[3] him to exact it from the *nokri*:

> XXIII:19. Thou shalt not lend upon usury (*neshek*) to thy brother (*l'aḥika*); usury of money, usury of victuals, usury of anything that is lent upon usury:

> XXIII:20. Unto a stranger (*nokri*) thou mayest lend upon usury; but unto thy brother thou shalt not lend upon usury,

[2] Elsewhere, the Bible proscribes increase or interest of any sort (*marbith* and *tarbith*, as well as *neshek*) from brothers. Lev. xxv:35-37. On numerous occasions, the Bible enjoins the Hebrews to treat the *gerim* as brothers. See, e.g., Ex. xxii:21; Lev. xix:33-34; Lev. xxv:35-37. Indeed, the last mentioned text seems to have forbidden the taking of usury in all forms from the *ger* and the *toshab*. See the remarks *ad loc.* in the commentaries on Leviticus by J. Smits, A. Bertholet, D. Hoffmann; also, P. van Hove, *Liber Deuteronomii*, II, 238-39. There is, however, a grammatical vagueness in the passage which permitted the *Mishnah* and the *Talmud* to conclude that the prohibition referred to the *ger*, but not to the individual they described as the *ger toshab*. See the *Mishnah, B.M.*, v. 6, in tr. of H. Danby, 356; *Babylonian Talmud, B.M.*, 70b-71a, in the new tr. issued at the Soncino Press under the general editorship of I. Epstein, 407-13. The phrase, *ger toshab*, occurs only once in the Bible: Lev. XXV:47. See *s.v.* "*ger*" and its variants in the concordances of Gesenius and Mandelkern. Indeed, many modern scholars incline to the view that originally the reference was to *ger ve-toshab* ("*ger* and *toshab*") in the usual fashion. The *Mishnah* and *Talmud*, however, proceed from this singular allusion to build a comprehensive distinction between the *ger* and the *ger toshab*, which helps to explain their aforementioned interpretation of the usury law of Leviticus. The *ger*, the Rabbis say, is a full proselyte. The *ger toshab* is defined in various ways. According to *R. Meir*, the term refers to a Gentile who foreswore idolatry in the presence of three devout Hebrew witnesses. The majority of scholars describe him as an incomplete proselyte who would not promise to abstain from forbidden foods: some authorities say that he undertook to observe only the seven Noachian commandments; others, that he swore to fulfill the whole *Torah*, with the exception of the dietary laws. See *Bab. Talmud, 'Abodah Zarah*, 64b, in the Soncino tr., ed. I. Epstein, 313-14. (I am indebted to Professor Boaz Cohen of the Jewish Theological Seminary for helping me in the final stages of this essay with the verification and interpretation of numerous Hebrew texts.)

[3] Maimonides (1135-1204), however, citing the second century *Sifre* on Deut., ed. M. Friedmann, §263, f. 121b, contends that Deut. xxiii:21 (20) constituted a positive commandment, rather than a permission. *The Book of Divine Commandments (The Sefer Ha-Mitzvoth of Moses Maimonides)*, tr. by Rabbi Charles B. Chavel, Vol. 1: *The Positive Command-*

that the Lord thy God may bless thee in all that thou settest
thine hand to in the land whither thou goest to possess it.[4]

I. Moralists of the Middle Ages found the double-edged
text a constant source of embarrassment, a simultaneous and

---

ments, no. 198, pp. 332-33; *idem, Mishneh Torah, Malveh ve-Loveh*, v:1-2.
Professor Baron observes: "This interpretation runs counter to the talmudic tradition to such an extent that Maimuni's juridical predecessors
and successors almost unanimously repudiated this view." See "The Economic Views of Maimonides," *Essays on Maimonides*, ed. Salo W. Baron,
226-27. For the references to the *Mishnah* and *Talmud*, see the preceding
note. Rashi (1040-1104) seems to lay stress on another portion of the
talmudic interpretation of Deuteronomy: the Hebrew may not *pay* interest
to his brother—by so doing, says Rashi, the debtor violates two negative
commandments and one positive commandment—but he may pay interest
to an alien. See *Pentateuch . . . and Rashi's Commentary*, tr. by Rev.
M. Rosenbaum *et al.*: *Deuteronomy*, 116. Sombart's summary of the significance of the Deuteronomic issue in the Middle Ages is doubly mis-
leading. See W. Sombart, *The Jews and Modern Capitalism*, tr. by M.
Epstein, 242-43; cf. the interesting remarks by Weber in *The Protestant
Ethic and the Spirit of Capitalism*, tr. T. Parsons, 271; *idem, General
Economic History*, tr. Frank H. Knight, 356-60 (these pages include the
excerpt quoted in the Foreword). Not only does Sombart misstate the
theoretical status and practical significance of the text among the medieval Jews, but he fails to do justice to the complex history of the law
and practice of restitution of usury and illicit gains in the Christian world.
For a preliminary discussion of the latter problem, see B. N. Nelson, "The
Usurer and the Merchant Prince," *The Tasks of Economic History*, VII
(1947), 104-22. A fuller treatment will be found in my forthcoming volume, *Restitution of Usury in Later Medieval Ecclesiastical Law*. It is
wrong, moreover, to exaggerate the economic, at the expense of the religious elements, in the explanation of Maimonides' poorly received innovation. He, like the *Talmud*, was concerned above all to insulate the
Hebrew community against contamination by foreign idolatries. Thus,
despite his attribution of commandatory character to the Deuteronomic
discrimination, he reiterates the talmudic reservations upon its application. Authoritative tradition is guided in this matter by the following
presumptions: debtors are generally anxious to avoid creditors; creditors,
on the other hand, are compelled willy-nilly to seek the company of
debtors. Therefore, any Hebrew may borrow at usury from a Gentile,
but loans to Gentiles are discouraged, being tolerated only to a limited
extent (not beyond what the lender needs for his livelihood) and, then
primarily, in the case of scholars, who are assumed to be proof against
heterodoxy. However, any Jew may exact the various "shades of usury"
from Gentiles. Much stronger limitations are put on the text by other
medieval rabbis. It is to be hoped that a scholar versed in medieval Hebrew

unparalleled challenge to the Church's general prohibition of usury and the Christian program of universal brotherhood. Medieval Christianity, aspiring to universalism, rejected the Deuteronomic discrimination against the alien as anachron-

---

literature and law will soon be inspired to undertake a documentary survey of the fortunes and significance of the Deuteronomic commandment in the Jewish community. Meanwhile, see Moses Hoffman, *Der Geldhandel der deutschen Juden während des Mittelalters bis zum Jahre 1350*, 76-77, 169-70; Joseph Jacobs, *The Jews of Angevin England*, 224-25; Israel Abrahams, *Jewish Life in the Middle Ages*, 237-39; D. Hoffmann, *Der Schulchan-Aruch und die Rabbinen über das Verhältniss der Juden zu Andersgläubigen*. Cf. notes 3, 7, 11, 34, and 49 in ch. I; also, pp. 99-100, 111-13.

[4] St. Jerome in the Vulgate generally renders *nokri* by *alienus*, *ger* by *advena*, and *toshab* by *peregrinus* or *inquilinus*. See *s.v.* "alienus," "advena," etc. in Bechis's Concordance; see also under appropriate passages in *Biblia sacra polyglotta*, ed. B. Walton; *Biblia sacra . . . Sixti quinti Pont. max. iussu; Biblia sacra . . . iussu Pii PP. XI*; but, above all, see notes and commentaries in the ed. by the Antwerp Franciscans toward the end of the 18th century. At Deut. xv:3, which involves the applicability of the Seventh Year release (*Shemittah*) to non-Hebrews, the Vulgate translates *nokri* by *advena et peregrinus*. See, esp., P. van Hove, *Liber Deuteronomii*, II, 59, 235-44; also, *ad loc.* in *Biblia sacra polyglotta*, and *Die Heilige Schrift*, ed. A. Bertholet.

The kinship basis of the Deuteronomic usury provision is emphasized by J. Hejcl, *Das alttestamentliche Zinsverbot*. For other modern renderings and interpretations of the passage under discussion here, see the commentaries on Deuteronomy by the following: S. R. Driver, 265-67; A. Bertholet, 74; E. König, 162-63; George Adam Smith. 274-75; D. Hoffmann, 42-43; H. Junker, 98-99; J. H. Hertz, 286-89; J. Reider, 218-19; cf. the excursus of H. Loewe, "On Usury," in *Starrs and Jewish Charters*, ed. I. Abrahams *et al.*, II, pp. c-ci; also, W. H. Bennett, *s.v.* "Usury (Jewish)," *Encyclopaedia of Religion and Ethics*, ed. J. Hastings, XII (1922), 555-56. The recent debate over the influence of the biblical anti-usury laws in the transactions recorded among the Adler papyri (134 B.C.-89 B.C.) emphasizes the need for a comparative study of interest-free loans in Antiquity and the Middle Ages. See *The Adler Papyri*, ed. E. N. Adler *et al.*, 3-6; cf. the critical comments by Ulrich Wilcken in *Archiv für Papyrusforschung*, XXX (1939), at 218-20, and the exchange of views between V. Tscherikower and F. M. Heichelheim in *Harvard Theological Review*, XXXV (1942), 25-44; also, Jacob J. Rabinowitz, "Some Remarks on the Evasions of the Usury Laws in the Middle Ages," *ibid.*, XXXVII (1944), 49-59. Eduard König minimizes the effectiveness of the Deuteronomic prohibition in the Jewish community at Elephantine. König, *Das Deuteronomium*, 162-63.

istic and obnoxious, and proposed to transcend the morality of clan by joining the "other" to the "brother."

II. The German Reformation marks the turning point in the fortunes of the Deuteronomic commandment. That age saw the issues of usury and brotherhood furnish the occasion for sanguinary social struggles between the conservative and radical elements of several Protestant nations. The alternatives at stake were posed in the following fashion: Were the fraternalistic institutions celebrated in the Old and New Testaments alike meant only for a day, or were they the expression of God's plan for all the ages? More precisely, were the Sabbatical and Jubilee releases, the prohibition of usury between brothers, and the love-communism of the Apostles in the early Jerusalem congregation mere expedients for special circumstances, or were they the supreme illustrations of God's eternal will?

The opposed groups answered these questions in entirely different ways. The radical preachers declared interest charges, usury, and in some cases even private property, to be anti-Mosaical and unchristian. In the New Jerusalem, as in the Old, brothers were to dwell together in a spirit of love, and not to exploit one another. The conservative reformers (Luther, Melanchthon, Zwingli, Bucer) took this program to be an invitation to social revolution and eventual anarchy. Rather than face the overturn of civil society and political government, they proclaimed the Mosaic law dead, without power to bind the conscience. The New Testament, they added, was not meant to serve as a civil constitution for the direction of this world. These propositions as such, it must be said, did not constitute an authorization of usury, or an abrogation of the idea of brotherhood, but they did speed the advent of the new order of Universal Otherhood.

III. Modern capitalism found the Deuteronomic law disserviceable in two different respects:

A. Within the circle of the in-group, Deuteronomy consecrated the rule of traditionalist restrictions which hampered the accumulation of capital and the progress of the capitalist spirit.

B. The assumption of hostility against the alien implied a world perpetually at war, in which the respect for the rights of property did not extend beyond the borders of the group.

Capitalism could not mature under such conditions. It required a society where uniform rules were observed wherever the game was played. At the same time, modern exegetes friendly to expanding capitalism cherished the isolated Deuteronomic exception as heaven-sent proof of their contention that their medieval predecessors had exceeded the Lord's mandate in proclaiming a universal prohibition of usury. Beginning with Calvin (1509-1564), they showed how it was possible to escape both horns of the Deuteronomic dilemma: they sloughed off the discrimination against the alien by appealing to the Christian brotherhood, and sloughed off the prohibition of usury, the inevitable corollary of the Hebrew and medieval exhortations to brotherhood, by triumphantly citing the Deuteronomic exception.

IV. No group was proof against the blandishments of the new interpretation. A formal disavowal of the double-edged standard by an official Jewish body came in the first decade of the nineteenth century. Soon after Napoleon's accession to the imperial throne, he called upon the Jews to renounce the antiquated commandment as a price of initiation into the brotherhood of Frenchmen.

In the Catholic world, Deuteronomy was dealt a crushing blow by innovating jurists in the middle of the eighteenth century. Notwithstanding the rough handling to which it was subjected at that time, however, the old text continued to lead a kind of spectral existence in traditionalist circles down to almost our own day. A desperate attempt to revive the ghost of the old Commandment is associated with the name of a quixotic priest, an exile from his native Ireland, who died on American soil on the eve of the outbreak of the Civil War (1861).

[xxiv]

In short, Western morality after Calvin reaffirmed the vocabulary of universalism, refused to concede that God could authorize or equity allow us to treat the Other differently from the Brother, assimilated the Brother to the Other, and eventuated in the Universal Otherhood.

In modern capitalism, all are "brothers" in being equally "others."

THE IDEA OF USURY

CHAPTER I

Medieval Universalism and the Deuteronomic Double Standard

T HE chronicle of the changing interpretations of Deuteronomy in Western exegesis begins with a dictum by St. Jerome (340-420), and an elaborate commentary in De Tobia[1] of St. Ambrose of Milan (340-397). They were the first authoritative Western theologians who strove to harmonize the irritating text with the ecclesiastical stand on usury. Jerome contended that the prohibition of usury among brothers in Deuteronomy had been universalized by the Prophets and the New Testament.[2] There was, in short, no scriptural warrant for taking usury from anyone.

[1] Ed. and tr. Lois M. Zucker (1933); cf. ed. K. Schenkl in CSEL, XXXII.2 (1897); Migne, PL, XIV.

[2] Comment. in Ezechielem, vi:18, in Migne, PL, xxv, col. 176. How difficult it was for some early Christian writers to arrive at a completely universalistic interpretation of the Deuteronomic laws is evidenced among the Greek Fathers by the failure of Clement of Alexandria (ca. 150-211/216) to go far beyond the exegesis of Philo Judaeus (ca. 30 B.C.-A.D. 45). Philo takes the term "brother" to mean "not merely a child of the same parents, but anyone who is a fellow-townsman (ἀστός) and fellow-tribesman (ὁμόφυλος); De virtutibus, XIV: 82, tr. and analyzed, now, in H. A. Wolfson, Philo, II, 365; cf. tr. by F. H. Colson, VII, 211. Josephus (37-95), incidentally, concludes from Deut. xxiii:19: "It is not just to draw a revenue from the misfortunes of a fellow countryman (τοῦ ὁμόφυλου)." Antiquities, IV: 266, ed. and tr. Thackeray, IV, 603-4. Clement declares that the Law, as exhibited in Deuteronomic prohibition, treats as a "brother" not only "one who was born of the same parents, but also whoever is of the same tribe, [namely] of the same faith, and who participates in the same logos [Logos?]." The Greek text reads: . . . οὐ μόνον τὸν ἐκ τῶν αὐτῶν φύντα γονέων, ἀλλὰ καὶ ὃς ἂν ὁμόφυλος ᾖ ὁμογνώμων τε καὶ τοῦ αὐτοῦ λόγου (Λόγου?) κεκοινωνηκώς, Stromata, ii, cap. 18, 84, 4 in Migne, PG, VIII, cols. 1023-24; in ed. O. Stählin, II, 157. I am deeply indebted to my colleague, Prof. Christian Mackauer, for his assistance in verifying the interpretation of the passages from Josephus and Clement. Evidence continues to mount that an unequivocally universalist treatment of the word brother in the Deuteronomic context did not become established in the West until the 12th and 13th centuries.

Ambrose proposed to account for the Deuteronomic discrimination against the alien by an appeal to Biblical antiquities. The true meaning and limits of Deuteronomy xxiii:20, he argued, were clear only in the light of the authorized war of the Chosen People against the tribes inhabiting the Promised Land. "The Law forbids you under any circumstances," Ambrose warned, "to exact usury from your brother." Who is he? Your brother is "your sharer in nature, co-heir in grace, every people, which, first, is in the Faith, then under the Roman Law." Who then, was the stranger? The Amalekite, the Amorite, the Canaanite: the notorious foes of God's people, who illegally withheld the lands which the Lord had promised to Israel for a habitation.

> From him, it says there, demand usury, whom you rightly desire to harm, against whom weapons are lawfully carried. Upon him usury is legally imposed. On him whom you cannot easily conquer in war, you can quickly take vengeance with the hundredth. From him exact usury whom it would not be a crime to kill. He fights without a weapon who demands usury: he who revenges himself upon an enemy, who is an interest collector from his foe, fights without a sword. Therefore, where there is the right of war, there also is the right of usury.[3]

The Carolingian Age saw the promulgation of a general prohibition of usury among Christians, whether lay or ecclesiastical. The moral overtones of the new legislation are less clearly exhibited in the Frankish capitularies, however, than in the commentaries of leading theologians.[4] An exceptionally clear illustration of the ambiguities in the Christian attempt both to spiritualize and to universalize the double-edged Hebrew Commandment is to be found in the gloss on

---

[3] *De Tobia*, xv:51, freely adapted from ed. and tr. L. Zucker, 66-67; ed. Schenkl, 547-48; Migne, *PL*, xiv, 779. In order to eliminate confusion in tracing the subsequent debate over Ambrose's exegesis among medieval writers, I have deliberately accepted their slightly variant reading of his text as a basis for the above translation.

[4] F. Schaub, *Der Kampf gegen den Zinswucher*, 26-75, esp. 33-40.

Deuteronomy associated with the name of the distinguished scholar, Rabanus Maurus (784-856).

Rabanus' exegesis makes no reference to Ambrose. But he, like Clement and Ambrose before him, strives with only partial success to find the basis for an unqualified universalist interpretation of the old Commandment. Deuteronomy xxiii: 19, Rabanus asserts, is proof of the benignity and justice of the Divine legislator in commending us to show charity rather than fraud and avarice to the indigent. By "brother," Rabanus continues, is meant any and every Catholic. According to the spiritual sense, we ought freely to provide the fruit of the Word to every Catholic brother inasmuch as he joins us in partaking of the celestial wafer. The "alien" in Deuteronomy, Rabanus explains, refers to infidels and criminals. To them we give money at usury when in compensation for the expenses incurred in preaching of the Word we demand the repentance of sins and, above all, faith together with good works. There are, in short, two meanings of the word "money" in the passage, Rabanus concludes. To take usury for the loan of "metallic money" is entirely forbidden; to ask usury for the offering of "spiritual" sustenance is legitimate.[5] A definitive rejection of Ambrose's formula was destined to be deferred until the Age of the Crusades.

With the beginning of the Crusades, alert churchmen were pained to discover that Ambrose's resolution opened the door

---

[5] Rabanus Maurus, *Enarratio super Deuteronomium*, lib. iii, cap. 12, in *PL*, CVIII, col. 934. For Rabanus' role in the Carolingian anti-usury legislation see Schaub, *op.cit.*, 61, n. 2. According to Schaub, the Deuteronomic issue received but brief and infrequent treatments in the Carolingian epoch. This was due, he thinks, to economic causes. *Ibid.*, 64-66. Rabanus' exegesis of Deut. xxiii constitutes a considerable advance over that of the Venerable Bede (672/673-735). Bede writes: "*nec fenerabis fruges*, id est legis; sed alieno, id est gentili populo." *PL*, XCI, 92. Bede's interpretation of the Sabbatical release in Deut. xv provides an interesting contrast to the tenor of the various inferences drawn from the passage in the Age of the Reformation. Says Bede: "Per septimum annum, quo dimittitur, activa vita exprimitur." *Ibid.*, 387; cf. Rabanus' fuller statement in the same spirit. *Ibid.*, CVIII, 390-95. The relations between the Hebraic releases, and the ideas of usury and brotherhood will be discussed in our next chapter.

to unwelcome economic and religious developments. They decided to throw off the double burden which his awkward defense of the Deuteronomic proviso had saddled upon Christianity by resorting to new exegetical strategies more in harmony with the economic interests of the Church and the universalist teachings of Christ.

All formulations of international economic policy were now seen to hinge on the adjustment of this issue. Unqualified acceptance of Ambrose's teaching authorized Christians to demand interest from Moslems—a few of the early commentators on Gratian's *Decretum* (*ca.* 1140)[6] pointed out that this was a useful economic weapon in recovering their rightful heritage as Christians from the modern Canaanites —but it also gave the Jews in Europe *carte blanche* to continue to exact usury from their Christian debtors.[7] There

[6] Enhanced publicity and authority were given to Ambrose's formula by its inclusion in the *Decretum*. See c. *Ab illo*, C.XIV, qu. 4, c. 12, headed by Gratian's dictum: "Porro a quo usurae exigendae sunt, Ambrosius testatur. . . ." Gratian fails to note Ambrose's subsequent intimation that by Luke vi:34-35 the *mutuum* is to be provided even to enemies. *De Tobia*, XVI:54. The editorial summary of cap. XVI in Migne, *PL*, XIV, cols. 780-81 goes somewhat beyond the text at this point.

[7] According to the chronicler, the monk Rigord (d. *ca.* 1209) of Saint-Denis, the Jewish usurers cited this text in self-defense. *Gesta Philippi Augusti*, ed. H. F. Delaborde, 24. Cf. the striking opinion of Rabbi Moses of Paris, who flourished not long before Rigord, which is cited by Joseph the Zealot (*Hamekanne*) in his polemical compilation of the last quarter of the 13th century:

They [the Gentiles] reproach us for doing usury and quote what David says (Ps. xv), "He that lendeth not at usury . . . he shall not perish." Answer: David was Moses' disciple, he could not, therefore, place himself in contradiction to his master by making additions or omissions in the Law: now Moses has said: "To the stranger thou mayest lend at interest, but to thy brother thou shalt not lend at interest." Our persecutors will perhaps pretend that they are our brothers in virtue of the verse, "Despise not the Idumean, for he is thy brother" (Deut. xxiii:8 [7]) but to that R. Moses of Paris has replied: "The prophet Obadiah has established that this brotherhood no longer exists, for he has said: 'Foreigners entered into his gates, and cast lots upon Jerusalem, even thou wast as one of them.' (Obad. verse 11). Now he is speaking of Edom, as may be seen from the beginning of his discourse."

Tr. in J. Jacobs, *The Jews of Angevin England*, 224-25, from Z. Kahn,

was the rub. In the eyes of the Popes, especially Innocent III (1198-1216), effective promotion of the crusades[8] required the curtailment of all usurers, Jewish as well as Christian, clerical as well as secular. Aided by formal government licenses and priestly collusion, these different but equally abhorred sorts of usurers were exploiting the opportunities for lush profits in commodity corners and loans on the security of lands which were thrown on the market by the crusade-bound nobility. The view of Ambrose allowed a loophole, also, for double-dealing Italian, South French, and Catalan merchants, who persisted, despite repeated papal fulminations, in providing the Saracen enemy with money and supplies.

Before long, these concerns were superseded by fears of a more radical challenge to the existing economic order and morality. By the end of the twelfth century, "manifest" Christian usurers were outstripping the Jews, and were well on their way to becoming an international menace. Like Judas Iscariot, contemporaries said, these parvenus stood ever ready to betray Christ and the Christian brotherhood for thirty pieces of silver. There were even those who dared to

---

"Étude sur le livre de Joseph le Zélateur . . . ," *Revue des études juives*, III (1881), 1-38, esp. 7-8, with the following observation: "It is an example how the lower minds among the Jews excused themselves for what they knew to be wrong. That the view was not shared by other Jews is shown by the comment: *There is nothing in it* [the argument] added by the compiler of the Book." (The above verse from Obadiah is cited here from the King James version for the sake of clarity.) Jacobs finds a reference to a "Mosse de Paris" in an English Liberate Roll dated 1204. H. Gross identifies R. Moses with the prominent Parisian Rabbi, Moses ben Jehiel ben Mattathiah, of the latter half of the 12th century. See Gross, *Gallia Judaica*, 513.

[8] For the link between usury and the crusades, first broached by Eugenius III in his bull, *Quantum praedecessores nostri* of 1145, see: E. Bridrey, *La condition juridique des croisés*; Edith C. Bramhall, "The Origin of the Temporal Power of the Crusaders," *American Journal of Theology*, V (1901), 279-92; A. Gottlob, *Kreuzablass und Almosenablass*. Innocent's actions against Jewish usurers in France may now be followed conveniently through the texts assembled and translated in S. Grayzel, *The Church and the Jews in the XIIIth Century*, esp. at 85-143.

cite God's word, Deuteronomy, against the Church prohibition of usury. Christian morality and feudal society were in the balance. Thus challenged, the Church felt called upon to check the economic revolution in the making by redefining the problem of the Brother and the Other.

The threat to the professed universalism of Christianity embodied in the Ambrosian analysis could no longer go unanswered. The double standard for the Brother and the Other appeared mysterious, paradoxical, anachronistic, and vicious to Christians, who were fascinated by the vision (or vocabulary) of a morality rooted in the Brotherhood of Man under the Fatherhood of God. It seemed altogether incompatible with Christ's summons to love our enemies. Had He not challenged Deuteronomy and pointed the new way in Luke vi:35:

> But love ye your enemies, and do good, and lend, hoping for nothing again; and your reward shall be great, and ye shall be the children of the Highest: for He is kind unto the unthankful and to the evil.

How mysterious the blood brotherhood morality of the Jews appeared to such Christians may be seen in the confession in St. Bruno of Asti's (d. 1123) *Expositio in Deuteronomium* that he could not perceive God's motives in permitting the Jews to take interest from aliens.[9]

---

[9] "Non vacat tamen a mysterio, quod alieno populo, Judaeis, fenerare ad usuram licet." Migne, *PL*, CLXIV, col. 528. It must be admitted, however, that when this passage is read in its context, it may not appear to mark so genuine a break with the exegesis offered by Rabanus Maurus. The following represents St. Bruno's complete assessment of the Deuteronomic passage: "Haec verba pietate et dilectione plena sunt, quibus admonemur, ut sine usura iis subveniamus, quos ut idem genus nostrum, et ejusdem religionis diligere debemus. Unde non minus in Novo, quam in Veteri Testamento feneratores damnantur. Non vacat tamen a mysterio, quod alieno populo, Judaeis, fenerare ad usuram licet. Nos enim ad usuram et legem, et prophetas ab eis accepimus: in usura enim non solum id quod datur, sed etiam id quod non datum est, per se luitur. Unde manifestum est, nos ad usuram legem et prophetas suscepisse, qui in eorum solutione praeter litteram, spiritualem quoque intelligentiam, solvimus. Sacra enim Scriptura et pecunia nobis est, et aurum, et argentum, et cibus, et potus,

Without venturing to iron out the Ambrosian difficulty, the Second Lateran Council of 1139 declared the unrepentant usurer condemned by the Old and New Testaments alike and, therefore, unworthy of ecclesiastical consolations and Christian burial.[10]

The influence of Rabanus Maurus is still strong in the *Glossa ordinaria,* currently said to be a compilation of the first half of the twelfth century. Though all are our neighbors, observes the *Glossa,* mercy is to be shown especially to those who together with us are members of Christ. The apparent legitimations of usury in both Deuteronomy xv and Deuteronomy xxiii apply only to the sort of "spiritual" usury approved in the Parable of the Talents (Matthew xxv: 14-30).[11]

Peter Lombard (*ca.* 1100-1160/1164) alluded neither to Deuteronomy nor to Ambrose in his discussion of usury. In the manner of the traditional exegesis, soon to be qualified, he lumps usury together with fraud, rapine, and theft as an "illicit usurpation of another's thing," plainly prohibited by the Mosaic commandment against theft. He suggests his

---

et frumentum, et vinum, et oleum, et similia." *Loc. cit.* See, however, St. Bruno's spectacular comment on the Sabbatical release of Deut. xv, *ibid.,* 457-58. This is closer in spirit to the left-wing of the Reformation (see below, ch. II) than it is to Bede's interpretation cited above, n. 5.

[10] J. D. Mansi, *Sacrorum conciliorum nova et amplissima collectio,* XXI, cols. 529-30, c. 13.

[11] *Glossa ordinaria,* on Deut. xv, in *PL,* CXIII, col. 466; *idem,* on Deut. xxiii:19, 20, in *ibid.,* 478-79. Customarily identified with the name of Walafrid Strabo (809?-849), the "preceptor of Germany," pupil of Rabanus, the *Gloss* is now declared to be a compilation of composite authorship dating from the 12th century. Beryl Smalley explains "that the *Gloss* on the Pentateuch is based on a compilation by Walafrid Strabo," but adds that the principal role in assembling the older materials and introducing new comments was played by Gilbert "the Universal," Bishop of London (1128-34). Smalley, *The Study of the Bible in the Middle Ages,* 44; cf. the same, "Gilbertus Universalis, Bishop of London (1128-34), and the Problem of the 'Glossa Ordinaria,'" *Recherches de théologie ancienne et médiévale,* VII (1935), 235-62; VIII (1936), 24-60. H. H. Glunz's earlier study places the *Gloss* in the second half of the 12th century; *History of the Vulgate,* esp. at 103-5.

general attitude on the Deuteronomic issue, however, by his treatment of the correlated problem of the plundering of the Egyptians by the Jews (Exodus iii:22). He follows St. Augustine in arguing that when the Jews carried off the precious vessels and vestments of the Egyptians, they acted on the command of God, and therefore incurred no imputation of theft or blemish of sin. There was, in short, no exception to the commandment against theft, and presumably against usury, which was merely a form of theft.[12]

Peter Comestor (d. 1179) created a new fashion by insisting that the taking of interest was not declared to the Jews as a precept, but conceded to them by God because He feared that if He refused them this, they would do worse—take usury from their own brothers. For a similar reason, the Lord sanctioned the bill of divorcement, the *libellus repudii* (Deut. xxiv:1-5): "What is said about the brother is a precept; what is said about the alien is a permission, which is also the case for what follows about the bill of divorcement."[13]

Exceptional interest attaches to the exegesis of the influential Parisian teacher, Peter Cantor (d. 1197). His expositions of the Bible, so vivid in their characterizations of the abuses in contemporary economic life, inspired one of the most intensive preaching campaigns against usury that the Middle Ages were to witness.[14] Moreover, his interpreta-

[12] *Liber sententiarum*, III: 37, *PL*, cxcii, col. 832.

[13] *Historia scholastica*, *PL*, cxcviii, col. 1256.

[14] For the anti-usury program of the Peter Cantor circle, see Peter Cantor's *Verbum abbreviatum*, *PL*, ccv, cols. 144-47, 255; Caesarius of Heisterbach, *The Dialogue on Miracles*, bk. II, ch. 33, in tr. by H. von E. Scott and C. C. Swinton Bland, I, 119-20; Stephen Langton, *Quaestiones*, excerpted from MS in F. M. Powicke, *Stephen Langton*, 16, n. 1; Matthew Paris, *Chronica majora*, ed. H. R. Luard, v, 404; V. Mortet, "Hugue de Fouilloi, Pierre le Chantre, Alexandre Neckam et les critiques dirigées au douzième siècle contre le luxe des constructions," *Mélanges d'histoire offerts à M. Charles Bémont*, 105-37; M. R. Gutsch, "A Twelfth Century Preacher," in *The Crusades and Other Historical Essays*, ed. by L. J. Paetow, 189-98; A. Cartellieri, *Philipp II. August, König von Frankreich*, III, 183-84.

tion of Deuteronomy xxiii is doubly notable: a) it provides an unusual insight into the exploitation of the ambivalent character of the Deuteronomic passage by princely patrons of usurers; b) it embodies a mode of analysis which was to recur, albeit with very different emphasis, in the writings of Luther. The detestable usurers, Peter cries in his *Verbum abbreviatum,* are now the bosom companions of princes and prelates, who surrender to the blandishments of the money bags and promote their sons to the highest posts in Church and State. The Christian usurers, to avoid annoyance, camouflage their faith and masquerade as Jews, and the princes will not suffer them to be charged with a crime, saying: "These are our Jews." Indeed, they are much worse than Jews, since the Jew is forbidden to take interest from his brother only, and permitted by the Lord's promise to take it from aliens; the Christian is charged by the Lord to refrain from taking usury from anyone.[15] Peter Cantor's allusion to the Lord's promise is clarified by the summary of his views offered by

[15] *PL*, ccv, col. 158: "Isti etiam nomen Judaeorum adepti sunt. Principes enim eos tuentes, non permittunt eos super aliquo crimine accusari, dicentes: 'Isti nostri judaei sunt,' imo pejores judaeis sunt, quia judaeus ex praescripto legis 'non foeneratur fratri (Deut. xxiii),' sed tantum alieno ex promissione; iste autem et proximo et alieno contra praeceptum Domini foeneratur." Sovereign authorities, secular and religious alike, resorted to Deuteronomy repeatedly in the Middle Ages to justify the exaction of usury by their Jewish subjects from Christians. It is not so well known, however, that the prohibition of usury between Jews was not a dead letter in Christian law. In a notable case in 1272, the English Court of the Exchequer of the Jews, staffed by Christian judges, acted on the assumption, to quote a recent writer, "that though it was permissible for a Jew to take usury from a Christian, it was unlawful for him to take usury from another Jew." The Prior of the "New Hospital without Bishopsgate," "vouched to warranty" in the trial, called for the voidance of a *starr* between two Jews, on the ground that "according to the Statutes of Jewry, Jew ought not to take usury from Jew, in like manner as according to the Law of the Land, Christian may not take usury from Christian." See J. M. Rigg, *Select Pleas, Starrs and other Records from the Rolls of the Exchequer of the Jews,* 65-68, cited in Rabinowitz, *Harvard Theological Review,* xxxvii (1944), 49. Regrettably, it is not clear what principles were entertained by the Court in defining usury in the case in question.

Robert de Curzon (d. 1219), one of his outstanding disciples. According to Robert, Peter Cantor seems to have read the reference to the alien in the light of the promise made to the Hebrews throughout the book of Deuteronomy. In short, Peter Cantor is reported to have said, the disputed text directs the following message to the Jew: "Thou shalt not lend to thy brother in the Holy Land; but there thou shalt enjoy such abundance that thou wilt lend at usury to the alien, that is, aliens will ask thee to lend to them."[16]

With his usual uncompromising severity the headstrong and quixotic de Curzon[17] threw the Ambrosian testimony out of court, on the ground that the text was morally obnoxious and anyway the work of the "pseudo-Ambrose," whoever he may have been.[18] Deuteronomy is to be interpreted in the light of Exodus xxii:21 and Leviticus xxv: 35-37, which protected the *ger*. Today the Jews ought not to take usury from us, who are strangers (*advenae*) rather than foreigners to them.[19] The text means, he argues, that although those who take interest from strangers or issue a bill of divorcement sin mortally against God, there is no law in force by which they may be punished.[20]

The conclusions of the vigorous Peter Cantor circle were sharpened by William of Auxerre (d. 1230/1232). The practice of usury, he insists, is a sin, *in se* and *secundum se*.

[16] *Le traité "De Usura," de Robert de Courçon*, ed. and tr. by G. Lefèvre, p. 7.

[17] The best studies to date are F. J. G. de La Porte du Theil, "Mémoire sur la vie de Robert de Courçon," *Notices et extraits des manuscrits de la Bibliothèque Nationale*, VI (1800-1801), 130-222, 566-616; B. Hauréau, "Notice sur le no. 3203," *ibid.*, XXXI, pt. 2 (1886), 261-74; Marcel and Christine Dickson. "Le Cardinal Robert de Courçon: Sa vie," *Archives d'histoire doctrinale et littéraire du moyen-âge*, IX (1934), 53-142. A new attempt to appraise his singular economic policies and his turbulent career will be found in my forthcoming *Restitution of Usury*.

[18] G. Lefèvre's inconclusive discussion of the readings; *Le traité*, 7, n. 1.

[19] *Ibid.*, 7. De Curzon argues, however, that "cum justum est bellum sicut illud quod committitur in terra sancta, signati ibi non rapiunt nec furantur bona aliorum, sed bona sua sibi assumunt . . . quia illa tota orientalis regio jure hereditario nostra est. . . ." *Ibid.*, 11.

[20] *Ibid.*, 7.

Although it was never licit for the Jews to take interest, they were yielded permission to do so for the same reasons for which they were accorded the resort to the bill of divorcement, in order to avoid a greater evil and because it was difficult to bring them to perfection all at once. In the opinion of many masters, he remarks, the canon *Ab illo* is the work of the "heretical" pseudo-Ambrose. The prohibition of usury is even more rigorous than the commandment against murder: there is no exception to the law against usury, whereas it is on occasion even meritorious to kill. The instance of the plundering of the Egyptians by the Jews is not relevant to the problem of usury, since in that case the Jews were but appropriating the wages which were long due them. Still following de Curzon, he asserts that the land inhabited by the infidels rightly belongs to Christians.[21]

Alexander of Hales's (d. 1249) review of the arguments exhibits a different emphasis. It was not licit, he declared, to take usury from an alien even in ancient times; it was merely permitted the Jews *propter duritiam cordis,* because of the hardness of their hearts.[22] God feared that they would commit the greater sin of taking usury from a brother. Secondly, as others have pointed out, Ambrose was not discussing usury properly speaking, but tributes, exacted from infidels to promote their conversion to the faith. If interest is to be taken only from those whom we have a right to kill, we ought hardly to call it interest at all, because those whom we have a right to kill have no proper title to their goods, and therefore usury does not constitute a usurpation—"tunc proprie loquendo in hoc sensu nomen usurae trahitur a propria significatione: quia non est usurpatio rei alienae."[23]

Usury is and always has been a sin by its own nature, *secundum se,* said Albertus Magnus (1193/1196-1280) and

---

[21] *Summa aurea in quattuor libros sententiarum* (Paris, P. Pigouchet, 1500), f. 223.

[22] A helpful definition of hard-heartedness is given by Bernard of Clairvaux, *On Consideration,* tr. by G. Lewis, bk. i, ch. 2, p. 19.

[23] *Summa theologiae,* pt. 3, qu. xxxvi, memb. 4, art. 2.

not because the prohibition by law made it such. He preferred the arguments based on the *libellus repudii* and the *duritia cordis Judaeorum* to the exoneration of Deuteronomy on the grounds that the Jews were engaged in recovering their own lands from the Canaanites. He dismissed the allusion to the Promised Land as a "bad example," and an unsafe counsel, since every kind of evil ought to be avoided. As for Ambrose, he was merely being paradoxical: his principle is obviously based on the "impossible hypothesis that we can desire to injure anyone without sinning."[24]

Thomas Aquinas's (1225-1274) summary is brief and clear:

> The Jews were forbidden to take usury from their brethren, i.e., from other Jews. By this we are given to understand that to take usury from any man is simply evil, because we ought to treat every man as our neighbour and brother, especially in the state of the Gospel, whereto all are called. . . . They were permitted, however, to take usury from foreigners, not as though it were lawful, but in order to avoid a greater evil, lest, to wit, through avarice, to which they were prone, according to Is. lvi:11, they should take usury from Jews, who were worshippers of God.[25]

The special permission granted to the Jews in Deuteronomy, he replied to the inquiring Duchess of Brabant, has long lapsed. They may not legitimately retain what they have exacted from others by usury, and are bound to restitution, despite all government decrees to the contrary.[26]

The same range of attitudes and scale of values are found in all the prominent theologians of the epoch.[27] Among ex-

[24] *In iii. Lib. sent.*, dist. 37, art. 3, ad 3m, in *Opera* (ed. Borgnet), XXVIII, 702.

[25] *Summa theologica*, 2ª. 2ᵃᵉ. 78. 1 ad 2m, from translation, with modifications, by the Dominican Fathers, x, 331-32.

[26] *De regimine Judaeorum*, in *Opera omnia* (Rome, 1570), XVII, 192v-193r; in ed. S. E. Fretté and P. Maré, XXVII, 413.

[27] See Franciscus de Mayronis (d. 1327), *Scriptum super quattuor libros sententiarum*, lib. iv, dist. 16, qu. 3, at f. 212; Alvarus Pelagius (d. 1352), *De planctu ecclesiae*, lib. ii, cap. 46, f. 92; Henricus de Hassia

egetes, the early Decretists[28] are the only ones who do not show an equal degree of impatience and displeasure with the Ambrosian resolution. Rarely troubling to reconsider the problem from the standpoint of moral philosophy, they followed Gratian in recording the *Ab illo* as a legitimate exception. According to Rolandus Bandinelli, who ascended the papal throne as Alexander III in 1159, laymen may exact usury from heretics, from infidels, and from those who openly attack the Church. Through the afflictions of usury, he felt, the enemy would be recalled to the unity of the Church.[29] The Saracens and heretics whom it has not been possible to conquer by arms, Rufinus suggested, would be compelled under the pressure of usuries either to yield to the Church or to cease to disturb it.[30] Bernard of Pavia (d. 1213) assumed the legitimacy of taxing the Saracen with usuries.[31] Huguccio (fl. 1188) and Johannes Teutonicus (fl. 1216)

(Heinrich von Langenstein, d. 1397), *Tractatus bipartitus de contractibus*, i:23-25 in Gerson, *Opera omnia*, IV, 195; cf. the canonist, Astesanus of Asti, *Summa de casibus conscientiae*, lib. ii, tit. 2, on c. *Ab illo*. Pelagius received the degree of *Dr. jur.* from Bologna, but he is noted chiefly as a theologian. Hurter, *Nomenclator*, 3d ed., II, col. 626. The assertion of J. Favre and some other French writers on the law of usury that Franciscus de Mayronis means to condemn only usury taken from the poor and implicitly allows increments taken from wealthy people and merchants is based on a faulty understanding of the Scotist presuppositions of Franciscus' mode of analysis. See J. Favre, *Le prêt à intérêt dans l'ancienne France*, 110; M. Mémin, *Les vices de consentement*, 173. A similar stricture applies to their interpretations of the views of Durandus de Sancto Porciano (d. 1332) and Chancellor Johannes Gerson (1363-1429). For a clearer presentation of the opinions of these later medieval theologians, see E. Schreiber, *Die volkswirtschaftlichen Anschauungen der Scholastik*, 172-76, 204-6.

[28] The best available descriptions, biographical and bibliographical, of the Decretists are to be found in the publications by Stephan Kuttner, especially his *Repertorium der Kanonistik (1140-1234)*. For the period after 1234, it is still necessary to consult the classic work of J. F. von Schulte, *Die Geschichte der Quellen und Literatur des canonischen Rechts.*

[29] See Rolandus, *Summa*, ed. F. Thaner, on C. XIV qu. 4, p. 29.

[30] *Summa decretorum*, ed. H. Singer, on C. XIV qu. 4, p. 342. This work was completed between 1157 and 1159.

[31] *Summa decretalium*, ed. E. A. T. Laspeyres, on X. v. 15. c. 5, p. 235.

foreshadowed, but did not themselves accept, a reformulation of the Ambrosian issue. Both legitimized the taking of usury from an enemy, "whether pagan, Saracen, Jew, heretic or Christian, when one has the right to wage war against him."[32]

A new source of indecision was bequeathed to canonists and Church authorities by the compromise decree (canon *Quanto amplius*) adopted by the Fourth Lateran Council of 1215. Embarrassed by the hostility shown by lay powers, especially in France, to efforts by the clergy to enforce a strong anti-usury program in conjunction with Innocent III's call for a crusade, the assembled Fathers chose to straddle the troublesome issue by threatening Christians with ecclesiastical censure if they persisted in associating with Jews who failed to make satisfaction for "heavy or immoderate usuries" (*graves immoderatasve usuras*).[33]

The qualifying phrase invited divergent constructions. Bishops and lay authorities issuing powers to Jewish moneylenders blandly cited the text in self-defense.[34] Jurists who

[32] T. P. McLaughlin, "The Teaching of the Canonists on Usury (*XII, XIII, and XIV Centuries*)," *Mediaeval Studies*, I (1939), 81-147, esp. at 137; II (1940), 1-22.

[33] X. v. 19. c. 18; Mansi, *Sacrorum conciliorum nova et amplissima collectio*, XXXI, 1054; Grayzel, *The Church and the Jews*, 306-9. See above, pp. 6-7.

[34] J. Aronius, *Regesten zur Geschichte der Juden im fränkischen und deutschen Reiche*, no. 741, p. 313. At various times in the Middle Ages, Jewish leaders undertook to justify the practice of moneylending at usury by their coreligionists. See Grayzel, *The Church and the Jews*, 46, notes 24-26. An especially impressive array of arguments seems to have been advanced by Rabbi Meir ben Simon of Narbonne in an audience in the closing months of 1246 before the "Chief Governor" (?) of Narbonne, protesting the recent ordinance of Louis IX against Jewish usurers. Regrettably, the principal summaries of the manuscript are too vague at critical points to inspire confidence. See: A. Neubauer in *Archives des missions scientifiques et littéraires*, ser. 3, I (1873), 551-61, esp. at 556-57; H. Gross, "Meïr b. Simon und seine Schrift Milchemeth Mizwa. Analekten," *MGWJ*, XXX, n.s. XIII (1881), 295-305, 445-52, 554-69. According to Neubauer, whose account seems to have been followed in its main outlines by all subsequent writers, Rabbi Meir proved, to the satisfaction of the "governor" (?) of Narbonne, that "the divine law forbids usury, but

were partisans of a total prohibition of usury, however, claimed that the adjectives were meant to describe all usury as heavy and immoderate. Earlier decrees of Innocent, particularly the canon *Post miserabilem*[35] were pressed into service to prove the obligation of Jews to make restitution of usuries.

The Decretalists generally took heart from Innocent's legislation and the new theological commentaries and broke with Decretist tradition. Raymond of Pennaforte (fl. 1234) put the problem as follows:

May Jews exact usury from Christians? And may Christians take usury from Jews, pagans, or other enemies of the Christian faith? Jews, he replies, in the first instance, sin mortally: they ought to be compelled to refund usuries in accordance with the decision of Innocent III's *Post miserabilem.*

This position, he admitted, seemed to contradict Ambrose's view. How, then, are we to understand Deuteronomy; how, Ambrose?

---

not interest," reminding him at the same time that the "codes" of the "Holy Emperor" in force among the Christians allowed two to three per cent annually (?). A. Neubauer, *op. cit.*, 556-57. Dubnow assumes that Rabbi Meir distinguished between excessive usury and reasonable interest, which the Rabbi is said to have insisted was forbidden neither by the Bible nor by the Christian Emperor. See S. Dubnow, *Weltgeschichte des jüdischen Volkes*, v, 31-32. Where in the Bible or the talmudic tradition would the Rabbi have found grounds for such a distinction, which was Christian and post-medieval in origin? Thirteenth century Christian canonists and theologians permitted *interesse* and forbade *usura*, but drew the line between them in a different fashion. *Interesse* and *usura* were different in kind, not in degree. Then again, was the Rabbi talking only of loans to Gentiles or of loans in general? In the former case, usury (*neshek*) was plainly permitted by the Bible and Talmud without regard to rate; in the latter case, the Rabbi could hardly have meant that a low rate of interest might be taken from a Jew. See above, p. xvi, n. 2. Finally, it would be desirable, also, to have the precise wording of Rabbi Meir's plea to Christian persecutors that all men were born in the image of God, their common Father. Did he in the course of his defense of "interest" speak of Jews and Christians as constituting a brotherhood?

[35] *PL*, ccxiv, cols. 308-12, excerpted in X. v. 19. c. 11.

Four glosses on the text have been proposed by previous writers, he declared. Some related it to ancient times, when the Jews were permitted to take usury from aliens. Others turned the tables on the Jews, saying *"Ab illo,* viz., from the Jew, demand usury, i.e., great rent." Many insisted that the text authorizes us to recover our rightful property from enemies of the republic, whether from pagans or from Jews, who are really our slaves and obligated to serve us. Nevertheless, the chief authorities argued that the passage does not sanction the taking of interest from Christian, Jew, pagan, or anybody else, and expounded Ambrose in this fashion: "From him demand usury, O you, whoever you may be, whom you rightly desire to harm: but you ought rightly desire to harm no one; therefore, you ought to demand usury from no one."[36]

Hostiensis (d. 1271) hedged; he included the Ambrosian formula, "cui velles iure nocere," in his mnemonic list of exceptions to the general prohibitions of usury, but disputed the right of Jews to take usury from Christians: he cited Deuteronomy xxviii:12 and 44 in clarification of xxiii:19-20.[37] Guillelmus Durantis, the "Speculator" (1237-1296), denied that it was legitimate to take usury from infidels.[38] Now and then in the later Middle Ages a canonist broke the ranks. Henricus Bohic (d. *ca.* 1350) authorized Christians to demand usury from enemies of the Church and the Roman Empire.[39]

In fifteenth-century Italy, economic expediencies com-

[36] *Summa* [*casuum*], lib. ii, tit. vii, in ed. of Verona (1744), 216. Raymond's discussion is followed by Monaldus (d. 1288/1289), *Summa perutilis atque aurea* . . . , f. 292r.

[37] *Summa aurea,* lib. v, rub. *de usuris,* col. 1623.

[38] J. Berthelé and M. Valmary, *Les instructions et constitutions de Guillaume Durand le Spéculateur,* 35.

[39] *In quinque decretalium libros commentaria,* on X. v. 19. c. 8, p. 174, cited in McLaughlin, *Mediaeval Studies,* I, 139, n. 468. Matheus Romanus (fl. 1320) is said by Zabarella (d. 1417) to have approved the taking of usury from enemies such as Saracens, if the creditor be animated by zeal and Christian charity, rather than by avarice. Perhaps, Matheus thought,

THE DEUTERONOMIC DOUBLE STANDARD

pletely overshadowed moral philosophy as a force in the propagation of Christian universalism. The Brotherhood of Man was the banner under which antisemitic friars, especially of the Franciscan Observants,[40] cloaked their demagogic appeals to expel the Jewish pawnbrokers, who had swarmed from Rome and Germany into the Italian towns in response to municipal invitations to set up shops, with licenses to take from 20 to 50 per cent on petty loans.[41] Paced by Bernardino da Feltre (d. 1494),[42] the Observantine preachers regurgitated the oft-discredited charges of ritual murder, incited mobs to attacks on Jewish life and property, and harangued the people and their magistrates to destroy the Jews, and establish Christian pawnshops, the *monti di pietà*. By 1509, eighty-seven such banks[43] had been set up in Italy with papal approval despite the insistent pleas of traditionalist theologians, chiefly Augustinians and Dominicans, that the interest charges taken by the *monti* were contrary to all tradition, natural and Divine law, and subversive of Christian brotherhood.[44]

In the heated polemic, which was not entirely silenced even by the decree of Leo X at the Fifth Lateran Council of 1515

---

those who could not be conquered by arms might be overcome by usuries. "Enemies" are defined as those upon whom the Emperor or Pope wages war. Zabarella, *Lectura super Clementinas*, on §*Sane*, c. *Ex gravi* [Clem., v. 5. c. 1. §a], f. 183, col. 2, no. 7, qu. 11.

[40] K. Hefele, *Der Hl. Bernardin von Siena und die franziskanische Wanderpredigt in Italien während des XV. Jahrhunderts.*

[41] The literature and developments are surveyed in H. Holzapfel, *Die Anfänge der Montes Pietatis (1462-1515)*; Maurice Weber, *Les origines des monts-de-piété*; V. Colorni, "Prestito ebraico e comunità ebraiche nell' Italia centrale e settentrionale con particolare riguardo alla comunità di Mantovà," *Rivista di storia del diritto italiano*, VIII (1935), 406-58; F. R. Salter, "The Jews in Fifteenth Century Florence and Savonarola's Establishment of a Mons Pietatis," *Cambridge Historical Journal*, v (1936), 193-211.

[42] L. de Besse, *Le bienheureux Bernardin de Feltre et son œuvre.*

[43] Salter, *Cambridge Historical Journal*, v, 205, n. 36.

[44] Nicholas Barianus, *De monte impietatis* (1496); Thomas de Vio (Cajetan), *De monte pietatis* (1498).

in favor of the *monti*,[45] none of the defenders[46] of the interest clause appealed to Deuteronomy or Ambrose, or disputed the ethic of universal brotherhood.

On the contrary, the attack upon the Ambrosian exegesis was conducted with redoubled energy by all parties to the controversy. In six *consilia,* written in condemnation of the public licensing of the Jewish loan shops, Alexander de Nevo (d. 1486.), Celsus of Verona, and Annius of Viterbo (d. 1502) come to the common conclusion that there is no sanction in morality, public welfare, or law for taking of interest by the Jews from Christians. It is the duty of the Church to step in and prohibit the practice, the duty of the faithful sons of the Church to avoid any relations with the accursed usurers. No one has the right to license Jewish usury, not even the Pope. Nor is it any argument to say that the Pope does in fact permit the Jews to practice their trade in his own territories, since not everything the Pope tolerates is *ipso facto* licit. Unfortunately, to avoid greater evils, the Holy Father is forced to permit even prostitution and tyranny. The magistrates and citizens of towns responsible for the framing of concessions to the Jews commit mortal sin, and are *ipso jure* excommunicate. God never ordered the Jews to take usury from aliens, insists Annius, "sed bene nomine usurae, iussit repetere sua a tyrannis alienis qui detinebant provincias alienas" in the same way that canon law permits clerics to take interest from laymen who illegally restrain Church properties.[47]

The taking of usury was never allowed to the Jews, Celsus reports, save as an aid or alternative method for the recovery

[45] *Inter multiplices,* ed. in *Bullarium, . . . (Taurinensis editio),* v, 621-23.

[46] Their arguments are given at length in Bernardino da Busti, *Defensorium montis pietatis contra figmenta emule falsitatis* (Hagenau, Henricus Gran, 1503).

[47] *Questiones due disputate super mutuo iudaico & civili & divino.* In *Pro monte pietatis: Consilia sacrorum theologorum ac collegiorum Patavii . . .* (Venice?, Johannes Tacuinus de Tridino?, 1498?).

of their own goods. No theologian or canonist has ever authorized usury *qua* usury. The Deuteronomic concession has lapsed along with the bill of divorcement.[48]

Alexander de Nevo expresses displeasure with the analogy to redemption or recovery of one's own goods, rejecting the applicability of Ambrose's formulation to contemporary conditions, "because in relation to the Jews, Christians are neither foreigners nor enemies; indeed, Christian piety tolerates Jews."[49]

[48] *Dissuasoria* (Verona, 1503).
[49] *Consilia contra Judaeos foenerantes* (Nuremberg, F. Creusner, 1479). They were written before Nov. 17, 1441. Guido Papa (d. 1487), Ambrosius de Vignate (fl. 1473), S. Giovanni da Capistrano (1384-1456), *et al.*, took similar positions. *Tr. univ. juris*, VII, fol. 51, 74, 95; cf. Colorni, *Rivista di storia del diritto italiano*, VIII (1935), 425. Panormitanus (d. 1453) observed that the Jews do not enjoy the right to declare war, and therefore have no just enemies. T. P. McLaughlin, *Mediaeval Studies*, I, 139. St. Antoninus of Florence (1409-1459) ascribes the following version of the old Ambrosian exegesis to Guido de Baysio (d. 1313), Gregory de Arimino (d. 1358), and Laurentius de Ridolfis (fl. 1403) : "sed ab hostibus [usura] licite recipitur non ratione mutui, sed iure domini." *Tr. univ. juris*, VII, f. 87r. S. Bernardino of Siena (1380-1444) indeed, defends the taking of usury from enemies (not by Jews, however) for reasons of "brotherly love": "Temporal goods are given to men for the worship of the true God and the Lord of the Universe. Where, therefore, the worship of God does not exist, as in the case of God's enemies, usury is lawfully exacted, because this is not done for the sake of the gain, but for the sake of the Faith; and the motive is brotherly love, namely that God's enemies may be weakened, and so return to him; and further because the goods they have do not belong to them, since they are rebels against the true faith; they shall therefore devolve upon the Catholics." *Opera omnia*, ed. J. de la Haye, II, 254, tr. in A. G. Ferrers Howell, *S. Bernardino of Siena*, 261-62.

Though, generally, later theologians and jurists carry on the discussion of the Deuteronomic issue in the usual grooves, now and then one of them strikes a new note or introduces a fresh sidelight worthy of mention. Conrad Summenhart (1465-1511) cites R. Salomon (Rashi?) for the view that the discriminatory features of Deuteronomy had been abolished by the Prophets. See *Opus septipartitum de contractibus* (Hagenau, H. Gran, 1500), qu. xxiv. Alfonso Villagut of Naples (1566-1623), though criticizing the *Ab illo* of Ambrose, rejects the absolute prohibition of Raymond of Pennaforte. In Alfonso's opinion, princes and others having authority to wage war may claim usury on loans to enemies, in the same way and for the same reasons as they exercise the *ius spoliandi*. See Villa-

All the defenders of the *monti* agreed that sums repaid by borrowers above the principal do not, in the least, constitute usury, *lucrum* taken in a *mutuum*. The so-called interest charges, they held, ought more properly to be described as contributions to defray the costs of operation, especially the salaries of the officials of the *monti*.

Some canonists went so far as to contend that Jews alleging the Deuteronomic text in defense of the view that they incurred no sin by lending at usury to Christians rendered themselves open to the charge of heresy under §*Sane,* canon

---

gut, *Tr. de usuris* . . . (Venice, 1589), qu. xxiv, pp. 235-43; reprinted in the collection, *Tr. . . . trium clarissimorum iureconsultorum,* at 544-54. Petrus Gregorius (1540-1597) of Toulouse offers an elaborate reassertion of the dominant medieval position, but takes away much of its force by the introduction of a novel qualification. Usury, he says, ought not to be exacted from an enemy, because the enemy is not eligible to receive a *mutuum,* which is a loan between friends. To extend a *mutuum* to enemies and foreigners is to offer them illicit aid. This practice, he declares, was rightly visited with the gravest penalties by Athenian law. See his *Tr. de usuris,* lib. ii, cap. 15, in *Tr. . . . trium clarissimorum iureconsultorum,* 160-61. According to Marquardus de Susannis, some say that the discrimination against the foreigner in Deuteronomy is an interpolation by the Jews and therefore possesses no authority. See his *De iudaeis et aliis infidelibus* . . . (Venice, 1568), 35. Sixtus Medices, a Dominican theologian of Venice, reports that a number of learned Rabbis had declared under oath to Filippo Archinto, then vicar of Rome, that the passage was to be construed in the passive mode after the fashion authorized by Rashi. See *De foenore iudaeorum* . . . (Venice, 1555), lib. 2, cap. 3, p. 22r; cf. above, p. xvii, n.3. Expanding the novel distinctions in the classification of enemies by Covarruvias (1512-1577) [see his *Opusculum variarum resolutionum, necnon practicarum quaestionum,* lib. iii, cap. 1], Bartolommeo Ugolini (d. 1610) condemns the extortion of usury from Indian aborigines when they have nothing belonging to Christians. See Ugolini, *Tr. de usuris* (Venice, 1604), cap. xii, pp. 91-92. That the Deuteronomic problem brought worries to the contemporary Hebrew authorities may be seen in the preface to the *Eternal Life* (Hebrew) of Rabbi Jehiel Nissim of Pisa, excerpted in Alexander Marx, "A Description of Bills of Exchange, 1559," *American Economic Review,* VI (1916), 609-14, reprinted in *Studies in Jewish History and Booklore* (New York, 1944), 167-73; cf. the text and summary of Jehiel's report of the decisions of a Jewish congress in Florence in 1428, excerpted in Cassuto, *Gli ebrei a Firenze,* 363. See also, the spirited discussion of the Deuteronomic discrimination in Joseph Albo (*fl.* 1425), *Sefer ha-'Ikkarim,* bk. iii, ch. 25, ed. and tr. I. Husik, III, 237-38.

Ex gravi of the Council of Vienne (1311-1312).[50] (Conventional impressions notwithstanding, unbaptized Jews were, under certain conditions, liable to condemnations as heretics; but that is another story.) Likewise heretical, Conrad Summenhart warned, was the pertinacious belief of Christians that it was not sinful for them to lend at interest to the Jews.[51]

Not once during this controversy, indeed, not once during the entire Middle Ages did anyone approach the contention, which was to become a commonplace of the modern exegesis, that since Deuteronomy singled out victuals for special mention, it was legitimate to assume that God meant to suppress only the usury taken from the destitute. On the contrary, medieval writers underscored the same fact to prove that all usury, not only usury of money was prohibited.

Much happened to the word usury from the time of the Fathers to the close of the sixteenth century.[52] Already in

[50] For the text of the canon, see *Clem.* v. 5. c. 1 (c. 15 of the Council of Vienne); cf. K. J. von Hefele, *Histoire des conciles*, tr. H. Leclerq, vi. 2, 694-95. Paulus de Liaziriis (d. 1356) went further than any other canonist in applying §*Sane* to the Jews, even to the point of contradicting the opinion expressed by the renowned Johannes Andreae (d. 1348) in his *Apparatus ad Clementinas*. Paulus advanced two arguments to prove that Deut. xxiii did not authorize Jews to take usury from Christians: a) the disputed text was to be understood clearly only in the light of Deut. xxvii:12; b) all men being the sons of Adam and therefore brothers, Jews might not allege, as Hostiensis had shown, that Christians were their enemies. See Petrus de Ancharano (*ca.* 1330-1416), *Super Clementinis facundissima commentaria* (Bologna, 1580), on §*Sane*, c. *Ex gravi*, f. 248, col. 2. Jews violating §*Sane* were declared subject to the Inquisition in the bull *Ab exordio nascentis ecclesiae* (Aug. 30, 1409) of Pope Alexander V, which was reissued and confirmed by Pope Martin V on Nov. 6, 1419. For the full text, see L. Wadding, *Annales minorum seu trium ordinum,* ed. J. M. Ribeiro da Fonseca, ix, f. 327-29; cf. J. Vidal, *Bullaire de l'Inquisition française au xive siècle et jusqu'à la fin du Grand Schisme,* 487-88.

[51] *Opus septipartitum,* qu. xxiv.

[52] The following studies should prove especially helpful in tracing this development: W. J. Ashley, *An Introduction to English Economic History*, ii, ch. vi; W. Endemann, *Studien in der romanisch-kanonistischen Wirthschafts- und Rechtslehre*; McLaughlin, *Mediaeval Studies*, i, 81-147;

the mid-thirteenth century, advanced theological and legal circles were tending to reserve their condemnations primarily to those contracts wherein profit was openly stipulated or secretly hoped for on a *mutuum*. A hexameter doggerel by Hostiensis mentions twelve exceptional cases in which it was permissible to take an increment above the principal.[53] After that date, moderately latitudinarian constructions steadily exempted novel arrangements, forged by developing business enterprise, from the stigma of usury. By the beginning of the fifteenth century, the doctors were agreed that increments given on public loans[54] were to be interpreted as compensation for *damna et interesse,* rather than *usura.*[55] In 1425 and 1455, respectively, Popes Martin V and Calixtus III handed down qualified authorizations of redeemable real and personal rent contracts (*census utrimque redimibilis*).[56] In

ibid. II, 1-22; Schreiber, *Die volkswirtschaftlichen Anschauungen.* An analysis of the major trends in the evolution of the theory and practice of restitution of usury in the later Middle Ages and Renaissance provides interesting sidelights on the changing impact of the ecclesiastical anti-usury program upon the every-day life of the medieval businessman. See B. N. Nelson, "The Usurer and the Merchant Prince," *The Tasks of Economic History,* VII (1947), 104-22.

[53] *Summa aurea,* rub. *de usuris,* esp. no. 8, col. 1623. An exemplary commentary of this doggerel from the formal standpoint is given by McLaughlin, *Mediaeval Studies,* I, 125-47.

[54] The older account of public credit in the Middle Ages by Endemann (*Studien,* II, 431-50) must now be supplemented by the following valuable documentary studies: A. von Kostanecki, *Der öffentliche Kredit im Mittelalter, passim;* H. Sieveking, *Genueser Finanzwesen,* I, esp. 37-40, 193-96; B. Barbadoro, *Le finanze della repubblica fiorentina,* esp. at 585, 611, 665; G. Luzzatto, *I prestiti della repubblica di Venezia, passim.*

[55] For a thorough defense of the practice and a history of the debate, see Laurentius de Ridolfis, *De usuris* [1403], in *Tr. univ. juris,* VII, 17r-50r; cf. St. Antoninus of Florence, *Summa theologiae,* pt. ii, cap. xi, cols. 159-91 (*De prestanza,* etc.), briefly summarized in C. Ilgner, *Die volkswirtschaftlichen Anschauungen Antonins von Florens,* 126-39.

[56] *Extrav. commun.,* III, 5. c. 1, 2, M. Neumann, *Geschichte des Wuchers,* 212-92, esp. 288-89, and tables of rates, 266-73. W. J. Ashley, *An Introduction to English Economic History,* II, 405-11 (note the correction of Neumann's views); 452-57; E. Schreiber, *Die volkswirtschaftlichen Anschauungen der Scholastik,* 194-96; P. Cleary, *The Church and Usury,*

1515, Pope Leo X attempted to cut short the bitter polemic among Franciscan, Dominican, and Augustinian theologians by pronouncing the legitimacy of the interest clause in the *monti di pietà*. At about the same time, Johann Eck (1486-1543) of Ingolstadt, Luther's notorious adversary, was making his way to the University of Bologna on behalf of the Fuggers to prove the legitimacy of the five per cent triple contract.[57] How far Catholic writers were to go during the next century with the aid of probabilist principles is familiar to anyone who has read Pascal's *Provincial Letters*.[58]

122-24. The aforementioned decretals indicate that a vast number of benefices, canonries, vicarages, prebends, dignities, altars, etc. were financed by such rents. Apparently, both in the diocese of Breslau (then attached to the Kingdom of Bohemia) and in various parts of Germany, the debtors, i.e., the "sellers of rents," were refusing to pay the charges, claiming that the *Zins* contracts were usurious. The two Popes rejected their contentions. Pope Martin, for example, writes: "Tamen nonnulli ex venditoribus ipsis, in arcum pravum conversi, cupientes cum alterius pecunia locupletari, huiusmodi census, hucusque per eos antea libere et absque ulla contradictione solutos, eisdem emptoribus tam ecclesiasticis quam saecularibus solvere contradicunt et recusant, confingentes, huiusmodi emptionis et venditionis contractus fore et esse usurarios et illicitos, ipsos emptores ecclesiasticos et saeculares, nec non collegia, canonicatus, et praebendas, et dignitates, personatus et officia, vicarias et altaria, ac beneficia huiusmodi ipsorum annuorum censuum spoliant perceptione, et detinent spoliatos in animarum suarum periculum, eorumque emptorum praeiudicium, damnum et gravamen." *Extrav. commun*, III, 5. c. I.

[57] Th. Wiedemann, *Dr. Johann Eck*, at 33, 54-55; Ashley, *An Introduction to English Economic History*, 441-47, and notes 211-26 on pp. 484-86. Summaries of two unpublished treaties by Eck (*Tractatus de contractibus usurariis* and *Tractatus de contractu quinque de centum*) are given by J. Schneid, "Dr. Johann Eck und das kirchliche Zinsverbot," *Historisch-politische Blätter*, CVIII (1891), 241ff. For the later history of the controversy see below, pp. 101; 104, n. 91.

[58] See the 8th letter in the ed. of H. F. Stewart, esp. at 83-86. A systematic and impartial survey of the moral and economic theories of probabilist theologians of the 16th and 17th centuries, chiefly of the Jesuit order, is badly needed. The recent studies of Fathers James Brodrick and Bernard Dempsey are often stimulating, but they must both be used with caution. See J. Brodrick, *Economic Morals of the Jesuits*; B. Dempsey, *Interest and Usury*. Both works, moreover, barely touch upon the significance of probabilism for the theory of usury. Valuable discussions of the economic views of some of the Jesuit moralists will be found

Unsympathetic readers of the canonists are wont to accuse them of having made way for morally dubious novelties by resorting to furtiveness and equivocation. However one might be inclined to assess the ethical character of their writings, one must acknowledge one decisive fact: not even the most accommodating of the casuists presumed at any time in the medieval period to call in question the historic assumption that the taking of usury was antithetical to the spirit of brotherhood. The proliferation of casuistry may have taxed the credulity of conscience,[59] but both conscience

in the following: W. Endemann, *Studien;* A. M. Knoll, *Der Zins in der Scholastik.* For a technical account of the Jesuit theories of usury by an avowed opponent of the probabilists, see the dissertation, *de mutuo et usura,* by Father Daniel Concina, O. P., in his *Theologia christiana dog-matico-moralis,* VIII, 326-541. Cf. below, 104-5.

[59] Recent controversialists, Catholic and Protestant alike, make much of the fact that Eck was in advance of Luther in economic matters. The truth in this observation has been exaggerated. Like latitudinarians before and since within the Church, Eck made way for a new contract; he did not reject the basic moral, legal, or theological assumptions of the anti-usury theory. For his traditionalist teaching on Deut. xxiii, see Schneid, *Historisch-politische Blätter,* CVIII, 323-24. There is a vast difference between casuistical concessions in details and outright rejection of an old morality in the name of a new conscience. It is not possible here to debate the case.

A classic critique of the Catholic casuistry of usury is given in Pierre Bayle: "Vous voyez qu'il [Antoine Favre] se vante du suffrage de tous les Théologiens, et qu'il traite Charles du Moulin de Mauvais Théologien pour avoir approuvé l'usure, mais il faut avouer de bonne foi que la plûpart des Casuistes de l'Église Romaine ruinent par leurs distinctions tout ce qu'il y a de pur Christianisme dans le Droit Canon sur cette matière. Voici deux vers où Marot se moque de leurs distinctions.

> On ne preste plus à usure
> Mais tant qu'on veut à l'intérest.

Il n'y a guères de sujet sur quoi leur doctrine puisse être plus justement nommée *l'art de chicaner avec Dieu.* On n'a qu'à lire les subtilitez dont le Docteur en Théologie (Le Correur) qui publia le Traité de la pratique des billets l'an 1682 se servit pour éluder tous les passages de l'Écriture, & des Pères, & des Papes & des Conciles, qui combattent son sentiment . . ." *Reponse aux questions d'un Provincial,* pt. iii, ch. 28, in *Oeuvres diverses,* III, 981.

For sympathetic appraisals of casuistry, see R. Thamin, *Un problème*

and casuistry clung tenaciously to the myth, if not the reality, of universal brotherhood. How embarrassing that myth could be, even when enveloped in clouds of dialectic, is a story that belongs to the Age of Reformation.[60]

---

moral dans l'antiquité; K. E. Kirk, *Conscience and its Problems: An Introduction to Casuistry.* Profound suggestions on the relations of casuistry to the spirit of capitalism will be found in Weber, *The Protestant Ethic,* 116-28; R. H. Tawney, *Religion and the Rise of Capitalism,* 98-102; Jeannette Tawney's introduction to her edition of excerpts from Richard Baxter's *Christian Directory;* and *C.O.P.E.C. Commission Reports,* XII, 108-11.

[60] As everyone knows, the moral problem broached in these pages was posed during the Middle Ages in other contexts, which had no immediate bearing upon the question of usury, and was resolved in ways contrary to the assumed emphasis on universalism in the medieval ethic. Only one or two of the relevant illustrations of ambivalence in medieval morality can be cited here. The noted maxim *"fides non servanda est ei qui frangit fidem,"* was customarily extended beyond its technical context and taken to imply that no promises made to an enemy of the Christian faith, whether infidel or heretic, need be kept, notwithstanding the contrary teaching of the c. *Noli* in the *Decretum* of Gratian (C. XXIII. qu. I. c. 3). See G. Boyer, *Recherches historiques sur la résolution des contrats,* 247-48; H. C. Lea, *A History of the Inquisition of the Middle Ages,* II, 469; also, I, 174; Marlowe, *The Jew of Malta,* II, 3, lines 175-218, 310-20; *Tamburlaine the Great,* 2nd part, II, I, lines 33-63; also, the commentary in the ed. of the latter work by U. M. Ellis-Fermor (London, 1930), at 42-43, 206, 209. An account of the difficulties experienced in transcending this concept of the *corpus Christianum* can be found in any of the standard histories of international law. See also the recent essays of F. L. Baumer, "The Church of England and the Common Corps of Christendom," *Journal of Modern History,* XVI (1944), 1-21; *idem,* "England, the Turk, and the Common Corps of Christendom," *American Historical Review,* L (1944), 26-48; *idem,* "The Conception of Christendom in Renaissance England," *Journal of the History of Ideas,* VI (1945), 131-56. The brother-other situation was involved, also, in the related discussions as to whether deception, lies, and other stratagems, attributed by the Old Testament to Jehu (ii Kings x:18-20) were permissible to Christians in the ferreting out of heretics. A striking justification of Jehu's tactics is found in a mid-thirteenth century *Summa* until recently attributed to Frater Clarus of Florence. See P. François-Marie Henquinet, "Clair de Florence, O. F. M., canoniste et pénitencier vers le milieu du xiiie siècle," *Archivum Franciscanum Historicum,* XXXII (1939), 31. This problem had bothered the Fathers, many centuries earlier. In the controversy between St. Jerome and St. Augustine, the former found Jehu's dissimulation "useful and timely" and the latter condemned it as impious. See K. E. Kirk, *Con-*

science and Its Problems, 183. (The relevance of Jehu's example for the solution of the Deuteronomic issue is explicitly rejected by Petrus Gregorius. See *Tr. . . . trium clarissimorum iureconsultorum,* p. 160.)

The invidiousness of feudal Christian morals which serves as a background for these dilemmas in medieval thought is exemplified by the behavior and beliefs of Christians with regard to Saracens and Jews. See Samuel C. Chew, *The Crescent and the Rose: Islam and England during the Renaissance*; C. Roth, "The Medieval Conception of the Jew: A New Interpretation," in *Essays and Studies in Memory of Linda R. Miller,* 171-90; Joshua Trachtenberg, *The Devil and The Jews: The Medieval Conception of the Jew and its Relation to Modern Antisemitism.*

CHAPTER II

Deuteronomy in Crisis: The German Reformers and the Mosaic Law

THE German Reformation witnessed the outbreak of the modern revolt against the Hebraic and medieval Christian prohibitions of usury. Within less than three decades after the day when Luther stood before the boy Emperor at Worms, there occurred a fateful desertion of a principle which had claimed the allegiance of men in the Judaeo-Christian tradition for more than two millennia, the principle that the taking of interest from a co-religionist was utterly antithetical to the spirit of brotherhood. This step was far from being the result of deliberate hostility or indifference to cherished Jewish and medieval Christian ways of conceiving the Lord's design for man. On the contrary, the sixteenth-century revolt against Deuteronomy was set in motion by the fact that in the Reformation, for the first time in the history of Western Christianity, the long-obscured premises of the inherited communalistic ethic were pressed to their ultimate conclusions.

Wherever the evangelical spirit took hold, visionary enthusiasts seized upon the fraternalistic core both of the Pentateuch and the Gospels to project a new Jerusalem, a Christian community so constituted that brothers should have no occasion to take usury from one another. In the critical hour, all of this proved anathema to the leaders of the Reformation (Luther, Melanchthon, Zwingli, Bucer)—a plot to discredit their own plans for a reform sponsored by the accredited civil magistrates. The Reformers met the challenge head on, accusing the extremists of conspiring to pervert the spiritual message of the Scriptures for the sake of their own carnal advantage. The Christian man, Luther cried, was free, under no obligation to observe dead Mosaic ordinances. As for the

Gospels, they were not intended to take the place of the civil law or to supplant existing authorities. These utterances mark a milestone in the history of the idea of the Brother and the Other. In circles under the influence of these official leaders, unauthorized attempts to reorganize society in the light of the injunctions of Moses and Christ were henceforth to be dismissed as utopian and, even, anti-Christian.

The Age of Luther and Calvin is the time of Deuteronomy's crisis and demise. In Luther's Germany, the authority of the old commandment suffered a blow from which there was little hope of recovery. In Calvin's Geneva, it was first wracked to yield a new and more acceptable meaning, then laid to rest. Let us now deal with Deuteronomy's crisis. The account of its demise is better deferred for the ensuing chronicle of the progress of the Universal Otherhood.

Properly to appreciate the evolution of Luther's attitude to usury,[1] it is necessary to read his declarations on economic

---

[1] Relatively little improvement has occurred in this department of Luther studies since the classic sketches of Gustav Schmoller (1860) and Heinrich Wiskemann (1861). See Schmoller, "Zur Geschichte der national-ökonomischen Ansichten in Deutschland während der Reformations-Periode," *Zeitschrift für die gesamte Staatswissenschaft*, XVI (1860), 461-716, esp. 554-72; Wiskemann, *Darstellung der in Deutschland zur Zeit der Reformation herrschenden nationalökonomischen Ansichten.* (It is well to consult these studies simultaneously as the former is arranged by subject and the latter by person.) The discussion in Grisar contains exaggerations of emphasis, but it is important for its awareness of the shifts in emphasis of Luther's teachings. See Grisar, *Luther*, tr. E. M. Lamond, VI, 80-98. See also: M. Neumann, *Geschichte des Wuchers*, 479ff.; W. Roscher, *Geschichte der National-Ökonomik*, ch. iii; Erhardt, "Die nationalökonomischen Ansichten der Reformatoren," *Theologische Studien und Kritiken*, LIII (1880), 666-719; R. H. Tawney, *Religion and the Rise of Capitalism*, ch. ii, §2, pp. 84-103; A. Hyma, *Christianity, Capitalism, and Communism*, ch. ii; G. Wünsch, "Luthers Beurteilung des Wuchers: Ein Beitrag zur reformatorischen Ethik," *Die christliche Welt*, XXIX (1915), cols. 26-31, 66-69, 86-91, 121-31; Th. Sommerlad, "Martin Luther und der deutsche Sozialismus," *Thüringisch-Sächsische Zeitschrift für Geschichte und Kunst*, XXII (1933), 1-38. For the general perspectives defining Luther's economic ethics, see: O. Dittrich, *Luthers*

issues chronologically against the background of the turbulent social politics of his day. Once Luther had launched
upon his career as a reformer, he ceased to think and act in
the stereotyped fashion of traditionalist exegetes. No one
who aspired to lead the German nation through a religious
revival could keep from becoming concerned over the critical
situation of the national economy. Germany was in the
throes of political and social upheaval. The Price Revolution
was working havoc in all sectors of the society. Peasants and
knights were already on the march. Everywhere there was
resentment against the operations of papal financiers, indulgence hawkers, and commercial companies engaged in
foreign trade. Town and country alike groaned under the
burden of monopoly prices and fixed interest charges on
loans.[2]

When Luther's declarations are read in their historical
contexts, they seem to fall into three periods, marked by
notable changes of emphasis.

1) The first period covers the early years of his career to
the spring of 1523. The principal allusions to usury in these
years are to be found in his *Open Letter to the Christian Nobility of the German Nation* (1519),[3] the two sermons on

---

Ethik; E. Troeltsch, *Social Teachings*, II, esp. 554-76, 870-79; F. Lau,
"Äusserliche Ordnung" und "Weltlich Ding" in Luthers Theologie; H.
Reymann, *Glaube und Wirtschaft bei Luther;* W. Betcke, *Luthers Sozialethik*, esp. 146-64; G. Wünsch, *Evangelische Wirtschaftsethik;* P.
Joachimsen, *Sozialethik des Luthertums.* For a notable criticism of the
exaggeration of the anti-capitalist character of Luther's statements in
many modern studies, see W. Elert, *Morphologie des Luthertums*, II,
477-85.

[2] See, e.g., K. Kaser, *Politische und soziale Bewegungen*, esp. 203-6;
J. S. Schapiro, *Social Reform and the Reformation*, esp. ch. i; H.
Crebert, *Künstliche Preissteigerung, passim*; W. Andreas, *Deutschland
vor der Reformation;* G. Franz, *Der deutsche Bauernkrieg.* For a detailed
account of the struggle against interest charges in Frankfurt, see W.
Lühe, "Die Ablösung der ewigen Zinsen in Frankfurt a. M. in den
Jahren 1522-1562," *Westdeutsche Zeitschrift für Geschichte und Kunst,*
XXIII (1904), 36-72, 229-72.

[3] *WA* (Unless otherwise indicated all subsequent references to Luther's

usury of 1519-1520,[4] and the *Preface to an Ordinance of a Common Chest* (1523).[5] During this period, Luther stands forth as the spokesman of the German nation against the "usurious" extortions of the Roman Church and the ecclesiastical foundations. All Germany, he charges, is being exhausted by usury, notably in the form of the *Zinskauf*. This diabolical invention, he says, was originally sanctioned by the Pope and continues to be practiced, above all, by the Roman clergy:

> . . . But the greatest misfortune of the German nation is certainly the traffic in annuities (*zynss kauff*). If that did not exist, many a man would have to leave unbought his silk, velvet, golden ornaments, spices, and luxuries of every sort. The system has not existed much over a hundred years, and has already brought almost all the princes, foundations, cities, nobles, and heirs to poverty, misery, and destruction. If it shall continue for another hundred years, Germany cannot possibly have a *Pfennig* left and we shall certainly have to devour one another. The devil invented this system, and the Pope by confirming it has injured the whole world.
>
> Therefore, I ask and pray that everyone open his eyes to see the ruin of himself, his children, and his heirs, which not only stands before the door but already haunts the house; and that Emperor, princes, lords, and cities arrange that this trade be condemned as speedily as possible and henceforth prevented, without considering the opposition of the Pope and all his justice and injustice, nor whether benefices or endowments depend upon it. Better a single benefice in a city based on an honest freehold revenue, than a hundred based on an annuity; yea, a single endowment based on an annuity is worse and more grievous than twenty based on freeholds. Truly this traffic in rents must be a sign and symbol that the world, for

---

Werke are to the Weimar edition), VI, 381-469, esp. at 466-67, tr. in Wace and Buchheim, *Luther's Primary Works*, 157-244, esp. at 240-41; also, in Luther, *Works*, ed. Jacobs (henceforth simply *Works*), II, 55-164, esp. at 159-61.

[4] *WA*, VI, 1-8; 31-60. The *Longer Sermon* is translated in *Works*, IV, 37-69.

[5] *WA*, XII, 11-30; tr. in *Works*, IV, 87-98 (89-91, intro.).

its grievous sins, has been sold to the devil, so that both temporal and spiritual possessions must fail us, and yet we do not notice it at all.[6]

Though hesitating to denounce all *census* arrangements as usurious, Luther is convinced that they can rarely be conducted "without violating the natural law and the Christian law of love."[7] Indeed, his criticisms of the contract go beyond the canon law in severity. This "new and slippery invention" is ruining all Germany, he contends, "as no usury could have done."[8] He calls upon the highest ecclesiastical and temporal authorities to abolish the practice; indeed, he summons each individual to do all in his power to prevent its continuance. He reminds creditors that it has "long since been men's duty to remit these charges." It is Christ's will, he protests, that the needy should be helped by loans and gifts, and not be constrained to sell incomes. Better that churches and endowments crumble for lack of funds than allow *census* contracts to remain unchanged, he insists.[9]

Indeed, in the spring of 1523, the Reformer warned the citizens of Leisnig that the Lord would not favor their proposed "common chest" unless they arranged to provide restitution of the usuries which had been taken by the ecclesiastical foundations, then being expropriated:

> Part of the possessions of monasteries and foundations, and a great part of the prebends are based upon usury, which now calls itself everywhere "interest [*widderkauf*]," and which has in but a few years swallowed up the whole world. Such possessions would have to be separated first of all, like leprosy, from those possessions which consist of simple bequests. . . . Interest bearing foundations . . . may rightly be regarded as usury; for I have never yet seen or heard of a right an-

[6] *WA*, VI, 466. The translation given above is freely adapted from both *Works*, II, 159-60 and Wace and Buchheim, *op.cit.*, 240.

[7] *WA*, VI, 51-52, tr. *Works*, IV, 56-57.

[8] *WA*, VI, 52-53, tr. *Works*, IV, 58. For the canon law treatment of the *census*, see above, p. 24, n. 56.

[9] *WA*, VI, 57, tr. *Works*, IV, 64-66.

nuity that bears interest. It would be necessary, therefore, in such a case, to make restitution of the usury, by returning to each one his interest payments, before allowing such a possession to go into a common chest; for God says, "I hate robbery for burnt offering" [Isaiah lxi:8]. If it prove impossible to find the persons who sustained loss by paying interest, the common chest might then receive the possession. . . . This matter is altogether one of the most urgent to which emperors and kings, princes and lords, and everyone else should give attention.[10]

Throughout the first period of his campaign against usury, Luther takes an extremely exalted view of Christ's teaching with regard to economic activities. He accuses the medieval doctors of turning the Lord's commandments into mere counsels. There are, he says, three Christian ways of acting with respect to temporal goods. The first is to submit meekly to repeated acts of violence and extortion, as we are counselled to do in Matthew v:40.[11] This is the most exacting of Christ's demands. The two less difficult charges laid on Christians are to give freely to those in need, and to extend loans without hope of return of the principal. These latter actions were so easy of accomplishment, Luther says, that they were even commanded to the Jews in the Old Testament.[12] Here the Reformer verges upon the issue of the Brother and the Other. Without explicitly citing the twenty-third chapter of Deuteronomy—he refers, instead, to Deuteronomy xv:4, 7 and xvi:11—he repeatedly emphasizes the fact that Luke vi obligated Christians to make no distinctions between friends, brothers, and enemies:

If we look the word of Christ squarely in the eye, it does not teach that we are to lend without charge, for there is no need for such teaching, since there is no lending except lending without charge, and if a charge is made, it is not a loan. He

10 *WA*, XII, 14-15; *Works*, IV, 96-97. Jacobs translates "widderkauf" as interest consistently through this page.
11 *WA*, VI, 36, tr. *Works*, IV, 37.
12 *WA*, VI, 42, tr. *Works*, IV, 44.

wills that we lend not only to friends, the rich, and those to whom we are well disposed, who can repay us again, by returning this loan, or with another loan, or by some other benefit; but also that we lend to those who cannot or will not repay us, such as the needy and our enemies. . . . Thus, too, the doctrine falls which says that we are not bound to lay aside the *signa rancoris*, as has been said above; and even though they (the *doctores*) speak rightly concerning lending, yet they turn this commandment into a counsel and teach us that we are not bound to lend to our enemies or to the needy, unless they are in extreme want. Beware of this![13]

2) The second period in Luther's campaign against usury extends from the summer of 1523 to the close of the Peasant Revolts in the winter of 1525. The stormy developments of these two years compelled Luther to institute a crucial modification of his former emphasis. In the first phase of his mission, he had appeared as the inspired champion of national evangelical revolt against foreign domination. His program appeared eventually to promise a drastic reorganization of society in the light of the scriptural injunctions to brotherly love. By the close of 1525, he was indelibly stamped as an ally of the territorial princes and of the annuity-owning creditors in their opposition to the demands of the lower classes and their radical preacher leaders.

In the hour of decision, Luther turned his back upon the utopian visions of a New Jerusalem. The cataclysm of 1525 forced him to reveal that he stood four-square against the radical claims that both individuals and government were eternally obligated to observe the Mosaic and Gospel prohibitions of usury.

During his first years as a Reformer, Luther had expressed himself with great abandon in the matter of usury. The evangelical character of his successive pronouncements, especially of his two sermons on usury of 1519-1520 had quickened the hopes of interest-ridden debtors. Many who professed to be

[13] *WA*, VI, 47-48, tr. *Works*, IV, 52.

his followers assumed that he would make no compromise with the civil or canon laws permitting usury, but that he would insist on the literal fulfillment of the word of Scripture. Some must have felt that he was not only not averse to a drastic revision of the terms of onerous *Zins* contracts, but that he even favored a cancellation, at least in part, of outstanding *Zins* charges. Luther seemed not to care that a great number of these contracts were held in the name of religious foundations. On the contrary, he gave the impression of considering that situation an incentive rather than a deterrent to radical reform.

Luther's left-wing followers took heart from his forceful sermons. Soon they were surpassing Luther in their insistence on the immediate application to the contemporary scene of Mosaic and Gospel teachings on social issues. A brief reference by Luther in his *Longer Sermon on Usury* to Deuteronomy xv served Karlstadt (*ca.* 1480-1541) as a point of departure for a sweeping proposal to adopt the principles of the Hebraic releases of the seventh year as an aid in the elimination of slavery and mendicancy.[14] Presently other evangelically minded preachers were to give new dimensions to the campaign against usury by pushing the Deuteronomic precedents into the forefront of their agitation. The most

[14] See Karlstadt, *Von Abtuhung der Bylder und das kein Betdler unther den Christen seyn sollen* (Wittenberg, 1522; foreword dated January 27, 1522), 25-29; cf. H. Barge, *Andreas Bodenstein von Karlstadt*, I, 394. The dependence of Karlstadt's social program on Luther's writings of 1519-20, especially his *Longer Sermon on Usury* and the *Open Letter to the Christian Nobility*, is stressed in K. Müller, *Luther und Karlstadt*, 31-48, 56-58. For our purposes, however, peculiar relevance attaches to Müller's comment on Karlstadt's challenging elaboration of Luther's reference to Deut. xv. Müller writes: "Auch die Stelle Deut. 15, die Karlstadt nachher in seiner Schrift *Von Abtuhung der Bilder* ausgiebig verwendet, hatte Luther im *Sermon vom Wucher* zuerst herangezogen. *Nur die Vorschriften über das Erlassjahr hat Luther nicht benutzt, aus guten Gründen.*" Müller, *op.cit.*, 57, n. 2 (italics mine). As we shall see in a moment it was the ascription by Karlstadt and others of eternal significance to the Deuteronomic precedents as a basis for Christian social organization which helped set the stage for the successive clashes between the left- and right-wings of the Reformation.

effective of the radical preachers to launch such a program was Dr. Jakob Strauss (*ca.* 1480/85-*ca.* 1533),[15] preacher at Eisenach.

The impetuous Strauss opened fire by issuing fifty-one tersely expressed theses against usury.[16] Some of these had highly inflammable implications. The taking of even one *Pfennig* above the principal was denounced as usury, antithetical in its nature to the love of neighbor and the precept of God. No respect was to be accorded to the evasive glosses on this head by theologians, jurists, and church councils, notably the "heretical" Council of Constance.[17] It was unchristian, Strauss insisted, for individuals to give, as well as to take, interest.[18] Hitherto, the common man had been

[15] For Strauss, see now H. Barge, *Jakob Strauss.* In common with other recent writers on Strauss—see, e.g., the comments of the editor in Luther, *BW*, III, 275-78—Barge shows a tendency to insist on the similarity of the views of Luther and Strauss. The account of Bossert is closer to the official fashion of earlier centuries of setting them in sharp opposition to one another. See G. Bossert, "Strauss, Jakob," *RE*, ed. 3, XIX (1907), 92-97; also, *The New Schaff-Herzog Encyclopedia*, ed. S. M. Jackson, XI (1911), 111-13. Several older surveys of Strauss's career are still indispensable reading. See, esp., G. Th. Strobel, *Miscellaneen*, III. 1, and G. L. Schmidt, *Justus Menius*, I, 113-29.

[16] See *Hauptstücke und Artikel christlicher Lehre wider den unchristlichen Wucher*, ed. Strobel, *op.cit.*, III. 1, 11-16. For a catalogue of Strauss's published writings, see Barge, "Die gedruckten Schriften des evangelischen Predigers Jakob Strauss," *Archiv für Reformationsgeschichte*, XXXII (1935), 100-21, 248-52; cf. F. Waldner, "Dr. Jakob Strauss in Hall und seine Predigt vom grünen Donnerstag (17. April) 1522," *Zeitschrift des Ferdinandeums für Tirol und Vorarlberg*, III Folge, Heft XXVI (1882), 1-39.

[17] Strauss, *Hauptstücke*, esp. theses 1-4, 8-10, 49, in Strobel, *Miscellaneen*, III. 1, 11-16.

[18] Strauss's *Hauptstücke*, esp. theses 24, 29, in Strobel, *op.cit.*, III. 1, 14. Schmoller is wrong to imagine that this proposition exhibits a novel and dangerous implication of Luther's teachings. Numerous medieval theologians can be cited for this view. See, e.g., Robert de Curzon, *Le traité* pp. 14, 55. A noteworthy reminiscence of this medieval attitude occurs in Antonio's first conversation with Shylock:

> *Ant.* Shylock, albeit I neither lend nor borrow
> By taking nor by giving of excess
> Yet, to supply the ripe wants of my friend,
> I'll break a custom. . . . *M. of V.*, I, iii, 62-65.

deceived by the teaching and example of the Antichrist. Now that he had come to the truth through the knowledge of the Gospels, he was no longer to pay usury, though he were commanded or constrained to do so, without registering some form of protest. In this matter, it was more important to obey God than man. Still, the Christian debtor was not to meet violence with violence, but to heed the word and example of Christ. If an oppressor seized his cloak, he was to let him take his tunic as well. Princes, on the other hand, were admonished not to compel anyone to pay interest unless they wished to be identified as tyrannical violators of Christ's rule.[19]

Many peasants and burghers of Eisenach took Strauss to mean that they might at once stop paying charges which were owing to their creditors. The Augustinian canons of the *Marienstift* at Eisenach, which had invested much of its funds in the purchase of annuities in the environs of the town, vigorously protested Strauss's sermons to the Elector, Duke Johann of Saxony. Without delay, the young Prince Johann Friedrich, acting for the Duke, his father, sent commissioners from Weimar to investigate the situation and to put pressure upon the Municipal Council of Eisenach and upon Strauss.[20]

Early in 1524, Strauss tried to correct the extremist interpretation of his views. At the suggestion of the Duke, he issued a supplementary treatise on usury. Its very title[21] de-

[19] *Haupstücke*, thesis 37 given in Strobel, *op.cit.*, III. 1, 15; cf. Barge, *Jakob Strauss*, 66.

[20] For the best documentary account of this crisis, we are advised to consult R. Jauernig, "D. Jakob Strauss, Eisenachs erster evangelischer Geistlicher, und der Zinswucherstreit in Eisenach," *Mitteilungen des Eisenacher Geschichtsvereins*, Heft 4 (1928), 30-48; cf. summary in Luther, *BW*, III, 275-78; Barge, *Jakob Strauss*, ch. vii.

[21] This work has not been available to me. It will henceforth be referred to in these pages as *Das Wucher zu nehmen*. See list of editions in Barge, *Archiv für Reformationsgeschichte*, XXXII (1935), 249-50. A summary of its main points will be found in Strobel, *Miscellaneen*, III. 1, 39-41; Barge, *Jakob Strauss*, 67-99; and in Luther, *BW*, III, 275-78.

cisively reasserts Strauss's conviction that the giving as well as the taking of interest was opposed both to Christian faith and brotherly love. In the text Strauss undertakes to define his views on the kind of resistance permitted to debtors in rent contracts. For the guidance of the consciences of all parties implicated in these arrangements, he lays down a comprehensive set of rules. These counsels amplify, but do not, save in emphasis, alter the position taken in his disputed theses. Debtors who contract to pay usury without explicitly demurring in some way are still declared to share the creditor's sin. Princes are again warned against incurring sin by their enforcement of the payment of usurious extortions. But, Strauss added, he wished now to state plainly that it was not his intention to provoke a revolt against the temporal authorities. If the magistrate commands the satisfaction of the improper charges, the debtors are to declare their awareness of the sinfulness of the proceedings, but not to resist, arms in hand.

Strauss's counsels to patience seem to have been effective for at least a short time in mollifying the turbulent debtors of Eisenach. The Eisenach archives have recently yielded evidence that the crisis was temporarily resolved during the summer of 1524.[22] From the larger standpoint of the fate of the Deuteronomic ideal, however, Strauss's role in effecting an arbitration of the Eisenach conflict and his subsequent disavowal of the Peasant Revolts[23] are less important than his vigorous affirmation of the authority of the fraternalistic injunctions of the Old Testament. Karlstadt's *Von Abtuhung der Bilder* and Strauss's *Das Wucher zu nehmen* were two of the earliest treatises clearly to focus a problem which was to be of paramount importance in every major crisis of Protestantism in the early modern epoch: What was the proper interpretation and embodiment of the Judaeo-Christian ideal of brotherhood? Or, to put the question in the terms used in

[22] See summary of Jauernig's essay in Luther, *BW*, III, 275-76.
[23] Barge, *Jakob Strauss*, 72-74.

the Age of the Reformation, to what extent was Christian Europe bound to emulate the fraternalistic institutions of the Hebrew Commonwealth?

Strauss hoped to make the brotherhood of man a social reality. All of God's children, he said, must display their devotion to their common Father by doing unto each the works of love. Evangelical faith was a mockery unless verified in evangelical practice. Early in 1523, in the course of his fifty-one theses, Strauss had attacked Johann Eck and others for proposing equivocal glosses on the fraternalistic injunctions of Deuteronomy xv and Luke vi.[24] In *Das Wucher zu nehmen*, Strauss boldly announced his support of the revival of the principles behind the Sabbatical and Jubilee releases. In the opinion of Strauss, Hebraic social legislation was the foundation of Christian brotherhood. True, Strauss says, some of the superficial details of the laws of Leviticus and Deuteronomy were "ceremonial" in character, and, therefore, anachronistic. He referred primarily to the emphasis on the seventh and fiftieth years. However, it was criminal to say that these commandments were intended only for the Jews. On the contrary, Christ came to fulfill, and not to destroy, these symbols of brotherly love. The releases and the related laws of the Jews were declared to the Jews as indispensable. Christians have worked shame in so blithely neglecting them.[25]

[24] *Hauptstücke*, thesis 49, in Strobel, *op.cit.*, III, 1, 16; cf. thesis 4, *ibid.*, p. 12; Barge, *op.cit.*, pp. 65-66, which supply the name of Eck and an additional phrase apparently omitted in Strobel's transcription.

[25] *Ibid.*, 72; cf. Luther, *BW*, III, 312-14. A detailed account of medieval Jewish and Christian attitudes to these releases does not appear to be available. Roughly speaking, however, it seems possible to establish the following contrast. In medieval Catholicism, the releases were translated into symbolical and spiritual terms as in the Jubilee Indulgence. Among the Jews, however, literal interpretation and application of the Sabbatical release in the case of loans continued to be demanded by many rabbis throughout the Middle Ages. See, e.g., A. Neuman, *The Jews in Spain*, I, 218-23. I am indebted to Prof. Boaz Cohen for a personal communication clarifying the medieval Jewish views on Hillel's *prosbol*.

The acts and declarations of Luther and Melanchthon during the Eisenach crisis are a turning point in the history of the Deuteronomic ideal. Luther, it is true, at first assumed a friendly and even conciliatory tone to Strauss. In two letters of October 18, 1523, one to Chancellor Gregor Brück,[26] of the Saxon court, the other to Strauss himself,[27] Luther confessed his underlying sympathy with Strauss's attack on outrageous rent contracts. Luther even pointed to his own record of opposition to this evil. The tone of his personal greetings and salutations to Strauss is cordial. Even his strictures against Strauss are presented with mildness. Yet, the affability of his manner does not conceal the undercurrent of his distrust of Strauss and Strauss's ways.

These first letters on the Eisenach crisis contain in embryo the seeds of Luther's subsequent revulsion against everything which savored of Strauss's program and of Mosaic literalism. In both letters, Luther warned the Eisenach preacher against sowing the whirlwind. In the first place, Luther said, not all rent contracts were usurious. Secondly, Strauss was playing a dangerous game by encouraging the common man to take matters into his own hands. A reform of the rent contracts was, doubtless, desirable, but it was the common man's duty to wait upon the princes to promulgate a general edict. To allow every man to act as judge in his own case was perilous. It was naive of Strauss to assume there were more than a few Christians in the world. Thirdly, Luther protested, neither the Gospels nor he had ever taught that debtors incurred complicity in the sin of usury by yielding payments to their creditors. To the contrary, Christ had commanded his followers to give their tunics as well as their cloaks to oppressors. For the common man, it was sufficient if he recognized and made known the fact that he was making a sinful payment.[28]

Luther's principal declarations on Strauss's program waited until May and June of 1524. The publication of *Das*

Wucher zu nehmen had a mixed effect on Luther. On the one hand, Luther was gratified to find that Strauss had publicly disowned the extremist interpretations of his theses.[29] On the other hand, Strauss had aggravated a troublesome issue in laying renewed emphasis on the Sabbatical and Jubilee releases and on the strict prohibition of usury between brothers.[30] Luther tried desperately in the months of May and June to formulate his position on these questions. Under the pressure of the agitation of Strauss and other preachers, Luther was inspired to entertain the idea of getting the princes to adopt the principles of the Hebraic release.[31] In the end, however, as we shall presently see, the disturbing turn of events in the latter half of 1524 forced him to admit his extreme horror of ultra-Mosaism.

Melanchthon seems to have spurred Luther on to effect a decisive reformulation of the official Protestant attitude on the power of scriptural ordinances to bind the Christian conscience. Venturing into Eisenach for a face-to-face disputation with Strauss, Melanchthon opened fire on the legalistic assumptions of Strauss's program. The "law of Christ," Melanchthon contended, was not necessarily to be taken as the basis of the organization of secular society. In the teaching of the Gospel, he said, temporal magistrates were entirely free to rule in accordance with civil laws.[32]

Luther hesitated to accept Melanchthon's position without qualification. He struggled throughout the years 1524 and

[29] See letter of June 27 (?), 1524 to Spalatin, *BW*, III, 312-14.

[30] Luther received a copy of Strauss's essay after June 24, 1524. For the link between Luther's proposals and the agitation of Strauss and Wolfgang Stein, see the editor's comments in *WA*, xv, 278-89; cf. Barge, *op.cit.*, 91, n. 241, for queries on the date of the *Von Kaufshandlung* and of the new conclusion to the *Longer Sermon*.

[31] See Luther's new conclusion of 1524 to the *Longer Sermon on Usury*, *WA*, xv, 321-22, tr. in *Works*, IV, 67-69; also, his letter to Prince Johann Friedrich of Saxony, *BW*, III, 305-8 of which an excerpt is translated in P. Smith, *Luther's Correspondence*, II, 236-38.

[32] See Melanchthon's own undated report in Luther, *BW*, III, 276-77, which corrects the account of the date and circumstances given in *CR*, I, 655-56.

1525 to establish a middle-of-the-road policy on the authority
of the "Mosaic" laws. Every one of his utterances of those
critical days reveals his indecision as well as his desire to
reconcile the antagonistic factions of the Great Revolt. In
the end, however, he shut the door against the Mosaic polity.

Luther and Melanchthon dreaded the ultra-Mosaism of
the left-wing reformers. In it they detected the harbinger of
social revolution. A thousand-and-one new slogans were in
the air. Some were pressing for the revival of the Hebrew
Shemittah and the Jubilee.[33] Others were to declare not only
interest taking, but even private property, to be incompatible
with brotherly love. In many areas beside Eisenach, extremist
elements were to suspend payments of interest charges to
creditors.[34]

[33] Strauss was not alone in his enthusiasm for the Hebraic releases.
Other notable partisans of these "Mosaic" institutions were Johann
Mantel (*ca.* 1468-1530) and Wolfgang Stein, preacher in Stuttgart and
court preacher at Weimar, respectively. For Mantel, see Ranke, *Deutsche
Geschichte*, II, 125-26; G. Uhlhorn, *Urbanus Rhegius*, 75; G. Bossert, *s.v.*
"Mantel, Johann," *RE*, ed. 3, XXIV (1913), 59-64, esp. 61. A letter from
Prince Johann Friedrich to Luther charges Stein with attempting to
seduce Duke Johann into affirming the primacy of the "Mosaic" laws.
See Luther, *BW*, III, 309-11; cf. Barge, *Jakob Strauss*, 94-95.

[34] Kaser, *Politische und soziale Bewegungen*, 205-6. For a remarkable
instance of severity on the usury question, see the *consilium* dated December 26, 1523, provided by Francis Lambert (d. 1530) of Avignon, to
Stephan Roth of Zwickau. See O. Clemen, "Zwei Gutachten Franz Lamberts von Avignon," *Zeitschrift für Kirchengeschichte*, XXII (1901), 129-
44, esp. at 138-43. (Lambert was for a short while preacher at Eisenach.)
The followers of Müntzer and Heinrich Pfeiffer at Mühlhausen confessed under examination that they had been taught to pay no more
interest on rents. It is not certain, however, that Müntzer derived communistic teachings from Acts ii:44 or Acts iv:34. See R. N. Carew Hunt,
"Thomas Müntzer," *Church Quarterly Review*, CXXVII (1939), 265, esp.
at n. 243 (for extracts from sources). The later Anabaptists of Münster
seem to have based their attack on usury on Scriptural suggestions of an
apostolic community of property. See, e.g., Bernhard Rotman's *Restitution
rechter und gesunder christlicher Lehre* (Münster, 1534), cap. xxii, in
modern reprint, *Neudrucke deutscher Litteraturwerke*, no. 77-78, at pp.
70-71; cf. the accounts of Rotman's views in Detmer, *Bernhard Rothmann*,
85-88; Erhardt, *Theologische Studien und Kritiken*, LIII (1880), 698. A
critical discussion of the use of the New Testament sources in the de-

Luther and Melanchthon flatly condemned all expressions of popular initiative in putting the Mosaic and Gospel laws into effect. If there was to be reform, Luther taught, it would have to come from the princes, and not the people. Luther, indeed, appears to have hoped, at one point, that the Emperor and princes would adopt the Old Testament principle of the proportionate tithe in the settlement of the *census* charges. He became especially active in advocating this measure in the summer of 1524,[35] soon after the appearance of Strauss's *Das Wucher zu nehmen*, when the peasant hosts were gathering. In the new conclusion of his *Longer Sermon on Usury* completed in the last week in June, he himself recommended the adoption of the principle behind the Jubilee year. Nevertheless, he simultaneously warned the people against taking matters into their own hands. Whatever Christ may have counselled, said Luther, in obvious reference to the situation at Eisenach and elsewhere, the civil authorities were right to use the sword against recalcitrant debtors.[36] He insists re-

velopment of the ideas of brotherhood and community of property among the Moravian Brethren will be found in Lydia Müller, *Der Kommunismus der mährischen Wiedertäufer*, 53-89.

[35] See Luther's letter of June 18, 1524, to Prince Johann Friedrich of Saxony, *BW*, III, 305-8; also the new conclusion to the *Longer Sermon on Usury*, *WA*, xv, 321-22, tr. *Works*, IV, 28. Attacking Karlstadt in January of 1525, Luther again recommended the adoption of Mosaic precedents: "Und ich wöllt, das man auch ettliche (scil. Exempel) mehr ynn welltlichen Sachen aus Mose neme, als das gesetz vom scheydebrieff, vom Hall iar, und vom Frey iar, von den zehenden und der gleichen, durch wilche gesetze die wellt das würde regirt denn itzt mit den zinsen, verkeuffen und freyen. . . ." Luther, *Wider die himmlischen Propheten*, in *WA*, xvIII, 81. Luther was not the only moderate Reformer to praise the principles of the release. Urbanus Rhegius, (d. 1549), for example, is chided by his modern biographer for having shown excessive sympathy for the idea of the Jubilee. See G. Uhlhorn, *Urbanus Rhegius*, 80, commenting on Rhegius's *Von Leibeigenschaft oder Knechtheit* (Augsburg, 1525).

[36] *WA*, xv, 302, tr. *Works*, IV, 22. To this Müntzer replied: "Er [Luther] saget aber imm buch von kauffsshandelung, dass die Fürsten sollen getrost undter die Diebe und Rauber streichen. Im selbigen verschweigt er aber den *ursprung aller dieberey.* . . . Sieh zu, die grundtsuppe des wuchers, der dieberey und Rauberey sein unser Herrn und Fürsten,

peatedly that Christians of the sixteenth century were no more bound by the "judicial laws" of Moses than they were by the ceremonial laws, such as the law of circumcision.[37] His private correspondence of 1525, indeed, finds him groping toward the propositions which were to receive their classic expression at the hands of Calvin. The Christian man, Luther was to say, was in the truest sense of the Gospel free to lend his money as he chose. Not the Gospels, but the economic situation and the considerations of public utility, were of paramount importance in finding clues for the regulation of loans at interest.[38]

3) Luther had little to say about usury and interest for almost fifteen years after the Revolt of 1525. Then, in the summer of 1539, in the midst of severe economic crisis, he

---

nemen alle creaturen zum aygenthumb. Die visch imm wasser, die vögel imm lufft, das gewechss auff erden muss alles ir sein. Esaie. 5. Darüber lassen sy dann gottes gepot aussgeen unter die armen und sprechen: Gott hat gepoten: Du solt nit stelen. Es dienet aber in nit. So sye nun alle menschen verursachen, den armen ackerman, handtwerckmann, und alles das da lebet, schinden unnd schaben. Micha. 3. So er sich dann vergreifft am aller geringsten, so muss er henken. So saget denn der Doktor Lügner: Amen. Die herren machen das selber, dass in der arme man feyndt wirdt, dye ursach des Auffrurss wollen sye nit weg thun, wie kann es die lenge gut werden? So ich das sage, muss Ich auffrurisch sein, wol hyn." Müntzer, *Hoch verursachte Schutzrede* (1524), cited in M. von Nathusius, *Die christlich-socialen Ideen,* p. 154, from modern reprint in *Neudrucke,* no. 118, p. 25. It is interesting to note that this passage has been taken as crucial by socialist thinkers from at least the time of Marx. See Marx, *Zur Judenfrage,* in *Der historische Materialismus,* ed. S. Landshut and J. P. Mayer, I, 260; cf. H. P. Adams, *Karl Marx,* 95; Engels, *The Peasant War in Germany,* 68; Kautsky, *Communism in Central Europe,* 136. O. H. Brandt accuses Müntzer of having entirely reversed Luther's own meaning. See Brandt, *Thomas Müntzer,* 246. Michael Freund comments: "Hier klingt so etwas wie die materialistische Geschichtsauffassung an. . . ." Freund, *Thomas Müntzer,* 126.

[37] See, e.g., his letter to Spalatin dated Wittenberg, March 14, 1524. *BW,* III, 254, freely tr. in Smith, *op.cit.,* II, 223.

[38] See especially Luther's letter to the City Council of Danzig, *BW,* III, 482-86, partially tr. in Smith, *op.cit.,* II, 310-11; cf. the favorable comments in M. von Nathusius, *op.cit.,* 145; also, Troeltsch, *Social Teachings,* II, pp. 870-71, n. 273.

once again took up the offensive. Two blasts against usurers and their princely patrons followed in short order: first, a sermon on Matthew xxv:23[39] denouncing noble practitioners of usury; then, the powerful *An die Pfarrherrn, wider den Wucher zu predigen*, issued on January 1, 1540.[40] These jeremiads, a number of letters, and the pungent declamations of the *Table Talk* constitute his last phase.[41]

For the purposes of this essay, it is not necessary to itemize the propositions of this last period. His productions after 1525 are, on the whole, more interesting for their rhetoric than for their content. By 1540, Luther was a disappointed man who retained little confidence in the willingness of the princes to extirpate usury. This is not concealed by the fact that he exhorted Protestant ministers in 1540 to use all the resources at their command to inculcate a horror of mammonism among their parishioners.

Preachers are called upon to fulfill their evangelical function of expounding the Gospel. They must teach unrelentingly that profit openly demanded on a contract of *mutuum*, whether from friend or foe, is a sin against all law, divine, natural, and civil. Communion and sacred burial are to be denied to shameless usurers.

Yet, Luther would not have the preachers usurping the functions of other authorities. Preachers are not to enter into elaborate discussions of the subtle legal issues which encumber the issue of usury. They are to cleave to the Gospel and to continue to denounce usury simply, leaving the resolution of fine points and the ambiguous contingencies of daily life to the jurists, the princes, and the individual conscience. Nor are the preachers to be indiscriminate in their attacks on usury. Special consideration is to be shown to the aged, wid-

---

[39] *WA*, XLVII, esp. 492-94. Hyma is wrong to date this sermon about 1537. See *WA*, XLVII, 493; also, *ibid.*, xi in "Einleitung."

[40] *WA*, LI, 325-424; cf. summaries in Schmoller, *Zeitschrift für die gesamte Staatswissenschaft*, XVI (1860) and in Grisar, VI, 87-88; Hyma, *Christianity, Capitalism, and Communism*, 61-62.

[41] See references indicated in the Weimar ed. of *Tischreden*, VI, 703.

ows and orphans, and other unfortunates, who perforce derive their income from returns on investments with merchants. Moreover, those who take only a little usury (*ein Wucherlein*), that is, those who ask but five or six per cent, are not to be treated as harshly as the gross extortioners. It is the hoarders of provisions and the gross usurers who are responsible for the fearful inflation which now weighs so heavily on the many, not themselves engaged in business, including the ministry, who depend on relatively stable incomes from *Zinsen*. Some creditors, he reports, were demanding as high as sixty per cent as interest; others—among them was at least one prince—were openly boasting that they were holding out for all that the traffic would bear. As far as the *Zinskauf* was concerned, Luther was willing in 1540 to allow eight per cent, so long as the contract was based on a redeemable security in land (*Unterpfand*).[42]

Luther might have done well to warn the preachers that due, in part, to his own influence, they might expect to meet with indifference and even retribution if they were to insist on interpreting his exhortations too literally. True, he had invoked them to use the dread medieval penalties against usurers, but he had also evinced some sympathy for those who were content with *ein Wucherlein* and warned against clerical attempts to usurp the functions of jurists, princes, and the individual conscience. How variously his words could be interpreted became evident soon enough in the several crises which broke out in Germany over the issue of usury during the half century following his tract of 1540. By 1587, five ministers of Regensburg were to be dismissed from their posts and exiled from the town by the Protestant magistrates of the municipal council for presuming to question the validity of the five per cent contract.[43]

The years 1523-1525 are preeminently the time of Deuteronomy's crisis. Fully to appreciate the extent of Luther's

[42] On Matth. xxii:25, in *WA*, XLVII, 493-94; cf. Hyma, *op.cit.*, 62-63.
[43] See below, pp. 93-94.

departure from the Hebraic and medieval Christian versions of the ideal of brotherhood, it is necessary to deal once more and in greater detail with the major pronouncements of that critical middle period of his economic thought.

A sense of storm and stress pervades all his actions and writings in these years. His *Deuteronomy with Annotations* (delivered in the years 1523-1524, but not published until a year later);[44] his *In Genesin Declamationes* (not printed until 1527-1528);[45] his *Von Kaufshandlung und Wucher* of June 1524; his actions in the Strauss case (October 1523-June 1524); his reply (June 18, 1524) to the inquiries of Prince Johann Friedrich of Saxony; his *Wider die himmlischen Propheten*, directed principally against Karlstadt;[46] his communications to the City Councils of Danzig[47] and Erfurt[48] of May and September 1525, respectively—all of these abound in hesitations and contradictions.

In these two troubled years, his every act appears to be marked by inconstancy of aim. His private correspondence presents a sharp contrast to his public utterances. At times, indeed, he seems to be working at cross-purposes in the manner of a beleaguered political leader. On the one hand, he appeals to the princes to "follow the law and example of Moses" in a number of crucial particulars. On the other hand, he cuts the ground from under the radical preachers who call for the New Jerusalem.

Especially impressive testimonies to the link between his anti-Mosaic attitude and the problem of usury are found in two of his letters: the reply to the inquiries of the young

[44] *WA*, xiv, 489-744, esp. the comments on Deut. xv (644-47) and Deut. xxiii:19, 20 (710, 713).

[45] *WA*, xxiv, *passim*, esp. 1-16.

[46] *Ibid.*, xviii, esp. at p. 81. The first part of the work was completed in January of 1525.

[47] *BW*, iii, 483-86.

[48] *WA*, xviii, 534-40; cf., comments of the editor in *BW*, iii, 577. Luther is here replying to the letter of September 9, 1525 (ed. *BW*, iii, 570-71). Cf. Th. Eitner, *Erfurt und die Bauernaufstände.*

Johann Friedrich of Saxony and his communication to the City Council of Danzig. In both of these documents, indeed, Luther manifests an inclination to enlarge the sphere of private conscience as against the claims of law in the matter of loans at interest. He advises the Prince to hold debtors to their obligations "and let the burden rest on the consciences of those who take unjust interest." He explains, further, that "interest which does not exceed four or five per cent" is not necessarily unjust.[49] In the memorandum to the Danzig councillors, he suggests that from the standpoint of evangelical religion each individual has a right to exercise his Christian liberty in the matter of making loans at interest. The only proper criterion for the regulation of usury would be to consider loans in terms of equity and the status of the parties involved.[50]

In September of 1525, he rejected the demand of the insurgents of Erfurt henceforth to make deductions of the interest payments in returning the principal of the debt. In mocking fashion, he boasts that if he had money available for investment he would never be tempted to make an advance under such conditions to a commoner of Erfurt.[51]

The *Von Kaufshandlung und Wucher* is invariably cited in modern discussions as an instance of Luther's stubbornly conservative opposition to forms of enterprise already tolerated by authoritative Catholic canonists.[52] True, in June of 1524, Luther is bitter against foreign trade, commercial companies, monopolists, and the Augsburg financiers. Indeed, on preliminary examination, the first part of the 1524 treatise seems more radical in its opposition to interest than either the *Shorter* or the *Longer Sermon on Usury* of 1519-1520. Yet closer study of the 1524 tract reveals a number of notable signs of a wish on his part to muffle the unworldly overtones

[49] *BW*, III, 306, tr. P. Smith, *Luther's Correspondence*, II, 237.
[50] *BW*, III, 483-86.   [51] *WA*, XVIII, 534-40; cf. *BW*, III, 577.
[52] See, e.g., the characterization in Tawney, *Religion and the Rise of Capitalism*, 97-98, 102.

found in his earlier essays. It is especially significant that, though he reiterates the formulae for the Christian ways of dealing with temporal goods, Luther goes out of his way on several occasions to warn against any attempt to translate his supra-ethical sentiments into legal terms. The three-fold way of Christianity is to be an ideal standard of measurement, not a program for action. He wastes no sympathy on utopian social reformers: the "red and bloody sword of the ruler," he insists, rather than the Gospel will alone guarantee peace in this world.[53] As if in reference to the Eisenach crisis, he declares:

> I have already said that Christians are rare in the world; therefore the world needs a strict, hard temporal government that will compel and constrain the wicked not to steal and rob and to return what they borrow, even though a Christian ought not demand it [the principal], or even hope to get it back. This is necessary in order that the world may not become a desert, peace may not perish, and trade and society may not be utterly destroyed: all which would happen if we were to rule the world according to the Gospel and not drive and compel the wicked, by laws and the use of force, to do and suffer what is right. We must, therefore, keep the roads open, preserve peace in the towns, and enforce law in the land, and let the sword hew briskly and boldly against the transgressors, as Paul teaches in Romans xiii. For it is God's will that those who are not Christians shall be held in check and kept from doing wrong, at least with impunity. Let no one think that the

[53] For Müntzer's comment on Luther's instructions on this, see above, p. 44, n. 36. Cf. the letter (Sept. 5, 1524) of Konrad Grebel of Zurich and his friends to Müntzer, available in Müntzer, *BW*, ed. Böhmer and Kirn, 92-101, esp. at 96; tr. Rauschenbusch, "The Zurich Anabaptists and Thomas Münzer," *American Journal of Theology*, IX (1905), 91-106. Interestingly enough, Grebel expresses enthusiasm for Strauss, Karlstadt, and Müntzer as against the "perverters of Scripture at Wittenberg." Moreover, Grebel urges Müntzer and Karlstadt to give up their benefices if they be tainted with usury: "If your benefices, as with us, are supported by interest and tithes, which are both true usury, and if you do not get your support from an entire church, we beg that you will give up your benefices. Ye know well how a shepherd should be supported." Rauschenbusch, *loc.cit.*, 94.

world can be ruled without blood; the sword of the ruler must be red and bloody; for the world will and must be evil, and the sword is God's rod and vengeance upon it.[54]

Unsteadiness marks every one of Luther's attempts in 1524-1525 to define his views on the significance and authority of scriptural allusions to remission of obligations. In the *Deuteronomy with Annotations*, he refers to the Sabbatical release as a "most beautiful and equitable law."[55] Were it to be adopted today, he says, the governors of the world would be saved endless legal business and disturbance. Trials, debts, acts, pacts—all would be terminated at one time and not be allowed to plague people forever. Moreover, men would be careful not to lend a greater sum of money than they could hope to have restored before the seventh year. Prodigals and bankrupts would thus be kept from foisting their debts and accumulated pacts on others.

True, Christians are commanded in Matthew v and Luke vi not to insist upon the repayment of loans; indeed, Christians are ordered to proffer loans without hoping to recover any equivalent. But, says Luther: "Christ is speaking to Christians, who are above all law and do more than the laws require." Moses, however, proclaimed civil laws for a people who were subject to the magistrate and to the sword, that evil might be checked and the public peace be served.

Hence the law must now be so administered that everyone who receives a loan must return it, even though he be Christian; if, however, the law does not come to the creditor's aid, and does not restore his loan, he should bear it with even spirit as the law allows no one to suffer injury and punishes the violent; nevertheless, a Christian will be patient if he is injured, and he himself will neither punish nor seek punishment, although he will not interfere with the rigor of sword of the vindicator, who knows the sword to be instituted for the punishment of evildoers.[56]

[54] *WA*, xv, 302; tr. in *Works*, IV, 22-23.
[55] *WA*, xiv, 654-55.
[56] *Ibid.*, 655.

A similar message is incorporated in his response of June 18, 1524, to the young Johann Friedrich of Saxony. The Prince had raised two questions: 1) Were governments obliged to observe the Mosaic law?; 2) Might a ruler allow the taking of usurious interest (*wuchrische Zinskauf*)? Luther replied:

> It would be a fine thing if tithes of all property were paid to the government every year, as was the custom in the ancient world. That would be the kind of interest (*zinse*) most in accordance with God's will, for that would lay no hardship on those who had to pay; if God gave much or little the tithe would be reckoned accordingly. Indeed it would be both tolerable and desirable that all other payments should be abolished, and a fifth or a sixth were collected from the people, as was done by Joseph in Egypt, but since there is no such orderly arrangement in the world, I must despair of this remedy and say that it is highly necessary that the taking of interest should be regulated everywhere, but to abolish it entirely would not be right either, for it can be made just. I do not advise your Grace, however, to protect people in their refusal to pay interest or to prevent them from paying it, for it is not a burden laid upon people by a prince in his law, but it is a common plague that all have taken upon themselves. We must put up with it, therefore, and hold debtors to it and not let them spare themselves or seek a remedy of their own, but put them on a level with everybody else, as love requires, even though it be at loss to themselves, until God puts it into the hearts of the princes to agree to some change.[57]

More sweeping attacks on the radical social theories of the devotees of Mosaism are found in other writings of the period directed explicitly against the turbulent masses and their left-wing leaders. Karlstadt and Müntzer are attacked along with Strauss for perpetrating pernicious misunderstandings of the Old Testament. Their teachings, Luther charges, force Christians to behave like Jews.

[57] *BW*, III, 305-8; cf. excerpt tr. in Smith, *Luther's Correspondence*, II, 237.

As for the revolting peasants, their appeal to the Old Testament is utterly misguided. The first chapters of Genesis cannot be cited as proof that "we are all baptized equal" and that "all things are created free and common." Moses is of no account in the New Testament. Christ puts us, both our bodies and our goods, under the control of the Emperor and the civil law.[58] Speaking for himself, Luther admits that if he were Emperor he might arrange to utilize the example of the Sabbatical and Jubilee releases. Christian rulers may, if they wish, adopt Mosaic regulations, but they are under no obligation to do so. The laws of Moses, Luther explains, are simply the Jewish *Sachsenspiegel*, having no more authority over the Germans of the sixteenth century than that compilation of Saxon customs had in the France of his day.[59]

An especially telling indication of the course of the development of Luther's ideas on usury is to be found in the contrast between two of his rare allusions directly to Deuteronomy xxiii:19-20 in the years 1516-1525. Luther's first important reference to the troublesome text is to be found in his sermon on the Seventh (Eighth) Commandment, which was preached to the people of Wittenberg during the Christmas holidays of 1516, about ten months before the posting of the Ninety-Five Theses. The second allusion occurs in the *Deuteronomy with Annotations* of 1523-1525. The two discussions are worlds apart.

In the *Sermons on the Ten Commandments*, Luther sounds little different from the writers of the twelfth and thirteenth centuries. In the manner of Peter Cantor, he contrasts Christians unfavorably with Jews. The Jews, he observes, were allowed to exploit only Gentiles. Christians, however, take usury from their own brethren.[60]

---

[58] *Wider die räuberischen und mörderischen Rotten der Bauern,* in *WA,* xviii, esp. at 358-59; cf. comments in Mackinnon, *Luther,* iii, 204.

[59] *Wider die himmlischen Propheten, WA,* xviii, 81; cf. *WA,* xxiv, 6-10.

[60] The *Sermons on the Ten Commandments Preached to the People of Wittenberg* were delivered from the end of June 1516 to the Shrovetide of 1517, while Luther was still in the fold of the Roman Church. The work

The *Deuteronomy with Annotations* represents a sharp break with the past. Unlike medieval writers, he seizes upon this passage to give vent to his ultra-nominalistic antinomianism, his intense antisemitism, and his horror of political and social equality.

God's actions, he begins, are not to be measured by man's understanding of good and evil. Far from being a species of iniquity, the Deuteronomic distinction between citizens, and foreigners and strangers rests on just grounds of public policy. In this world all cannot be equal. There must be respect of persons and inequality. Otherwise, there cannot be public peace. Not all can be kings, princes, senators, rich, and free; some must be slaves and laborers.

Luther applauds the Deuteronomic discrimination for still another reason. The Jews, he observes, were not only authorized by law to recover loans from one another but were also charged to lend at interest to Gentiles. Luther, indeed, finds the latter provision even more excellent than the former. There can be no question of God's authority to make such a concession. For God is Lord of all, who takes anything He chooses from whomsoever He wishes and distributes it in whatever way He pleases. This applies not only to money and goods, but also to kingdoms and empires. If, therefore, desiring to punish the Gentiles by usury and interest, God ordered the Jews to do this on His behalf, the Jews did well to render themselves His obedient instruments and to execute His wrath by claiming usury from the Gentiles. In the same fashion He ordered the Jews to expel the Amorites and Canaanites.

God allowed the Hebrews to take usury from alien peoples, says Luther, not because usury was meritorious or a part of the common law, but because He wished thus to indicate His wrath against the Gentiles. Nor should the Jews have been

---

was published on July 20, 1518. See, *WA*, 1, 394-98 (intro.), 398ff. (text), esp. at 502.

treated any better than were the Gentiles if God in His mercy had not chosen the Jews as His agents. In short, if the matter be rightly considered, it was not the Jews, but God, who did the usury, and persecuted the Gentiles. He made the Jews a promise to insure their mastery over other peoples so long as they observed His precepts. Once they disobeyed Him, the tables were turned. Now, the Jews are fittingly exposed to contempt and suffering at the hands of other peoples.

> This is easily proved since when the Jews became disobedient and sinful, He gave them back to the Gentiles not only to be subjected to usury, but also to be vexed by every manner of contumely no less severe than had been previously allotted to the Gentiles, just as He predicted in the twenty-eighth chapter of this book (Deut. xxviii:15-68). He promised them that if they failed to heed the word of God, not only would they not lend to any nations, but they would be more miserable than the Gentiles. Today, when the Jews are no longer the people of God, the law has been removed and they, deserving of God's wrath through their impiety and blasphemy, are not permitted usury, but are forced to observe the laws of the Gentiles among whom they live. Forsooth, if you carefully examine the text, you will observe that He did not order them to lend at usury but rather made them a promise, namely, "If thou shalt hear the words of the Lord, thou shalt lend to many nations." It is not for men to fulfill the words of a promise, as they do the words of law. God alone carries out the promise.[61]

Luther's justification of the Deuteronomic discrimination against the alien and his praises of social inequality were, doubtless, intended by him to convey his repudiation of utopian extremism. Christ's teaching was not to be adopted as a code in this world. If sinful man were left on his own to

[61] *WA*, xiv, 654-56. A more universalistic note is sounded in the remarks on Deut. xxiii: "Frater non est premendus usura sed alienus, idest, iusto non est lex posita, quae exigit opera, sed iniusto, ut humilientur impii agnitione peccati. Nam officium legis est exigere usuram, plusquam possimus, donec fidem suspiremus et fratres facti liberemur ex usura, psal. 71." *Ibid.*, 713; cf. *ibid.*, 710. It is interesting to observe how markedly Luther transforms the exegesis suggested by Peter Cantor, cf. above, pp. 11-12.

fulfill the Lord's commandments, anarchy would surely ensue. Here below, civil government, positive law, and the sword must hold sway.[62]

Melanchthon wrote numerous disquisitions on usury.[63] He rarely, however, stops to debate the Deuteronomic issue. His most sustained allusions to the disputed text seem to be concentrated in the early years of his career. In the first version of his *Loci theologici* (1521), he suggests that the universal prohibition of usury is part of the natural and divine law. Thus, statutes allowing usury may not be issued.[64] The Mosaic discrimination against aliens has been superseded. Now no one is an outsider, all are kinsmen.[65]

Melanchthon returned to the theme several years later, in his commentaries on the *De officiis* of Cicero. His remarks on that occasion recall Luther's on *Deuteronomy with Annotations* in their apparent readiness to admit the rationale of the ancient discrimination against the alien. Indeed, Melanchthon seems to suggest that Christ's commandment on loans (Luke vi:35) was intended to apply only among fellow-citizens in the fashion of the Mosaic legislation. Regrettably, Melanch-

[62] I regret that I cannot at this time undertake to collate my findings with those of Paul Althaus's striking volume, *Communio Sanctorum*. According to Althaus, Luther's interpretation of the *communio sanctorum* testifies to a restoration of the original Gospel concept of the Church as a "Liebesgemeinschaft" which had become corrupted in the Middle Ages by the ecclesiastical identification of religion with "good works" and the "treasury of merit."

[63] The following passages are particularly valuable in this connection: *In officia Ciceronis Prolegomena* (1525), *CR*, XVI, esp. at 575-94; *Commentarii in aliquot politicos libros Aristotelis* (1530), *ibid.*, 428-30; *Philosophiae moralis epitomes libri duo* (1538), *ibid.*, esp. 128-42; *Dissertatio de contractibus* (1545), *ibid.*, 495-508; *Ethicae doctrinae elementorum libri duo* (1550), *ibid.*, 248-59. The dates just cited refer to the first editions of these works. It is not, however, easy to tell from the bibliographic introductions in the *CR* what alterations occurred from edition to edition. For an interesting evaluation of Melanchthon's economic and social teachings, see Roscher, *Geschichte*, 72-73.

[64] *CR*, VIII, 31-32.

[65] *Ibid.*, 75, 146.

thon does not trouble to indicate the inferences to be drawn from this extraordinary conclusion.

His analysis bears repetition. The Deuteronomic prohibition, he says, represents an attempt on the part of Moses to guarantee the communication of good offices among fellow-citizens. One is more obligated to a fellow-citizen, than to a stranger (*peregrinus*) or to an enemy. Therefore, loans to fellow-citizens are gratuitous. In the same way, the law forbidding the recovery of debts in the seventh year does not apply to strangers. It seems, likely, Melanchthon thinks, that many Jews failed to treat their brothers in accordance with the Mosaic injunction against usury. Christ, therefore, summoned them to heed the word of the law. Christ, like Moses, had in mind the establishment of good offices among citizens. Scriptural rulings about loans embody a natural law, namely, that a person who is able to provide a loan to an indigent person for an honest purpose without himself incurring some notable loss ought not to receive usury. "All who are members of the Church are without the striving for profit and without usury." Injurious loans, more precisely, loans involving a recompense for damages incurred by the creditor (*mutuationes damnosae*), Melanchthon explains, may be made to strangers, since one is not obliged to render them courteous services.[66]

[66] *Ibid.*, XVI, 579. "De hac officiosa mutuatione simpliciter servandum est dictum (Luke vi:35): Mutuum date, nihil inde sperantes. Loquitur enim Christus de officio inter cives, sicut lex Moisi ante praeceperat. Credibile est multos Iudaeos nec erga cives servasse leges. Retrahit igitur Christus suos ad vocem legis. Et habet lex rationem naturalem. Officium quod volens ultro praestat sine suo incommodo, nequaquam debet esse captatio lucri: dans mutuo volens sine suo incommodo, ac recipiens ad certum tempus quantum dederat, vult existimari officiosus, ergo non debet amplius petere, alioqui nomen officii transfertur ad insidias, et ad avaritiae praetextum. Vult igitur lex Moisi inter cives hoc officium gratuitum esse, quia civis in communicatione rerum, quae communicari possunt, plus obligatus est civi, quam peregrino et hosti, sicut lex Deuteron. xv, (2, 3) vetat anno 7. peti debitum a cive; sed a peregrino expresse concedit. Item praecipit Hebraeum servum dimitti, natum in alia gente non oportebat dimitti. Ita multa sunt officia, quae Deus vult cives civibus praestare,

Other aspects of Melanchthon's attitude to the usury question are illustrated in his observations on the Mosaic law of the Jubilee. Like Luther, Melanchthon repeatedly proclaims the irrelevance of the Hebrew polity for sixteenth-century Christians. The custom of the Jubilee, he concurs, was as peculiarly an ordinance of the Hebrew people as circumcision. Among the Hebrews, the Jubilee had a reason for existence and provided an example of humanity. To insist on transferring that custom to present-day republics is seditious. We are bound only by our own laws, which are compatible with reason and approved by the magistrates.[67]

---

quae non necesse est hostibus aut peregrinis praestare. Qui igitur utrinque sunt membra Ecclesiae, sint sine captatione lucri et sine usura: ut si pius homo vere egens petiverit ab alio dari mutuo frumentum aut pecuniam, et non egens illi dederit mutuo volens et certo tempore receperit, nihil petat amplius, quia Deus sic praecipit de mutuatione, quae est officium inter cives, quod debet esse gratuitum et sine insidiis.

"Sunt et mutuationes damnosae, cum principes petunt magnam pecuniam a subditis, qua sine detrimentis subditi carere non possunt et nulla constituunt tempora reddendi, cum ad naturam mutuationis pertineat constitui certum tempus ad reddendum. Tales mutuationes similes sunt illi generi, de quo lex divina loquitur, cum concedit usuras peti a peregrinis. Non est enim ibi officii ratio, quia nec dans mutuo prorsus sponte id facit, nec facit virtute, ut illi egenti opem ferat, et accipiens multo plus petit, quam quantum sine compensatione alter sustinere possit. Talis contractus certe non est officiosa mutuatio, ut quidam disputarunt esse innominatum contractum: Do ut des, quia hoc deest, quod ad naturam mutuationis pertinet, ut ad certum tempus sors reddatur." *Ibid.*, XVI, 579-80. The distinction between *mutuationes officiosae* and *mutuationes damnosae* is presented in a more generalized way in Melanchthon's later statements. Cf. his *Dissertatio de contractibus, ibid.*, 505-6. Also, see below, pp. 63-65.

[67] *CR*, XVI, 131, 136-37, 255, 503-4. In 1549, one year before the Roman Jubilee of 1550, Melanchthon made a new attempt at a formal Protestant interpretation of the Hebraic releases. On that occasion, he simultaneously denounced the Roman Church and the revolting peasants of 1524-25 for having derived two contrasting but equally absurd sets of inferences from the Old Testament passages. The Jubilee, he claimed, provides no basis either for ecclesiastical indulgences from penitential satisfactions nor for rustic demands to be released from rent charges. Among the Hebrews, and, for that matter, among the Greeks, he observes, legislation in favor of remissions performed a worthwhile social function. The coming of the Church, however, means the advent of a continual and everlasting

Disputing with Strauss in 1524, he issued a similar warning about the Gospel. Political affairs, he insisted, need not be judged according to the law of Christ. "The Gospel permits us liberty in using civil laws, Roman laws, and others, to the extent required for the public peace."[68]

In the following year, this time taking Aristotle as his text, Melanchthon issued a stronger admonition in the same vein.[69] Only the unlearned and the fanatical imagine, he charged, that the Gospel embodies a political doctrine according to which cities must be governed. Politics, like medicine, is a specialized art, entirely consonant with reason, albeit far removed from the Gospel. Preachers ought not to presume to sit in judgment on political issues. Their duty, rather, is to persuade men to obey the civil laws religiously. It is as foolhardy for a preacher of the Gospel to interfere in politics as it would be for a theologian to practice medicine. Indeed, ministers are to be deemed seditious who go beyond their function to suggest laws concerning the "division of estates, tributes, contracts, and the punishments of criminals." In this connection, he explicitly accuses Wyclif (1320-1384), Capito (1478-1541), Zwingli, and the Anabaptists of fomenting disturbance.[70]

Jubilee. The literal release of the Old Testament served mainly to prefigure God's offer to men, "because of the mediator," of unending absolutions "from sin, from the judgment of the law, that is from condemnation, from death and from all miseries." *Disputatio de iubileo,* esp. no. 37.

[68] See Luther, *BW,* III, 266-67; also, *CR,* I, 655-56.

[69] See the entire introductory discussion of the *Commentarii in aliquot politicos libros Aristotelis, CR,* XVI, 417-22.

[70] "Vere enim seditiosi iudicandi sunt isti, qui cum doceant Evangelium, irrumpunt in alienam functionem, ferunt leges de divisione haereditatum, de tributis, de contractibus, de poenis maleficiorum. Sicut multis locis concionatores vetant suspendi fures, ferunt leges de decimis, damnant publice receptos contractus etc. Wicleff valde tumultuatur et contendit decimas non esse solvendas otiosis sacerdotibus. Capito contendit ut principes remittant aliquid de annuo tributo. Cinglius vocat vectigalia Harpyias; alii venationes publicas, Anabaptistae damnant iudicia etc. Hi errores praeterquam quod impii sunt, etiam labefaciunt tranquillitatem

Again and again, Melanchthon defends the pact of purchase of a rent with promise to resell (*cum pacto de reven-
dendo*).[71] His arguments at this point, as well as his strictures
against taking the Old Testament or the Gospel as a norm for
civil law, are aimed at those left-wing sectaries of the
Reformation who were inspired by the egalitarian features
of the Hebrew Commonwealth. Even more explicitly than
Luther, he is concerned to discredit the claim of the radicals
that the taking of interest in any form was incompatible with
Christian brotherhood. He asserts unequivocally that erroneous views on the interest question plunged the peasants
into the excesses of the 1525 Revolt.[72] Strauss's theses of
1524, he charges, were directly responsible for the rising in
Thuringia.[73]

Melanchthon writes as an ecclesiastical statesman intent
upon serving the civil government, rather than as an over-
wrought religious leader of turbulent masses. He seems to
have had much less sympathy for the burdens of the under-

---

publicam. Quare prodest adversus hanc impietatem bene munitum esse, et
recte tenere discrimen Evangelii et politices, ac scire quod Evangelium ad
cordis iustitiam pertineat, non pertineat ad civilem statum. Imo approbet
omnes formas rerum publicarum, modo sint consentaneae rationi, sicut
approbat architectonicam, aut medicinam rationi consentaneam.

"Pauci in Ecclesia fuerunt scriptores, qui satis perspexerunt hoc discrimen. Itaque pontifices invaserunt imperia, arrogaverunt sibi ius trans-
ferendi regna. Nos igitur diligenter observemus maximum intervallum
inter Evangelium et politicam esse. Et politias omnes approbari ab
Evangelio, si cum ratione consentant. Ac videte quae sit stultitia. Si quis
theologus velit medicinam exercere, nonne hunc omnes irriderent, quia
artem, quam non didicisset, profiteretur? Ita iure irridentur concionatores,
qui volunt civitates gubernare, quum nunquam in republica versati sint."
Ibid., 419-20.

[71] *CR*, XVI, 132-36, 250-55, 499-503.

[72] "Anno 1525 alicubi classicum seditionum erant clamores indoctorum,
qui vociferabantur sine discrimine, reditus qualescunque usuras esse."
Ibid., XVI, 250; cf. *ibid.*, 498. Commenting upon the *De officiis*, Melanchthon recalls that numerous revolutions occurred in Greece and Rome
"because of the magnitude of the usuries." *Ibid.*, 610.

[73] *Ibid.*, 131; cf. *ibid.*, 415-22. Rejecting Strauss's thesis, Melanchthon
writes: "Caeterum qui solvit usuras, non peccat." *Ibid.*, 129.

privileged than Luther. Thus, Melanchthon never betrays himself into encouraging either the agitation against the *Zinskauf* or the pleas for a restoration of utopian Mosaic laws. To the contrary, he accepts, and even goes beyond, the most advanced economic views of medieval theologians and jurists. For example, he elaborates upon Chancellor Gerson's declaration that contracts which are customarily practiced in any region are not lightly to be condemned.[74] Shedding the reservations maintained even by latitudinarian Italian civilists, like Paul de Castro (d. 1441),[75] he "was ready to allow that interest (*interesse*) might justly be demanded even when there was no delay in repayment, that is, that it might be bargained for from the very day that the loan was contracted."[76]

Melanchthon's views on the traffic in annuities are much more advanced than those of Luther.[77] He approves even of the contract whereby the rent was constituted on the whole complex of the borrower's property rather than on a specific estate yielding a permanent income (*res frugifera*).[78] This arrangement had seemed an abomination to Luther, and, soon it was to be outlawed by Pius V in the bull *Cum onus* (1568).[79] Melanchthon, however, professes to find authority

[74] *Ibid.*, 131, 501; cf. *ibid.*, 429-30. On a number of occasions Melanchthon expresses approval of other distinctions advised by Gerson to ease the burdens on conscience. *Ibid.*, 111, 113, 248. It is interesting to observe that Gerson is praised for the same propositions by the notorious apologist of the Jesuit "laxists," G. Pirot. See the latter's *L'apologie pour les casuistes,* p. 99. For Gerson's views on usury, see his *De contractibus,* in *Opera,* ii, 167-96; also, Schreiber, *Die volkswirtschaftlichen Anschauungen der Scholastik,* 204-6.

[75] Ashley, *op.cit.*, ii, 402-3.

[76] *Ibid.*, 453; cf. *CR*, xvi, 138-40, 257. A similar view is attributed to the contemporary canonist, Martinus Navarrus (d. 1586), and to Sigismund Scaccia. Ashley, *op.cit.*, ii, 403, 453, 457. Melanchthon claims to find authority for his latitudinarian analysis of extrinsic titles in the following jurists: Hostiensis on c. *Salubriter,* X. v. 19. c. 16; Baldus, on l. *Acceptam, Cod. Iust.,* iv. 32.19; Panormitanus, on c. *Naviganti,* X. v. 19. c. 19.

[77] Wiskemann, *Darstellung,* 65.

[78] *CR*, xvi, 134-37, 252-55, 500-1.

[79] For the text, see *Lib. Sept.,* ii, 12. c. *un.,* ed. J. H. Boehmer, 79. Ashley puts the fate of this bull tersely: "The moral theologians of the

in the views of Innocent IV and Baldus for the conclusion that this transaction was a genuine sale. In contrast to Luther, Melanchthon takes occasion to praise the rulings on this head of Martin V and Calixtus III.[80]

On several notable occasions, Melanchthon publicly came to the defense of civil laws allowing a limited rate of usury. In the disputations at the Diet of Regensburg in 1541, he supported the ordinance of Charles V.[81] Twelve years later, in the midst of great disturbances over the interest question in Denmark, he provided that country's King, Christian III, with an important opinion approving a civil regulation of the interest rates.[82] Both times he argued for a sharp distinction between morality and law in the settlement of the usury question. Though preachers remain bound to protest against all usury as sinful, he said, secular powers are free to restrict punishment only to excessive usury.[83] Soon after, he acknowledged the legality, with some reservations, of the Bres-

---

order of Jesus, and chief among them Molina in Spain (1535-1600), Lessius in the Netherlands (1554-1623), and Azorius in Germany (1533-1603), set themselves to minimize the purport of the bull. They maintained that in those countries where it had not been properly published it was not in force, and accordingly argued that it had no validity in France, the Netherlands, and Germany; in the two Sicilies its operation was suspended by a bull of Gregory XIII, confirming that of Nicholas V." *Op.cit.*, II, 452-53. Cf. the full discussion in Honoratus Leotardus, *Liber singularis de usuris*, qu. 44, pp. 205-7. Incidentally, a similar fate overcame the same Pope's ruling on *cambia*, the c. *In eam pro nostro*, of Jan. 28, 1571. See *Lib. Sept.*, II, 11, c. *un.*, ed. Boehmer, 78-79; also H. Denzinger, *Enchiridion*, nos. 1081-82, pp. 336-37, where it is given as V. 13. 2; cf. Lessius, *De iustitia et iure*, lib. ii, cap. 23, dub. 11, p. 323.

[80] Wiskemann, *Darstellung, 65.*

[81] *CR*, VIII, 86.

[82] *Ibid.*, 84-88. Cf. the summary of Melanchthon's letter to Zacharias Ursinus in the latter's letter of February 27, 1577, to Crato: "ante aliquot annos cum in Dania essent magni tumultus de usuris se in hanc sententiam scripsisse ad Regem et eam probatam fuisse Cancellario magis quam aliorum." J. F. A. Gillet, *Crato von Crafftheim*, 2te Th., 474. For the influence of German theologians and jurists on the Danish controversy over *Zinsen*, see A. Rubow, *Renteforhold i Danmark*, 27-51.

[83] *CR*, VIII, 86-87.

lau law concerning the investment of funds of wards. Replying to the inquiries on this head by Zacharias Ursinus, he recalled that Luther, though condemning usury, had permitted a *"Wucherlein."*[84]

Notable signs of the latitudinarian drift of Melanchthon's attitude toward the usury question are to be found in two sets of *consilia* issued by him in 1554-1555. The first set of responses was sent to the municipal council of Regensburg;[85] the second[86] was issued to Christoph Fischer, then embroiled in the controversy over usury in Thuringia in his capacity as *Generalsuperintendent* in Schmalkalden and Meiningen.[87]

Melanchthon's formula in both responses rests on the expansion of a distinction, made previously by him in less decisive form, between two types of loan, one *officiosa,* the other *damnosa.* The former transaction occurs, for example, Melanchthon now explains, when a man borrows a sum from his neighbor which the latter can dispense with for a short time. Being *officiosa,* this loan ought to be gratuitous. It is of this kind of loan, says Melanchthon, of which Christ speaks. On this matter the teachings of Christ and the laws of Moses are one.

Truth to tell, the contrast between *mutuationes officiosae* and *mutuationes damnosae* had been present to Melanchthon's

---

[84] Gillet, *Crato von Crafftheim,* 2te Th., 469-75, esp. at 474. In the course of this letter, Melanchthon recommends the reading of the discussion of usury in his recently re-issued commentaries on Cicero's *De officiis.* See *CR,* XVI, 575-94. He makes reference, also, to his letters on the subject of usury to the King of Denmark and to the town of Brunswick.

[85] *CR,* VIII, 368-72, esp. at 370-71 (wrongly numbered 377).

[86] For description and text, see Georg Arndt, "Ein bisher unbekanntes Gutachten Philipp Melanchthons, Georg Majors und Paul Ebers in Sachen des Thüringer Wucherstreites aus dem Jahre 1555(?)," *Beiträge zur thüringischen Kirchengeschichte,* 1 (1929/30), 158-61. Melanchthon was author of the responses; his two aforementioned colleagues were simply subscribers.

[87] For Fischer's role in the controversy over usury in Thuringia, see Arndt, "Christoph Fischer und seine Tätigkeit als Generalsuperintendent im Thüringer Lande," *Beiträge zur thüringischen und sächsischen Kirchengeschichte,* 295-326, esp. 315-21.

mind for at least thirty years. In 1525, however, the distinction is presented in a restricted fashion and in the special setting of the Deuteronomic debate. The difference between this earlier version and the analysis given in the *responsa* under discussion is seen most clearly by comparing successive illustrations of the *mutuationes damnosae*. In his earlier essay, Melanchthon identifies the *mutuatio damnosa* by two marks: 1) the loan is forced by a prince from his subjects; 2) the time for repayment is not fixed. In other words, Melanchthon means to argue, the involuntary character of the transaction, the undergoing of specific loss, and the uncertainty of the date of repayment entitle the creditor to compensation for *damnum*. Indeed, he observes, some are disposed to describe this transaction as an "innominate contract," rather than a *mutuum,* since the hallmark of a *mutuum,* to their way of thinking, the fixed term of maturity, is lacking.[88]

The later *responsa* bear no trace of special connection with the Deuteronomic issue. In addition, they represent a significant extension of the canonist mode of analysis. In illustration of the *mutuatio damnosa,* he now mentions not merely involuntary subventions but also sums freely invested with merchants in the form of a partnership. The precise terms of Melanchthon's analysis will bear repetition. The *mutuatio damnosa,* he explains, refers to large loans over long and not clearly determinate periods. In such cases, the lender cannot extend his money without suffering damage. Therefore, the rule of equality demands that he receive a compensation, which is called *interesse,* amounting to no more than five per cent. Many such interest-bearing loans, Melanchthon reports, are made by the treasurers of churches and other honest men. Princes are frequently offered such arrangements and the moneys of orphans are invested in a similar fashion in the cities.

True, Melanchthon adds that he does not mean to extend

[88] For the text, see above, note 66, at p. 58.

his approval indiscriminately to all mercantile contracts. Indeed, he cautions, each arrangement needs to be examined on its own merits. Nevertheless, it is apparent that Melanchthon's treatment of the *mutuatio damnosa* in 1554-1555 is additional proof of his readiness to exceed the canonists in the liberalization of the laws of usury.[89] Without saying so in so many words, Melanchthon's formula implies the increasing bifurcation of human relations into distinct spheres: one, the world of friendship and free services; the other, the world of commercial intercourse and the economic calculus.

Zwingli (1484-1531),[90] like Luther and Melanchthon, seems loathe to concede that a strict prohibition of usury might be inferred from Scriptures. To deny the name of Christians to those who extend loans with a hope of profit is to torture the texts, he declares.[91] The Swiss Reformer, also, opposes the utopian teachings of the Anabaptists.[92] The

[89] An interesting fusion of old and new viewpoints is to be found in the response to the fourth question, where Melanchthon discusses the treatment to be accorded to practitioners of "notorious usury." See Arndt, "Ein bisher unbekanntes Gutachten," *Beiträge zur thüringischen Kirchengeschichte,* 1 (1929/30), 161.

[90] The best available study of Zwingli's economic ethics known to me is Paul Meyer's *Zwinglis Soziallehren,* a dissertation done at Zurich under the supervision of Walther Köhler. Two works on related themes deserve special mention. W. Classen's *Schweizer Bauernpolitik im Zeitalter Ulrich Zwinglis* has valuable statistical material on rent contracts. Ernst Correll's *Das schweizerische Täufermennonitentum* is an outstanding account of the views of the Swiss Anabaptists. Other works are indicated in subsequent notes.

[91] On Luke vi:34-35, in *Werke,* ed. M. Schuler and J. Schulthess, vi, 589. Bullinger (1504-1575) reports that the Swiss Anabaptists took Luke vi:35 to be a commandment against usury and interest. See Correll, *op.cit.,* 47. For Bullinger's criticisms of utopian teachings on usury, see his *Von dem unvershampten fraefel,* bk. iv, pp. 151-54; *idem, Wider die Widertoeuffer,* esp. bk. ii, ch. 2, ed. 1560, pp. 37ff.; *idem, The Decades, decas* iii, *sermo* i, Vol. ii (*Parker Society Publications,* vii), 40-44.

[92] W. Herding, *Die wirtschaftlichen und sozialen Anschauungen,* 41. According to some accounts, the Swiss Anabaptists held that it was the duty of a Christian to pay interest if it were decreed by the civil authorities, but that no Christian was free to accept it. See texts in Correll, *op.cit.,* 47.

critical years, 1523-1525, find him repeatedly emphasizing his objections to radical proposals on the twin issues of tithes and usury. The world, he insists, cannot be governed according to Divine Justice. Once private property has been established in human society, it becomes theft to withhold payment of interest charges or rents.[93] Not even the civil authorities may thereafter compel anyone to provide loans gratis. The obligation to pay interest flows directly from the Lord's commandment "to render to all their dues."[94] Nevertheless, Zwingli, in common with the other Reformers, inveighs against the exploitation of the people by Jewish and other professional usurers.[95]

Zwingli has little sympathy for extremist attacks on private property and the prerogatives of civil government. The reception of the Gospel, he says, must not become the occasion for withholding another's goods.[96] In the matter of the *Zins* contracts, Zwingli seems closer to Luther than to Melanchthon.[97]

[93] See: *Auslegen und Gründe der Schlussreden* (1523), *CR*, LXXXIX, art. 67, p. 454; *idem, Wer Ursache gebe zu Aufruhr, CR*, XC, 387-90, and Köhler's remarks at 356, 363-64; Zwingli, *Von göttlicher und menschlicher Gerechtigkeit* (1523), *CR*, LXXXIX, 515-21; cf. Hyma, *op.cit.*, for translations of extracts from these *loci;* also, Wiskemann, *Darstellung,* 71; Schmoller, *Zeitschrift für die gesamte Staatswissenschaft*, XVI (1860), 571-73.

[94] Romans xiii:7. Zwingli writes: "Zins ist man ouch schuldig ze bezalen by dem gbott gottes. . . . Denn für das die eigenschafft ingebrochen ist, so mag ein obergheit nieman zwingen das er das sin one trost des widergeltens oder nutzes usslyhe (cf. Luke vi:35)." *CR*, LXXXIX, 515, tr. in Hyma, *op.cit.*, 115.

[95] *CR*, LXXXIX, 520; cf. Wiskemann, *Darstellung,* 71.

[96] See Zwingli's letter of Sept. 6, 1530, to Ambrose Blaurer: "Postremo dixi: nobilitatem atque rusticos diversis nonnunquam mediis ad idem scelus tendere. Ut cum rustici evangelium recipiant, ut omne aes alienum omneque debitum vi antiquent." See *CR*, XCVIII, no. 1091, p. 121, cited from earlier ed. in Herding, *op.cit.*, 43-44.

[97] Meyer, *Zwinglis Soziallehren,* 58-62; Wiskemann, *Darstellung,* 71-72. Köhler's summary of Zwingli's treatment of the bitterly disputed problems of the tithes and usury deserves citation: "Die Stärke der Opposition gegen die Zins-und Zehntenzahlung lag im Evangelium, das doch die Reformation unter Zwinglis Führung restituieren wollte. An der Norm

Luther, Melanchthon, and Zwingli do not expressly depart from the ethic of brotherhood. To do this, they would have had to redefine the character of the fraternal bond between men. But they did help to encourage the conviction that the ethic of brotherhood could not be the basis of civil society.

Few men have been so insistent as Luther in proclaiming that men were incorrigibly depraved and the world a theatre of their demonic aggressions. He insisted upon the sharpest possible divorce between the Christian ethic and the character of political organization. With him, the prophetic elements in the Old Testament and the Gospels become a utopian ethic, rather than a substratum of the common law of Christianity. In exalting "conscience" at the expense of "law" and "casuistry," he helped to demolish the very armature which conscience inevitably generates in its effort to become effective in the world. In insisting upon man's total unworthiness to merit grace and in throwing man entirely upon God's mercy, he made it possible for many the more easily to justify their egoism and irresponsibility in social life.

In terms of the specific history of Deuteronomy xxiii: 19-20, neither Luther's nor Melanchthon's exegesis can be said to have been germinal. Luther's gory description of God's wrath, first against the Gentiles, then against the Jews, did violence to the sense that the Lord was the fount of equity, justice, and universal love; his intense antisemitism and anti-egalitarianism worked only to enhance the discriminatory aspects of the Deuteronomic commandment. Melanchthon's mature interpretation, too, was particularistic,

---

der Bergpredigt z.B. gemessen, ist Zins und Zehnten nicht zu halten. Zwingli hat das hier vorliegende ernste und schwere Problem gespürt, Evangelium und Kultur klaffen in 'göttlicher' und 'menschlicher Gerechtigkeit' auseinander, aber er entscheidet die Frage mit einem Machtspruch:hier hat die Obrigkeit das letzte Wort, ist ihr zu gehorchen. Dass diese Kapitulation vor der Praxis der Kultur die auf die Höhenlage der Restitution des Evangeliums Gestimmten nicht befriedigt, versteht man. Daher musste diese Frage eine Unruhe in der Zürcher Reformationsbewegung bleiben." See *CR*, xc, 363.

rather than Christian in character. From the standpoint of the capitalist spirit, the crying need was to transcend, rather than to buttress, the double-edged rule. In the later history of the Deuteronomic commandment, Calvin, and not Luther or Melanchthon, is the principal source of inspiration.

Yet one last detour is required before it will be proper to focus on the true author of the new ethic. Something must first be said about Martin Bucer (1491-1551), the Reformer of Strassburg.[98]

Bucer comes closer than any other representative of the first generation of the Reformation to sponsoring a decisive break with medieval interpretations of the idea of brotherhood and usury. Indeed, in the opinion of one student, whose work has been unduly neglected, Bucer, rather than Calvin, deserves to be described as the architect of the new Protestant theory of usury.[99] A fresh review of the relevant sources, however, fails to substantiate this extreme view. Truth to tell, intimations of many of Calvin's major conclusions, to be discussed presently in their own right, are found earlier in Bucer. Yet a chronicler of the career of Deuteronomy will feel justified in retaining the name of Bucer as the last of the witnesses to Deuteronomy's crisis, rather than to substitute his name for that of Calvin at the opening of a fresh chapter in the history of the relations of the ideas of usury and brotherhood.[100]

[98] For a convenient bibliography of Bucer's published writings, see F. Mentz, *Bibliographische Zusammenstellung der gedruckten Schriften Butzer's*. For recent accounts of Bucer's social teachings, see C. Hopf, *Martin Bucer and the English Reformation*, esp. 122-27; W. Pauck, *Das Reich Gottes auf Erden*.

[99] Klingenburg has contended that all of Calvin's reputed innovations with respect to the idea of usury are anticipated in the writings of Bucer. See G. Klingenburg, *Das Verhältnis Calvins zu Butzer*, pp. 22-41, 79-81, 83, 85-92. Interestingly, Klingenburg is not the first writer to identify Bucer as the founder of the Protestant doctrine of usury. The priority of Bucer is asserted in the *Traité de l'usure* by Bossuet (1627-1704), for example. See Bossuet, *Oeuvres*, xxx, 677.

[100] Klingenburg's claim has been unreservedly rejected as absurd by

Three reasons may be alleged for this conviction. Firstly, Bucer nowhere provides an array of arguments on usury so well-panoplied, both for offensive and defensive uses, as to guarantee a decisive breach in the medieval tradition. The all-important reasons for Bucer's novel conclusions are either omitted altogether or are offered in too casual a fashion to serve as a secure base from which to venture a new start. Secondly, a number of the newer theses, prerequisite to the destruction of the older medieval doctrines, were not brought into action by Bucer until 1550-1551,[101] five years after the epochal letter of Calvin to Claude de Sachins.

Thirdly—and this seems decisive to a chronicler of the career of Deuteronomy—Bucer's confrontation of the historic double-edged commandment failed to produce in him a heightened tension or elicit from him a noteworthy response. How different was the case with Calvin! As we shall presently see, it was Calvin's response to Deuteronomy, as much as, if not more than, his spectacular rebuff to scholastic versions of Aristotle's theory of money, which finally spelled the dislodgement of the millennial theory of usury.

The source of Bucer's principal emphasis would appear to have been Luther. It is Luther's voice whose echoes are heard in Bucer's proclamations of the authority of conscience,

---

Doumergue. See E. Doumergue, *Jean Calvin*, v, 688-89; cf. Hyma, *Christianity, Capitalism, and Communism*, 112. Though I cannot share the convictions of Klingenburg, I am convinced that less than justice is done to his quite original essay by the biographer of Calvin. Actually, Bucer does go quite far, farther than any of his contemporaries among the Reformers, in the direction ultimately defined by Calvin. For our purposes, however, it is not Bucer, but Calvin who signalizes in an explicit fashion the rejection of the Hebraic and medieval versions of the ethic of brotherhood, in terms of which the millennial opposition to usury had expressed itself. I do not find that Bucer came in any of his writings directly and deliberately to turn his back on the traditional definitions of brotherhood. This is true even of the treatise of 1550, which appeared five years after the epochal pronouncement of Calvin in 1545.

[101] See Bucer, *Tractatus de usuris*, ed. in *Scripta anglicana*, 789-96.

informed by the Golden Rule, to serve as the guide to right conduct and the ultimate criterion of legal institutions.[102] In Bucer, the Lutheran rejection of Mosaic and medieval legalism is expressed with enhanced self-confidence. He betrays no lingering doubts as to the intention or authority of the Old and New Testaments with regard to usury and the releases of the Sabbatical and the Jubilee years. In Bucer's opinion, ordinary people had been and were still being betrayed into an erroneous understanding of the Gospels by an assortment of ignorant and partisan commentators. The "mad Anabaptists" were no less blameworthy in this regard than the perverse mythologists and presumptuous canonists at the beck of the Pope. With utter forthrightness, Bucer claims that the sole test of the legality of loans is the Golden Rule. After the fashion of Luther he contends that Matthew v:42 treats not of usury, but of capital. We are adjured in that passage, says Bucer, not simply to abstain from taking usury from our needy neighbors, but even to abstain from hoping for the restoration of our capital. Indeed, says Bucer, usury is nowhere forbidden *per se*; nowhere is usury declared iniquitous in itself. The Old Testament forbids only biting usury (*neshek*). Indeed, there is nothing to keep the Christian from observing the rules laid down by the Emperor Justinian.[103]

Bucer's commentary upon Psalms xv:5 flatly rejects the view that all forms of usury were proscribed by the Old Testament. Surely one should not cry usury when a debtor is asked to provide his creditor some portion of the income which the loan has yielded. There is no law or moral principle to forbid widows, orphans, and studious clergy from

[102] See Bucer, *In Evangelion Matthaei enarratio,* on cap. v, esp. at pp. 179-81: "Unde probe animadvertendum est, quod in Luca mox subiectum legitur, prout vultis ut vobis faciant homines, et vos facite illis similiter. Haec unica erit regula, omnis donationis, mutui, et cessionis." Cf. *idem, In epistolam ad Ephesios,* at p. 60.

[103] *In Evangelion Matthaei enarratio,* 182-83.

receiving a share of the profits made by merchants in investing their funds.[104]

Yet, Bucer, no more than Luther before him or Calvin after him, meant to authorize unlimited usury. Like all the other reformers, Bucer was in opposition to the practices of Jewish moneylenders. In an opinion submitted to the Landgrave Philip of Hesse in 1539, Bucer demanded the strictest governmental control of Jewish usuries and the reduction of the rates which Jews were allowed to take.[105]

The fullest discussion by Bucer of the problem of usury is to be found in his *Tractatus de usuris* of 1550. Here he records his replies to a number of pious youths who had consulted him in the hope of pacifying their own consciences with reference to the issues posed by the question of usury. Five years before the issuance of this treatise, Bucer had been attacked for his views by his traditionalist colleague at Cambridge, the polemical master of Pembroke Hall, John Young (1514-1580), in the course of public lectures and disputations at Canterbury.[106] Bucer's replies are once more characterized by his supreme conviction in the decisive importance of the Golden Rule. The laws of God are in no way breached by the rates authorized by the civil law of Justinian. Indeed, Bucer claims, persons living in England may rightly claim ten per cent interest under the law.[107] The objections to usury in the Old Testament apply not to all increments on loans, but properly to biting usury upon usury. Luke vi, he maintains, has nothing to do with usury as such, nor for that matter are the remarks against usury in the writings of St.

---

[104] Klingenburg, *op.cit.*, 34-35.

[105] *Ibid.*, 35, citing Bucer's *Von den Juden* (1539), 3, 13.

[106] For Young's polemics against Bucer, see J. B. Mullinger, *The University of Cambridge*, II, 122; also A. W. Ward, *s.v.* "Butzer, Martin" in *DNB*, VI (1886), 172-77 and A. F. Pollard, *s.v.* "Young, John," *ibid.*, LXIII (1900), 379. Young's defense of the traditionalist view of usury is unpublished. See reference to *MS* of Young's work in *DNB*, LXIII, 379.

[107] See Bucer, *Scripta anglicana*, 792. Bucer is here recognizing the legality of the Act of 37 Henry VIII, c. 9 (1545).

Basil and Demosthenes to be referred to every form of interest on loan.[108]

In short: Bucer was the bridge from Luther to Calvin. Now to Calvin himself.

[108] It is interesting to note that one of the charges made by Andrew Perne (1519-86) in the course of his sermon on the occasion of the burning of the remains of Bucer was the latter's toleration of usury *among Christians.* Perne declared: "de mordacibus item usuris quasi is eas licere inter Christianos sentiret, et aliis permultis." Bucer, *Scripta anglicana,* 930-31.

CHAPTER III

The Road to Universal Otherhood:
From Calvin to Blackstone

WITH John Calvin we stand on the threshold of a "transvaluation of values." In demolishing the inherited exegesis of Deuteronomy, Calvin departs even farther from the medieval morality than has been suspected. To Ashley,[1] Calvin's attack on the Aristotelian, more correctly the patristic and scholastic, concept of the sterility of money seemed a "turning point in the history of European thought"; Weber declared that his recasting of the doctrine of "calling" and his enunciation of the program of *innerweltliche Askese* were the foundations of the modern capitalist spirit; and Hauser[2] hailed him as the pioneer in the introduction of sociological relativism into the interpretation of history and ethics. But no one has noticed that Calvin, self-consciously and hesitantly, charted the path to the world of Universal Otherhood, where all become "brothers" in being equally "others."

Calvin is the first religious leader to exploit the ambivalence of the Deuteronomic passage in such a fashion as to prove that it was permissible to take usury from one's brother.

---

[1] *An Introduction to English Economic History*, II, 459.

[2] *Les débuts du capitalisme*, 50. According to Hauser, Calvin and du Moulin (1500-1566) exhibited profound economic realism by broaching the usury question in terms of the structure of society. They found a precedent for this approach, he observes, in the commentary on Psalms xv by Johannes Aepinus (Johann Hoeck), which was published at Strassburg and Mainz in 1543. (Aepinus was the first Lutheran Superintendent at Hamburg.) It seems relevant to point out here that the core of Aepinus' analysis, the tripartite grouping of classes, appears almost a century earlier in the works of the defenders of the *monti*. See, e.g., Annius of Viterbo in *Pro monte pietatis: Consilia*, p. 8v. Cf. Aepinus, *In Psalmum XV Davidis*, esp. at f. 27v. Calvin stressed this perspective to the point of breaking the bounds of the medieval theory of interest.

His exegesis spells the demise of Deuteronomy. He succeeded in legitimizing usury without seeming to impair the vitality either of the universalism or the fraternalism of the Christian ethic. Trained as a jurist, he was able to lend precision to the notion, crudely anticipated by Luther and Bucer, that the Mosaic and Gospel rules were to be translated in the light of the individual conscience, the equity of the Golden Rule, and the requirements of public utility.[3]

Calvin on Deuteronomy became a Gospel of the modern era. Everyone from the sixteenth to the nineteenth century who advocated a more liberal usury law turned to Calvin for support. Even those who would not or could not mention his name were compelled to speak his words. If today we do not appeal to his teachings, it is because we have learned his lessons too well. Religious or even ethical vocabulary is no

[3] Had Weber had the opportunity to pursue the insights of his last lectures, he might well have hit upon the fact that Calvin's view of usury was one of the first monuments of the Universal Otherhood, whose characteristics he had so well envisaged. For reasons too complex to recall here, it was not until the end of his life that he detected the fruitfulness of taking the usury question as a point of departure for the history of the capitalist spirit. In this respect, his *General Economic History* presents the strongest possible contrast with the tenor of *The Protestant Ethic* and of his replies to the criticisms of it by F. Keller and Sombart. See *The Protestant Ethic*, 200-203.

Most attacks on the "Weber thesis" neglect to mention the important changes of emphasis in his successive expositions. But that is petty misdemeanor compared with the graver felonies committed against his classic treatise. Careless critics have accused him again and again of ignoring the medieval origins of capitalism and of imagining that the capitalist economy was an emanation of the capitalist spirit. Weber was guilty of neither charge. To see this clearly, it is simply necessary to observe his care in delimiting his claims and declaring his methods. (Indeed, the present author is minded at this point to reiterate these disclaimers on his own behalf, since it is not possible for him in these pages to debate the myriad issues relevant to this sketch.) It is pleasing at this juncture to report that a more judicious estimate of the master's aims and achievements is now gaining currency in the scholarly community. See, esp., E. Fischoff, "The Protestant Ethic and the Spirit of Capitalism: The History of a Controversy," *Social Research,* xi (1944), 53-77 (summarizes a chapter of the same author's unprinted doctoral dissertation submitted to the New School for Social Research in New York in 1942).

longer needed to justify the moral and economic postulates
which he helped to establish.

The new coordinates assumed in Calvin's schema are exposed in the reply to Claude de Sachins' inquiry on the problem of usury in the closing months of 1545,[4] and in the
sermons and commentaries on various books of the Old
Testament during the following decades.[5]

"If we wholly condemn usury," he begins, "we impose
tighter fetters on the conscience than God himself." Scriptures forbid only biting usury (*neshek*), usury taken from
the defenseless poor. Luke vi:35 has been perverted to imply
that He commanded us to lend gratuitously, and without
any hope of gain.

> . . . As elsewhere in speaking of the sumptuous feasts and
> ambitious social rivalry of the rich He commands rather that
> they invite in from the streets the blind, the lame and the poor,
> who cannot make a like return, so here, wishing to correct the
> vicious custom of the world in lending money, He directs us
> to lend chiefly to those from whom there is no hope of re-
> covery.[6]

As for Deuteronomy xxiii:19—God had no other object
in view "except that mutual and brotherly affection should
prevail amongst the Israelites."[7] The precept to lend without
usury was plainly a part of the Jewish polity and not a uni-

---

[4] *Opera*, x.1 (*CR*, xxxviii.1), cols. 245-49; tr. freely in Georgia Harkness, *John Calvin*, 204-7.

[5] See the sermons and commentaries on the following passages: On
Ex. xxii:25, Lev. xxv:35-38; Deut. xxiii:19-20 in *Mosis reliqui libri
quatuor in formam harmoniae digesta, Opera*, xxiv (*CR*, lii), 680-83, tr.
by C. W. Bingham in Calvin, *Commentaries on the Four Last Books of
Moses*, iii, 128-32; on Ps. xv:5, in *Opera*, xxxi (*CR*, lix), 147-48; on
Deut. xxiii:18-20, in *Opera*, xxviii (*CR*, lvi), 111-21; on Ezek.
xviii:5-9, esp. 8, in *Opera*, xl (*CR*, lxviii), 425-33, tr. in *Commentaries
on . . . Ezekiel*, ii, 225-28. Other references in the letters will be cited
below.

[6] *Opera*, x.1 (*CR*, xxxviii.1), 245, tr. Harkness, *John Calvin*, 205.

[7] *Opera*, xxiv (*CR*, lii), 680, tr. Bingham, iii, 128.

versal "spiritual law." Else, God would not have allowed the
Hebrews to lend at usury to Gentiles. The spiritual law does
not admit such discriminations. The peculiar turn of the
Deuteronomic text cannot be justified by appealing to God's
promise to the Hebrews in respect to Canaan. The peoples
of this area were not singled out for special mention. Rather,
God spoke generally of all the nations of the world, including
Egypt and Syria, and all the islands of the sea, in short, of
all who traded with the Jews.[8]

God has permitted many things *"pour la police des Juifs"*
which are in themselves not good; therefore, He did not mean
to legitimize the taking of usury from strangers. He merely
left it unpunished. God showed this indulgence to the Jews,
"since otherwise a just reciprocity would not have been preserved, without which one party must needs be injured."
God had laid the Jews alone and not foreign nations under
the obligation of the law against usury.[9]

> In order, therefore, that equality (*ratio analogica*) be pre-
> served, He accords the same liberty to His people which the
> Gentiles would assume for themselves; for this is the only
> intercourse that can be endured, when the condition of both
> parties is similar and equal.[10]

Today, the Deuteronomic law must be applied to the profit
of the Christians, rather than be allowed to justify the exploitation of Christians by Jews. On a correct interpretation,
the text can hardly give comfort to Jewish usurers. (Here,
indeed, Calvin undertakes to show how the Deuteronomic
discrimination, rightly understood, reacts against the Jews of
his own age.) Modern Jews are wrong, he explains, to assume that everything is permitted them so long as they
practice no extortion among themselves.

> Indeed, they are doubly to be condemned. For they ought to
> be joined with us since God has opened the door to His

[8] *Opera*, xxviii (*CR*, lvi), 116.
[9] *Opera*, xxiv (*CR*, lii), 680, tr. Bingham, iii, 128.
[10] *Ibid.*, 681, tr. Bingham, iii, 129.

church. But now the Jews have quit the place, they have been deprived and banished from the Kingdom of God, and, therefore, we [Christians] are reputed the Sons of Abraham, even though we be not descended according to the flesh of this race. Though then, the Jews anciently had the privilege to exercise usury against pagans, it does not mean that today they ought to burden and molest the children of God, even those who have been driven from His house and have been disowned in consequence of their rebellion and disobedience.[11]

Thus, the specific content of the judicial law which was given to the ancient people is abrogated. There remains as residue only what is dictated by the rules of charity, equity, and justice, from which, in the first place, the old law springs, namely, the injunction not to show harshness to our needy brethren.[12]

The law of Moses (Deut. xxiii:19) is political, and does not obligate us beyond what equity and the reason of humanity suggest. Surely, it should be desirable if usuries were driven from the whole world, indeed that the word be unknown. But since that is impossible, we must make concession to the common utility (*utilité commune*).[13]

However, Calvin admits, both Ezekiel xviii:5-9[14] and Psalms xv:5[15] seem to express universal opposition to usury, and what is more, to condemn the taking of *tarbith* as well as *neshek*. If, however, we take recourse to the infallible norm of justice, we discover that usury does not conflict with the law of God in every case. Hence, it follows that not all usury need be damned. There is a grave difference between taking usury in the course of business and setting up as a usurer. If a person takes profit on a loan on only one occasion, he is not called a usurer. This is not mere word play, Calvin

---

[11] *Opera*, xxviii (*CR*, lvi), 116.
[12] *Ibid.*, 115.
[13] *Opera*, x.1 (*CR*, xxxviii.1), col. 246.
[14] See *Opera*, xl (*CR*, lxviii), 425-33, tr. *Commentaries on ... Ezekiel*, ii, 225-28.
[15] *Opera*, xxxi (*CR*, lix), esp. 147-48.

insists. Men invent cavils, thinking to fool one another by the construction of "specious titles," but God does not admit such deceptions.

It must, nevertheless, be granted, that usury is not allowed indiscriminately in every case, at all times, under all forms, from everybody (*neque passim, neque semper, neque omnia, neque ab omnibus*). For example: an excessive rate is objectionable; one who takes usury constantly has no place in the Church of God; interest taken from the poor is prohibited. In short, it is important to cling to the rule: usury is permissible if it is not injurious to one's brother.[16]

Lastly, the crucial question: May it not be objected, Calvin asks, that usury ought to be outlawed today for the same reason that it was forbidden to Jews, "because among us there is a fraternal union (*conjunction fraternelle*)?" His reply is epoch-making:

> There is a difference in the political union, for the situation in which God placed the Jews and many other circumstances permitted them to trade conveniently among themselves without usuries. Our union is entirely different. (*Nostre conjunction n'a pointe de similitude.*) Therefore I do not feel that usuries were forbidden to us simply, except in so far as they are opposed to equity or charity.[17]

[16] *Opera*, XL (*CR*, LXVIII), 431-32.

[17] *Opera*, X.I (*CR*, XXXVIII.I), 245-49, esp. at 247, tr. Harkness, *John Calvin*, 206. In an illuminating footnote, Josef Bohatec remarks that this sentence refers to the "conjunction fraternelle" as well as to the "conjunction politique." He reminds Hauser also that anticipations of Calvin's historical relativism are found in antiquity. See Bohatec, *Calvins Lehre von Staat und Kirche*, p. 698, n. 214. The importance of relativistic assumptions for medieval thought also must not be overlooked. See G. La Piana, "Joachim of Flora: A Critical Survey," *Speculum*, VII (1932), 257; Thomas Aquinas, *S. th.*, 2.ª2.ªe62.3.; Pierre Dubois, *De recuperatione terrae sanctae*, ed. Langlois, §48, pp. 39-40. To lend money only to those from whom one may expect return is simply to practice the carnal friendship (*carnalis amicitia*) of the pagan, Calvin elsewhere explains. G. Wünsch, "Calvins Beurteilung der Zinswirtschaft," *Die christliche Welt*, XXIX (1915), col. 687. Thus, Calvin devalues the content of the traditional notion of brotherhood while seeming to insist on an elevated standard of friendship. For the implication of this point, see the Appendix, pp. 141-64.

Today, the "wall of partition which formerly separated
Jew and Gentile is . . . broken down," the discrimination
against the alien abrogated. "Nous sommes frères, voire sans
aucune distinction." Yet, since it is abundantly clear that the
prohibition of usury among the ancient peoples was merely a
part of their political constitution, it follows that

> usury is not now unlawful, except in so far as it contravenes
> equity and brotherly union. Let each one, then, place himself
> before God's judgment seat, and not do to his neighbor what
> he would not have done to himself, from whence a sure and
> infallible decision may be come to. To exercise the trade of
> usury, since heathen writers counted it amongst disgraceful
> and base modes of gain, is much less tolerable among the
> children of God; but in what cases, and how far it may be
> lawful to receive usury upon loans, the law of equity will bet-
> ter prescribe than any lengthened discussions.[18]

[18] *Opera*, xxiv (*CR*, lii), cols. 680-83, esp. at 683; tr. Bingham, iii,
128-32. It will be recalled that a similar warning against applying the
Gospel as an external secular rule in the matter of interest to the derogation of Christian liberty is to be found in Luther's letter of 1525 to the
municipal council of Danzig. See above, p. 45, n. 38. But, Hyma clearly
falls into excess when he writes that "Calvin's arguments resembled
Luther's opinion in almost every word." *Christianity, Capitalism, and
Communism*, 78. The summary of the evidence for this argument (*ibid.*,
79-80 and ch. iii, *passim*) though a helpful corrective of those writers who
magnify the differences between the two Reformers goes to the opposite
extreme of denying the novelty even of Calvin's authentically original
contributions (such as the refutation of the so-called Aristotelian theory
of sterility of money, his revolutionary exegesis of Deuteronomy, his
systematic analysis of equity, etc.). Moreover, Luther's theories were for
the most part concerned with one institution, the *census* contract. Calvin,
however, treated of money loans in general, as they functioned in ordinary
commerce. In any event, as we have indicated above, Calvin, rather than
Luther, was the authority for subsequent critics of the medieval usury
laws.

Interesting sidelights on Calvin's attitude toward usury are to be found
in four related documents, which do not explicitly involve the Deuteronomic issue.

A) In the ordinances of February 3, 1547, for the country parishes of
the government of Geneva, Calvin and his fellow ministers fixed the
maximum rate of "usury" at five per cent, on penalty of confiscation of

It hardly seems necessary to elaborate any further on the niceties of Calvin's theory of usury. Reminiscences of his novelties will be found in virtually every writer to be discussed henceforth in the course of the present work. It does seem desirable, however, to add one remark—this by way of assessment or evaluation of the impact of his exegesis on the meaning and subsequent history of the idea of fraternity in the West. There is, of course, no warrant for imagining that Calvin renounces the traditional Christian summons to universal brotherhood and *caritas*. If anything, he feels called on to disallow the tampering with these precepts which

---

the principal, plus a fine in accordance with the exigencies of the case. *Opera,* x.1 (*CR,* xxxviii.1), 56-57.

B) On November 26, 1549, the Fleming, Utenhove, wrote to Calvin to tell of the difficulties he had experienced while in London in the attempt to recover a debt owing to Calvin by Pierre de la Guerce. Utenhove takes the opportunity, also, to enclose the opinion he had prepared on the legality of the ordinance of Henry VIII allowing a rate of ten per cent on loans. (For the reference to the text of the decree, see below, p. 83.) Though Utenhove's memorandum is not available, it is apparent that he approved the new ruling on the ground that a legislator had the right to take into account the diverse situations of different areas. Utenhove reports that he himself had invested his money with a "good man" so as not to let it lie idle in his own hands. Calvin, *Opera,* xiii (*CR,* xli), 462. Calvin's answer is not to be found in the *CR.* According to Hauser, however, Calvin replied that the king was empowered to issue such a decree, and that anyone might obey it in safe conscience. "L'économie calvinienne," *Bulletin de la Société de l'histoire du protestantisme français,* lxxxiv (1935), 228.

C) In a letter to an anonymous correspondent of April 28, 1556, Calvin is concerned to protect the poor from exploitation. Sometimes, Calvin says, even the slightest increment may not be demanded on a loan without doing offense to God and injury to one's neighbor. Even though in the town of Geneva there is an authorized rate of interest, it does not follow that a creditor may with good conscience exact a profit from a poor man, which might in any way oppress him. The most secure course of action is to follow the dictate of natural law and the will of Christ, the best expression of which is the Golden Rule. *Opera,* x.1 (*CR,* xxxviii.1), 264.

D) In his letter to Francis Morel, pastor at Gien, in January of 1560 or 1562, Calvin gave ministers limited permission to lend money at interest. Here, as elsewhere, one finds Calvin hesitant about extending approval to contracts involving interest. However, it seems to him better for a minister to make a living in that fashion than to engage in trade or to practice

he felt was countenanced by medieval authorities.[19] Still, the specific gravity of the claim of brotherhood is radically altered by his support of the taking of interest and his reinterpretation of the Deuteronomic issue. Such a substitution impels our use of the phrase "Universal Otherhood." This is only one instance of the process of re-evaluation of the moral currency which has unnumbered illustrations in the history of morality. Calvin, it is true, appeals intensely for brotherhood; but there is a world of difference between a brotherhood in which interest is abominated and a brotherhood in

---

an occupation which would distract him from his office. He hoped, he said, that ministers would act in moderation and not demand a fixed profit, but that they would invest their moneys with reputable merchants and trust to the faith and loyalty of the latter to return an equitable share of the gains. This letter is available in two versions: the Latin is dated Jan. 10, 1560; the French, 1562. See, respectively: *Opera*, x.1 (*CR*, XXXVIII.1), 262-63; *Opera*, XIX (*CR*, XLVII), 245-46. For an earlier expression by Luther to this effect, see his letter of March 7, 1532, to Dorothea Jörger, in *Werke*, Erlangen ed., LIV, 277-78, cited Grisar, VI, 92. Cf. *BW*, ed. Enders, IX, no. 1981, p. 160.

May we take this opportunity, however, at the outset of our account of the path of Calvin's influence, to explain that we do not consider the modern temper to have arisen merely by a process of "progressive stripping off of legal and moral restraints upon the anti-social greed of the individual." We have adopted the word *Otherhood* precisely because we mean to imply that modern liberalism, at its best, looks, at the very least, to the advent of a certain kind of Brotherhood, a Brotherhood in which all are brothers in being equally others.

In summing up our first chapter (see p. 27, n. 60), we made it plain that the apparent stress on the universal brotherhood in medieval Christianity was violated in innumerable ways at other points in the medieval ethic. So, in approaching the modern situation, it is desirable to realize that the dominant accent on individualism is qualified in myriad ways by the morality, custom, and law of the several Protestant nations. In any case, we have no desire to encourage the fashionable charge that modern liberalism stands opposed to humanitarian fellow-feeling, benevolence, and fraternalism. For an especially valuable critique of overdrawn indictments of the Protestant ethic and laissez-faire liberalism, see O. H. Taylor, "Tawney's *Religion and Capitalism* and Eighteenth-Century Liberalism," *Quarterly Journal of Economics*, XLI (1927), 118-31. (I am indebted to my colleague, Prof. Gerhard E. O. Meyer, for calling my attention to this stimulating paper.)

[19] See esp., *Institutes of the Christian Religion*, bk. ii, ch. 8, §55-56; also, iii, 7, §6.

which it is authorized. Neither the Hebrews nor the Christians of the Middle Ages would have been able to understand the latter kind of brotherhood.[20]

Now that an outstanding religious leader had dealt a resounding blow against the burdensome medieval doctrine of usury, merchants, lawyers, and other spokesmen of the business community rushed in to take the initiative in assuring its demise. Though the divines continued to command respect into the next century, it is already evident that in the more aggressive centers of business enterprise they were no longer dictating so much as echoing public opinion. If the once inarticulate laymen were now so forward in challenging the

[20] The significance of this transition is generally overlooked in standard modern accounts of Calvin's doctrine of usury. See, e.g., G. Klingenburg, *Das Verhältnis Calvins zu Butzer*; E. Doumergue, *Jean Calvin*, v, 679-90, esp. at 681; K. Holl, "Die Frage des Zinsnehmens und des Wuchers in der reformierten Kirche," *Gesammelte Aufsätze zur Kirchengeschichte*, III, 385-403; G. Wünsch, "Calvins Beurteilung der Zinswirtschaft," *Die christliche Welt*, XXIX (1915), cols. 687-89; H. Hauser, *La modernité*, 97; A. Hyma, *Christianity, Capitalism, and Communism*, ch. iii.

In the opinion of many religious writers of the early modern era, however, the new exegesis contained implications which breached basic Christian teachings. Numerous texts will be cited in the course of the present chapter to indicate that conservatives, both Protestant and Catholic, detected a severe shrinkage of moral values in Calvin's innovations in the matter of usury. Only one illustration of this assessment need be cited here, the pointed declarations from the *Decretum* issued by the Gallican clergy in 1683 under the direction of Bossuet:

"Usura sive foenus, hoc est ex mutuo lucrum, Mosaicis, propheticis et evangelicis Scripturis universim inter fratres vetitum; Ecclesia Catholica semper intellexit, eaque constans et perpetua patrum omnium et saeculorum omnium traditio est.

"Heterodoxi scripsere Mosaicum de usura interdictum antiquae legis finibus coerceri, nec permanasse ad populum christianum, magna christiani nominis contumelia, quod in moralibus, ipsaque fraterna charitate exercenda, justitia Pharisaeorum plusquam Christianorum abundare intelligatur, cum Christus dixerit: *Nisi abundaverit justitia vestra plusquam Scribarum et Pharisaeorum, non intrabitis in regnum coelorum* (Matt. v:20). In eo ergo abundaverit justitia christiana quod a christiana fraternitate nemo sit alienus, sed omnes homines pro fratribus habeantur." Bossuet, *Oeuvres*, VII, 306. Cf. *ibid.*, 332, for the decree of the Assembly of 1700.

traditional exegesis, it is because they felt that they had for too long a time been dominated by cloistered visionaries who had no knowledge of the world of affairs. In the pamphlets of the late sixteenth century, we are no longer in the atmosphere of the confessional; we are in the counting house. Henceforth, the controversy over the legitimacy of interest tends more and more to be carried on in eminently secular contexts, free of the otherworldly associations which had clung to the issue in the past. In many lands, the debate henceforth eventuates in parliamentary statutes and royal decrees aimed to destroy the medieval usury doctrine and legislation. The Commercial Revolution in Western and Northern Europe had entirely altered the picture.

The first rehearsal of the new campaign against classic interpretations of Deuteronomy occurs, naturally enough, in Elizabethan England. Traditionalists[21] continued to compare usurers to idle drones, spiders, and bloodsuckers, and the dramatists[22] identified them as Sir Giles Overreach, Messrs. Mammon, Lucre, Hoard, Gripe, Bloodhound, & Co. But when in 1571 the "marchaunts and occupiers" pressed for the abrogation of the Bill Against Usury of 5 & 6 Edward VI, c.20 (1552), which had repealed the rate of 10 per cent allowed by the Act of 37 Henry VIII, c.9 (1545), they borrowed their arguments from Calvin. In the discussion at the second reading of the Bill in the House of Commons, Mr. Molley, "a lawyer for the business interests in London,"[23] expressed the laymen's approval of the new exegesis:

[21] C. T. Wright, "Some Conventions Regarding the Usurer in Elizabethan Literature," *Studies in Philology*, XXXI (1934), 176-97; *idem*, "The Usurer's Sin in Elizabethan Literature," *ibid.*, XXXV (1938), 178-94; J. W. Draper, "Usury in *The Merchant of Venice*," *Modern Philology*, XXXIII (1935), 37-47.

[22] A. B. Stonex, "The Usurer in Elizabethan Drama," *PMLA*, XXXI (1916), 190-210; *idem*, "Money Lending and Money Lenders in England during the 16th and 17th Centuries," *Schelling Anniversary Papers*, 263-85; L. C. Knights, *Drama and Society in the Age of Jonson*, 127-30, 164-68.

[23] Mr. Molley is so described in A. Hyma, *op.cit.*, 193. The evidence for the characterization is not indicated.

Experience hath proved the great mischief which doth grow by reason of excessive taking, to the destruction of young gentlemen, and otherwise infinitely; but the mischief is of the excess, not otherwise. Since to take reasonably or so that both parties might do good, was not hurtful; . . . God did not so hate it that He did utterly forbid it, but to the Jews amongst themselves only, for that He willed they should lend as Brethren together; for unto all others they were at large; and therefore to this day they are the greatest Usurers in the world. But be it, as indeed it is, evil, and that men are men, no Saints, to do all these things perfectly, uprightly and brotherly; yet *ex duobus malis minus malum eligendum*; and better may it be born to permit a little, than utterly to take away and prohibit Traffick, which hardly may be maintained generally without this.

But it may be said, it is contrary to the direct word of God, therefore an ill law; if it were to appoint men to take usury, it were to be disliked; but the difference is great between that and permitting or allowing or suffering a matter to be unpunished.[24]

Mr. Robert Bell, representing King's Lynn, thought that "though it (usury) were a sin, yet it was to be punished here on earth according to the good or bad, or rather according to the greater or less hurt which groweth thereby." An anonymous colleague concluded that "God did not absolutely forbid Usury, which surely if it had been utterly ill, he would have done."[25]

In a last stand, the traditionalists marshalled the vast array of argument against usury which medieval thinkers had painfully built up by appeals to Plato, Aristotle, Cato, the Roman law of *mutuum*, the Divine Law, the vicious eco-

[24] The original source is *A Compleat Journal of the Votes, Speeches and Debates, Both of the House of Lords and House of Commons throughout the Whole Reign of Queen Elizabeth* . . . Collected by . . . Sir Simonds D'Ewes (London, 1693), 171-74. Reprinted in R. H. Tawney and E. Power, *Tudor Economic Documents*, II, 154-60; J. B. Kelly, *A Summary of the History and Law of Usury*, 215-24.

[25] Tawney and Power, *op.cit.*, 158-59; Kelly, *op.cit.*, 219-20.

nomic consequences of usury on the peasantry, social solidarity, the religious life. A new ardor gave the hackneyed
citations fresh poignancy. Some matched blow for blow with
the upstart exegesis of Calvin, in the hope of showing that
his interpretations of *neshek,* Luke vi and Deuteronomy
xxiii were philologically unjustifiable, logically absurd, and
morally corrupt. Nothing availed them. Neither scholarship
nor threats could frighten the merchant of Thomas Wilson's
Discourse upon Usury (1572) out of his cynical complacency
or the lawyer out of his argument, advanced without regard
for any of the legal technicalities involved, that

> if usurie weare against nature, it should be universallye evell,
> but god hath said that to a stranger, a man may put out his
> money for usury, but if it had bene againste nature, god would
> not have graunted that libertie . . . in gods lawe, if I be not
> deceived, usury is not forbidden. For is it not in S. Lukes
> ghospell that god said he would come and aske the money lent
> with the usury, blaming him that did not put it forthe for
> gaine?[26]

Nicholas Sanders,[27] Philip Caesar,[28] Miles Mosse,[29] Henry
Smith,[30] Roger Fenton,[31] Gerard Malynes,[32] and a host of
others[33] tried to stem the tide by reminding the usurers and

[26] Ed., with an historical introduction, by R. H. Tawney (London,
1925), 237.

[27] *A Briefe Treatise of Usurie* (Louvain, 1568), p. 3v.

[28] *A general Discourse against the damnable sect of Usurers . . .*
(London, 1578).

[29] *The Arraignment and Conviction of Usurie* (London, 1595).

[30] "The Examination of Usury: The First Sermon," in *The Works of
Henry Smith,* I, 88-100. The sermon is to be dated before 1591, when
Smith died.

[31] *A Treatise of Usurie* (London, 1611).

[32] *Consuetudo, vel, Lex mercatoria* (3d ed., London, 1686), 227. The
first edition appeared in 1622. For his views on usury, see E. A. J. Johnson,
Predecessors of Adam Smith, ch. iii.

[33] For the opposition of other Puritan and High Church divines to the
Bill of 1571, see H. M. Robertson, *Aspects of the Rise of Economic Individualism,* 123-38; Helen C. White, *Social Criticism in Popular Religious Literature of the Sixteenth Century,* 189-223; cf. M. M. Knappen,
Tudor Puritanism, 417-23.

their supporters that Deuteronomy xxiii was a double-edged sword. True, it allowed the Jews to take usury from aliens; but it absolutely forbade them to take it from their brothers. "Of a stranger, saith God," Smith admitted, "thou mayest take usury; but thou takest usury of thy brother; therefore this condemneth thee, BECAUSE THOU USEST THY BROTHER LIKE A STRANGER." Here stranger "doth signify the Jews enemies, they were commanded to destroy; therefore mark how much this maketh against usury which they object for usury ... I hope usurers will allege this Scripture no more."[34]

Is there perhaps a veiled allusion to the conflict over Deuteronomy in *The Merchant of Venice*? Did Shakespeare mean to join the debate by contrasting the self-sacrificing Antonio, who "lends out money gratis" with the hardhearted Shylock, the "alien," "misbeliever," "stranger cur"? Antonio does not expect that Shylock will grow kind and extend friendship, that the "Hebrew will turn Christian," as later, at the point of death, he will counsel Bassanio not to try "to soften that—than which what's harder?—his Jewish heart." Enraged at Shylock's protestations, he cries:

> I am as like to call thee so [dog] again,
> To spit on thee again, to spurn thee too.
> If thou wilt lend this money, lend it not
> As to thy *friends*,—for when did *friendship* take
> A breed for barren metal of his friend?—
> But lend it rather to thine *enemy*:
> Who if he break, thou mayst with better face
> Exact the penalty.[35]

[34] *The Works of Henry Smith*, I, 97-98; cf. Wilson, *A Discourse upon Usury*, 360. In a similar vein, Bishop John Jewel (1522-1571) ridiculed another argument in Calvin's contention. If Scripture explicitly forbids usury only from the poor, how does it follow that it may be taken from the rich? "Scripturis pugnandum erat, non illis rationibus quae nihil probent. Quae enim est ista dialectica: Non licet usuras exigere a paupere; *ergo* licet exigere a divite? Nam eodem modo prorsus possis dicere: Non licet affligere pauperem in judicio; *ergo* licet affligere divitem: atque etiam pueri in scholis hoc sciunt, ex negativa non recte concludi affirmativam." *De usura*, in *Works*, ed. Ayre, IV, 1294.

[35] *M. of V.*, II, I, 131-37. Though A. Tretiak rightly stresses the im-

A true friend not only takes no usance on a loan—indeed, the loan (*mutuum*) is an occasion for the expression of charity and brotherly love—but even waives his legal right to exact the penalty if the debtor break. The true friend

---

portance of the alien problem in *The Merchant,* he does not detect the Deuteronomic overtones in the play. See his *"The Merchant of Venice and the 'Alien' Question," Review of English Studies,* v (1929), 402-9. Even if we follow his lead in accepting the authority of the learned collaborators of *Shakespeare's Hand in The Play of Sir Thomas More: Papers by Alfred W. Pollard, et al.* (Cambridge, England, 1923), for the Shakespearian authorship of the disputed 147 line fragment in the D hand, there is still not sufficient warrant for his contention that Shylock is symbolically "the French, Walloon or Flemish refugee," and the play (especially Portia's great speech) "an appeal both to Queen Elizabeth for mercy and to the Protestant refugees from France and Holland, residing in London, to seek a sort of *modus vivendi* with the original citizens." Tretiak, *loc.cit.,* 402-4.

An emphasis on the contrast between brotherhood and enmity, if not explicit allusion to the Deuteronomic locus, is found in the other Elizabethan treatments of the Bond of Flesh story. The fullest discussion of the evolution of this tale is by B. V. Wenger, "Shylocks Pfund Fleisch. Eine stoffgeschichtliche Untersuchung," *Sh.J.,* LXV (1929), 92-174. See also B. N. Nelson and Joshua Starr, "The Legend of the Divine Surety and the Jewish Moneylender," *Annuaire de l'Institut de philologie et d'histoire orientales et slaves,* VII, 289-338, esp. at 335, n. 60. Truculento, the Christian creditor in Anthony Munday's *Zelauto* (1580), demands that Justice grant him the forfeit of the right eyes of the two debtors on the ground that they committed perjury by breaking their promise to repay on time the 4000 crowns which he had lent them because of "firme affection, and pure zeal of friendship." The Judge pleads with him:

Why Truculento . . . respect you cruelty more than Christian civilitie, regard you rigor more than reason. . . . Is this the love you beare to your brother? The Turke, whose tyranny is not to be talked of: could but exact to the uttermost of his crueltie. And you a branch of that blessed body, which bare the burden of our mannifolde sinnes how can you seem to deal so sharply with yourselfe? seeing you should use to all men as you would be dealt withall. (Text in F. Brie, "Zur Entstehung des 'Kaufmann von Venedig.'" *Sh.J.,* XLIX [1913], 116, 118.)

The Jewish creditor in the ninety-fifth *Declamation* of Lazarus Pyott's translation of Alexander Silvayn's *Orator* (1596) makes reference to the morality of brotherhood and interracial relations in the course of his claim to a pound of flesh from his Christian debtors. In some countries, he declares, not only

shows "human gentleness and love"; sympathizes with the debtor, compelled to "break" by an act of God; "looses the forfeiture," nay more, forgives "a moiety of the principal,

---

the whole bodie but also al the senses and spirits are tormented, the which is commonly practiced not only betwixt those which are in sect or Nation contrary, but also even amongst those that are all of one sect or nation, yea amongst neighbors and kindred, and even among Christians it hath been seene, that the son hath imprisoned the father for monie.

To this and to other arguments of the Jew, the Christian replies:

It is no strange matter to here those dispute of equitie which are themselves most unjust; and such as have no faith at all desirous that others should observe the same inviolable . . . this Jew is content to lose nine hundred crownes to have a pound of my flesh, whereby is manifestly seen the ancient and cruell hate which he beareth not only unto Christians but unto all others that are not of his sect: yea, even unto the Turks. . . . What did not the verie Patriarchs themselves, from whom they have their beginning? They sold their brother and had it not been for on(e) amongst them, they had slaine him even for verie enemie. . . . *Absalon* did not he cause the persecution of his father? . . . What may one hope of them now, when they have neither faith nor law, but their rapines and usuries? And that they beleeve they do a charitable work, when they do some wrong unto anie that is not a Jew. (Reprinted in *M. of V.*, ed. H. H. Furness, 310-13.)

In the earliest Byzantine and Latin forms of the story of Theodore and Abraham, which became known in numerous Western and Eastern versions as "The Jew Who Took as Surety the Image of Our Lord," the pious Abraham, an analogue of Shylock, twice provides the Christian merchant and shipmaster, Theodore, with loans free of any interest, pawn, or collateral. He extends this friendship, it must be underscored here, despite the fact that the only surety is the icon of Jesus, over whom, the Jew reminds Theodore, there is enmity between their peoples. See Johannes Monachus, *Liber de miraculis*, ed. M. Hoferer, cap. xvii, p. 20.

The only explanation offered for this extraordinary courtesy is the fact that the Jew respects the "pure and strong faith" of Theodore. Indeed, when on the first venture in Sidon and Tyre, Theodore hits a reef and loses his cargo, Abraham advances a second loan. The contract between Abraham and Theodore is a very model of the Christian *mutuum*. The instrument mentions neither the date of repayment, nor any pledge or security (save for the surety, the icon of Christ), stipulations for eventual damages, forfeitures, costs, interest, expenses, penalty of the double, nor renunciations of exceptions available to the debtor by Roman, canon, or customary law. The conduct of Abraham is exemplary and puts to shame by contrast Theodore's Christian merchant-banker friends, who

glancing an eye of pity on his losses."[36] Only the enemy, who cannot be expected to entertain such scruples, let alone exercise such charity, may exact the penalty "with better face."

The Lutheran theologians and jurists of Germany lagged behind the English in adopting the newer arguments on behalf of the legality of interest.[37] In general, it would appear

---

not only denied him an ordinary interest-bearing maritime loan, but even refused to stand surety for him to the infidel Jew.

At the close of the story, Abraham is persuaded by a miracle to be converted to Christianity. He accepts baptism, together with the seventy-five members of his household; and honors the surety (*Antiphônétés*) by building a chapel, to which he is appointed a presbyter and his two brothers are attached as deacons by the Patriarch. In the familiar Western versions of the story, which were written under the impulse of the antisemitic tendencies of the crusading epoch, the character of the Jew and the point of the tale are twisted almost beyond recognition. (For a survey of the history of this tale and a consideration of its similarities to and possible influences on certain variants of *The Merchant of Venice* cycle, see the essay by B. N. Nelson and J. Starr, cited above in this note.)

Even if it be held that Shakespeare did not intend to allude to Deuteronomy in the speech under discussion here, Antonio's reference to the irreconcilability of friendship and usury nevertheless involves the problem of the double standard in the ethics of intragroup and intergroup relations. See the Appendix below, pp. 141-51.

I beg to be allowed to reserve for the future a systematic exegesis of the passage in question, since the technical meanings and symbolic penumbra of "friend," "enemy," "break," and "penalty" in medieval law and literature are legion.

[36] See the Duke's speech: IV, I, 20-38. Does Shakespeare mean to counterpose Luke vi:35 to Deuteronomy? I am tempted to think so. Cf. Cotton Mather's treatment of a similar situation in his *Durable Riches* (Boston, 1695), pt. ii, p. 10, cited by E. A. J. Johnson, *American Economic Thought in the 17th Century*, 216-17. For an extraordinary text, much earlier in date, in which a creditor waives his just claim to one hundred per cent interest in deference to "the law of friendship," see Sidonius Apollinaris, (*ca.* 431-*ca.* 484), *Epistolae*, iv:24, tr. by O. M. Dalton, *The Letters of Sidonius*, II, 42-45. Here, the classic friendship *ethos* had more profound influence on the actions of the parties involved than either the Church legislation on usury or the Christian ideals of brotherhood and mercy. This point is not mentioned in the otherwise exemplary commentary on the letter by A. Esmein, "Sur quelques lettres de Sidoine Apollinaire," *Mélanges d'histoire du droit*, 359-92.

[37] Brief but valuable accounts of the victory of a liberal policy among Lutheran theologians of the late 16th and early 17th centuries will be found in W. Elert, *Morphologie*, II, 487-90, and E. Uhl, *Die Sozialethik*

that a strictly traditionalist view lingered longest among the pastors and preachers of the humbler sort. In the mid-sixteenth century these older attitudes on usury continued to be shared by a significant number of prominent theologians and jurists, such as Johann Brenz (1499-1570),[38] Hieronymus Schurpf (1481-1554),[39] Dietrich Schnepf (1525-1586),[40] Nikolaus Gallus (1516-1570),[41] and Martin Chemnitz (1522-1586).[42]

The liberal interpretation appears to have been accorded a more favorable reception by the faculties of the major universities[43] and by a group of influential Church superin-

---

Johann Gerhards, 103-4. Most of the sources—see the references in Elert —appear in the form of *consilia* in the following collections: *Consiliorum theologicorum decas* I [*decas* II, etc.], ed. F. Bidembach, and the *Thesaurus consiliorum et decisionum*, ed. G. Dedekennus, II, sectio 8, "de negotiationibus et usuris. . . ." The variations of theological and legal opinion suggested by these *consilia* must not, however, be studied *in vacuo*. Without exception, the *consilia* on usury were inspired by or had great bearing on the bitter controversies over usury in most of the German towns throughout the latter half of the 16th century.

[38] See Brenz's *consilium* "Von wucherlichen Contracten und Zinssgelt" in *Consiliorum theologicorum decas* I, ed. F. Bidembach, 20-22; cf. W. Köhler, *Bibliographia Brentiana*, no. 730, pp. 344-45; also, "Vom Wucher Unterricht Johannis Brentii an einen guten Freund wie es N. N. aus seiner Handschrifft abgeschrieben hat," ed. in W. Köhler, *op.cit.*, no. 735, pp. 348-49. See, also, *Thesaurus consiliorum*, ed. Dedekennus, II, p. 146.

[39] See references to Schurpf's writings against usury in Th. Muther, *Aus dem Universitäts-und Gelehrtenleben im Zeitalter der Reformation*, 419.

[40] See B. Anemüller, *M. Bartholomäus Gernhard*, 17; cf. *RE*, ed. 3, XVII, 674.

[41] Gallus's *Zwo Predigten wider den Wucher aus dem XV. Psalm . . .*, preached at Regensburg on March 10 and 17, 1569, were edited by Wolfgang Waldner and published at Jena in 1572; cf. Köhler, *Bibliographia Brentiana*, no. 735, p. 348. For the influence of Gallus's views on the opponents of usury in the 1587 episode—to be described presently—see the essay by F. Loy in *Beiträge zur bayerischen Kirchengeschichte*, XXXI (1925), esp. at 14-18.

[42] See Chemnitz's *Locorum theologicorum*, pars 2, *locus de paupertate*, cap. 6, *de usura*, at pp. 430-62.

[43] We do not mean to suggest that university faculties were universally or even generally sympathetic to new statutory decrees of interest. Indeed, in many cases, learned respondents, whether theologians or jurists,

tendents who perforce became involved in the widespread controversy over the usury question.[44] The authorities to whom the liberal constructionists proudly appealed were: Luther, Melanchthon, Bucer, Aepinus, du Moulin, Calvin, Hotman, and a number of lesser lights. Luther supplied the innovators with animadversions against Mosaism[45] and justifications of numerous exceptions to the prohibition of usury;[46] Melanchthon provided arguments on behalf of the customary civil contracts[47] and made available a distinction between gratuitous and interest-bearing loans, which were conceded to merit a five per cent return if authorized by the civil law;[48] Aepinus,[49] du Moulin,[50] and Calvin appeared to offer a telling social and historical refutation of the foundations of the medieval doctrine of usury. Additional aid and comfort were drawn from the arguments and reputations of other notable writers.[51]

---

differed among themselves, the opposed parties issuing separate responses. See, e.g., the replies of the universities in the Rudolstadt crisis; B. Anemüller, *op.cit.*, 13ff. Notwithstanding, the university theologians and jurists appear to have had little sympathy for hot-headed traditionalist pastors.

[44] Among the superintendents who showed indulgence to newer views of usury were: Johannes Aepinus, Christoph Fischer, and Jakob Andreae.

[45] See, e.g., the *consilium* of Gerhard in Dedekennus, *Thesaurus*, II, at pp. 163-164, where a vigorous case is made out also against the pertinence for Christians of the Sabbatical and Jubilee releases.

[46] See, e.g., the *consilium* submitted by the Jena theologians during the Rudolstadt crisis. Anemüller, *op.cit.*, 14.

[47] Note the warnings to preachers made in the Leipzig response against presuming to mix in civil affairs. Interestingly, Melanchthon's colloquy with Jakob Strauss is recalled. Anemüller, *op.cit.*, p. 14.

[48] See the *consilium* submitted by the theologians of Wittenberg during the Rudolstadt crisis. Anemüller, *op.cit.* 13; also, the *Censura juridicae Facultatis in Academia Tubingensi super Ratisbonensi Controversia*, cited by Hunnius, *In epistolam D. Pauli ii ad Cor.* cap. viii, p. 340.

[49] See, e.g., the version of the tripartite classification of society in Hunnius's *consilium* in Dedekennus, II, 148-49.

[50] See the statements of the Tübingen Law Faculty concerning the Regensburg controversy, cited in Hunnius, *In epistolam D. Pauli ii ad Cor.*, p. 340.

[51] For the influence of Bucer, see letter of Z. Ursinus to Crato von

Most prominent among the Lutheran advocates of the legality of interest-bearing loans were Jakob Andreae (1528-1590),[52] Aegidius Hunnius (1550-1603),[53] and Johann Gerhard (1582-1637).[54] Hunnius's[55] categorical denial of the sterility of money and Gerhard's overturning[56] of Chemnitz's interpretation of Deuteronomy are clear testimony to the adoption, albeit somewhat belated, by Lutheranism of the Calvinist interpretation of the scriptural passages on usury. A complete lack of sympathy with "papal superstitions on usury" will be found in the official survey of ecclesiastical jurisprudence by Benedict Carpzov (1595-1666).[57]

The two most poignant expressions of the losing fight of the traditionalist interpretation of Luther's views on usury are associated with the crises of 1564-1565 and 1587 in Rudolstadt and Regensburg, respectively.

Crafftheim sent from Zurich, January 13, 1561. Neumann, *Geschichte*, 491, in notes.

[52] If our secondary authorities can be trusted, Andreae would appear to have experienced a change of heart on the five per cent issue. In 1564 he joined Schnepf, Osiander, Brenz, and Balthasar Bidembach in a strongly conservative *consilium*. Anemüller, *op.cit.*, 17. As we shall see presently, twenty-three years later, in 1587, he directed the pro-five per cent forces in Regensburg.

[53] See his *consilium* of 1576 in Dedekennus, *Thesaurus*, II, 148-150; cf. Elert, *Morphologie*, II, 488.

[54] E. Uhl, *Die Sozialethik Johann Gerhards*, 103-4. Considerable interest attaches to Uhl's harsh verdict on Gerhard's teaching on usury: "denn damit, dass er das Zinsnehmen und die Fruchtbarkeit des Geldes lehrte, stand er nicht in der lutherischen Tradition. . . . Wo es sich darum handelt, das Zinsnehmen zu rechtfertigen, ist Gerhard jede Bundesgenossenschaft recht. Imo ipse Socinus wird zitiert. . . ." Uhl, *op.cit.*, 103, n. 2. Cf. Elert, *Morphologie*, II, 490. For the views of Faustus Socinus (1539-1604) see his letter to Christopher Morstinus, dated "Cracow, March 8, 1597," ed. in F. Socinus, *Opera*, I, 457-58.

[55] See *consilium* in Dedekennus, *op.cit.*, II, 148-50. Elert, *Morphologie*, II, 489-90.

[56] Gerhard, *Loci theologici*, loc. 24, *de magistratu politico* no. 236 in ed. Preuss, VI, 391. Also *consilium* in Dedekennus, II, 151-71, esp. at 163-64.

[57] *Jurisprudentia ecclesiastica*, lib. ii, tit. 20, def. 319, pp. 492-94.

The Rudolstadt episode[58] centers about the battle on behalf of a strict prohibition of usury by the quixotic Bartholomäus Gernhard (d. 1600), pastor of the church of St. Andreä in Rudolstadt.

Gernhard's troubles began when he and other clergymen of the Church, acting under the inspiration of Luther's *An die Pfarrherrn* of 1540, denied communion to two nobles, Georg von Schonbergk and Georg von Schonfeld, on the ground that they had taken interest of four to six per cent on loans. The nobles replied that they had no other way of supporting themselves. Being without landed estates, they said, they had to make their living by investing their funds in interest-bearing loans. The two nobles claimed to be justified, also, by the civil laws which permitted five per cent. Gernhard and his supporters were unmoved by these pleas. The matter dragged on for over two years, ending with Gernhard's retirement from his post and his self-imposed exile from the town. Before the issue was resolved in favor of the pro-interest parties, Rudolstadt and the surrounding regions in Thuringia and elsewhere were in turmoil. *Consilia* were solicited and received from the most prominent university faculties and theologians of the epoch, including the faculties of the universities of Wittenberg, Leipzig, Jena, Tübingen, Erfurt and Marburg, and such theologians as Maximilian Merlin (1516-1584), Nikolaus von Amsdorff (1483-1565), Cyriacus Spangenburg (1528-1604), Hieronymus Mencelius, Jakob Andreae, Dietrich Schnepf, Luke Osiander, the Elder (1534-1604), Johann Brenz and Balthasar Bidembach (1533-1578).

The 1587 crisis in Regensburg[59] witnessed an open breach

[58] The agitation in Rudolstadt and other towns of Thuringia in 1564-1565 is described in B. Anemüller, *M. Bartholomäus Gernhard und der Rudolstädter Wucherstreit im 16. Jahrhundert*; G. Arndt, "Christoph Fischer . . . ," *Beiträge zur thüringischen und sächsischen Geschichte*, ed. A. Cartellieri *et al.*, 315-21.

[59] For the Regensburg affair, see especially F. Loy, "Der Regensburger Wucherstreit," *Beiträge zur bayerischen Kirchengeschichte*, XXXI

between the municipal magistrates and a group of five preachers who relentlessly attacked the practice of usury. Lenders who took five per cent in accordance with civil law regulations, said the preachers, in medieval fashion, were comparable to thieves or murderers, and were unworthy of ecclesiastical consolations. In the contest, the preachers, notably Michael Linsenbarth and Dietrich Rosinus, like Gernhard before them, claimed the authority of Luther, particularly of his tract of 1540. They appealed also to the tradition of the Regensburg church, as it appeared to be evidenced in the critiques against usury by Nikolaus Gallus. The latitudinarian opposition to the preachers was directed by Christopher Binder, who had been assigned to Regensburg at the recommendation of the powerful superintendent, Jakob Andreae. Binder denied that any prohibition of usury could be derived from Luke vi and appealed to Luther's toleration of *interesse* in numerous special circumstances. So great was the restlessness among the common people, we are told, that the *Rath* decided to impose a decree of silence on the traditionalist preachers. Rosinus and his colleagues paid no attention to the decree and continued to excoriate usurers from the pulpit. Challenged, the *Rath* summoned Andreae to Regensburg in the hope that he might discredit the arguments of the preachers. When conferences between Andreae and the preachers failed to shake their resolution, the councillors decreed their expulsion. A battle of pamphlets ensued, but the victory in fact rested with the magistrates. Again, the broad interpretation of the teaching of the Scriptures and of the leaders of the Reformation had won the day.[60]

(1925), 3-28; cf. B. Duhr in *Zt. für katholische Theologie*, XXXII (1908), 608-10. The older accounts may still be consulted with profit. See: J. G. Walch, *Historische und theologische Einleitung in die Religions-Streitigkeiten der evangelisch-lutherischen Kirchen*, IV (1739), 426-33; G. Arnold, *Unpartheyische Kirchen-und Ketzerhistorien*, esp. *Th.* ii, *Anhang.* no. 49, Vol. I, pp. 1148-50.

[60] Loy's study deserves to be better known. It is valuable not merely for its survey of the Regensburg crisis, but also for its attempt, recalling

By the middle of the seventeenth century the traditionalist forces had been thoroughly routed in Protestant lands. The Jewish hardness of heart, to which the medieval exegetes had pointed in extenuation of the Mosaic bill of divorcement and discrimination against the alien, is gradually generalized to allow usury among Christians. Again and again, as in Francis Bacon (1561-1626)[61] and Robert Burton (1577-1640),[62] all men are assumed to have equally hard hearts. Whenever the arguments over the Deuteronomic issue are rehearsed by jurists, theologians, directors of conscience of Holland,[63] Germany,[64] Great Britain[65] or colonial America,[66] the refrain is the same.

---

that of Luther himself, to grapple with the ethical and political issues involved in the creation of a Christian policy on the usury question. Like Luther, Loy is unable to resolve the antagonism between Christian liberty and scriptural law. Thus, he concludes by vindicating both Binder and the five exiled preachers. For an interesting link made by Loy between the Regensburg conflict and the anti-usury program of the *National-Sozial-istische Arbeiter Partei*, see *loc.cit.*, 27.

[61] *The Essays or Counsels, Civil and Moral, of Francis Bacon*, ed. S. H. Reynolds, no. cli, p. 288.

[62] *The Anatomy of Melancholy*, I, 120-21; in *Seventeenth Century Essays*, ed. Jacob Zeitlin, 201. An approach to this position had already been made by Cino da Pistoia (*ca.* 1270-*ca.* 1337) and Bartolus (1314-1357), who argued that the Emperor is not to be considered a heretic for permitting usury in civil law since Moses did likewise on account of the people's hardness of heart. See their comments and those of other civilists on *Cod. Iust.* IV.32 and on the Authentic *Ad haec* (-*Novella* 34); cf. McLaughlin, "The Teaching of the Canonists on Usury," *Mediaeval Studies*, I (1939), 84-95; C. N. S. Woolf, *Bartolus of Sassoferrato*, 47.

[63] Grotius, *Annotationes in quatuor Evangelia et Acta Apostolorum*, on Luke vi:35, in *Opera omnia theologica*, II.1, 380-82; *idem, De jure belli ac pacis*, lib. ii, ch. xii, sect. 20, tr. by F. W. Kelsey *et al.*, p. 356. Unless we may assume that in the latter locus Grotius is speaking after the fashion of Calvin, whom he does not cite, his teaching on usury is unclear. On the one hand, he contends that "human laws [e.g., the Roman-Dutch interest laws] which allow that a return may be agreed on for the *use* of money or of anything else . . . are not inconsistent with natural or divine law." On the other hand, he insists that Christians are required to fulfill the Hebrew law against usury from brothers in a universalist fashion. In proof of the claim that "the Gospel has removed all distinctions between peoples," Grotius cites Arnobius' view [*Adversus gentes*, iv:35]

It is absurd to argue that usury is intrinsically evil, since God permitted the Jews to take it from aliens. It is fantastic to imagine that by aliens God meant the enemies of the Jews. It is horrible to suppose that it is lawful to discriminate against an enemy.[67] The Ambrosian argument is historically unsound, economically ludicrous, and morally perverse.[68]

The Deuteronomic text may once have served to protect the poor farmer and grazier of the rudimentary Hebrew economy against the usurer and to enable the nation as a whole to compete with its hostile neighbors, who were not minded to observe Mosaic scruples about interest.[69] Now it is merely an expression of positive law, which has long out-

---

that Christians "share their possessions with all men whom union joins in the bonds of brotherhood." See also the three works by Claude de Saumaise (1588-1653) published in successive years at Leyden by the Elzevir Press: *De usuris liber* (1638), *De modo usurarum liber* (1639), and *Dissertatio de foenore trapezitico, in tres libros divisa* (1640); cf. E. Laspeyres, *Geschichte der volkswirtschaftlichen Anschauungen der Niederlander und ihrer Litteratur zur Zeit der Republik*, 256-68.

[64] Johann Gerhard, *Loci theologici* . . . , ed. E. Preuss, VI, 396-402 is an exhausting parade of the texts; S. von Pufendorf, *De jure naturae et gentium libri octo*, lib. v., ch. 7, in tr. by C. H. and W. A. Oldfather, 753-55, cf. Johann Alsted, *Theologia casuum*, p. 393.

[65] W. Ames, *De conscientia et eius iure, vel casibus, libri quinque* (Amsterdam, 1631), 385; Richard Baxter, *A Christian Directory*, pt. iv, ch. 19, tit. 4, §§19-23, in ed. of 1673, at 126-27, in ed. J. Tawney, p. 125; Gabriel Towerson, *An Explication of the Decalogue* . . . (London, 1676), 438; Bishop Edward Stillingfleet, *A Letter to a Deist* . . . (London, 1677), 119-20. John Dormer (pseud.), *Usury* . . . ; or Conscience Quieted in the Case of Putting out Mony at Interest (London, 1695/6), 78-80; *The Table Talk of John Selden*, ed. S. H. Reynolds, §ccxv, pp. 188-89; Lord Chief Justice Ley (1550-1629) on Saunderson *v.* Warner, 2 Rolle, 239, in *English Reports*, Vol. LXXXII: *King's Bench Division*, X, 772-73, cited in J. B. Kelly, *A Summary of the History and Law of Usury*, p. 7; cf. Richard B. Schlatter, *The Social and Religious Ideas of Religious Leaders, 1660-1680*, 217-22.

[66] See the decision of an assembly of Puritan Divines of 1699 in Cotton Mather, *Magnalia Christi Americana*, II, 259; also, E. A. J. Johnson, *American Economic Thought in the 17th Century*, 213-20.

[67] Ames, *De conscientia*, 385.

[68] Dormer, *Usury Explain'd*, 78.

[69] *Ibid.*, 80.

lived its purpose.[70] Notwithstanding "Popish" rules, a regulated usury is justified by every law of necessity, utility, equity and parity.[71]

John the Baptist's reply to the publicans (Luke iii:13) and Christ's Parable of the Talents plainly showed that neither Prophet nor Saviour were prejudiced against bankers or loans at interest.[72] We should give alms, not loans, to the destitute.

De Saumaise, indeed, turns the Ambrosian argument on its head. Wars among Christians ought not to be perpetual or result in the subjection of the vanquished, or in their expulsion from their land. It is fitting that the rival kings arbitrate the issues under dispute as private persons do. So long as two Christian countries are in a state of war, loans at interest (*foenus*) cannot be carried on between them any

---

[70] Stillingfleet, *A Letter to a Deist*, 120. Cf. Pufendorf, *De jure naturae*, tr. by C. H. and W. A. Oldfather, 755. Gilbert Burnet (1643-1715) argued that the prohibition of usury among the Hebrews assured them of prosperity and an ample food supply, by directing the flow of capital into foreign trade and manufactures; see Schlatter, *op.cit.*, 220. Richard Baxter puts the legal situation bluntly: "And if it had been forbidden in *Moses* Law only, it would not extend to Christians now, Because the law of *Moses as such* is not in force. The matter of it is much of the law of Nature indeed; but, *as Mosaical*, it was proper to the Jews and Proselytes, or at least extended not to the Christian Gentiles, as is plain in ii Cor. iii.7, Gal. iii.19, 24, and v.3, Eph. ii.15, i Tim. 1.7, Heb. vii.12, 16, 19. *Moses* Law as such never bound any other Nations, but the proselytes that joined themselves to the Jews (nor was all the world obliged so to be proselyted as to take up their laws). Much less do they bind us that are the servants of Christ, so long after the dissolution of their Commonwealth. So much of them as are part of the law of Nature, or of any positive law of Christ, or of the Civil Law of any State, are binding as they are such *Natural, Christian,* or *Civil Laws* But not one of them as Mosaical: Though the *Mosaical* Law is of great use to help us to understand the law of nature in many particular instances, in which it is somewhat difficult to us." (*A Christian Directory*, pt. iv. ch. 19, tit. 4, in ed. of 1673, at pp. 126-27; in ed. J. Tawney, p. 123.) For helpful surveys of medieval and early modern conceptions of the hierarchy of laws, see Jan Kosters, *Les fondements du droit des gens*; Troeltsch, *Social Teachings*, II, *passim*.

[71] Cotton Mather, *Magnalia Christi*, II, 259.

[72] *Ibid.*

more than any other type of business. Once the war is over, all trade, including usury, is naturally resumed. *Loans at interest are proper therefore only among friends, not enemies.*[73]

By the seventeenth century, the old arguments had grown wearisome. The mercantilist theorists were concerned about the economic consequences of different *rates* of interest. There was nothing in Scriptures to guide them on that issue. Yet given the religious cast of much of the culture of the time, they naturally make the usual bow to theological tradition by deferentially leaving "the proof of the unlawfulness of usury to the Divines."[74] Locke anticipates Bentham and Ricardo in insisting that the "price of the hire of money" cannot be regulated, that lowering the rate of interest by law would destroy trade, ruin "widows and orphans," and inspire general perjury; such a law would enrich only bankers (for with the money of the "ignorant and the lazy" in their hands, they are always skillful enough to get interest "above the legal").[75]

On one occasion, at least, during the century the Deuteronomic issue assumed exceptional importance. When the enemies of Cromwell's plan[76] to resettle the Jews in England recalled the records of Jewish usury in England before the expulsion of 1290 and denounced the supposed Hebraic an-

[73] *De usuris*, 666-67.

[74] Thomas Culpeper, *A Small Tract against Usurie* (1621), reprinted in Josiah Child, *A New Discourse of Trade* (London, 1690), 235; cf. Sir James Steuart, *Works*, III, 151.

[75] *Some Considerations of the Consequences of Lowering the Interest, and Raising the Value of Money In a Letter Sent to a Member of Parliament, 1691.* Reprinted in *The Works of John Locke*, V, 3-130, esp. at 4-18. See the remarks of Eli Hecksher, *Mercantilism*, II, 289.

[76] The contemporary debate is described in Lucien Wolf, *Menasseh ben Israel's Mission to Oliver Cromwell*; Max J. Kohler, *Menasseh ben Israel and Some Unpublished Pages of American History*; S. B. Liljegren, "Harrington and the Jews," *K. Humanistiska Vetenskapssamfundets I Lund Årberättelse*, IV (1931-32), 65-92; N. Osterman, "The Controversy over the Proposed Readmission of the Jews to England (1655)," *Jewish Social Studies*, III (1941), 301-28.

tagonism to the alien,[77] the Jewish spokesman, Rabbi Menasseh ben Israel (1604-1657), offered an official explanation of the Deuteronomic text:

> As for usury, such dealing is not the essential property of the Iews, for though in Germany there be some indeed that practise usury; yet the most part of them that live in Turky, Italy, Holland and Hamburg, being come out of Spaigne, they hold it infamous to use it; and so with a very small profit of 4 or 5 per cent, as Christians themselves do, they put their money ordinarily in Banco: *for to lay out their money without any profit, was commanded only toward their brethren of the same Nation of the Iews: but not to any other Nation.* And however by this Charity is not hurt: for it stands in good reason, that every on[e] should gaine and get some advantage with his money, to sustaine his owne life: and when any one to supply his own wants doth take some course of Marchandise, by which he hopes to gaine by other mens moneys taken up on trust, 'tis no inhumanity to reckon and take from him use: For as no man is bound to give his goods to an other; so is he not bound to let it out, but for his owne occasions and profit, and not to leave himself destitute of the profit he could make of the moneys. Onely this must be done with moderation, that the usury be not biting and exorbitant, which the Christians themselves use, amongst themselves; as even in the Mounts of Piety at Padua, Vicenza and Verona is to be seen, where they take 6 par Cent, and elsewere yet much more. This in no manner can be called Robbery, but is with consent and will of the Contracter; and the same Sacred Scripture, which allows usury with him that is not of the same Religion, forbids absolutely the robbing of all men whatsoever Religion they be of. In our Law it is a greater sinne to rob or defraud a stranger, than if I did it to one of my owne profession; because a Jew is bound to shew his charity to all men: for he hath a precept, not to abhorre an Idumean, nor an Egyptian; and that he shall love and protect a stranger that comes to live in his land. If notwithstanding there be some

[77] See, e.g., William Prynne's *A Short Demurrer to the Jewes Long Discontinued Barred Remitter into England* (London, 1656).

that do contrary to this, they do it not as Iewes simply, but as wicked Iewes, as amongst all nations there are found generally some Usurers.[78]

In Catholic circles, the decisive break with the traditional doctrine of usury came in the mid-eighteenth century with the effort of latitudinarians, both among the clergy and laity, to insinuate a new extrinsic title, the *lex civilis* (less familiarly known as *consuetudo* or *statutum principis*) as a justification for the taking of interest upon a *mutuum*. During the Middle Ages, the authority of the civil law to permit interest was consistently denied by the Church.[79] Roman imperial regulations were declared to have been merely opportunistic concessions to the hardness of men's hearts and to have been abrogated by Justinian's declaration of adherence to the Council of Nicea. Medieval statutes allowing interest were held to be null and void. Indeed, sponsors and partisans of such legislation were rendered subject to excommunication by the canon *Ex gravi* of the Council of Vienne (1311-1312).[80] Nevertheless, an occasional jurist or theologian

---

[78] *To His Highnesse the Lord Protector of the Commonwealth of England, Scotland, and Ireland, The Humble Addresses of Menasseh Ben Israel, a Divine and Doctor of Physick, in behalf of the Jewish Nation*; reprinted by H. M. Dwight, 19-20; L. Wolf, *op.cit.*, 100-101. Menasseh's noted coreligionist and contemporary, Leo of Modena (1551-1648), also, takes pains to disprove the slander that Jews take oaths to cheat and rob Christians. See Leo of Modena's *Historia de riti hebraici* (1st ed., Paris, 1637), in tr. by S. Ockley, *The History of the Present Jews . . .* (London, 1707), pt. ii, ch. 5, §2, p. 89. For the Biblical grounds claimed for such allegations, see H. Eells, "Bucer's Plan for the Jews," *Church History*, VI (1937), 127-35. A century after Cromwell, on the occasion of the debate and agitation over the Naturalization Act of 1753, similar attempts were made to defend the Jews against disadvantageous interpretations of the Deuteronomic law. One of the most noteworthy apologies for the Jews will be found in the writings of the eminent Anglican divine and economist, the Rev. Josiah Tucker (1713-1799). Tucker charged the Hudson Bay Company with exacting more extortionate profits than did the Jewish usurers of Anglo-Norman England. See Tucker, *A Second Letter to a Friend concerning Naturalizations* (London, 1753), 36. For Tucker's sufferings on behalf of his pro-Jewish views, see R. L. Schuyler, *Josiah Tucker*, 40.
[79] McLaughlin, *Mediaeval Studies*, I (1939), 84-95.
[80] *Clem.* v. 5. c. 1.

approached the modern view by arguing that the interpreters and administrators of the Church legislation would do well to permit the widest possible latitude to the varying customs of different regions.[81]

Credit for having pioneered the title *lex civilis* in the current form is attributed to Father Jacobus Ledesma, S.J. (d. 1575), who played a leading role in the General Congregation of the Jesuits at Rome in 1573, which attempted to end the strife within the order over the "triple contract."[82] He is said to have contended that it was permissible in conscience to take five per cent interest in triple contracts, where such arrangements were approved by custom and law. This would hold true, especially, he said, for "miserable persons,"[83] who

[81] For example, the renowned civilist, Jason de Mayno (d. 1519), argues that since the contract of *retrovenditio* is customary in Fermo, it should not be treated as usurious there. See *consilium* 153, no. 16, in his *Consiliorum*, IV, 86v-87r.

[82] Ashley, *An Introduction to English Economic History*, II, 441-47; B. Duhr, S.J., "Die deutschen Jesuiten im 5%—Streit des 16. Jahrhunderts: Nach ungedruckten Quellen," *Zeitschrift für katholische Theologie*, XXIV (1900), 209-48; *idem*, "Noch einige Aktenstücke zum 5% Streite im 16. Jahrhundert," *ibid.*, XXIX (1905), 178-90; *idem*, "Der 5% Streit im protestantischen Regensburg: Ausweisung vom 5 Predigern," *ibid.*, XXXII (1908), 608-10. The account of Father Brodrick, *Economic Morals of the Jesuits*, especially the summaries of the decisions of the commissions of 1573 and 1581 (pp. 135, 149-50), must be supplemented by A. M. Knoll, *Der Zins in der Scholastik*, 105-59. The principal sources used by Duhr are now available in *Beati Petri Canisii Societatis Jesu Epistulae et Acta*, ed. O. Braunsberger. See Vol. VIII in indices, *s.v.* "contractus," "foeneratio." Allusions to archival materials will be found also, in the influential *Dissertationes* of F. X. Zech, generally known under the title, *Rigor moderatus doctrinae pontificiae circa usuras a Sanctissimo D. N. Benedicto XIV per Epistolam encyclicam episcopis Italiae traditus* [1747-51]. The two editions available to me differ in details. See the appendix to Honoratus Leotardus, *Liber singularis de usuris* (Venice, 1761-62); also, Migne, *Theologiae cursus completus*, XVI, cols. 765-996. The latter publication arranges the work into two, rather than three, dissertations and prints the defense of Father Pichler's thesis (*vide infra*) separately under the name of Franz Josef Barth, Zech's disciple.

[83] For a full-length account of the law of "miserable persons," see the *De privilegiis miserabilium personarum* of the Luccan jurist, Johannes Maria Novarius. Novarius served as consultant to many Neapolitan ecclesiastical courts in the first quarter of the seventeenth century.

had no opportunities for profitable investment other than the triple contract.[84]

Though, soon after the decision of the Congregation, the distinguished Jesuit theologian, Franciscus Toletus (1532-1596), asserted that he would not contradict those who affirmed Ledesma's view,[85] further development of this line of argument was delayed for over a century. Philibert Collet's *Traité des usures*, which appeared at Paris in 1690, argued that the civil law had the power to make usury legal or illegal at will. In 1743 the Jansenist, Nicholas Broedersen, writing in Holland, contended that "though charity may prohibit usury when taken from the poor, yet there is no sin against charity or justice in taking it from a rich man at the rate of return allowed by law or by custom."[86]

In the following year, the Marquis Scipione Maffei of Verona, an intimate of Pope Benedict XIV, published his *Dell' impiego del danaro libri tre*[87] in defense of the four per cent interest charges on the Veronese state loan of 1740.[88] His position was substantially that of Broedersen. The Pope was anxious to stop the debate that had been aroused by Maffei's contention. He, therefore, issued an encyclical, *Vix pervenit* (November 1, 1745),[89] to the Italian hierarchy, laying down five rules for the determination of usury, which purported to represent the conclusions of a special commission he had established for the clarification of the usury problem. The letter was general in scope. No attempt was

---

[84] Zech, *Rigor moderatus*, diss. ii, cap. 1, sect. 5, §142, no. 10, ed. in appendix to Leotardus, *Liber singularis*, p. 37; Barth, *De statuto principis*, art. ii, 25:10, in Migne, *Theologiae cursus completus*, xvi, col. 1016. Cf. Knoll, *Der Zins in der Scholastik*, 133-34.

[85] Migne, *Theologiae cursus completus*, xvi, col. 1016; also, appendix to Leotardus, *op.cit.*, p. 37.

[86] Patrick Cleary, *The Church and Usury*, 158.

[87] I have used the second edition, enlarged, of Rome, 1746.

[88] Cleary, *loc.cit.*; Knoll, *op.cit.*, 60-61.

[89] *Codicis iuris canonici fontes*, ed. P. Card. Gasparri, i, 939-43; see also Maffei's letter to the Pope, dated Nov. 12, 1745, from Verona, in *Dell' impiego*, ix-xv.

made to decide the dispute between Maffei and his opponents, notably Pietro Ballerini (d. 1769).[90]

Undaunted by the rebuff apparently dealt to Maffei, Father Franz Xaver Zech (1692-1772), leader of the school of Jesuit canonists at Ingolstadt, and his disciples, continued to strive for the adoption of a latitudinarian reform. Nothing in their approach, they insisted, was incompatible with the *Vix pervenit*, which they took to represent a spur to a moderate rather than a rigorist view of the tradition. As their point of departure, they took a novel defense of the *lex civilis*, which had been proposed by Father Vitus Pichler, S.J. (d. 1736), Zech's teacher. Every link in the historic thesis was affected by the new line of argument. The first and the most important link to be transformed was the millennial interpretation of Deuteronomy.

Pichler contended that though usury is forbidden by natural and divine laws, it is probably not outlawed so absolutely that human magistrates may not in certain circumstances permit it by statute for the general good, provided, however, it is moderate, and not opposed to the prescribed spirit of charity.

Taking a leaf from the Protestants, Pichler allows his claim that usury is not utterly prohibited by the law of nature to rest heavily on the Deuteronomic exception. In the manner of Luther, he explains that the permission to the Jews to take usury from aliens simultaneously illustrates and is explained by the Lord's supreme power over men's goods. Similar considerations empower human magistrates to permit usuries for the common good. Do not they have eminent, albeit restricted, *dominium* over the property of the state's subjects? If, as Deuteronomy suggests, I may take usuries from one whose goods I may appropriate against his will, may not magistrates authorize me to receive usuries from a

[90] For his labors on behalf of the conservative interpretation, see H. Hurter, *Nomenclator*, 3d ed., v, cols. 107-8. Ballerini's *Vindiciae juris divini* (1747) offers a systematic critique of Broedersen's theses.

willing and consenting fellow citizen? Such increments are indeed no longer to be called usuries in the strict sense, since I receive them by a just title.

To this, the Dominican rigorist, Father Daniel Concina of Venice (1676-1756) replied bitterly that it was shocking that a Catholic, especially a religious, should at this late day dare to revive sophisms exploded so long ago by St. Ambrose and St. Thomas. No believer before Pichler dreamed of allowing to princes the sort of power that was God's as the Supreme Lord. Because God permitted the Hebrews to carry off the goods of the Egyptians, could princes authorize theft? If the Lord allowed the patriarchs to have many wives, might a prince allow polygamy? Was Pichler prepared to follow in the footsteps of Bucer and Luther in approving polygamy for the public good? How, indeed, did Pichler's teaching differ from that of Calvin, du Moulin[91] and de Saumaise, which had been condemned by the Church?

[91] For Concina's linking of Pichler to the heretics, du Moulin and de Saumaise, see: Zech, *Rigor moderatus*, diss. ii, cap. i, sect. 5, §179, in appendix to Leotardus, *op.cit.*, p. 40; Barth, *De statuto principis*, art. iv, §62, no. 26, in Migne, *Theologiae cursus completus*, xvi, col. 1024. Du Moulin's *Tractatus commerciorum et usurarum* first appeared in 1547, according to Doumergue and Hauser; see Hauser, *Les débuts*, 61-62. The 1576 printing, bearing the name of "Gaspar Caballinus," passed in many places for an authorized departure from tradition, and had an extraordinary influence on the outcome of the five per cent controversy among the Jesuits. Strangely, H. M. Robertson and Father Brodrick, the two most recent writers on the debate, miss the link between Caballinus and du Moulin. Their contrasting estimates of the work provide an interesting object-lesson in the pitfalls of historical research. On the strength of three contemporary statements by leading Jesuits, Robertson guessed that "Caballinus had gone at any rate as far as Calvin in denying the complete prohibition of usury." *Economic Aspects*, 144-45. Father Brodrick countered: "Caballino" [whom he simply calls an "Italian jurist"] "did not, as Dr. Robertson erroneously puts it, 'throw overboard the traditional teaching of the Catholic theologians,' but he argued vigorously for the lawfulness of accepting interest in a large number of cases." See Brodrick, *Economic Morals of the Jesuits*, 144. The true authorship of the book was known to many outstanding theologians and jurists of the sixteenth and seventeenth centuries. Du Moulin's *Opera* were put on the Index by Pius IV in 1559 and again by Clement VIII in 1602. The heretical nature of his views on usury was proclaimed by Martinus Navarrus, Johannes Azorius

Zech and his disciple, Franz Josef Barth, countered that what the Jews took from aliens was not usury in the strict sense. Ambrose, they explained, had justified it by the law of war; Johannes de Medina (1496-1546) had called it a divine concession to the Jews in the rights of others; Johannes Major (1469-1549/1550) had underscored the argument of the Promised Land held by the Canaanites; Gabriel Biel (d. 1495) had insisted that it would not be usury if the Lord were to allow the Jews to take something above the loan in a *mutuum*. Therefore, the ruler who permits his subjects to take usury from one another is merely imitating the Lord. Does not the prince have the right for the public good to transfer some charge on his subjects to another? May he not demolish houses in order to build roads? This does not necessarily mean, as Concina suggests, that the prince may do whatever God may. The prince is given power only in those instances which involve the proper government of the republic. Usury legalized by magistrates, in keeping with Pichler's view, is not usury on a *mutuum* in the strict sense, which alone is prohibited by natural law. Concina's fears that such authorization implies a right to license polygamy

---

(d. 1603 or 1604), Sigismund Scaccia, etc. See Scaccia, *Tractatus de commerciis et cambio* [1619], (Venice, 1650), §1, qu. 1, no. 402ff., p. 71. A more moderate rejection of du Moulin's thesis will be found in Lessius, *De iustitia et iure* (Antwerp, 1621), lib. 2, cap. 20, dub. 4, pp. 249-50. Justus Henning Boehmer expresses amusement at the confusion in Catholic circles over du Moulin's work. He writes: "Licet enim hoc nomen adeo damnent rigidiores pontificii, vt a designatione eius olim abstinuerint, euius rationem tradidi *tit. de haeret.* §*119.in f.* eius scripta iuridica tamen in pretio habuerunt, MOLINAEI nomine abstinentes, & MODERNI PARISIENSIS, FACHINAEI exemplo *lib.* II. *c.* 9., DAMNATI PARISIENSIS laudatione vtentes. Quid? quod praedictus *de vsuris* tractatus mutato *per falsum* nomine sub tit. CASPARI CABALLINI in terris Catholicorum editus sit, quem per imperitiam multi a MOLINAEI tractatu distinxere." (*Ius ecclesiasticum protestantium*, lib. v, tit. 19, *de usuris*, §2, Vol. v, 310.)

Truth to tell, Caballino was a minor 16th century Italian jurist, whom Pius V deputed to "correct" the *Tractatus* on du Moulin's death! . . . From here on, the learned A. Lattes must be allowed to tell his own tale; see *Archivio giuridico*, XCV (1926), 7-19.

are groundless. In point of fact, the Pope has the power to dissolve consummated marriages and even to allow a man to have more than one wife, in the same way as he may permit a bishop to have many sees. If by usury Concina means any moderate increment above the capital, God might certainly allow the Jews to take it from one another. Why he did not do so it is not for us to explain. Ours is not to reason about the will of God.[92]

That the Ingolstadt Jesuits should have felt free to exploit the analogy from the Deuteronomic text reveals how far removed they were from the spirit of the medieval moralists. Did not Pichler, Zech, Barth, and the others realize that their argument involved the tacit admission that the citizens of a

---

[92] Zech, *Rigor moderatus*, diss. ii, cap. 1, sect. 5, §195, in Appendix to Leotardus, *op.cit.*, 42-43 (provides references for citations from Medina, Major, *et al.*) ; Barth, *De statuto principis*, ed. in Migne, *Theologiae cursus completus*, XVI, cols. 1016-17, 1019, 1032. Pichler's own analysis has not been available to me. It will be found in his *Summa jurisprudentiae sacrae universae*, etc., better known under its subtitle, *Ius canonicum secundum quinque decretalium* . . . , at X.v.19, n. 8; see also the appendix thereto. He makes no reference to his novel thesis in the last edition published before his death of his supplementary volume of "cases." See his *Jus canonicum practice explicatum, seu decisiones casuum selectorum centum octoginta quinque* (Ingolstadt, 1735), on X.v.19, c. 9, *decisio* 163, pp. 638-41. For Pichler's bibliography and the controversy on his thesis, see Augustin and Aloys de Backer, *Bibliothèque de la Compagnie de Jésus*, ed. C. Sommervogel, VI, cols. 706-14. Some version of Pichler's position seems to have been taught by Ingolstadt Jesuits since the time of Father Adam Tanner (d. 1632) and Christopher Haunold (d. 1689). See Knoll, *Der Zins in der Scholastik*, 149-51. Indeed, the faculty was notorious for its indulgence in the matter of usury as far back as the latter half of the 16th century. The activities of Johann Eck and Gregorius de Valentia (1551-1603) on behalf of the five per cent contract are memorable in this connection. In the opinion of Knoll, Gregorius de Valentia was the "Begründer dieses anticanisianischen [i.e., anti-Petrus Canisius] neuen Geistes, der die Ingolstädter Akademie zur Pflanzschule eines 'katholischen Kapitalismus' formte . . ." *Ibid.*, 148. Concina's three principal polemics, all issued in 1746, have not been accessible to me, but I have consulted his long dissertation, *de mutuo et usura*, in his *Theologia christiana dogmatico-moralis*, VII, 326-541.

state stood in relation to one another as did the Hebrews to their enemies?[93]

The initial installment of the story of the progress of the Universal Otherhood comes to a fitting close with two authoritative Protestant jurists, the German, Justus Henning Boehmer (1674-1749), and the Englishman Sir William Blackstone (1723-1780). Their words read like obsequies over the corpse of the old commandment.

Boehmer blames the unreasonably long life of Deuteronomy upon the "totalitarian" designs of the Catholic Church. The Deuteronomic prohibition, he observes, was simply a civil law of the Jewish Republic; on the other hand, the right to take usury from aliens stemmed from the *ius gentium*. The Roman curia, he continues, simply took over the theocratic assumptions of the Jews, and organized the Church as a "Christocracy," composed of all Christians under the direction of the Supreme Pontiff. The adoption of the noxious Hebrew text served chiefly to foster the overweening political and hierarchical interests of the medieval Popes and canonists.[94]

By the time of Blackstone, Calvin's views of usury had come a long way. The English jurist takes it as axiomatic that

[93] The title *lex civilis* is now formally recognized by the Church. See *Codex iuris canonici*, c. 1543, in ed. of Rome, 1917, at p. 448. Moral theologians of the late 19th and early 20th centuries have gone far beyond the *mutuum*-extrinsic title analysis and recognize the fruitfulness of money in modern capitalism. The traditional rules are understood to have been a temporary adaptation to the less developed economy of the Middle Ages. Indeed, Catholics are now allowed to take interest without regard to whether civil law allows it; see Father Victor Cathrein, S.J., *Philosophia moralis in usum scholarum, editio undecima et duodecima ab auctore recognita* (Freiburg im B., 1921), thesis lxvi, pp. 341-48. For the modern developments, see A. M. Knoll, *op.cit.*; F. Zehenthauer, *Das Zinsproblem nach Moral und Recht*. Father Thomas Slater, S.J., finds nothing wrong with 60 per cent, but he believes 433 per cent per annum altogether extortionate and unjust; *Cases of Conscience for English Speaking Countries*, I, 326-27. Cf. his essay "Liberalism and Usury," *Questions of Moral Theology*, 78-98.

[94] Boehmer, *Ius ecclesiasticum protestantium*, lib. v, tit. 19, §25, ed. 174? v, 339-40.

the progress of capitalism was deeply indebted to the Protestant ethic, notably to Calvin's attack on Deuteronomy and Aristotle. He sums up his historical convictions simply, as though he were recording familiar equations. The total interdiction of usury, he says, was the work of the "Dark Ages," the time of "monkish superstitions and civil tyranny," when "commerce was at its lowest ebb." A credit economy and its "inseparable companion," the "doctrine of loans upon interest," both owed their rebirth to the "revival of true religion and real liberty" in the Reformation.[95]

Appropriately, Blackstone's conclusions carry us back to the historic document with which the present chapter begins, Calvin's letter of 1545 to Claude de Sachins.

[95] Blackstone, *Commentaries*, bk. ii, ch. 30. This second book was published in 1766.

CHAPTER IV

The Ghost of Deuteronomy (1770-1840)

IDEAS die hard. They linger long after their native soil has been supplanted. To their loyal devotees, the case for them never appears entirely hopeless. Every conceivable kind of reinforcement is called upon to save them from utter extinction. Decaying fibres are reanimated by the infusion of new blood. A fresh enchantment is provided for their faded exterior by the liberal application of symbolism and casuistry. In truth, no idea ever becomes so obsolete that it cannot in some form or other, at some time or other, reawaken the enthusiasm which was once its portion. So long as ideas survive in memory, they preserve a hold upon life, however tenuous. Seemingly dead ideas sometimes lead extremely active spectral existences. This was the case with the Deuteronomic law of usury.

The ghost of Deuteronomy began the last stage of its restless wanderings in France and the British Isles. From there it was transported by the last of its defenders, the quixotic Father Jeremiah O'Callaghan (ca. 1780-1861), first to Rome, the capital of the Old World, and finally, by a curious turn of fortune, to the shores of this country, where it quickly ended its posthumous career.

The world it beheld on its final journeys was unlike anything it had ever before known—a world being made over by the Industrial Revolution, laissez-faire economics, utilitarian morality, and a new nationalism. The effort to accommodate itself to these changed times inevitably exhausted the old commandment. Soon after 1840 it disappeared from view.

In France, the old commandment was roughly handled by Turgot and Napoleon. The former rejected the medieval interpretations of the Deuteronomic prohibition as a vestige of an age in which theologians had dominated the economic life to the detriment of men of good sense. The latter pronounced the Deuteronomic discrimination incompatible with the egalitarian foundations of the youthful French nation. He summoned the Jews to forswear Hebraic tribalism on penalty of standing outside the fraternity of Frenchmen.

In the British Isles, the center of the new industrialism, the commandment was called upon to do a double chore: to serve as a whipping-post for the followers of Calvin and the newfangled utilitarianism; and to provide a pretext for an extraordinary attempt to dress up Catholicism as a religion preeminently equipped to serve capitalism.

The last recorded attempt to resuscitate the dead commandment is associated with the name of Father O'Callaghan. Father O'Callaghan began his stormy career as a parish priest in Ross Carbery in the south of Ireland. He ended his life as a missionary in the state of Vermont. The story of his exile and martyrdom on behalf of the Deuteronomic commandment stamps him as a sort of Don Quixote of the capitalistic epoch.

Turgot subjected the scholastic casuistry to ridicule. He was incensed at the persistence of the anachronistic prejudices and laws against usury revealed by an investigation in Angoulême. Any person with common sense, he insisted, will agree that in Luke vi and Deuteronomy xxiii, Christ had no intention of condemning all loans at interest. Had He so wished, He would not have expressly permitted the Jews to practice on strangers what is manifestly prohibited by natural law. God cannot authorize injustice. Theologians have violated good sense in trying to prove the contrary, but their scandalous responses merely reveal their embarrassment and give the objection the force of a true demonstration in the eyes of those who have "sane notions of God and Justice."[1]

[1] Turgot, *Mémoire sur les prêts d'argent*, §xxviii, in *Oeuvres*, ed. G. Schelle, iii, 180-83.

In France, the Deuteronomic problem was recalled to the spotlight of European political discussion once again in 1806. Aroused by the protests of the peasantry, especially in Alsace, against the practices of Jewish moneylenders, and eager to complete the unfinished business of Jewish emancipation, Napoleon convoked an Assembly of Jewish Notables at Paris.[2] He directed it to reply to twelve queries, five of which involved the ancient text.[3] He called upon the representatives to repudiate the double-edged teaching of Deuteronomy and to renounce clannishness by a proclamation that Jews and Frenchmen are brothers.

Now at last, on the threshold of modern nationalism, it was the turn of the Jews to disavow the Deuteronomic teaching. The deputies were in a quandary over the answers to be made to the eleventh and twelfth queries, which dealt directly with xxiii:19-20. They could neither accept the Maimonidean exegesis that they must demand usury from Gentiles, nor reassert literally the scriptural rule that they could not take it from their own brethren. Moreover, they could not afford to support the Calvinist argument that *neshek* meant *excessive* interest, lest they be trapped by Molé, the hostile instigator and chief commissioner of the Emperor's inquiry, into the admission that they could take *usury* from aliens and merely *interest* from their brothers.[4]

In the first week of August 1806, the Assembly adopted the following responses:

Deuteronomy xxiii is currently misunderstood. *Neshek* did not mean usury (excessive interest), but simply any interest, like the Latin *foenus*. Verse 19 was one of the many precepts of charity, which made the Bible so humane a document for its time. The *Talmud* made it clear that the prohibition of interest among brothers referred only to loans given to the needy, and not to commercial loans which entail risk of the

[2] R. Anchel, *Napoléon et les Juifs*, ch. ii-v.
[3] *Ibid.*, 166-67, esp. queries 11 and 12.
[4] *Ibid.*, 126.

capital. The law was designed to strengthen the bonds of fraternity among an isolated people. Since the Dispersion, however, it has not been necessary to abide by this precept. On the authority of the *Talmud*, the Jews have lent at interest to Jewish merchants as well as to Gentiles.[5]

Verse 20, the notables went on, merely makes it permissible for Jews to take interest, not excessive profit or usury, from foreigners. Any other reading of the passage contradicts the numerous exhortations in Scripture to show friendship to the stranger. Moses could not reasonably have forbidden the Hebrews to take interest from aliens. Nations not bound by his legislation would then have had an unfair advantage over the Hebrews. He therefore allowed them to take interest from aliens, while forbidding them to take it from their brothers. Clermont-Tonnerre of the Constituent Assembly, Pufendorf, and many others had exploded the notion that Jewish law sanctioned the taking of usury. Maimonides, it is true, read the text as an imperative prescription,[6] but his opinion is no more binding on the Jews than that of a solitary theologian on Catholics. Finally, the notables protested, there are fewer usurers among the Jews than is commonly believed. Under any circumstances the vice of one ought not to be imputed to all.

"La France est notre patrie, les Français sont nos frères. . . ."[7]

The Emperor defined his attitude in a communication to M. de Champagny, Minister for Foreign Affairs, on August 23, 1806.[8] It contained instructions on the procedure to be employed in the formation of a Great Sanhedrin.

[5] *Ibid.,* 176.

[6] Anchel is incorrect in saying that this passage of Maimonides is an interpolation. *Ibid.,* 177, n. 1.

[7] *Ibid.,* 173.

[8] *Correspondance de Napoléon* [I], XIII, no. 10686, pp. 122-26, tr. in J. M. Thompson, *Napoleon Self-Revealed in Three Hundred Selected Letters,* 155-59.

It is the first time, since Titus' capture of Jerusalem, that so many enlightened men belonging to the religion of Moses have been able to foregather. . . . Certain questions will then be proposed to this gathering [the Great Sanhedrin], and the answers given will be made into theological rulings or instructions, so that they may have the force of ecclesiastical and religious law, and form a second Jewish dispensation, preserving the essential character of that of Moses, but adapting itself to the present condition of the Jews, and to the customs and usages of the day. . . .

The Sanhedrin, after recognizing, as the Assembly has done, that Frenchmen and Jews are brothers . . . must prohibit usury in dealing with Frenchmen, or with the inhabitants of any countries where the Jews are allowed to enjoy civil rights. It will expound the Mosaic Law on these lines, laying it down that the Jews ought to behave, in all places where they are citizens, as though they were in Jerusalem itself; that they are strangers only where they are persecuted or ill-treated by the law of the land; and that it is only in such places that illicit gain can be tolerated by religious legislation. When this point has been regulated by the Sanhedrin on these lines, we must look further into the matter for some means of limiting and repressing this habit of speculation, which is nothing but a system of fraud and usury.[9]

. . . I am anxious to do all I can to prevent the rights restored to the Jewish people proving illusory—in a word, . . . I want them to find in France a New Jerusalem.[10]

The "infamous" Imperial edict of March 17, 1808, which imposed discriminatory regulations against the economic and political opportunities of the Jews,[11] left no doubt how "anxious" the Emperor had been.

[9] Thompson, op.cit., 155-58.   [10] Ibid., 158.

[11] Anchel, op.cit., 277-84, and ch. ix, "Un régime d'oppression." In French ecclesiastical circles, the polemic over usury and, incidentally, over Deuteronomy, showed little signs of abatement for some time to come. See, for example, Abbé Bouyon, Réfutation des systèmes de M. l'abbé Baronnat et de Mgr. de la Luzerne sur la question de l'usure (Clermont-Ferrand, 1824). According to Abbé Bouyon, Abbé Baronnat derived his false position from the formula (de la doctrine judaique) presented to the Imperial government by the Assembly of Jewish Notables. Bouyon,

Across the Channel, the final apparitions of Deuteronomy commence in an atmosphere of deep mystery. The year 1774 saw the publication at an unnamed press in London of the pseudonymous *Letters on Usury and Interest*, which claim to have been printed previously in the *Edinburgh Weekly Magazine*. The circumstances and the participants in the debate are wrapped in obscurity. There is no way of telling whether the various letters are the work of a single author or editor or whether the many pseudonyms are the *noms de plume* of different correspondents.[12] Indeed, the very point of the work as a whole does not emerge until one is nearly at the end of the correspondence. Only then does it become evident that the publication of these *Letters* constitutes one of the earliest and most ingenious attempts known to prove that Catholicism rather than Calvinism effectively reconciles the interests of modern capitalism with the spirit of sacred traditions.

The work is divided into two parts. The first part offers a pungent recital of the historic criticisms of the Catholic teachings on usury. Most of the *motifs* are, inevitably, drawn from Calvin, but use is made also of Grotius,[13] Pascal,[14] and,

---

op.cit., 186-93. Bouyon's survey of the history of the arguments over usury is rendered especially notable by the directness with which he makes a charge, which is found frequently in modern apologetics. He claims that the heretical Patarini and Cathari were the first to defend the legitimacy of interest and that Calvin took over his doctrine from the latter sect. *Ibid.*, p. xv. It is not possible to rehearse the evidence for these claims here. See, e.g., A. P. Evans, "Social Aspects of Medieval Heresy," *Persecution and Liberty: Essays in Honor of George Lincoln Burr*, 93-116, esp. at 101, 113-14, 116; C. H. Haskins, *Studies in Medieval Culture*, 199 n. 3, 217 n. 1, 239. It is sufficient on this occasion to say that, in the opinion of the author, the materials are too fragmentary and partisan to permit the conclusion that the Cathari or any other of the medieval heretical sects proclaimed the legitimacy of usury or were peculiarly addicted to the practice of usury.

[12] The British Museum Catalogue gives it as London, J. P. Coghlan, 1774.

[13] See *Letters on Usury*, p. 28.

[14] *Ibid.*, 47-50: "Doppio Ju to the Editor, &c."

probably, Locke and Hume. All the letters of this section appear to have an authentically Calvinist ring. The juxtaposition of hoary bits of Calvinist exegesis by the side of the stridently secular contentions of utilitarian economics and morality indicate the degree to which Calvin's reformulation of the Deuteronomic issue had served to ease the progress of the capitalist spirit. The fine points of Reformation theology are recalled, here, chiefly by way of introduction, in order to remove the lingering scruples of a "Bible-bred Christian, John Simple." The principal note of this first part, however, is a proud declaration of the progress of English commerce.

The Catholic orientation of the work comes to the surface only in the second part. The slanders against "papists," frequent in the first part, are denounced as anachronistic and inhumane. Innocent X (1644-1655) and Benedict XIV are commended for the excellence of their rulings on usury. The second section might well have been composed by a skillful theologian trained in the Jesuit schools. It is characterized by two theses: 1) the Protestant strictures against the scholastic interpretations of the key texts are untenable; 2) the traditional (Catholic) distinction between usury and interest is more suitable to the workings of a system of commercial and industrial capitalism than either the unscriptural (Calvinist) defenses of usury or the supposedly advanced views of secular moralists, such as Francis Hutcheson (1694-1746),[15] teacher of Adam Smith.

The Deuteronomic text plays a leading role throughout the work. In the first part, the Deuteronomic discrimination against the alien is presented as the stumbling block to the Catholic assumption that the prohibition of usury was grounded in divine and natural law. In the second part, the apparent discrepancy in the celebrated text is held to be a supreme illustration of the "precision" of the Divine Legislator in suiting his laws to the needs of the Hebrew Commonwealth. Indeed, the double-edged ordinance, preeminently, is

---

[15] *Ibid.,* 113-15.

claimed to embody a lesson essential for all times, namely, that, though usury is intrinsically evil, *interest* may be taken where there exist adequate grounds, notably in the form of extrinsic titles, for such compensation.

"John Simple" introduces the opening series of letters by professing that his conscience has been disturbed since the day a friend reminded him of the numerous biblical passages prohibiting interest in any form. A host of correspondents promptly undertake to submit proof that Simple's doubts are groundless. The correspondent, "Marcellus," observes that the purpose of the Old Testament prohibition was to protect the simple farmers of the Hebrew Republic from falling prey to the temptation of foreign luxuries and heathen superstitions. For this reason, and to assure their subsistence, he explains, the Hebrews were all allotted "equal portions of the land."[16] As for the discrimination against the alien: "this liberty of taking usury from strangers was undoubtedly intended to keep up the idea of distinction, and to maintain in their minds that superior degree of esteem and regard which was due to their countrymen."[17]

The entire battery of Calvin's arguments against the medieval interpretations of Deuteronomy xxiii is offered in evidence by another correspondent. All the ceremonial and political laws of the Hebrews, "A.B.C." recalls, were merely temporary and binding upon that nation only.

> I am persuaded this Gentleman [Mr. Simple's counselor] will not imagine, even in a morning dream that ever God would give express allowance to a thing unjust in itself . . . [The breach of God's laws by the Hebrews] incurred his [God's] displeasure, and exposed the breakers to severe judgment until he [God] dissolved the obligation by breaking down the middle wall of partition:—and therefore let Mr. Simple stand forth in the liberty wherewith he, as a Christian, is made free, and let him not be intangled in the same yoke of bondage.[18]

[16] *Ibid.,* 7.   [17] *Ibid.,* 32.   [18] *Ibid.,* 15.

Surely the learned traditionalist could not be right in holding that abstaining from usury is "an express condition of
salvation."

> Alas! what shall become of thousands of good British Chris-
> tians, who support their families on the interest of their
> money! Will this man of so much probity excommunicate
> them all from the society of the blessed, and ingross salvation
> to himself? I am fatally mistaken if Salvation descends not
> to us in a different manner, "not by work of righteousness
> which we have done, but according to His mercy He saved
> us."[19]

The claims based on Luke vi are rejected in a similar fashion. "Marcellus" states the case most effectively:

> If this verse proves anything, it proves too much; for it will
> imply that we are to part with both capital and interest, as
> evidently appears from the context. In order to elucidate this
> matter, it will be proper to reflect on the particular situation
> of the primitive christians, and from thence we will find a key
> to these moral instructions, which are seemingly too rigid for
> practice. The christians in that early period were inevitably
> to be exposed to the hardest trials and dangers; they were to
> suffer persecution from Jews and Gentiles, to be banished
> their native country, and reduced to the most deplorable cir-
> cumstances of misery and distress. In order to give the world
> a favourable idea of that spirit which animated christianity,
> it was necessary to kindle up the warmest sentiments of love
> and affection, and to inculcate the principles of humanity and
> charity in their strongest terms. They were to consider them-
> selves as one body, and united by the most indissoluble bonds
> of love and interest: in short, as the children of one common
> parent. They were not to mingle with the political connections
> or interests of the world, but to place their affections on a
> heavenly reward.[20]

Evidently, "Marcellus" continues, "the political situation
of this world has suffered a great revolution." Men no longer,

[19] *Ibid.*, 16.   [20] *Ibid.*, 8-9.

he seems to say, need to regard themselves as "the children of one common parent" or to center their hopes on a "heavenly reward."

> In this country, for instance, we live under a regular form of government, and are abundantly secured against injustice and persecution. Commerce is carried on to a great extent, and there are numberless occasions for borrowing and lending. The merchant who has acquired a handsome fortune in trade, perhaps chuses to retire, and to enjoy the fruits of his labor and attention; as he is naturally inclined to provide for his posterity, as well as himself, he will take care not to break upon the capital, but will lend it out perhaps to those who are possessed of the same commercial spirit.[21]

A.B.C. concurs in this view:

> ... I am afraid, that to secure his title to heaven on this plan, he [Mr. Simple] will be obliged to lose both interest and capital.[22]

In other words, Luke vi, as well as the Deuteronomic passage, hardly applies to the present day. Calvin's claim that Christ's summons was supererogatory in character, that it called for the abandonment of capital as well as interest in dealings with the indigent, is suggested only in order to emphasize the unsuitability of the commandment to eighteenth-century England. How, moreover, could so exacting a demand be a requirement for salvation?

Mr. Simple, it is claimed, has merely to reread the Parable of Talents to realize how wide of the mark his notions are. He must beware, also, of drawing false conclusions from the reference in the Gospel of Matthew (xxi:13) to Christ's expulsion of the moneychangers and thieves. "Christ's indignation," says "Marcellus," "was not so much levelled at their usury itself, as at the dishonest and oppressive manner in which they carried on the forbidden commerce."[23] Only biting usury was prohibited for the sake of securing the poor

[21] *Ibid.*, 9-10.   [22] *Ibid.*, 16-17.   [23] *Ibid.*, 36.

against oppression. If we are to divine the true meaning of Scriptures, we must pay heed, above all, to the Golden Rule, "the solid basis of all equity and justice between man and man."[24]

"Simon Sober" clinches the argument by calling attention to the "infallible" principle of utility:

Here, then, is a sure and infallible rule to judge of the lawfulness of a practice. Is it useful to the State? Is it beneficial to the individuals that compose it? Either of these is sufficient to obtain a tolerance; but both together vest it with a character of justice and equity. *Utilitas semper justi prope mater et aequi.* In fact, if we look into the laws of different nations concerning usury, we shall find that they are all formed on the principle of public utility. In those States where usury was found hurtful to society, it was prohibited. In those where it was neither hurtful nor very beneficial, it was tolerated. In those where it was useful, it was authorized. In ours, it is absolutely necessary.[25]

From this standpoint the "present practice of lending money to interest in Great Britain" is not oppressive of the poor, hurtful to society or contrary to nature and the laws of the State, and consequently is not the usury prohibited by Scriptures and condemned by the Fathers. Interest is not only beneficial to the needy; it also prevents many persons "from falling into poverty, otherwise inevitable"; it is useful to younger sons, gentlemen of broken estates, widows, unlucky traders, colonists, projectors, landholders, and peers. In short:

the practice of lending money to interest is in this nation, and under this constitution, beneficial to all degrees; therefore it is beneficial to society. I say in this nation; which, as long as it continues to be a commercial one, must be chiefly supported by interest; for interest is the soul of credit and credit is the soul of commerce.[26]

[24] *Ibid.*, 13.   [25] *Ibid.*, 41-42.   [26] *Ibid.*, 40-41.

The second set of letters issues in a similar conclusion. Yet the argument of the second section differs in fundamentals from that of the first section. Interestingly enough, it is Simon Sober, spokesman for utilitarianism and the commercial interests, who is the principal butt of the criticisms of Calvin by "Michael Meanwell," the reputed author of all but one of the second set of letters.

Meanwell writes:

> The Scriptures condemn usury, not only because it is oppressive of the poor, but also because it is unjust and dishonest in itself, and therefore intrinsically unlawful, whether done to rich or poor.[27]

Only one text seems to cast doubt on the intrinsic iniquity of usury: Deuteronomy xxiii. For the understanding of this passage, however, "there is no need of having recourse to a dispense from the law of nature," as Simon Sober suggests; we need merely observe how the major Catholic theologians distinguish between usury and interest. The latter is entirely justified when based on titles extrinsic to the loan.

Whether or not a gain on loans of money is to be allowed depends on the historical circumstances. From this standpoint, there are three principal types of economy:

> If any nation or constitution were found in which the grounds of interest could have no existence, it is plain, that under such a constitution, all gain whatsoever arising from the loan of money must be absolute usury, iniquitous and unjust in itself, and therefore to be entirely prohibited. Again, if any other nation were found, in which the grounds of interest sometimes did, and sometimes did not accompany the loan of money, the taking of interest here must be properly regulated, so as on the one hand to prevent usury, and on the other to secure a just and lawful interest to those who have a real title to receive it. And lastly, if any other nation be found, in which the loan of money scarce can exist, without someone or other

27 *Ibid.,* 76-77.

of the grounds of interest accompanying it, in such circumstances the taking of interest must be universally established.[28]

The original institutions of the Hebrew people afford an admirable instance of the first of these cases:

They [the people of God] were all one family, the children of one common father, and according to the spirit of their laws, both civil and religious, they were obliged to support one another as brethren, and with a liberal hand to supply one another's wants: Nay, Almighty God, their divine lawgiver not only commands this in the strictest terms, but it is in a particular manner on condition of their complying with this duty, that he engages himself to give them his most ample benedictions, as he himself declares at large in the 15th chapter of Deuteronomy. The more effectually to cement this harmony and fraternal union among them, they were forbid all commerce or communication with other nations; nay, they were taught to look upon them with abhorrence, as impious and profane, and as enemies to their God and to their religion. Hence it was, that living entirely by themselves, and in manner sequestered from the rest of the world, trade had no being among them, and the whole nation, from the princes of their tribes, to the lowest of the people, were all shepherds or husbandmen.[29]

Among the Hebrews, perpetual alienation of immovable goods was impossible, and the contracting of debts, very difficult. Engrossing of lands was forbidden by the Jubilee law, and the greedy were further restrained by the Sabbatical release. "The whole nation was upon a kind of equality with regard to their riches, as well as in their birth and nobility." In short, among them the grounds on which the lawfulness of interest on loans is founded, namely, the extrinsic titles, could have no existence.

The inspiration of their laws was to promote fraternal love. The precision with which the Divine Wisdom acted is revealed, above all, in their laws with regard to strangers and

[28] *Ibid.*, 118.   [29] *Ibid.*, 119.

foreigners. When they lent to strangers, there they were in danger of losing all or part of the capital or of being put to trouble in recovering it. For this reason, they were allowed to demand compensation from strangers. In the same way, they were allowed to recover their just debts from foreigners, notwithstanding the Sabbatical Year.[30]

In short, there is no injustice in the fact that the Jews were allowed to take gain on loans to strangers.

... By the word usury, when forbid to the Jews, is understood usury only in its proper and criminal sense; and by the same word usury, when allowed to be taken from strangers, is signified that just and equitable recompence for the risk they run in lending to strangers, which in modern language is distinguished by the name interest. Thus the scriptures is easily reconciled to itself without the least torturing or straining.[31]

By the same token, the lending of money "in a commercial nation can scarce ever be unattended by some or all the grounds of interest." A law fixing the rate of interest may be freely established in Great Britain.

Meanwell concludes on a polemical note. Hutcheson's formula basing the rate of interest on the rate of profit is denounced as "superficial and inaccurate." This would mean, he alleges, that "where no profits are made, no interest could be demanded at all."[32]

The disingenuousness of Meanwell's manner and the

[30] *Ibid.*, 121-23. For a vigorous expression of a similar point of view by an earlier writer, see Josiah Tucker, *A Second Letter*, 37.

[31] *Letters on Usury*, 129.

[32] *Ibid.*, 114-15. For Hutcheson's economic views and his influence on Smith, see: W. R. Scott, *Francis Hutcheson*, 230-43; A. Smith, *Lectures on Justice*, ed. E. Cannan, xxv-xxvi (in intro.); *idem, Wealth of Nations*, ed. E. Cannan, xxxvi-xli (in intro.). One of Hutcheson's comments on the Deuteronomic prohibition is worth comparing with Calvin's pronouncements. Hutcheson writes: "The prohibition of all loans for interest would be destructive to any trading nation, tho' in a democracy of farmers, such as that of the Hebrews was, it might have been a very proper prohibition." See Hutcheson, *A Short Introduction to Moral Philosophy*, bk. ii, section 7, ch. 13, pp. 208-9.

subtlety of his casuistry almost obscure the extent of his indebtedness to Calvin for many of the nodal points in his apology for Catholicism. At bottom, the unknown author or editor is more faithful to the letter than he is to the spirit of the traditional view of usury. He is warm in his praises of the Hebrew Commonwealth, yet he tacitly assumes that its fraternalistic institutions are not to be emulated in eighteenth-century England.

Unembarrassed adherence to Calvin's teaching marks the incisive review of the usury question by the celebrated Archdeacon Paley (1743-1805):

> There exists no reason in the law of nature, why a man should not be paid for the lending of his money, as well as of any other property into which the money might be converted.
>
> This prohibition [based, Paley notes, on Deuteronomy] is now generally understood to have been intended for the Jews alone, as part of the civil or political law of that nation, and calculated to preserve amongst themselves the distribution of property, to which many of their institutions were subservient; as the marriage of an heiress within her own tribe; of a widow who was left childless, to her husband's brother; the year of jubilee, when alienated estates reverted to the family of the original proprietor; regulations which were never thought to be binding upon any but the commonwealth of Israel.
>
> This interpretation is confirmed, I think, beyond all controversy, by the distinction made in the law between a Jew and a foreigner: . . . a distinction which could hardly have been admitted into a law, which the Divine Author intended to be of moral and of universal obligation.[33]

There was little left for Bentham (1748-1832) to do save paraphrase such sentiments. He finds it strange "that the liberty of making one's own terms in money-bargains" should be restricted in free England. "In a word," he declares,

[33] *The Principles of Moral and Political Philosophy* (1785) bk. iii, ch. 10, ed. in *The Works of William Paley*, IV, 106-7. Cf. the spirited estimate of Paley by Alfred Cobban in *Encyclopedia of the Social Sciences*, XII (1933), 535-36.

the proposition I have been accustomed to lay down to myself on this subject is the following one, viz. that *no man of ripe years and of sound mind, acting freely and with his eyes open, ought to be hindered, with a view to his advantage, from making such bargain, in the way of obtaining money, as he thinks fit: nor,* (what is a necessary consequence) anybody hindered from supplying him upon any terms he thinks proper to accede to.

Were this proposition accepted, he insists, it would at once sweep away all existing barriers to such money-dealing contracts.[34]

A concluding reminiscence of the Deuteronomic issue occurs in Father Jeremiah O'Callaghan's story of the calamities he had suffered on behalf of the medieval usury prohibition.[35] Father O'Callaghan had been successful early in his career (1819), in enforcing restitution by a dying retailer, "whose time price was much higher than his ready-money price."[36] Soon after, the Father's indiscreet attacks on usurers aroused strong opposition among both the laity and clergy. He was declared suspended from office and benefice by order of his superior, Bishop Coppinger of Cloyne and Ross. The principled Father requested and was granted an *exeat*. This permitted him to depart without censure from Ross Carberry and to exercise his sacerdotal functions elsewhere. Now he was free "to ascertain the doctrine of foreign countries on the subject of usury." A brief visit across the Channel yielded the encouraging conviction that usury was detested through-

[34] *Defence of Usury*, Letter 1, dated "Crichoff, in White Russia, January, 1787," in ed. of 1816, at p. 2; cf. Bentham, *Works*, ed. J. Bowring, III, 3.

[35] Father O'Callaghan's major work, *Usury . . .* , appeared four times in the decade, 1824-34. The editions vary considerably. The first appeared in New York in 1824. In the following year the work was published in London by C. Clement. Three years later, William Cobbett re-issued it with an ironical dedication to the "Society of Friends." This printing was the first to contain Father O'Callaghan's story of his life. I have consulted three editions, those of 1825, 1828, and 1834. Hereafter, references to these volumes will be by date of publication.

[36] *Usury*, pp. 6-7 (1828).

out France.[37] He hastened back to Ireland with high hopes, only to be ordered to submit on pain of being blacklisted throughout the Church of Ireland. Father O'Callaghan appealed unsuccessfully against this ultimatum to the Metropolitan and to the Primate.

Without honor in his native land, he submitted his case to Rome on August 15, 1822. He was certain of his vindication, knowing little of the compromises that had been achieved by the theologians and jurists since the compilation of the Decretals.[38] He seems even to have been unaware of the wish of the Vatican to allay public controversy while deferring final decision.

Father O'Callaghan's letter fell on deaf ears. Rome had

[37] *Ibid.*, 8-9.

[38] "Amongst all the profane, unscriptural terms invented by the Prince of Darkness to palliate the deformity of usury, and the eternal flames decreed against it in both Testaments, 'Ceasing Gain and Emergent Loss' produce the greatest uncertainty; . . . Collet [Pierre?, 1693-1770 (Migne, *Dictionnaire*, I, 1045-47)], Natalis Alexander [1639-1724 (Hurter, *Nomenclator*, ed. 3, IV, 1179-85)] Genetto [François Genet?, 1640-1702?/03? (*ibid.*, col. 944)], Bailey [Louis Bailly?, 1730-1818 (*ibid.*, V, 507, 591-93)], Denns [Pierre Dens?, 1690-1775 (*ibid.*, 46)] and so forth, seem to be puzzled on them; no two fully agreeing when they explain the conditions; some require three or four; others, six, and sometimes seven; and even explain these according to their respective notions on right and wrong. Nothing but disagreement and contradiction could indeed be expected, when neither of them takes any Christian rule, *scripture* or *tradition*, during the exposition. How could they? Scripture makes no mention whatever of such barbarous terms; all antiquity is silent on them; being mentioned nowhere prior to the seventeenth century. But it is really astonishing what gave rise to them since that time. Then the New Light of philosophy began to dawn; the miserable time foretold by the Apostle, 2 Tim. iv. 3, seemed then fast approaching. 'There will be time when they will not endure sound doctrine, but will, according to their own desires, heap together doctors having itching ears, and they will indeed turn the hearers from the truth, they will be converted to *fables.*'" (O'Callaghan, *op.cit.*, 119-20 [1828].) Only one so innocent of the writing of medieval jurists and theologians as Father O'Callaghan would have escaped discovering that the *damnum emergens* and *lucrum cessans* were Roman law concepts taken up and adopted by commentators on the law of usury as early as the 13th century. See McLaughlin, *Mediaeval Studies*, I, 144-46.

already committed itself to another course. Only a month earlier, on July 3, 1822, the Holy Office of the Inquisition, through Cardinal Galleffi, had issued a letter to an unnamed woman of Lyons, relieving her of the obligation to make restitution of interest increments, for which she alleged no other justification than the prevailing civil law rules.[39] Though she was given to understand that response to her question was to be postponed until the proper time, she was declared eligible for absolution. In Father O'Callaghan's case, Rome maintained silence for seven months. Trusting that America, "the garden of liberty," would grant him an opportunity to resume his clerical vocation, he set sail from Cork, on March 8, 1823. He sought refuge in New York and Baltimore, only to discover that America lay prostrate before usury.[40] Despite the fact that the highest ecclesiastical au-

---

[39] See *Litterae monitoriae DD. Bellicensis episcopi ad clerum suae dioecesis directae, circa quoddam opus de mutuo recenter editum,* in Migne, *Theologiae cursus completus,* XVI, cols. 1065-90, esp. at 1065. The story of the "non esse inquietandos" formula deserves telling.

[40] "I started in the month of September [1823], to try my fortune in Baltimore. The Archbishop of that See, Dr. Mareschall [Maréchal], related to me a melancholy story.

"He was, he said, a native of Lyons in France, was four years a teacher of divinity in the Diocesan School of Baltimore, and that during that time he taught his pupils that usury or interest is against the law of God, and destructive to souls; but that since his accession to the mitre, he was forced to connive at the practice, for fear of throwing everything into confusion!! That he knew several pious divines who have, notwithstanding the prevalence of the measure, their fears and scruples about it; that, for instance, he received a letter from Bishop Flagett, of the Western States, beseeching, in the most impressive manner, to be informed of his sentiments on the question; and that also, on his return from Rome, a couple of years before, he had another letter from a young ecclesiastic in Lyons, praying, for God's sake, to let him know the modern doctrine of the Holy See in that regard, promising secrecy if he, Bishop Mareschall, would desire it. God has said, *Seek and you shall find.* A copy of my little book was carried to the pious Flagett, by a young gentleman from Dublin, who went out to him as a missionary; and one of his own clergy, the Rev. Mr. Badin, who arrived two years ago in London, from America, bought another copy at 183 Fleet Street, and sent it to him. Does not this verify the saying of Providence, *Seek and you shall find.* But when I continued to ask the Archbishop whether he allowed usury to be condemned

thorities in Quebec and Montreal saw eye to eye with him on the usury question, they hesitated to give him a post in Canada. On top of these disappointments came a communication from Rome dated July 5, 1823. Rome was sending him the *Vix pervenit*, with a letter signed by Cardinal Consalvi on behalf of the Holy Office, advising him that he would surely gain Bishop Coppinger's forgiveness if he would embrace the five rules on usury embodied in Benedict's XIV's Bull and would promise henceforth to obey his superior. He immediately handed the letter to his printer in New York for insertion in his forthcoming book on usury, which was to tell the story of his martyrdom for the sake of the traditional doctrine of usury.

To Father O'Callaghan, the *Vix pervenit* seemed a patent confirmation of his views. He hastened to return to Ireland. Directly on arrival, he offered to comply with the conditions laid down by the letter from the Congregation. The Bishop bluntly rejected his overtures. After a serious "self-consultation," the disappointed priest felt he had no recourse but to go to Rome to make a personal appeal to the Pope. En route he left a copy of his *apologia* in the Fleet Street office of William Cobbett, who was so smitten with its argument that he republished the book and assigned all the profits to the author.

---

yet in the same seminary? He replied, 'Yes.' 'Your Divines then,' continued I, 'learn in the school a doctrine, which they must lock up in their breast on the mission, to conform to the world, for fear of throwing everything into confusion! How do you get over the saying of Christ, Luke vi.35, *Lend, hoping for nothing thereby*'? Appearing deeply affected, he made no other reply, but put an end to our conversation." O'Callaghan, *op.cit.*, 10-11 (1828).

"To New York the very focus of usury, the great emporium of North and South America, flock greedy speculators from all the extensive regions. You would see there Jews, Quakers, Tunkers, Socinians, with nominal Christians prostrate in full devotion to the idol, *Mammon*; money-changers, bankers, brokers, auctioneers of all hues, climes, and creeds on the alert to hook the simple prey; in Wall Street of that city Satan seems to have fixed his eternal abode." *Ibid.*, 18 (1834), cf. p. 12 in ed. of 1828.

(In the following year, indeed, Father O'Callaghan became a tutor in Cobbett's household.)

Father O'Callaghan arrived in Rome on December 10, shortly before Pope Leo XII's opening of the Grand Jubilee of 1825.[41] He presented his book, together with a memorial to the Cardinals, praying either to be redressed or to be ordered to conform to Bishop Coppinger's doctrine. "Such was my faith in the infallibility of Peter's chair," he tells us, "that I would not hesitate even one moment to admit usury if they had ordered me to do so."[42] The Cardinals wrote to the Bishop requesting him to submit his version of the case. In the meantime, they granted Father O'Callaghan a pension in Rome. The Bishop's letter of defense arrived five months later. It contained a flat denial of Father O'Callaghan's charge that he had received "any one shilling of interest in the course of his life." Two of the Bishop's agents corroborated their superior's story. Father O'Callaghan tells us that no attempt was made either by the Bishop or his representatives to put up any defense of usury in general. They did, however, undertake to justify the practices of the retailer whom Father O'Callaghan had persuaded to restitution. They made two claims:

1. That the trader in question was entitled to compensation for the risk which he incurred with the time purchases.

2. "That the clergy would, by now opposing a deep rooted and general custom, fall into contempt and be despised upon all questions."[43]

The Sacred Congregation, Father O'Callaghan continues, rejected these arguments and sent Bishop Coppinger "peremptory orders to suppress altogether the extortion in his diocese."[44]

---

[41] *Ibid.*, 38 (1834).   [42] *Ibid.*, 19 (1828).   [43] *Ibid.*, 39 (1834).

[44] Father O'Callaghan adds: "Accordingly the Prelate issued in the year 1825 a Circular Letter to the clergy of Ross Carberry to dissuade all traffickers in the name of the Holy See from such extortion for the future. The Circular was duly published in the Churches of that vicinity. Thus that abuse which I had always opposed and for opposing which I had

At this juncture, Father O'Callaghan was called upon to defend himself against Bishop Coppinger's charge that the profits he was regularly receiving from the publication of his book by Cobbett in London rendered him ineligible to accept the pension in Rome. Notwithstanding presentation of evidence to the contrary, Father O'Callaghan was unable to clear himself in the eyes of the Cardinals. Becoming reconciled to the failure of his mission in Rome, he decided to return to Ireland. Selling some of his linen, he set out for home in May 1825.

He visited Rome a second time four years later (April 29, 1829).[45] On June 7th he requested the Reverend C. H. Boylan, Superior of the Irish College in Rome, to intervene on his behalf with the Congregation, promising among other things that he would allow his hearers to practice legal interest, "that is to say, the interest allowed by the human laws for money loans," provided the Sacred Congregation said to him that he could, "with safe conscience do so."[46] Four days later, Father Boylan replied that the Propaganda had "no disposition to recede on the decisions already given." This communication sent Father O'Callaghan reeling.[47] He knew

---

been deprived in 1819, is condemned by the Pope and by the very Bishop in 1825; thus are the flocks recalled into the path of Christ; though the buyers and sellers manifest no discontent, or disregard towards their pastors." *Ibid.*, 39-40.

[45] *Ibid.*, 56-63.   [46] *Ibid.*, 59.

[47] His confusion was aggravated by the fact that in addition to receiving much favorable comment in England, Ireland, and America, his book was well known in Rome, through the issuance there of an Italian translation of Cobbett's *History of the Protestant Reformation*, which proudly reported Cobbett's sponsorship of the work in London. Indeed, had not Cobbett's *History* received the approval of the Roman censors, of whom one was Cardinal Cappellari, elevated to the Papal Throne in 1831 as Gregory XVI? Father O'Callaghan wondered: "Would the Holy See, always so tenacious of the faith, re-edit said History or affix the note to my name, if my principles on usury were erroneous? Why does not Rome, that knows full well the sinfulness of usury, openly come out against it; is the infection so inveterate that there is no prospect of a remedy; or have they as the lamb did with the wolves, formed a truce with

of no decision he might be expected to obey, with the exception of the letter he had been sent in explanation of the forwarding of the Bull of Benedict XIV. He left Rome on July 27, 1829, never to return.

On April 28, 1830, he set sail for New York for a second time. Soon after his arrival there he was presented to Bishop Fenwick of Boston, who gave him an appointment to Vermont. The newly arrived Irish immigrants of that state were without a Catholic pastor. Here a new life started for him. In the annals of American Catholicism Father O'Callaghan is remembered today, if at all, as the "Apostle of Vermont."[48]

Father O'Callaghan repeatedly denounces Protestant interpretations of Deuteronomy, in the several editions of his work from 1824 to 1856:

> The usurers and their advocates say that the Jews were, by this text, forbidden to charge usury only to their brethren; we will therefore charge every person with it, excepting neither friends nor foes; natives nor aliens. This is curious logic. How contrary to the arguments of the Saints Thomas, Ambrose, and Anthony! . . . The Saints would hold all mankind as brethren and friends under the law of Christ, the usurers would treat them all as strangers and foreigners. They say, "the law of Moses allows to charge strangers interest; therefore we, Christians, charge it to mankind in general, friends as well as aliens." The truth is, if this or any other dispensations that are granted in favour of particular persons, or certain portions of the community, have the effect of repealing the general law, neither canon nor civil decrees can bind any longer. The prerogative of the crown and of the sceptre to grant dispensations and pardons, when the general welfare require it, is not contested by any man. . . .[49]

Will any man take upon himself to say that the Absolute Ruler

---

the usurers?" *Ibid.*, 61. For Cobbett's high estimate of Father O'Callaghan's views, see Cobbett, *op.cit.*, Letter xiv, Vol. i, par. 403.

[48] See the sketch of Father O'Callaghan by Richard J. Purcell in *Dictionary of American Biography*, xiii (1934), 613-14.

[49] *Ibid.*, 8-9 (1825).

THE GHOST OF DEUTERONOMY

of the Universe, though he dispensed under the Old Law with
the Jews to receive usury from strangers, *could* not or *has* not
forbidden it to all mankind, under the New Law?[50] With what
facility does the reformer pass by the rest of Scriptures, until
he comes to this text, Deut. xxiii.19. The Jews got permission or dispensation from God himself to receive usury from
strangers. Henry VIII and the reformers permitted therefore his followers to receive it from friends and foes; from
strangers and natives.[51]

Blessed be the Holy Catholic Church which teaches, that we
are bound, under the law of Christ, to look upon all mankind
as our brethren; that we must love our enemies; do good to
them that hate us; in order to be children of our Father, who
is in heaven, who maketh his sun to rise upon the good and
bad, and raineth upon the just and the unjust. Cursed be the
Calvinistic school that teaches like the heathens, to love those
that love us, to salute our brethren only; cursed be the Calvinistic School that teaches that we need not do any good
works at all—that we need not lend, without interest, to friend
or to foe; to native or alien; that usury is permitted, where
any person, but an Israelite, is concerned.[52]

Without apparently being aware of it, Father O'Callaghan's critique of Blackstone's treatment of the Deuteronomic issue incorporated a condemnation of the Ingolstadt
argument for the *statutum principis*:

Where is his [Blackstone's] proof for saying that it was a
political, not a moral precept? or upon what authority makes
he a distinction between both precepts? A moral precept seems
to regulate men's manners (*mores*) in society; a political precept, regards the manners or mutual relations of the multitude (*polus, multus*), consequently both precepts, moral and
political, seem to signify one and the same thing. . . . If the
Jews were permitted to take usury from strangers, not from
their brethren the Jews; from what logic will he allow Christians to exact it from their brethren and strangers—from
Christians and Jews; from friends and foes; from natives and
aliens. And as God himself, the absolute Ruler of our life and

[50] *Ibid.*, 42 (1828).   [51] *Ibid.*, 127 (1825).   [52] *Ibid.*, 76-77 (1834).

property permitted the hardened Jews to exact usury from strangers, will Blackstone say that to take moderate usury is not *malum in se*—"an evil in itself"? The Reformer by similar argument may say, whereas the Omnipotent God transfers human life and property when, and how he pleases, it is not an evil in itself, if the Reformers do the same thing when and how it pleaseth them. Upon what authority does he foist in the adjective *moderate*, for the text which he quotes from, DEUT. makes no such distinction. . . .[53]

Father O'Callaghan's appeal elicited no response from the Vatican, nor from anywhere else in the world. He was a voice crying in the wilderness. Deuteronomy had passed into limbo.

Bentham's "self-evident propositions," Napoleon's flight into exegesis, and Father O'Callaghan's quest for justice provide a fitting close to the meanderings of Deuteronomy in the western world. Under the impact of changing economic and ideological requirements, the ancient text had been pressed into a bewildering variety of services, until, exhausted, it consumed itself.

Deuteronomy had been all things to all men.

The medieval exegetes, who identified the Jew with the usurer—they labelled Christian usurers as "baptized Jews" —repudiated verse 20 on the ground that it was a temporary concession by the Lord to innate Jewish greed.

The exegetes of the Reformation, embarrassed by the loyalty of left-wing Protestants to the reputed egalitarianism of the Hebrew Commonwealth, discarded verse 19 as a vestige of an antiquated version of the ideal of brotherhood.[54]

[53] *Ibid.,* 252 (1834).

[54] This is not intended as a denial of the familiar views of Heine, Matthew Arnold, Max Weber, Sombart, *et al.,* on the significance of Old Testament sources for the Calvinist patterns of ethic and sentiment. The evidence for the influence of Mosaic precedent on Reformation political theory and law is overwhelming. Nevertheless, as we have intimated above, a more refined analysis of the problem is in order. It needs to be recalled that opposed economic and political groups emphasized different

Catholic traditionalists continued for some time to offer stubborn resistance to this innovation. Slowly but surely, however, a latitudinarian view came to prevail in official circles. Though no casuist would presume to deny that mankind was a brotherhood in which usury was forbidden, the Deuteronomic prohibition came to be neutralized by a devious exegesis. Among Catholics, just as among the Protestants, the Deuteronomic discrimination was invoked to discredit the universality of the Deuteronomic prohibition. It was to the Deuteronomic exception to which the innovating theologians and jurists turned when promoting novel extrinsic titles by which the old commandment was finally, albeit only tacitly, renounced.

---

features of the Hebraic polity. We must be careful to distinguish between the Hebraism of Bucer, Calvin, Cromwell and the Pilgrim Fathers, for example, and that of the Anabaptists, the Diggers, the Fifth Monarchy Men, the Quakers, *et al.* Aristocratic and middle-class cadres in the opposition to absolute monarchy professed to emulate the political structure of the Hebrew Commonwealth, e.g., the Sanhedrin, and the rule of magistrates and judges. From time to time, the Hebrew polity was differently conceived: now as oligarchic, now as democratic. The left-wing sectaries of the Reformation were more prone to appeal to the Hebrew Commonwealth as a model of social and economic egalitarianism and reaffirm Hebraic messianic and millennarian aspirations. Hebraic precedents were, in short, the inspiration for profoundly different moralities and policies: for the repressive criminal laws of oligarchic Massachusetts and New Haven, and for Gerrard Winstanley's Utopian *Law of Freedome in a Platform* (1651-52). How the Hebraizing Puritans dealt with the Hebraizing Diggers is a familiar story.

For the contrast between the social outlook of these groups, see R. B. Schlatter, *The Social and Religious Ideas of Religious Leaders, 1660-1680, passim*; John Winthrop, *A Modell of Christian Charity* (1630). [The neo-Platonic and medieval sources of Winthrop's appeal to divine sanctions for eternal class stratification are patent. See A. O. Lovejoy, *The Great Chain of Being*.] The Diggers claimed to be Hebrew in origin and stressed the living heritage of Old Testament communalistic brotherhood. See L. H. Berens, *The Digger Movement,* esp. at pp. 14, 37, 82, 92; E. Bernstein, *Cromwell and Communism*; Gerrard Winstanley, *Works*, ed. G. Sabine. This feature of Digger thought is not sufficiently highlighted in H. Holorenshaw, *The Levellers* or D. W. Petegorsky, *Left-Wing Democracy in the English Civil War,* but see the *Tyranipocrit* cited in the latter work, p. 233.

Finally, under the pressure of modern capitalism and modern nationalism, the Jews were compelled explicitly to disavow the historic interpretation of *both* verses and the principles on which they had been based.

In all of its roles, the double-edged text had acquitted itself with distinction: as a bulwark of Hebrew tribalism, as a challenge and incentive to medieval universalism, and as a last obstacle and trump card in the struggle to promote the universal otherhood of modern capitalism.

The Brother and the Other: An Epilogue

CONTEMPORARY students of moral evolution have charted the transition from tribalism to universalism in radically different ways. Which of their conclusions, if any, are warranted by the record of the odyssey of Deuteronomy?

Rationalist liberals have set the highest value on the enlargement of the moral community. The successive steps in the consolidation of world society have appeared to them to bespeak continual progress. Once, it is recalled, the ideals of friendship and brotherhood were confined to the circle of the kindred; today, these ideals serve to unite the whole of mankind. If the seemingly interminable clan feuds of tribal times have been rendered obsolete with the advance of civilization, may we not hope, ask the liberals, that soon eternal peace, friendship, and brotherhood will prevail among the peoples and the nations of the earth?

Writers with organicist leanings have tended to reject this version of history as an expression of capitalist ideology. In their estimation, the process of moving from community to society[1] has involved vastly more loss than gain. The vital harmonies of the organic community have been displaced by the *bellum omnium contra omnes*, carried on under the fragile masks of equal opportunity and equal law. Modern economic morality represents a perversion of the golden rule of the tribal kindred. The superficial expansion of the moral community cannot compensate for the baneful distortions in the quality of the moral bond.

We do not find it possible to subscribe without reservation to either of these points of view. The liberals have been too prone to take the abstract forms of the moral order for its living substance. There is more to moral progress than the scrapping of authoritarian controls on individual freedom.

[1] See F. Tönnies, *Fundamental Concepts of Sociology (Gemeinschaft und Gesellschaft)*, tr. and supplemented by Charles P. Loomis.

The increase in the size of the moral community has not meant the automatic extension of old and valid moral ideals. Here the organicists have been right. But, having admitted that, we must at once take leave of their company. A Paradise of mythical "communities" provides no secure refuge from the processes of history. There has been too much of "club law" to permit us the thought of ever again consigning men to a disunited world of antagonistic "fraternities." One must go forward to recapture the original purity of the moral bond, not backward. Love and prudence—and not mere resentment,[2] as the organicists say—spur men on to democracy, humanitarianism, cosmopolitanism, and universal brotherhood.

Thus we return to our point of departure. The road from clan comradeship to universal society is beset with hazards. When two communities merge and two sets of others become one set of brothers, a price is generally paid. The price, as this essay suggests, is an attenuation of the love which had held each set together. It is a tragedy of moral history that the expansion of the area of the moral community has ordinarily been gained through the sacrifice of the intensity of the moral bond, or, to recall the refrain of this sketch, that all men have been becoming brothers by becoming equally others.[3]

[2] Nietzsche's view is reformulated in Max Scheler's *L'homme du ressentiment*, tr. from *Vom Umsturz der Werte*, I, ch. 2.

[3] Modern imperialism faces the issue of the Brother and the Other every day. Successful penetration of undeveloped areas often requires dislocation of tribal communalism and the overcoming of native hostility to the stranger. A graphic twentieth-century illustration of the problem is provided by Mr. A. M. Miller's testimony before the South African Native Commission on the policies to be adopted by the British government of the Swaziland Protectorate: "Every act of the legislature that tends to preserve his [the Swazi native's] old time communistic life welds an additional fetter that will bind him helplessly in the struggle that is ahead of his race. . . . I feel with deepest conviction that if the native problem is to be solved, the solution will only be found when the Administration is strong enough to cut itself free from all the trammels of tribal precedent, to ignore the existence of traditions, interesting rather

Still, we need not end our survey of the wanderings of Deuteronomy on a note of despair. A society which embodies recognizable norms for people in general is ethically superior to one in which there are privileges for the insiders, temporary concessions for good neighbors and strangers, and no obligations at all toward distant "barbarians." Better a prize ring under Marquis of Queensberry rules than gang brawls with no holds barred. Better the abhorred "atomized individualism of bourgeois liberalism" than conflicting "Brotherhoods of Blood and Soil."

Better still the Brotherhood of Man.*

---

than useful, of laws as incongruous and unsuitable in juxtaposition with twentieth century civilization as the feudalism of Northern England, and customs as moss-grown as the memories of the Hebrew Patriarchs." *Report of the South African Native Commission, 1903-1905*, Vol. v, p. 250, cited in Brian Marwick, *The Swazi*, 301-2. It is common knowledge that such penetration has frequently been effected by practices which have strained the universalist teachings of Christianity. Pareto cites the pungent testimony of a former Commissioner of Indian affairs, Robert G. Valentine: "It is astounding to note that whites follow different moral modes according as they are dealing with other white men or with Indians. People who would never think of stealing from their white neighbors find it quite natural to swindle an Indian." *The Mind and Society*, ed. A. Livingston, II, 627. Emerson's "Emancipation Address" (1844) recalls that in an imperialist world even 'men of good will' may become unwitting accessories to moral duplicity.

* In the eleventh hour, I have come to see how much I owe to that neglected Victorian, Sir Henry Sumner Maine. It is now evident to me that Maine must have been a central, if not the ultimate, source of many of the distinguished masters of the social sciences, whose views have been under consideration in the latter stages of the writing of the present work. Above, in the Foreword, it will be recalled, the place of honor was given to a passage from Max Weber. This passage now appears to have been anticipated in a spectacular fashion in Maine's forgotten Rede Lecture for 1875. There Maine writes:

"Whenever a corner is lifted up of the veil which hides from us the primitive condition of mankind, even of such parts of it as we know to have been destined to civilisation, there are two positions, now very familiar to us, which seem to be signally falsified by all we are permitted to see—All men are brothers, and all men are equal. . . . Each fierce little community is perpetually at war with its neighbour, tribe with tribe, village with village. . . . Yet, even amid all this cruelty and carnage, we find the germs of ideas which have spread over the world. There is still a place and a sense in which men are brothers and equals. The universal belligerency is the belligerency of one total group, tribe, or village, with another; but in the interior of the groups the regimen is not one of conflict and confusion but of ultra-legality. The men who composed the primitive communities believed themselves to be kinsmen in the most literal sense of the word; and surprising as it may seem, there are a multitude of indications that in one stage of thought they must have regarded themselves as equals.

"There are other conclusions from modern enquiry which ought to be stated less confidently, and several of them only in negative form. Thus, whenever we can observe the primitive groups still surviving to our day, we find that competition has very feeble play in their domestic transactions, competition (that is) in exchange and acquisition of property. This phenomenon, with several others, suggests that Competition, that prodigious social force of which the action is measured by political economy, is of relatively modern origin. Just as the conceptions of human brotherhood and (in a less degree) of human equality appear to have passed beyond the limits of the primitive communities and to have spread themselves in a highly diluted form over the mass of mankind, so, on the other hand, competition in exchange seems to be the universal belligerency of the ancient world which has penetrated into the interior of the ancient groups of blood-relatives. It is the regulated private war of ancient society gradually broken up into indistinguishable atoms." (Maine, *Village-Communities*, 3d ed., 203-39, esp. at 225-27).

In citing this passage, I by no means desire to suggest my approval of the details either of its characterization of early society or its estimate of the ethical foundations of competition. The former has been modified in essential respects by modern anthropology and the latter needs to be qualified in the light of Maine's essential evaluation of the "movement from status to contract" in the "progressive societies." I chiefly wish to indicate that I am grateful to Maine for strengthening my conviction that the history of moral development in the West must not be described, as has, unfortunately, so often been done, as a simple passage from darkness to light or from light to darkness. Thus, it may be noted, I have taken pains in the foregoing pages to avoid the impression that the ethos of modern society represents an unmitigated corruption of a stainless past. Above all, I have had no desire to support the currently fashionable myth that all our ills can be traced to a "fatal misstep" which our forefathers were seduced into taking under the baneful influence of one or another misguided leader, whether he be Luther, Calvin, Descartes, Rousseau, or someone more recent. Only those who are confirmed Manichees are free to write history in that fashion.

APPENDIX

APPENDIX*

Some Remarks on the Parallel Fate of the Ideals of Friendship and Brotherhood in Early Modern Times

THE sixteenth century witnesses a reevaluation of the ideal of friendship[1] which parallels the vicissitudes of the Deuteronomic concept of brotherhood surveyed in the foregoing pages. Only a selected number of instances of the early modern doctrine of friendship will be considered here:

A. Antonio, "the royall merchant of Venice," will be shown to have exemplified the true friend in a manner scorned as anachronistic and utopian by the worldly-wise among his contemporaries. The depreciation of friendship by the capitalists and courtiers of England's Golden Age is seen to mark a milestone in the adoption of a universalist morality. The world of hostile clusters of friends and enemies gives way to a more drab, but more egalitarian environment, ruled by a frankly prudential calculus.

B. Antonio's suretyship for Bassanio vis-à-vis Shylock will be found to illustrate medieval, rather than Reformation ideals of conduct. Indeed, behavior like Antonio's had been

---

* See above, note 35, at pp. 86-89.
[1] A documentary history of the ideal of friendship has still to be written. The following are among the more helpful studies: L. Dugas, *L'amitié antique;* R. Egenter, *Gottesfreundschaft: Die Lehre von der Gottesfreundschaft in der Scholastik und Mystik des 12. und 13. Jahrhunderts;* Ruth Eglinger, *Der Begriff der Freundschaft in der Philosophie;* T. J. Haarhoff, *The Stranger at the Gate: Aspects of Exclusiveness and Co-operation in Ancient Greece and Rome, with Some Reference to Modern Times;* F. Irmen, *Liebe und Freundschaft in der französischen Literatur des 17. Jahrhunderts;* P. Kluckhohn, *Die Auffassung der Liebe in der Literatur des 18. Jahrhunderts und in der deutschen Romantik;* L. J. Mills, *One Soul in Bodies Twain: Friendship in Tudor Literature and Stuart Drama;* L. Schücking, *Die Familie im Puritanismus;* W. W. Tarn, *Alexander the Great and the Unity of Mankind;* Eva Thaer, *Die Freundschaft im deutschen Roman des 18. Jahrhunderts.* Other studies are listed at relevant points in the notes below.

denounced by Luther as a challenge to God's total authority over the lives of men. Antonio's way of standing surety appears to the Reformer an inexcusable effort to imitate Christ's inimitable goodness. The seeming impracticality of Luther's doctrine of suretyship should not obscure the fact that its moral assumptions were not unwelcome to the German burgher.

C. A simultaneous universalization and devaluation of friendship will be found to have been effected by some of the pioneers of international law. In the transfer of the category of friendship from the moral to the juridical sphere, the celebrated stories of classic pairs of ideal friends were rejected as edifying fictions, unsuitable for emulation by states. Through the work of such writers as Alberico Gentili (1552-1608) and Samuel von Pufendorf (1632-1694), there was accomplished a shift from exacting double-edged norms of friendship, conceived in the spirit of personal relations, to general sociability in which all men and all states are treated with calculated benevolence. An analogous reformulation of the meaning of Christ's call to love of neighbor and God (charity) is detected among influential moralists of the seventeenth and eighteenth centuries, notably Jeremy Taylor (1613-1667) and William Paley.

A. *Antonio's Friendship in the Light of the Prudential Morality of Elizabethan Capitalists and Courtiers*

IN THE history of the ideal of friendship, Shakespeare stands at the parting of the ways. The ancient and Renaissance ideal of friendship, as well as the medieval ideal of sworn brotherhood or *compagnonnage*,[2] was ambivalent and invidious. Friends and sworn brothers are supposed to share all goods,

---

[2] See, for example, J. Flach, "Le compagnonnage dans les chansons de geste," *Études romanes dédiées à Gaston Paris*, 141-80; Marc Bloch, *La société féodale: La formation des liens de dépendance*, 190-207, 355 (splendid quotations from the sources).

services, and sentiments, including hatred of one another's enemies. By Shakespeare's day the worldly-wise were already denying the usefulness of "exaggerated" manifestations of friendship. For Shakespeare, the Friendship-Surety motif and the contrast between the true friend, personified in Antonio, and the false friend or enemy, incarnate in Shylock, are crucial.[3] He evokes the whole range of romantic, moral,

[3] L. J. Mills has subtly depicted the opposition of the true friendship of Antonio-Bassanio to the feigned proffer of friendship of Shylock; see *One Soul in Bodies Twain*, 268-75. Shylock, he explains, receives deserved punishment because, Judas-like, he makes a mockery of friendship in behaving like an enemy. Nothing new is to be found in the dissertation of H. Burre, *Das Freundschaftsmotiv und seine Abwandlung in den Dramen Shakespeares.*

The surety-hostage theme is integral to all the principal ancient and medieval friendship stories. This may readily be seen by tracing the history of such tales as Petrus Alfonsi's *The Complete Friend*, the *Amicus and Amelius, Valentine and Orson,* as well as the literary fortunes of classic friendship pairs like Orestes and Pylades, *et al.* The legal basis and moral and theological implications of this pervasive motif have not been exploited. The following studies may serve as orientation to the documents and problems of diffusion: R. Basset, "Contes et légendes de la Grèce ancienne," *Revue des traditions populaires* xxII (1907), 10-11; K. Kelling, *Das Bürgschaftsmotiv in der französischen Literatur;* L. Sorieri, *Boccaccio's Story of Tito e Gisippo in European Literature;* H. G. Wright, *Early English Versions of the Tales of Guiscardo and Ghismonda and Titus and Gisippus from the Decameron;* A. Dickson, *Valentine and Orson: translated from the French by Henry Watson; idem, Valentine and Orson: A Study in Late Medieval Romance;* B. Aubé, *Polyeucte dans l'histoire; Amis et Amiloun,* ed. M. Leach; M. A. Potter, "Ami et Amile," *PMLA,* xxxIII (1908), 471-85. For the possible linkages between the friendship-surety stories and the Dioscuric legends, see: A. H. Krappe, "The Legend of Amicus and Amelius," *Modern Language Review* (1923), 152-61; *idem,* "The Molionides," *Amicitiae Corolla,* ed. H. G. Wood, 133-46; J. Rendel Harris, *The Cult of the Heavenly Twins; idem, Boanerges.* The suretyship concept assumed profound significance in Hebrew religion and literature. See the series of articles by A. Abeles in the *MGWJ,* LX (1916), 213-26, 263-78; LXVI (1922), 279-94; LXVII (1923), 35-53, 122-30, 170-86, 254-57. For helpful remarks, from the standpoint of literary history, on the origin of the friendship-surety motif in the Bond of Flesh cycle, see the following: J. O. Halliwell, *The Remarks of M. Karl Simrock on the Plots of Shakespeare's Plays,* 45-63; J. L. Cardozo, "The Background of Shakespeare's *Merchant of Venice,*" *English Studies,* xiv (1932), 182-84; G. Huet, *Les contes populaires,* 162; N. Delius, "Die Freundschaft in Shakespeare's Dramen," *Sh. J.,* xix

and theological implications available in these themes. Though Bassanio is presented as a carefree young lover oblivious to his obligations, Antonio remains ever ready to make the last sacrifice for him.

Shakespeare does not, like his principal source, Giovanni Fiorentino, have Antonio return to Belmont to marry one of Portia's serving-ladies. This is vulgar enough in the *Pecorone*

(1884), 25-26; D. H. Müller, *Die Mehri-und Soqoṭri-Sprache*, I, 217-26.

Shakespeare's most significant departure from his sources is to be found in his treatment of the surety's (Antonio's) willingness to undergo death on behalf of his friend. It is at this point that we are best able to detect the strength of Shakespeare's attachment to medieval modes of evaluating friendship and to sense his lack of sympathy for the kind of assumptions contained in the denunciations of suretyship by Luther (see below, pp. 151-53) and by the courtiers and capitalists of his own day. (The author will be pardoned if, in the effort to make this contrast more vivid, he ventures to anticipate some of the conclusions of a work in progress.) Shakespeare's Antonio appears to imitate and symbolize the Christ. Antonio's heroic suretyship to Shylock for Bassanio finds its prototype in Christ's act in serving as "ransom" to the Devil for all mankind. See the hints to this effect in B. N. Nelson and J. Starr, "The Legend of the Divine Surety and the Jewish Moneylender," *Annuaire de l'Institut de philologie et d'histoire orientales et slaves,* VII (1939-44), 289-338, esp. at 326-38. A striking, albeit very incomplete, selection of texts illustrating the medieval identification of the self-sacrificing friend with the example of Christ is cited by Gollancz in two stimulating essays, which must be used with caution. See I. Gollancz, "Bits of Timber: Some Observations on Shakespearian Names—'Shylock,' 'Polonius,' 'Malvolio,'" *A Book of Homage to Shakespeare,* 170-78; *idem, Allegory and Mysticism: A Medievalist on The Merchant of Venice.* Printed for Private Circulation by George W. Jones (London, 1931). I am indebted to Dr. Samuel A. Tannenbaum for use of his copy of the latter work. Further evidence of the atonement symbolism in *The Merchant* is provided by the fact that the Trial Scene can be traced to one or another of the many medieval renderings of Satan's suit against the Redeemer before God's tribunal, probably to the *Processus Satanae,* the best known version of which is attributed to the jurist, Bartolus. Hope Traver and J. D. Rea deserve the credit for making the preliminary discoveries along these lines. See: Traver, *The Four Daughters of God,* esp. at p. 94, n. 18; *idem,* "The Four Daughters of God: A Mirror of Changing Doctrine," *PMLA,* XL (1925), 44-92; Rea, "Shylock and the Processus Belial," *PQ,* VIII (1929), 311-13. A full length statement of the proof and implications of Shakespeare's indebtedness to the *Processus Satanae* complex will have to be deferred for a later occasion.

(*ca.* 1378)[4] but would be indecent and gross in Shakespeare. In the strange last scene, Shakespeare prefers to emphasize again and again Antonio's willingness to lay down his life, nay his soul, for his lover.[5] Antonio is never linked to any woman during the play. He is absorbed completely in his friend. He is the Complete Friend.

Digeon has noted that the friendship of Antonio and Bassanio both exemplifies the criteria of friendship celebrated by Montaigne and reflects a conflict between *l'amour et l'amitié*.[6] This formulation hardly captures the profound ways in which the friendship-ideal is integrated with the other motifs of the play. In the first place, there is a strong confirmation of our stress on the Friendship-Surety situation in Sonnet cxxxiv, which reads almost like a scenario of *The Merchant*. Then again, Digeon has failed to see how Shakespeare's emphasis serves to create the sharpest possible contrast between the friendship and *brotherhood* of the two Christians with the malevolent *enmity* of the alien Shylock. How subtly this combines with and heightens the conflict over usury and the hostility between the Jew and the Christian in the play should, by now, be apparent.

Antonio and Bassanio are friends and bosom lovers. They may be compared to Damon and Pythias. Like the heroes of

---

[4] Ed. in *Classici italiani*, xxv, 168-96; text and tr. in J. P. Collier, *Shakespeare's Library*, ed. W. C. Hazlitt, pt. 1, Vol. 1, 319-53; for tr. and commentary, see the *M. of V.*, in Variorum ed. of Furness (1916), 297-303, and Arden ed. of C. K. Pooler, pp. xx-xxx, based on the modern rendering by W. G. Waters, *The Pecorone of Ser Giovanni*, 1, 111-56, reprinted in the same author's *The Italian Novelists Now First Translated into English*, v, 111-56.

[5] *Antonio* I once did lend my body for his wealth,
   Which but for him that had your husband's ring,
   Had quite miscarried; I dare be bound again,
   My *soul upon the forfeit*, that your Lord,
   Will never more break faith advisedly. (v, 249-53)

The diffusion of one of the medieval forfeit of soul stories is traced in R. Köhler, "L'âme en gage," *Kleinere Schriften*, ed. J. Bolte, II, 220-23.

[6] A. Digeon, "Le jeu de l'amour et de l'amitié dans *Le Marchand de Venise*," *Revue anglo-américaine*, XIII (1936), 219-31.

the classic fable, they outdo each other in protestations of self-sacrifice. Each is ready to "make incision" for his love. It is even possible that Shakespeare's play found inspiration in Richard Edwards' earlier drama of the Pythagorean friends, which was performed before Queen Elizabeth during the Christmas season of 1564-1565.[7]

The medieval quality of Antonio's friendship is revealed by comparing it with the depictions of faithful sureties in the thirteenth-century book of letter forms by Boncompagnus of Florence (*ca.* 1218). Great men and nobles, Boncompagnus explains, are compelled to resort to borrowing for a variety of reasons, not the least important of which is the need to defray the losses they have incurred in standing surety for a friend. In one letter, a surety writes to remind the principal debtor that the time for repayment at the fairs is fast approaching, and expresses the hope that the principal debtor will not permit him to suffer any loss. Another letter catalogues the complaints of a surety to the principal debtor. He resents being called a perjurer on account of the borrower's failure on five successive occasions to observe the times for repayment. Having already incurred many expenses and paid usuries for previous prorogations, he no longer knows what to do since he may not request further extensions. Another surety writes: "*Dedi salaria, duplicavi usuras, consumpsi mobilia, possessiones distraxi, et nunc filii mei detinentur in carcere vinculati.*" Now, in short, after having advanced a thousand marks and obligated his sons on behalf of his friend, he pleads with the latter to come to his defense and to rescue his sons from detention.[8]

[7] See ed. in Joseph Quincy Adams, *Chief Pre-Shakespearean Dramas*, 571-608; also, R. Dodsley, *A Select Collection of Old Plays*, I, 175-262. For commentary and background material, see L. J. Mills, *Some Aspects of Richard Edwards' Damon and Pithias;* J. F. L. Raschen, "Earlier and Later Versions of the Friendship Theme," *MP*, xvii (1919), 105-9; *idem*, "The Hostage: An Arabian Parallel to Schiller's Ballad 'Die Bürgschaft,'" *ibid.*, 351-60.

[8] L. Rockinger, *Briefsteller und Formelbücher des elften bis vierzehnten Jahrhunderts*, I (*Quellen und Erörterungen*, IX.I), 166-68.

Antonio's suretyship for the debt of Bassanio has the
flavor of a romantic archaism when set in contrast to the
shrewd maxims of contemporary businessmen and statesmen. In John Lyly's *Euphues and his England* (1580), Cas-
sander, the "lewd usurer," warns his son Callimachus:

Enter not into bands, no not for thy best friends: he that
payeth another man's debt seeketh his own decay, it is as rare
to see a rich Surety, as a black Swan, and he that lendeth to
all that will borowe, sheweth great good will, but lyttle witte.
Lende not a penny without a pawne, for that will be a good
gage to borowe.[9]

Lord Burghley (1520-1598) tells his son Robert:

Beware of suretyship for thy best friends; he that payeth
another man's debts seeketh his own decay; But if thou canst
not otherwise choose, rather lend thy money thyself upon
good bonds, although thou borrow it; so shalt thou secure
thyself, and pleasure thy friend; neither borrow money of a
neighbor or a friend, but of a stranger, where paying it, thou
shalt hear no more of it, otherwise thou shalt eclipse thy credit,
lose thy freedom, and yet pay as dear to another. But in borrowing of money be precious of thy word, for he that hath
care of keeping days of payment, is lord of another man's
purse.[10]

Sir Walter Raleigh (*ca.* 1552-1618) instructs his son and
posterity:

Amongst all other things of the world take care of thy estate, which thou shall ever preserve, if thou observe three
things; first, that thou know what thou hast, what every thing
is worth that thou hast, and to see that thou art not wasted by
thy servants and officers. The second is, that thou never spend
any thing before thou have it; for borrowing is the canker and
death of every man's estate. The third is, that thou suffer not
thyself to be wounded for other men's faults, and scourged for
other men's offences, which is the surety for another; for
thereby millions of men have been beggared and destroyed,

[9] John Lyly, *The Complete Works*, ed. R. W. Bond, II, 16.
[10] J. N. Larned, *A Multitude of Counsellors*, 242.

paying the reckoning of other men's riot, and the charge of
other men's folly and prodigality; if thou smart, smart for
thine own sins; and, above all things, be not made an ass to
carry the burdens of other men: if any friend desire thee to be
his surety, give him a part of what thou hast to spare; if he
press thee further, he is not thy friend at all, for friendship
rather chooseth harm to itself than offereth it; if thou be bound
for a stranger, thou art a fool: if for a merchant, thou putteth
thy estate to learn to swim: if for a churchman, he hath no in-
heritance: if for a lawyer, he will find an evasion, by a syllable
or word, to abuse thee: if for a poor man thou must pay it
thyself: if for a rich man, it need not: therefore from suretyship, as from a manslayer or enchanter, bless thyself....[11]

Charles G. Smith seems to me to fall into an exaggeration
at one point in his appraisal of the significance of the Elizabethan ideal of friendship. According to him, the theory that
friends' goods are common goods is "usually disapproved"
in Renaissance literature. "Perhaps," he continues, "this is
accounted for by the fact that communistic theory was taboo
in England in the sixteenth century."[12] His own catena of
citations does not sustain this view. Under any circumstances,
a "communistic" theory of friendship was almost never interpreted in antiquity, the Middle Ages, the Renaissance or
Reformation to imply an appeal for a communistic society,
any more than Christian Liberty and Freedom (in St. Paul,
the medieval theologians, Luther, *et al.*), modern nationalism, *Liberté-Egalité-Fraternité*, current *Volksgemeinschaft*,
democratic political equality, or "Union Now" are felt to involve communal ownership of property.[13]

[11] "Instructions to His Son and to Posterity," in *Works of Sir Walter
Raleigh*, II, 351-52; Larned, *op.cit.*, 256-57. Cf. the sentiment in Francis
Osborne's *Advice to a Son*, in *Works of Francis Osborne*, §30, p. 13.

[12] *Spenser's Theory of Friendship*, 50.

[13] It must be admitted that classic theories of friendship entered into
the complex of the communistic ideas of Sebastian Franck (*ca.* 1499-*ca.*
1543) and of the Münster Anabaptists, notably Bernhard Rotman. See H.
von Schubert, *Der Kommunismus der Wiedertäufer in Münster und seine
Quellen*, 14, 29-32. A similar appeal to friendship-communism is found in
the defense of the Brethren of the Common Life by Gerard Zerbolt of

Need it be pointed out, at this stage, that Plato, Aristotle, Cicero, and others do not regard "friendship-communism" as incompatible with private property and slavery? In the ancient and medieval worlds,[14] "friendship" always savoured of exclusiveness and upper-class solidarity. Readers of Cicero will recall how frequently the ambivalent character of friendship proved a source of embarrassment to him. How could he prosecute Brutus, the friend of his friend, Atticus, for unconscionable usuries without violating his friendship with Atticus? Then again, was not the friendship of Tiberius Gracchus and Blossius of Cumae inimical (in the eyes of Cicero) to the claims of "justice"?[15]

The Ciceronian quandaries suggest that ancient friendship, like the later medieval sworn-brotherhood, preceded and outranked generalized justice.[16] The conflicts with justice of

---

Zutphen (1367-1398). There, however, as in the usual *encomia* of the monastic life, communism is assumed to exist only within the circle of the brethren. See Gerard's *Super modo vivendi devotorum hominum simul commorantium*, ed. A. Hyma, *Archief voor de geschiedenis van het Aartsbisdom Utrecht*, LII (1925), 1-100, esp. at 32-33. It is interesting to note that Melanchthon protests against communistic inferences drawn from the institution of friendship. He writes: "Amicorum omnia sunt communia, scilicet virtute, non obligatione seu iure civili. Cum autem dicitur virtute, intelligitur voluntaria communicatio rerum communicabilium, cum habet probabilem causam seu officii rationem, sine mutatione politici ordinis, ut hospes Davidis in exilio Galadites, praebebat Davidi et eius amicis hospitia et sine mutatione politici ordinis. . . ." *Prolegomena in officia Ciceronis, CR*, XVI, 551.

[14] L. Dugas, *L'amitié antique*, 156-70.

[15] For illuminating pages on the implications of the idea of *amicitia* for the development of the doctrines of agency, suretyship, *consilium*, etc., in Roman private law, which do not, however, exhaust the role of the antinomies of ancient friendship, see Fritz Schulz, *Principles of Roman Law*, 233-37. Much still remains to be done in the way of probing the socio-moral aspects of the doctrines of *mutuum, nexum,* and *mandatum* in the Roman law. The significance of the double-standard ethics for the Roman theory of loan has been detected by G. Salvioli, *Le capitalisme dans le monde antique*, 28-29; and C. Appleton, "Contribution à l'histoire du prêt à intérêt à Rome: Le taux du 'fenus unciarium,'" *Nouvelle revue historique de droit français et étranger*, XLIII (1919), esp. 484-85.

[16] *De officiis*, i:5.

friendship-pairs like Orestes-Pylades and Tiberius Gracchus-Blossius of Cumae are cases in point. But there is another side to this story. On the Ciceronian definition of justice, a struggle to encourage a "universal friendship," by the device, let us say, of a Gracchan agrarian law—though this was far from contemplating community of property—was by its nature unjust, since justice consisted *"in tribuendo suum cuique et rerum contractarum fide."* Max Radin has observed that the Stoic idea of distributive justice, the *suum cuique*, may not always be "pleasant," may require the "enslavement of man by man," and may be consistent with the repudiation of a Kantian formula of justice.

> This justice [he adds] may indeed be distributive, but it is hard to call it a virtue when the distribution is so very unequal that it gives all to one man and nothing to his fellow, and harder still to understand how so evil a consequence can flow from what is the fundament of society and the linchpin of the universe. . . . In other words, justice in this its proper sense, the demand by a man for his own and no more than his own, is not based on a moral foundation at all. It is δίκη; it points out where the thing lies that may be claimed. It exercises no moral censure over the claim.[17]

[17] "A Juster Justice, A More Lawful Law," *Legal Essays in Tribute to Orrin Kip McMurray*, ed. Max Radin and A. M. Kidd, 537-64, esp. at 540. Another interesting statement of the conflict between the claims of friendship and the demands of Justice is to be found in Saint-Evremond (1610-1703), who writes: "Mais, pour conserver une chose si précieuse que l'amitié, ce n'est pas assez de se précautionner contre les vices, il faut être en garde, même contre les vertus; il faut être en garde contre la justice. Les sévérités de la justice ne conviennent pas avec les tendresses de l'amitié. Qui se pique d'être juste, ou se sent déjà méchant ami, ou se prépare à l'être. L'Évangile ne recommande guère la justice, qu'il ne recommande aussi la charité; et c'est, à mon avis, pour adoucir une vertu, qui seroit austère, et presque farouche, si on n'y mêloit un peu d'amour. La justice, mêlée avec les autres vertus, est une chose admirable: toute seule, sans aucun mélange de bon naturel, de douceur, d'humanité, elle est plus sauvage que n'étoient les hommes qu'elle a assemblés; et on peut dire qu'elle bannit tout agrément de la société qu'elle a établie." See his epistle "Sur l'amitié. A Madame la Duchesse Mazarin" (1676) in *Oeuvres mêlées de Saint-Evremond*, ed. Ch. Giraud, I, 147-48; cf. R. de Planhol, *Les utopistes de l'amour*, 97.

Is this not another instance of the type of ambivalent transvaluation of values we have been describing in this paper?
When exclusivistic blood kinship, sworn brotherhood, and
friendship, all involving intragroup cooperation and sharing
of goods and services, give way to society and generalized
justice (*suum cuique*), all men become brothers by becoming
equally others.

To return to Mr. Smith's thesis, the derogation of friendship was not so much the work of poets and moralists who
were frightened by the "spectre of communism," but of the
sober and plain-dealing statesmen, shopkeepers, and courtiers
of nascent capitalism and the modern state. Elizabethan prudence and self-preservation are the prelude to the later "un-
masking" of friendship by La Rochefoucauld (1613-1680),
Mandeville (1670-1733), Marie Huber (1695-1753),[18] Hel-
vetius (1715-1771) and others. By the close of this transvaluation of values, popular wisdom seems to be summed up
as never before in the adage "God helps those who help themselves." In short, the deflation of friendship is a stage in the
development of a universalist morality. When friends are
depreciated, all men become equally others.

B. *Luther and Shakespeare:*
Agape and Eros

To REALIZE how completely Shakespeare is maintaining the
classic and medieval friendship morality, in the face of the
egoistic implications of the spirit of capitalism, Renaissance
Realpolitik, and Protestant theology, we need only contrast
the ethical pattern exemplified in Antonio's conduct with
Luther's doctrine of suretyship. Luther writes:

> . . . There is a common error, which has become a widespread
> custom, not only among merchants but throughout the world,
> by which one man becomes the surety for another; and al-

[18] See, especially, her *The World Unmasked: Or, the Philosopher the
Greatest Cheat in Twenty-Four Dialogues* . . . Tr. from the French
(London, 1736).

though this practice seems to be without sin and looks like a virtue springing from love, nevertheless it causes the ruin of many and brings them irrevocable injury. King Solomon often forbade and condemned it in his Proverbs. . . .

See with what strictness and vehemence the wise King forbids in Holy Scripture that one become surety for another, and the German proverb agrees with him, *Bürgen soll man würgen*; as if to say, "Standing surety should be slain." It serves the surety right when he is caught and has to pay, for he acts thoughtlessly and foolishly in standing surety. Therefore it is decreed in Scripture that no one shall become surety for another unless he is able and entirely willing to assume the debt and pay it. It seems strange that this practice should be wrong and be condemned, though many have discovered the folly of it when it has made them scratch their heads. Why, then, is it condemned? Let us see.

Standing surety is a work that is too lofty for a man; it is unseemly, for it is presumptuous and an invasion of God's rights. For, in the first place, the Scriptures bid us to put our trust and place our reliance on no man, but only on God; for human nature is false, vain, deceitful, and unreliable, as the Scriptures say and as experience teaches every day. But he who becomes surety puts his trust in a man, and risks life and property on a false and insecure foundation; therefore it serves him right when he falls and fails and goes to ruin.

In the second place, a man puts trust in himself and makes himself God, for that on which a man puts his trust and reliance is his god. But of his life and property a man is not sure and certain for a single moment, any more than he is certain of the man for whom he becomes surety, but everything is in God's hand only, and He will not allow us a hair's breadth of power or right over the future or have us for a single moment sure or certain of it. Therefore the man who becomes surety acts unchristianlike, and deserves what he gets, because he pledges and promises what is not his and is not in his power, but in the hands of God alone . . . these sureties act as though they did not need to be on speaking terms with God or to consider whether they were sure of tomorrow for their life and property. They act without fear of God, as though their life and property were their own, and were in their power as long as they wished to have it; and this is nothing but a fruit of unbelief. . . . Wherefore He has bidden us, in the Lord's Prayer, to pray for nothing more than our daily bread today, so that we may live and act in fear and know that at no hour are we sure of either life or property, but may await and receive everything from His hands. This is what true faith does.

After describing the "Christian" way to lend and trade, without making use of security and suretyship, Luther continues:

> . . . if there were none of this becoming surety and lending on security, many a man would have to keep down and be satisfied with a moderate living, who now aspires day and night after the high places, relying on borrowing and standing surety. This is the reason that everyone now wants to be a merchant and get rich.

Finally, becoming surety is condemned as one of the three "sources" of "abomination, injustice, treachery and guile."[19] This doctrine is a choice instance of Luther's "theology of crisis" and of his "theocentric" rejection of what Anders Nygren[20] has described as the *"eros* dynamic in the *caritas-*synthesis" of medieval religion. Although no one would think of taking it as an explicit approval of "capitalist" business practice, Luther's hostility to the older friendship *ethos* can easily be harnessed to the service of a self-regarding capitalist morality. The ambivalence of this schema, a persistent feature of the thought of both Luther and Calvin, suggests the extreme peril of hazarding generalizations about the economic ethics and social teachings of the leaders of the Reformation. This is not meant in criticism of Max Weber,

[19] *Von Kaufshandlung und Wucher* (1524), ed. *WA*, xv, 298-305, tr. *Works*, iv, esp. 18-24. Cf. references indicated in *Luthers Werke für das christliche Haus*, ed. G. Buchwald *et al.*, iv, 4th ed., 52, n. 2; 522, n. 1.

[20] *Agape and Eros*, tr. A. G. Hebert, esp. ii, ch. 6. Roscher is not unjustified, however, in his insistence that Luther's discussion of suretyship here and elsewhere is not oblivious to considerations of economic prudence. W. Roscher, *Geschichte*, 65.

who, unlike many of his disciples and critics, understood how impressionistic and restricted his brilliant sketch truly was. If his suggestions are to continue to bear fruit, new and more intensive forays into the sources must be made. A concentration on the theories of love, friendship, and suretyship is likely to produce almost as rich a harvest as was yielded by Weber's focus on *Beruf* and *innerweltliche Askese*.[21] A survey of the idea of suretyship, which is a form of vicarious atonement, would involve consideration of every basic motif in the moral and theological systems of the historic religions.

Such a perspective brings out the contrast between the Catholic *caritas* structure with its call to imitate Christ and the Protestant emphasis on superethical justification by God's *agape*. For Luther and Calvin, the chasm between man and

[21] Weber offers a provocative comment on the influence of related Calvinist ideas on the view of friendship among the Puritans, notably Richard Baxter. Weber writes: "Here the belief that the Christian proved . . . his state of grace by action *in majorem Dei gloriam* was decisive, and the sharp condemnation of idolatry of the flesh and of all dependence on personal relations to other men was bound unperceived to direct this energy into the field of objective (impersonal) activity. The Christian who took the proof of his state of grace seriously acted in the service of God's ends, and these could only be impersonal. Every purely emotional, that is not rationally motivated, personal relation of man to man easily fell in the Puritan, as in every ascetic ethic, under the suspicion of idolatry of the flesh." *The Protestant Ethic*, 224 (citing Baxter's opinion that "to love any one farther than reason will allow us . . . often taketh up men's minds so as to hinder their love of God."). In a subsequent note, Weber asserts that in the Puritan ethic "the duty to love one's neighbour is satisfied by fulfilling God's commandments to increase His glory." "The neighbour thereby receives all that is due him, and anything further is God's affair. Humanity in relation to one's neighbour has, so to speak, died out." *Op.cit.*, 226. Cf. the remarks in Troeltsch, *Social Teachings*, II, 894, n. 344. Wolfdietrich Rasch records the fears of Baxter, Pascal, the Pietists, and a number of medieval German mystics including Tauler, that friendship for man, a mere creature, is a danger to pure inwardness and love of God. *Freundschaftskult und Freundschaftsdichtung im deutschen Schrifttum des 18. Jahrhunderts*, esp. ch. ii. Such deprecations of human friendship as slights to the love of God, though frequent enough in the Middle Ages, are generally—though not so often in the great German mystics—sublimated by the emphasis on the imitation of Christ, the Divine Surety.

God was infinite. Their insistence on man's incorrigible depravity in will and his utter inability to win salvation by his acts implied the shattering of the merit system, the moral casuistry, and the *exemplarist-imitationist* axis of medieval Catholicism. The anxiety to present an uncontaminated doctrine of justification *sola fide* committed Protestantism to formulae which could readily be converted into a morality serviceable to capitalism. How Luther's pessimistic anthropology and his horror of a perfectionist "invasion of God's rights" affected Protestant views on the ordering of secular society is evident even from the extract cited above. The ease with which the practical consequences derived from this theocentric doctrine of the pioneer reformers led to abuse in the subsequent social teachings of the Protestant churches, holds a moral for those who are today promoting a revival of the "Reformation theology."

C. *The Devaluation of "Ideal Friendship" and "Christian Charity" in International Law and Moral Philosophy (16th-18th centuries)*

THROUGHOUT the seventeenth century, critiques directed against the exorbitant demands exacted by the classic and medieval canons of friendship occur in widely separated contexts, and with such frequency as to suggest a turning-point in the history of moral sentiments. The dominant theme in this chorus of complaint is that the older models were keyed too high, were too "Utopian" for emulation in this world. Prudence and hard common sense seemed to dictate a scaling down of the code of friendship. The celebrated "ideal friendships" were relegated to the realm of fable, and new and less exacting criteria were taken as the basis for a reconstructed *ethos*. Two samples will have to suffice here to show the significance for the history of morality of this devaluation of the demands of friendship:

1. The seventeenth century witnessed a sustained attempt

to apply the ideas of personal morality to international law. Such an extension could not easily be effected without deflating the content of moral notions like friendship. The value of the traditional "ideal friendships," which "philosophy invents for our benefit," was repudiated in favor of "friendships of which our law takes cognizance, that is, those within the experience of mankind." If the friendships of "real life" were to be imitated, it was suggested, it would be seen that international amity need not be based upon the story-book view that "all the possessions of friends are common property." Unlike their latter-day followers, the pioneers of international law were still too close to the traditional meanings of hallowed ethical ideals to feel free of embarrassment when referring the notion of friendship to collective egoisms like nations. The anatomy of this uneasiness is nicely brought out in Alberico Gentili:

> If friendship is contracted, or an agreement is made that it shall not be contracted with others, by this term something of no slight importance is designated. And that certain services are due is shown by the treaty contracted by the Romans with the Lacedemonians, in which it was said that the latter should live under their own laws and should render nothing by way of tribute except friendly services. These, however, appear to have been something moderate, for the most part a tribute of gifts, such as the Rhodians paid even though they were free. So, too, an agreement to be brothers, although it does not make men brothers, surely has some effect, as we infer from certain decisions of Decio rendered to the noble landgraves of Hesse. And it is known from Caesar and others what the Romans thought that their relations with the Haeduans were because they had given the Haeduans the title of brothers.

> Will not therefore an agreement about friendship, which makes nations friends, furnish something greater? Or does the agreement regarding fraternity also imply that the parties to it are joined by as great a friendship as if they were brothers? Alciati, following others, decided that by an agreement to be brothers it was meant that a general union of all

public and private advantages had been formed. An agreement of fraternity and friendship at the same time will bind even more closely, and we know that such an agreement was made by the Romans with the valiant Batavians; for we read upon an ancient stone: "The Batavians, friends and brothers of the Roman people." Therefore we ought not to listen to Bodin, who thinks that no aid is due because of a contract of friendship. And Baldus decided that because of friendship two states actually became one body.

Bodin is also proved wrong by the constant usage of the Romans, who invariably considered it their duty to make war in behalf of their friends. If this is not so, what is gained by that agreement and the title of friendship? Certain it is that among private individuals, if one friend did not lend aid to another, he would seem to have inflicted a severe wound upon the laws of friendship. Why should it not be the same with states? And we are speaking of the friendships of individuals which we see all about us, not drawing arguments from those ideal friendships which philosophy invents for our benefit, none of which we actually see, but at best we have merely read about some of them. Those ideal friendships regard all the possessions of friends as common property, and there are many other differences between such friendships and those of real life. We are speaking here of friendships of which our law takes cognizance; that is, those within the experience of mankind.[22]

No systematic attempt to answer Gentili's questions will be found in subsequent classics of international law. Grotius and his successors are distressingly vague in their occasional references to the notion of friendship. We are rarely permitted to apprehend its meaning or its sphere of operation.

As a whole, the trend of doctrine reveals admirable moral elevation, strong universalistic impulses, but a predominantly negative concept of "friendship." All nations not formally allies or enemies seem to be reckoned as friends. It is held to be natural, desirable, and mutually profitable for all men and

[22] Gentili, *De iure belli libri tres,* bk. iii, ch. 18, in tr. by John C. Rolfe, 387-88.

all nations to be friends. However, little more seems to be meant by this proposition than that nations and individuals, alike, are obliged to do their best not to make others hostile to themselves.

Grotius does not pretend to offer a comprehensive theory of the legal significance of friendship. Individuals, he insists, are drawn to friendship spontaneously, by their own nature, and not by need. "Regard for others," he observes, "often warns me, sometimes commands me to put the interest of many above my own."[23] His two sections on friendship are relegated to his chapter "On Good Faith in Ending War."[24] They fail to fulfill the promise of their titles; we are never shown "what falls under the term friendship." We are simply told that "acts which are contrary to friendship break a treaty which was entered into under the terms of friendship"; that it is not contrary to friendship for one nation to admit individual subjects or exiles of another nation.

Reminiscences of medieval attitudes and sixteenth-century theological debates are found in Grotius' extended discussion of aid to allies. If a nation's allies are at war, he writes, its actions are to be regulated by a weighing of the justice in the case. If the causes are unjust on both sides, neither ally is to receive assistance. If one party appears to have the just cause, it alone must be supported. If both parties can claim a just cause, money and men will have to be sent to both. "But if the individual cooperation of the one who promised is required, reason demands that preference be shown to the ally with whom the treaty is of longer standing. It is right that friendships be so established that the more ancient friendship and alliance be not violated."[25]

Pufendorf's explicit treatment of friendship and love[26]

---

[23] Grotius, *De jure belli ac pacis*, bk. ii, ch. 1, sect. 9, art. 3, in tr. by F. W. Kelsey *et al.*, 177.

[24] *Ibid.*, bk. iii, ch. 20, sect. 40-41, pp. 818-20.

[25] *Ibid.*, bk. ii, ch. 15, sect. 13, p. 404.

[26] *De jure naturae et gentium libri octo*, bk. ii, ch. 3, §§17-18, in tr. by C. H. and W. A. Oldfather, 213-14.

savors more of the moral philosopher, than of the jurist. He rejects the Hobbesian anthropology in order the better to demonstrate man's natural capacity for society and the mutual benefit of friendship between nations. Nevertheless, he seems unable to provide the notion of association with positive content. The "general sociable attitude and peace," for which he appeals, calls for little more than the abstention "from unjust injuries" and the "mutual advancement and division of advantages and profits, so far as more binding obligations make it possible. . . ."

> All this makes perfectly clear the reply to be made to the following objection: "If a man loved another man naturally, that is, as a man, there would be no reason why every man should not love every other man equally, as being equally a man, or why he should associate himself more closely with those in whose society more than that of others he is accorded honor and profit." In this statement a general sociable attitude is confused with particular and more limited societies, and general love with that which arises from particular causes, for, as a matter of fact, no reason is required for this general love other than that a person is a man. Nature, indeed, for the reasons cited above, has in fact ordained a certain general friendship (*generalem aliquam amicitiam*) between all men, of which no one is to be deprived, unless some monstrous iniquities have made him unworthy. But, although by the wisdom of the Creator that natural law has been so adapted to the nature of man, that its observance is always connected with the profit and advantage of man, and therefore also this general love tends to man's greatest good, yet in giving a reason for this fact, one does not refer to the advantages accruing therefrom, but to the common nature of all man.

The existence of general love and friendship do not, however, preclude our entertaining greater affection for one man rather than another. To cultivate the society of those among whom we are accorded special honor or profit is both natural and legitimate. The pursuit of personal advancement involves no necessary injury to the public welfare.

Now, indeed, there are not a few circumstances above and beyond this general friendship (*communem illam amicitiam*) which makes a person cherish one man with greater affection than another. For instance, because there is a greater congeniality of mind between them along certain lines of conduct; because one is more fitted or inclined than another to work to your advantage; or because they have close relations of birth or residence. But the reason why a man more gladly associates himself with those in whose society he is accorded more honour or profit than another, lies in the fact that no man can avoid setting his heart upon his own advancement, so far as he recognizes it correctly. But such a setting of one's heart is by no means repugnant to the social order of man, provided it does not disturb the harmony of society. For nature has not commanded us to be sociable, to the extent that we neglect to take care of ourselves. Rather the sociable attitude is cultivated by men in order that by the mutual exchange among men of assistance and property, we may be able to take care of our concerns to greater advantage. And even though a man, when he joins himself to any special society, holds before his eyes, first of all, his own advantage, and after that the advantage of his comrades since his own cannot be secured without that of all, yet this does not prevent his being obligated so to cultivate his own advantage, that the good of the society be not injured, or harm offered its different members; or at times to hold his own advantage in abeyance and work for welfare of society.

Bynkershoek's discussion[27] of friendship is more limited in scope and more juridical in character. His principal allusions to the notion are made in the course of an attempt to diminish the obligations upon neutrals in the course of a war.

When hostilities have broken out between a nation's friends, he says, in opposition to Grotius, it is not required to choose between them; indeed, neutrals may lend aid to neither part for fear of helping one more than the other. On the whole, Bynkershoek tends to define friends negatively as

[27] *Quaestionum juris publici libri duo* (1737), bk. i, ch. 9, in tr. by T. Frank, 60-61.

nations which are not specifically allies, confederates, or enemies.

Wolff (1679-1754) explicates the bearings of Pufendorf's analysis in the sphere of international relations. To Wolff, friendship among nations is a principle of natural law, and is grounded in the Christian precept of love.[28] The harmony of national self-interest and the general welfare is assured by fulfilling the Christian teaching. The original duty of a nation is to itself. It must, in the first instance, seek its own preservation and development. Then, in accordance with the Christian teaching, it is to extend the same love and the same services to its neighbors, that is, to other nations.[29]

The obligations of friendship are defined negatively. A nation manifests friendship, primarily, by doing "its best not to make others hostile to itself."[30] "Treaties of friendship" are described as "those which are arbitrated for the performance of the duties of humanity, or not to do injury."[31]

Wolff's French disciple, Vattell (1714-1767), is equally convinced that Nature impels and private advantage counsels mutual love among individuals, and, therefore, among nations. Friendship between nations is "a duty of humanity"; the mark of true friendship is "mutual affection." "Every nation is bound to cultivate the friendship of other nations, and to avoid carefully what might arouse their enmity."[32]

Through such reevaluations, the concept of friendship has come to have little more than a rhetorical content in the current parlance of international law. Today "bonds of eternal friendship" ally nations with momentarily similar interests against real or potential common enemies. No modern state has felt itself bound by an "eternal pact," which has caused it even slight inconvenience. Still, diplomats will

[28] *Jus gentium methodo scientifica pertractatum*, ch. ii, §156, in tr. by J. H. Drake, 84.
[29] *Ibid.*, ch. ii, §161, Drake, *op.cit.*, 86.
[30] *Ibid.*, ch. ii, §172, p. 9.
[31] *Ibid.*, ch. iv, §394, p. 204.
[32] *Le droit des gens. . .* , bk. ii, ch. 1, in tr. by Ch. G. Fenwick, 116-17.

continue till the end of time to prefer the vocabulary of amity to less orotund and less idealistic alternatives. This deceives only the gulls who persist in unfounded hopes without regard for evidence. Nations know well enough to treat their friends as if they were on the verge of becoming enemies.

2. A similar lowering of the moral standard is to be observed in the fortunes of the ideals of friendship and *caritas* among theologians and moralists of the seventeenth and eighteenth centuries.

The old and the new stand side by side in Jeremy Taylor's profound discourse on friendship. Following upon a reference to Pollux's division of immortality with Castor, Taylor writes:

> . . . and you know who offered himself to death being pledge for his friend, and his friend by performing his word rescued him as bravely. And when we find in Scripture that "for a good man some will even dare to die"; and that Aquila and Priscilla laid their necks down for St. Paul; and the Galatians "would have given him their very eyes," that is, everything that was most dear to them; and some others were near unto death for his sake; and that it is a precept of christian charity, "to lay down our lives for our brethren," that is, those who were combined in a cause of religion, who were united with the same hopes, and imparted to each other ready assistances, and grew dear by common sufferings; we need inquire no further for the expressions of friendship. "Greater love than this hath no man, than that he lay down his life for his friends"; and this we are obliged to do in some cases for all christians; and therefore we may do it for those who are to us, in this present and imperfect state of things, that which all the good men and women in the world shall be in heaven, that is, in the state of perfect friendships. This is the biggest; but then it includes and can suppose all the rest; and if this may be done for all, and in some cases must for any one of the multitude, we need not scruple whether we may do it for those who are better than a multitude. . . . it is not easily and lightly to be

done; and a man must not die for humour, nor expend so great a jewel for a trifle . . . ; we will hardly die when it is for nothing, when no good, no worthy end, is served, and become a sacrifice to redeem a foot-boy.[33]

Taylor goes on to explain that we may not give our life to redeem another unless "the party for whom we die" is a "worthy and useful person, better for the public, or better for religion, and more useful to others than myself." Commenting on a passage in Seneca, he continues:

I will die for a prince, for the republic, or to save an army, as David exposed himself to combat with the Philistine for the redemption of the host of Israel: and in this sense, that is true. . . . "Better that one perish than a multitude." A man dies bravely when he gives his temporal life to save the soul of any single person in the christian world. It is a worthy exchange, and the glorification of that love by which Christ gave his life for every soul. Thus he that reproves an erring Prince wisely and necessarily, he that affirms a fundamental truth, or stands up for the glory of the Divine attributes, though he die for it, becomes a worthy sacrifice. These are duty, but it may be heroic and full of christian bravery, to give my life to rescue a noble and brave friend, though I myself be as worthy a man as he; because my preference of him is an act of humility in me, and of friendship towards him. . . .

A more profound departure from the accents of the past is made in the discussion of charity in Paley's authoritative *Principles of Moral and Political Philosophy*.[34] He writes:

I use the term Charity neither in the common sense of bounty to the poor, nor in St. Paul's sense of benevolence to all mankind: but I apply it at present, in a sense more commodious to my purpose, to signify *the promoting the happiness of our inferiors.*

[33] See *A Discourse of the Nature, Offices and Measures of Friendship. . .* , in *The Whole Works of the Right Rev. Jeremy Taylor, D.D.*, III, 32-44, esp. at 37-38.
[34] Bk. iii, pt. 2, ch. i, in *Works*, I, 153-72, esp. at 153.

Charity, in this sense, I take to be the principal province of virtue and religion: for, whilst worldly prudence will direct our behaviour towards our superiors, and politeness towards our equals, there is little beside the consideration of duty, or an habitual humanity which comes into the place of consideration, to produce a proper conduct towards those who are beneath us, and dependent on us.

There are three principal methods of promoting the happiness of our inferiors.

1. By the treatment of our domestics and dependants.
2. By professional assistance.
3. By pecuniary bounty.[35]

Thus by the eighteenth century the historic precept of Christian love had become a shadow of its former self. In the very circles which might have been expected to meet the challenge of advancing capitalism by reiterating the call to love with ever increasing emphasis, it had turned into a lukewarm exhortation *"to promote the happiness of our inferiors."*

[35] Almost a half-century earlier, Hume had written: "In general, it may be affirmed that there is no such passion in human minds, as love of mankind, merely as such, independent of personal qualities, of services, or of relation to ourself . . .; public benevolence, therefore, or a regard to the interests of mankind cannot be the original motive to Justice." *A Treatise of Human Nature* (1739-1740), bk. iii, pt. 2, §1, pp. 44, 46. See Henry Sidgwick, *Outlines of the History of Ethics*, 211, also 195, 205.

BIBLIOGRAPHY

ABBREVIATIONS

B.M.	*Baba Metzia.* Title of a tractate both in the *Mishnah* and the *Babylonian Talmud*
BW	*Briefwechsel*
C.	*Causa,* a subdivision in pt. 2 of Gratian's *Decretum*
c.	canon, *capitulum*
C.I.L.	*The Classics of International Law.* Edited by James Brown Scott
Clem.	*Corpus iuris canonici: Clementinae*
Cod. Iust.	*Corpus iuris civilis: Codex Iustinianus*
CR	*Corpus Reformatorum*
CSEL	*Corpus scriptorum ecclesiasticorum latinorum*
DNB	*Dictionary of National Biography*
E.E.T.S.	*Early English Text Society*
Extrav. comm.	*Corpus iuris canonici: Extravagantes Decretales quae a diversis Romanis Pontificibus post Sextum, emanaverunt*
Extrav. Jo. XXIII	*Corpus iuris canonici: Extravagantes D. Iohannis Papae XXIII*
Lib. sent.	Peter Lombard, *Liber sententiarum*
Lib. sept.	*Liber septimus*
MGWJ	*Monatsschrift für die Geschichte und Wissenschaft des Judenthums*
PG	J. P. Migne, ed., *Patrologiae....Series graeca*
PL	J. P. Migne, ed., *Patrologiae....Series latina*
PMLA	*Publications of the Modern Language Association of America*
PQ	*Philological Quarterly*
RE, ed. 3	*Realencyclopädie für protestantische Theologie und Kirche*
Sh. J.	*Shakespeare Jahrbuch*
Tr.	*Tractatus*
tr.	translation, translated by
Tr. ... trium clarissimorum iureconsultorum	*Tractatus de usuris triplex, trium clarissimorum iureconsultorum*
WA	Luther, *Werke.* Weimarer Ausgabe
X.	*Corpus iuris canonici: Decretales Gregorii IX.* (Thus, e.g., X.v.19, c. 5 is *Decretals ...,* lib. v, tit. 19, canon [*capitulum*] 5.)

BIBLIOGRAPHY

The following list mainly comprises works cited in the foregoing footnotes. Titles which contain especially helpful references to additional literature are indicated below by asterisks. I have made no attempt to be exhaustive.

ABELES, A. "Die Bürgschaft als Motiv in der jüdischen Literatur." *MGWJ*, LX (1916), 213-26, 263-78.
———. "Der Bürge nach biblischen Recht." *MGWJ*, LXVI (1922), 279-94; LXVII (1923), 35-53.
———. "Bürge und Bürgschaft nach talmudischen Recht." *MGWJ*, LXVII (1923), 122-30, 170-86, 254-57.
'Abodah Zarah. Tractate in Talmud. Translated by A. Mishcon and A. Cohen; edited by I. Epstein. London, 1935. In *The Babylonian Talmud*, translations under the editorship of I. Epstein.
ABRAHAMS, ISRAEL. *Jewish Life in the Middle Ages*. Philadelphia, 1896. There is a revised and enlarged edition, with different pagination, by Cecil Roth. London, 1932. I have used the first printing.
ADAMS, HENRY P. *Karl Marx in his Earlier Writings*. London, 1940.
ADAMS, JOSEPH QUINCY, ed. *Chief Pre-Shakespearean Dramas*: A Selection of Plays illustrating the History of the English Drama from its Origin down to Shakespeare. Boston and New York, 1924.
Adler Papyri, The. The Greek Texts, edited by Elkan Nathan Adler, John Gavin Tait and Dr. Fritz M. Heichelheim; the Demotic Texts, edited by Francis Llewellyn Griffith. London, 1939.
AEPINUS, JOHANNES. *In Psalmum XV Davidis Iohannis Aepini commentarius, in quo de iustificatione, de vita Christiani hominis, de votis et iuramentis*. . . . Strassburg, 1543.
ALBERICUS DE ROSATE. *Dictionarium juris tam civilis quam canonici*. . . . Venice, 1591.
ALBERTUS MAGNUS. *Opera omnia*. Edited by A. Borgnet. 38 vols., Paris, 1890-1899.
ALBO, JOSEPH. *Sefer ha-'Ikkarim (Book of Principles)*. Critically edited on the Basis of Manuscripts and old Editions and provided with a Translation and Notes by I. Husik. 4 vols. in 5, Philadelphia, 1929-1930. "Schiff Library of Jewish Classics."

ALEXANDER OF HALES. *Summa theologiae.* 4 vols., Venice, 1576. I have also used the 4 volume edition of Nuremberg, 1481-1482. A modern edition: Vol. 1, Quaracchi, 1924. In progress.

ALEXANDER DE NEVO. *Consilia contra Judaeos foenerantes.* Nuremberg, F. Creusner, 1479.

——. *Consilia famosissimi necnon pontificii caesareique iurisconsultissimi . . nunc primum in lucem aedita.* Venice, 1560.

ALFONSI, PETRUS. *Die Disciplina clericalis des Petrus Alfonsi (das älteste Novellenbuch des Mittelalters) nach allen bekannten Handschriften.* Edited by A. Hilka and W. Söderhjelm. Heidelberg, 1911. Sammlung mittellateinischer Texte, hgb. von A. Hilka, 1.

ALPERT, HARRY. "Emile Durkheim and the Theory of Social Integration." *Journal of Social Philosophy,* VI (1941), 172-84.

ALSTED, JOHANN HEINRICH. *Theologia casuum.* Hanover, 1630.

ALTHAUS, PAUL. *Communio sanctorum: Die Gemeinde im lutherischen Kirchengedanken.* Vol. 1, Munich, 1929. Forschungen zur Geschichte und Lehre des Protestantismus, Reihe 1, Band 1.

ALVAREZ DE VELASCO, GABRIEL. *De privilegiis pauperum et miserabilium personarum.* 3rd edition. 2 vols. in one, Lausanne and Geneva, 1739. Includes two works by Novarius: *De privilegiis miserabilium personarum* and *De incertorum et male ablatorum privilegiis.*

ALVARUS PELAGIUS. *De planctu ecclesiae libri duo.* Venice, 1560.

AMBROSE OF MILAN, ST. *De Tobia.* Edited and translated by Lois M. Zucker. Washington, D.C., 1933. The Catholic University of America: Patristic Studies, Vol. XXXV. Also edited by K. Schenkl in *CSEL,* XXXII, pt. 2 (1897) ; and in Migne, *PL,* XIV.

AMBROSIUS DE VIGNATE. *De usuris.* In *Tr. univ. juris,* VII, 50-66.

AMES, WILLIAM. *De conscientia et eius iure, vel casibus, libri quinque.* Amsterdam, 1631.

——. *Opera quae Latine scripsit omnia.* 5 vols., Amsterdam, 1658.

Amis et Amiloun. Edited by MacEdward Leach. London, 1937. E.E.T.S., original series, no. 203 (for 1935).

Amis et Amiloun zugleich mit der altfranzösischen Quelle. Nebst einer Beilage: Amícus ok Amilíus Rímur. Herausgegeben von Eugen Kölbing. Heilbronn, 1884. Altenglische Bibliothek, Band II.

BIBLIOGRAPHY

ANCHARANO, PETRUS DE. *Super Clementinis facundissima commentaria.* This is Vol. IV of: *In quinque Decretalium libros [et in sextum] facundissima commentaria, a plerisque erratis.* 7 vols. in 4, Bologna, 1580-1583.

ANCHEL, ROBERT. *Napoléon et les Juifs; essai sur les rapports de l'état français et du culte israélite de 1806 à 1815.* Paris, 1928.

ANDREAE, JOHANNES. *Apparatus ad Clementinas.* In *Constitutiones Clementis Papae quinti una cum apparatu domini Iohannis Andreae.* In *Corpus iuris canonici,* III. Venice, 1604.

ANDREAS, WILLY. *Deutschland vor der Reformation, eine Zeitenwende.* Stuttgart and Berlin, 1932.

ANDREWES, LANCELOT. *De usuris, theologica determinatio.* . . . London, 1629. In *Opuscula quaedam posthuma.* Oxford, 1852.

ANEMÜLLER, BERNHARD. *M. Bartholomäus Gernhard und der Rudolstädter Wucherstreit im 16. Jahrhundert; zugleich ein Beitrag zur Geschichte der Gräfin Katharina "der Heldenmüthigen," nebst einigen durch den Druck noch nicht veröffentlichten Briefen derselben.* Rudolstadt, 1861. "Rudolstadt Programm," 1861.

ANGELUS CARLETUS DE CLAVASIO. *Summa angelica de casibus conscientiae.* Nuremberg, 1488.

———. *Tractatio de restitutionibus.* 2 vols., Rome, 1771.

ANNIUS OF VITERBO, JOHANNES. *Quaestiones super mutuo judaico et civili et divino.* In *Pro monte pietatis: Consilia sacrorum theologorum ac collegiorum Patavii.* . . . Venice ?, Johannes Tacuinus de Tridino ?, 1498 ?.

ANTONINUS OF FLORENCE, ST. *Summa theologica.* 4 vols., Verona, 1740-1741.

———. *De usuris per modum praedicationis.* In *Tr. univ. juris,* VII, 78v-91v.

ANTWERP FRANCISCANS, eds. *Biblia sacra vulgatae editionis, versione belgica, notis grammaticalibus, literalibus, criticis, &c. Elucidata per FF. Minores recollectos Musei Philologico-Sacri Antwerpiensis.* See: Hove, Petrus van; Smits, F.

APPLETON, C. "Contribution à l'histoire du prêt à intérêt à Rome: Le taux du 'fenus unciarium.'" *Nouvelle revue historique de droit français et étranger,* XLIII (1919), 467-543.

ARNDT, GEORG. "Christoph Fischer und seine Tätigkeit als Generalsuperintendent im Thüringer Lande." In *Beiträge zur thüringischen und sächsischen Kirchengeschichte: Fest-*

schrift für Otto Dobenecker zum siebzigsten Geburtstage am 2. April 1929. Jena, 1929, pp. 294-326.

————. "Ein bisher unbekanntes Gutachten Philipp Melanchthons, Georg Majors und Paul Ebers in Sachen des Thüringer Wucherstreites aus dem Jahre 1555 (?)." *Beiträge zur thüringischen Kirchengeschichte,* I (1929/30), 158-61.

ARNOBIUS *(Afer). Adversus nationes libri VII.* Edited by A. Reifferscheid. Vienna, 1875. *CSEL,* IV. Also known as the *Adversus gentes.*

ARNOLD, GOTTFRIED. *Unpartheyische Kirchen- und Ketzer-Historien, vom Anfang des Neuen Testaments biss auf das Jahr Christi 1688.* 3 vols. in 4, Schaffhausen, 1740-1742.

ARONIUS, JULIUS. *Regesten zur Geschichte der Juden im fränkischen und deutschen Reiche bis zum Jahre 1273.* . . . Bearbeitet unter Mitwirkung von A. Dresdner und L. Lewinski. Berlin, 1887-1902.

*ASHLEY, W. J. *An Introduction to English Economic History and Theory.* 2 vols., London, 1903.

ASTESANUS OF ASTI. *Summa de casibus conscientiae.* Strassburg, Johann Mentelin, not after 1473.

AUBÉ, B. *Polyeucte dans l'histoire.* Paris, 1882.

AZORIUS, JOHANNES. *Institutionum moralium.* . . . 3 vols., Lyons, 1616-1625. I (1625), II (1622), III (1616).

Baba Metzia. Tractate in *Talmud.* Translated by S. Daiches and A. Freedman. London, 1935. In *The Babylonian Talmud,* translations under the editorship of I. Epstein.

————. Also see *Mishnah, The.*

Babylonian Talmud, The. Translated into English with notes, glossaries and indices, under the editorship of I. Epstein. 34 vols., London, 1935-1949. Soncino Press.

BACKER, AUGUSTIN and ALOYS DE. *Bibliothèque de la Compagnie de Jésus: 1) Bibliographie par les pères Augustin et Aloys de Backer. 2) Histoire par le père Auguste Carayon.* A new edition of the whole by C. Sommervogel. 11 vols., Brussels and Paris, 1890-1932.

BACON, FRANCIS. *The Essays or Counsels, Civil and Moral.* Edited with an introduction and illustrative notes by Samuel Harvey Reynolds. Oxford, 1890.

BALDUS DE UBALDIS. *Super quarto et quinto codicis.* Lyons, 1539.

*BALLERINI, PIETRO. *De jure divino et naturali circa usuram* *libri sex*. 2 tomes in one, Bologna, 1747. Tome 2 subtitled: *Vindiciae juris divini, ac naturalis circa usuram quae veluti liber septimus haberi possunt, adversus opus novissime editum de usuris . . . Nicolai Broedersen . . .*

BARBADORO, BERNARDO. *Le finanze della repubblica fiorentina: Imposta diretto e debito pubblico fino all'istituzione del Monte*. Florence, 1929.

BARGE, HERMANN. *Andreas Bodenstein von Karlstadt*. 2 vols., Leipzig, 1905.

*———. "Die gedruckten Schriften des evangelischen Predigers Jakob Strauss." *Archiv für Reformationsgeschichte*, XXXII (1935), 100-21, 248-52.

———. *Jakob Strauss: Ein Kämpfer für das Evangelium in Tirol, Thüringen und Süddeutschland*. Leipzig, 1937. Schriften des Vereins für Reformationsgeschichte, no. 162.

BARIANUS, NICHOLAS. *De monte impietatis*. Cremona, 1496. Reprinted in the appendix to Dorotheus Asciani (pseud. for Matthias Zimmermann), *Montes pietatis*. . . . Leipzig, 1670.

BARON, SALO W. "The Economic Views of Maimonides." In *Essays on Maimonides: An Octocentennial Volume*, edited by Salo W. Baron. New York, 1941, 127-264.

BARTH, FRANZ JOSEF. *De statuto principis*. In Migne, *Theologiae cursus completus*, XVI. See Zech, Franz.

BARTOLUS DE SAXOFERRATO. *Omnia, quae extant, opera*. 11 vols. in 10, Venice, 1590-1602.

———. *Processus . . . inter Virginem Mariam advocatam humani generis ex una parte, et diabolum contra genus humanum ex alia parte*. In *Opera*, X, 127v-29v.

BASSET, R. "Contes et légendes de la Grèce ancienne." *Revue des traditions populaires*, XXII (1907), 9-12.

BAUMER, FRANKLIN L. "The Church of England and the Common Corps of Christendom." *Journal of Modern History*, XVI (1944), 1-21.

———. "The Conception of Christendom in Renaissance England." *Journal of the History of Ideas*, VI (1945), 131-56.

———. "England, the Turk, and the Common Corps of Christendom." *American Historical Review*, L (1944), 26-48.

BAXTER, RICHARD. *A Christian Directory: Or, A Summ of Practical Theology and Cases of Conscience*. 4 parts, London, 1673.

———. *Chapters from A Christian Directory*. Selected by Jeannette Tawney. With a Preface by The Right Rev. Charles Gore, D.D. London, 1925.

BAYLE, PIERRE. *Oeuvres diverses . . . contenant tout ce que cet auteur a publié sur des matières de théologie, de philosophie, de critique, d'histoire et de littérature; excepté son Dictionnaire historique et critique.* 4 vols., The Hague, 1727-1731.

――――. "Réponse aux questions d'un Provincial." In *Oeuvres diverses*, III, 501-1084.

BECHIS, MICHAEL. *Repertorium biblicum, seu totius Sacrae Scripturae concordantiae.* . . . 2 vols., Turin, 1887-1888.

BEDE, THE VENERABLE. *In Deuteronomium.* In Migne, *PL*, XCI.

Beiträge zur thüringischen und sächsischen Geschichte: Festschrift für Otto Dobenecker zum siebzigsten Geburtstage am 2. April 1929. Edited by A. Cartellieri, G. Fischer, H. Koch, Th. Lockemann, and G. Mentz. Jena, 1929.

BENNETT, W. H. "Usury (Jewish)." In Hastings, *Encyclopaedia of Religion and Ethics*, XII (1922), 555-56.

BENTHAM, JEREMY. *Works.* Published under the superintendence of his executor, John Bowring. 11 vols., Edinburgh, 1843.

――――. *Defense of Usury; showing the impolicy of the present legal restraints on the terms of pecuniary bargains: In Letters to a Friend. To which is added, A Letter to Adam Smith, Esq. LL.D. on the Discouragements opposed by the above restraints to the Progress of Inventive Industry.* In *Works*, III, 1-29.

BERENS, L. H. *The Digger Movement in the Days of the Commonwealth.* London, 1906.

BERNARD OF CLAIRVAUX, ST. *On Consideration.* Translated by G. Lewis. Oxford, 1908. "Oxford Library of Translations."

BERNARD OF PAVIA. *Summa decretalium.* Edited by E. A. T. Laspeyres. Ratisbon, 1860.

BERNARDINO DA BUSTI. *Defensorium montis pietatis contra figmenta emule falsitatis.* Hagenau, Henricus Gran, 1503.

BERNARDINO OF SIENA, ST. *Opera omnia.* Edited by Johannes de la Haye. 5 vols. in 2, Paris, 1634-1635. Also Venice, 1745.

BERNSTEIN, EDUARD. *Cromwell and Communism: Socialism and Democracy in the Great English Revolution.* London, 1930. Translated by H. J. Stenning.

BERTHEAU, CARL. "Aepinus, Johannes." *RE*, ed. 3, 1, 228-31 ; *Idem, The New Schaff-Herzog*, 1 (1908), 59-60.

BERTHELÉ and VALMARY, eds. See Durantis, Guillelmus.

BERTHOLET, ALFRED. *Die Stellung der Israeliten und der Juden zu den Fremden.* Freiburg and Leipzig, 1896.

————, ed. *Die Heilige Schrift des Alten Testaments.* In Verbindung mit . . . Budde . . . Guthe . . . Übersetzt von E. Kautzsch. 4th edition, 2 vols., Tübingen, 1922.

————, ed. *Leviticus erklärt.* Tübingen and Leipzig, 1901. In *Kurzer Hand-Commentar zum Alten Testament* in Verbindung mit I. Benzinger, A. Bertholet, K. Budde, B. Duhm, H. Holzinger, G. Wildeboer, hgb. von D. Karl Marti. Abteilung III.

————, ed. *Deuteronomium erklärt.* Freiburg and Leipzig, 1899. In *Kurzer Hand-Commentar zum Alten Testament*, . . . , Abteilung V.

*BESSE, L. DE. *Le bienheureux Bernardin de Feltre et son oeuvre.* 2 vols., Tours, 1902-1903.

BETCKE, WERNER. *Luthers Sozialethik: Ein Beitrag zu Luthers Verhältniss zum Individualismus.* Gütersloh, 1934.

Biblia sacra iuxta latinam vulgatam versionem ad codicum fidem iussu Pii XI cura et studio monachorum Sancti Benedicti commissionis Pontificiae a Pio PP X institutae sodalium praeside Aidano Gasquet S.R.E. Cardinale edita. Vol. 1, Rome, 1926. In progress.

Biblia sacra polyglotta. Edited by Brian Walton. 6 vols., London, 1655-1657.

Biblia sacra vulgatae editionis Sixti quinti Pont. max. iussu recognita atque edita. Antwerp, 1603; Venice, 1611-1624; Antwerp, 1624. Often reprinted.

BIDEMBACH, FELIX, ed. *Consiliorum theologicorum decas I.* Frankfurt, 1608. (*Decas II-IV*, Frankfurt, 1608; *decas VI*, Darmstadt, 1609; *decas VII*, Frankfurt, 1611). Not accessible to me. See W. Köhler, *Bibliographia Brentiana*, 344, no. 730.

*BILLETER, GUSTAV. *Geschichte des Zinsfusses im griechisch-römischen Altertum bis auf Justinian.* Leipzig, 1898.

BLACKSTONE, SIR WILLIAM. *Commentaries on the Laws of England.* 1st edition, 4 vols., Oxford, 1765-1769. Edited by William Draper Lewis, 4 vols., Philadelphia, 1902.

BLAU, LUDWIG. *Prosbol im Lichte der griechischen Papyri und der Rechtsgeschichte.* Budapest, 1927. Sonderabdruck aus

Festschrift zum 50Jährigen Bestehen der Franz-Josef-Landesrabbinerschule in Budapest.

BLAXTON, JOHN. *The English Usurer. Or, Usury Condemned, By The most Learned, and famous Divines of the Church of England.* . . . 2nd edition, London, 1634.

BLOCH, ERNST. *Thomas Münzer als Theologe der Revolution.* Munich, 1921.

BLOCH, MARC. *La société féodale: la formation des liens de dépendance.* Paris, 1929.

BOEHMER, JUSTUS HENNING. *Ius ecclesiasticum protestantium: usum hodiernum iuris canonici.* 2nd edition, 5 vols., Halle, 1745.

————, ed. See *Corpus iuris canonici.*

————, ed. See *Liber septimus.*

BOHATEC, JOSEF. *Calvins Lehre von Staat und Kirche, mit besonderer Berücksichtigung des Organismusgedankens.* Breslau, 1937. *Untersuchungen zur deutschen Staats- und Rechtsgeschichte,* begründet von Otto von Gierke, hgb. von Dr. Julius von Gierke, Dr. Karl G. Hugelman und Dr. Eugen Wohlhaupter, 147.

BOHIC, HENRICUS. *In quinque decretalium libros commentaria.* Venice, 1576.

BOSSERT, G. "Mantel, Johann." *RE,* ed. 3, XXIV (1913), 59-64.

————. "Strauss, Jakob." *RE,* ed. 3, XIX (1907), 92-97.

————. *Idem. The New Schaff-Herzog,* XI (1911), 111-13.

BOSSUET, JACQUES BÉNIGNE. *Oeuvres.* 43 vols., Versailles, 1815-1819.

————. *Decretum de morali disciplina, quod erat a clero gallicano publicandum in comitiis generalibus anni 1682.* In *Oeuvres,* VII, 257-322.

————. *Traité de l'usure.* In *Oeuvres,* XXX, 643-98.

BOUYON, ABBÉ. *Réfutation des systèmes de M. l'abbé Baronnat et de Mgr. de la Luzerne sur la question de' l'usure.* Clermont-Ferrand, 1824.

————. *Examen du système de feu Mgr. le Cardinal de la Luzerne sur le prêt de commerce.* Clermont-Ferrand, 1826.

BOYER, GEORGES. *Recherches historiques sur la résolution des contrats: Origines de l'article 1184 C.civ.* Paris, 1924. Thèse pour le doctorat en droit. Université de Toulouse. Faculté de droit.

BRAMHALL, EDITH C. "The Origin of the Temporal Power of the Crusaders." *American Journal of Theology,* V (1901), 279-92.

BRANDT, OTTO H., ed. *Thomas Müntzer: Sein Leben und seine Schriften.* Jena, 1933.

BRAUNSBERGER, O., ed. See Canisius, Petrus.

BRENTANO, LUJO. *Der wirtschaftende Mensch in der Geschichte: Gesammelte Reden und Aufsätze.* Leipzig, 1923.

BRENZ, JOHANN. *In Leviticum librum Mosi commentarius.* Frankfurt, 1562.

———. See Walther Köhler, *Bibliographia Brentiana.*

BRIDREY, E. *La condition juridique des croisés et le privilège de croix: étude d'histoire du droit français.* Paris, 1900.

BRIE, F. "Zur Entstehung des 'Kaufmann von Venedig.'" *Sh.J.,* XLIX (1913), 97-121.

BRODRICK, JAMES, S.J. *The Economic Morals of the Jesuits: An Answer to Dr. H. M. Robertson.* London, 1934.

BROEDERSEN, NICOLAUS. *De usuris licitis et illicitis vulgo nunc compensatoriis et lucratoriis, secundum ius naturale, divinum, Veteris atque Novi Testamenti, ecclesiasticum et civile, ac juxta doctrinam sanctorum veterumque Patrum . . . libri XII.* s.l., 1743.

BRUNO OF ASTI, ST. *Expositio in Deuteronomium.* In Migne, *PL,* CLXIV.

BUCER, MARTIN. *Enarrationum in evangelia Matthaei, Marci et Lucae, libri duo.* Strassburg, 1527.

———. *Epistola D. Pauli ad Ephesios. . . .* Without imprint. Dedication: Strassburg, 1527.

———. *In sacra quatuor evangelia, enarrationes perpetuae.* Basel, 1536.

———. *Praelectiones doctiss. in Epistolam D. Pauli ad Ephesios.* Edited by Immanuel Tremelius. Basel, 1562.

———. *Scripta anglicana fere omnia; Iis etiam, quae hactenus vel nondum, vel sparsim, vel peregrino saltem idiomate edita fuere adiunctis.* Basel, 1577.

———. *Tractatus de usuris.* In *Scripta anglicana,* 789-96.

———. Also see Lenz, Max, ed.

Bullarum, diplomatum et privilegiorum sanctorum romanorum pontificum Taurinensis editio . . . 25 vols., Turin, 1857-1882.

BULLINGER, HEINRICH. *The Decades.* Translated by H. I. and edited for the Parker Society by the Rev. Thomas Harding. 5 vols. in 4, Cambridge, 1849-1852. Parker Society Publications, VII-X.

———. *Adversus Anabaptistas libri sex, nunc primum e germanico sermone in Latinum conversi per Iosiam Simlerum Tigurinum. . . .* Addita est etiam *Anabaptistarum Apologia,* in qua causas exponunt cur non ad ecclesias seu sacros coetus nostros accedant, eodem interprete. Zurich, 1560.

———. *Der Widertoeufferen: Ursprung, Fürgang, Secten . . .* Zurich, 1560. Cited herein as *Wider die Widertoeuffer.*

———. *Sermonum decades quinque.* 3 vols. in one, Zurich, 1562.

———. *Von dem unvershampten fraefel ergerlichem verwyrren unnd unwarhafftem leeren der selbsgesandten Widertoeuffern vier gesspraech Buecher zu verwarnen den einfalten.* Zurich, 1531.

BURRE, H. *Das Freundschaftsmotiv und seine Abwandlung in den Dramen Shakespeares.* Marburg, 1938.

BURTON, ROBERT. *The Anatomy of Melancholy.* Edited by the Rev. A. R. Shilleto. With an introduction by A. H. Bullen. 3 vols., London, 1903-1904. "Bohn Standard Library."

BUTLER, SIR GEOFFREY B. and SIMON MACCOBY. *The Development of International Law.* London, 1928.

BYNKERSHOEK, CORNELIUS VAN. *Quaestionum juris publici libri duo.* 2 vols., Oxford, 1930. C.I.L., no. 14. Vol. II: A Translation of the Text, by Tenney Frank, with an introduction by J. de Louter.

CABALLINUS, GASPAR. See Du Moulin, Charles.

———. See Lattes, Alessandro.

CAESAR, PHILIP. *A general Discourse against the damnable sect of Usurers.* London, 1578.

CAESARIUS OF HEISTERBACH. *The Dialogue on Miracles.* Translated by H. von E. Scott and C. C. Swinton Bland, with an Introduction by G. G. Coulton. 2 vols., London, 1929.

———. *Dialogus miraculorum.* Edited by J. Strange. 2 vols., Cologne, 1851.

CALVIN, JOHN. *Opera quae supersunt omnia.* Edited by W. Baum, E. Cunitz and E. Reuss. 59 vols., Brunswick (Braunschweig), 1863-1900. In *CR*, XXIX-LXXXVII.

———. *Commentary on the Book of Psalms.* Translated from the original Latin, and collated with the author's French version, by the Rev. James Anderson. 5 vols., Edinburgh, 1845-1849. "The Calvin Translation Society."

———. *Commentaries on the First Twenty Chapters of the Book of the Prophet Ezechiel.* Now first translated from the original Latin, and collated with the French version, by Thomas Myers. 2 vols., Edinburgh, 1849-1850. "The Calvin Translation Society."

———. *Commentaries on the Four Last Books of Moses, ar-*

ranged in the form of a Harmony. Translated from the original Latin, and compared with the French edition, with annotations, etc., by the Rev. C. W. Bingham. 4 vols., Edinburgh, 1852-1855. "The Calvin Translation Society."

———. *Institutes of the Christian Religion.* Translated from the original Latin, and collated with the author's last edition in French, by John Allen. 4th American edition, revised and corrected. 2 vols., Philadelphia, 1843. Often reprinted.

*CANISIUS, HENRICUS. *Praelectiones academicae in duos tit. singularis iuris canonici.* Ingolstadt, 1629.

CANISIUS, PETRUS, ST. *Epistulae et acta.* Edited by Otto Braunsberger. 8 vols., Freiburg, 1896-1923.

CANNAN, EDWIN. "Who Said 'Barren Metal'?." *Economica,* II (1922), 105-11. A Symposium by Prof. E. Cannan, W. D. Ross, Dr. J. Bonar, and Dr. P. H. Wicksteed.

CANTOR, PETER. *Verbum abbreviatum.* In Migne, *PL,* ccv.

CARDOZO, J. L. "The Background of Shakespeare's *Merchant of Venice." English Studies,* XIV (1932), 177-86.

CARPZOV, BENEDICT. *Jurisprudentia ecclesiastica seu consistorialis rerum et quaestionum in serenissimi ac potentissimi principis electoris Saxon. senatu ecclesiastico et consistorio supremo.* . . . Leipzig, 1685.

CARTELLIERI, ALEXANDER. *Phillip II. August, König von Frankreich.* 4 vols., Leipzig, 1899-1922.

*CASSIMATIS, GRÉGOIRE. *Les intérêts dans la législation de Justinien et dans le droit byzantin.* Paris, 1931.

*CASSUTO, UMBERTO. *Gli ebrei a Firenze nell' età del Rinascimento.* Florence, 1918. Pubblicazioni del R. Istituto di Studi Superiori Pratici e di Perfezionamento in Firenze, Sezione di Filosofia e Filologia.

CASTELL, EDMUND. *Lexicon heptaglotton.* . . . 2 vols., London, 1669.

Catalogue of Books Printed in the XVth Century now in the British Museum. Parts I-VII, London, 1908-1935.

CATHREIN, VICTOR, S.J. *Philosophia moralis in usum scholarum.* Editio undecima et duodecima ab auctore recognita. Freiburg, 1921.

CAUSSE, ANTONIN. *Du groupe ethnique à la communauté religieuse: le problème sociologique de la religion d'Israël.* Paris, 1937.

CELSUS OF VERONA. *Dissuasoria.* Verona, 1503.

CHEMNITZ, MARTIN. *Locorum theologicorum . . . quibus et loci communes D. Philippi Melanchthonis perspicue explicantur et quasi integrum Christianae doctrinae corpus, ecclesiae Dei syncere proponitur.* 3 vols., Frankfurt, 1604.

CHEW, SAMUEL. *The Crescent and the Rose: Islam and England during the Renaissance.* New York, 1937.

CHILD, JOSIAH. *A New Discourse of Trade.* London, 1690.

CIARDINI, MARINO. *I banchieri ebrei in Firenze nel secolo XV e il monte di pietà fondato da Girolamo Savonarola.* Appunti di storia economica con appendice di documenti. Florence, 1907.

CICERO, MARCUS TULLIUS. *De officiis.* Latin text with English translation by W. Miller. London, 1913. "Loeb Classical Library."

CINO DA PISTOIA. *Super codice et digesto veteri lectura.* . . . Lyons, 1547.

CLARK, BERTHA W. "The Huterian Communites." *Journal of Political Economy,* XXXII (1924), 357-74, 468-86.

CLASSEN, WALTER. *Schweizer Bauernpolitik im Zeitalter Ulrich Zwinglis.* Weimar, 1899. Zeitschrift für Social- und Wirtschaftsgeschichte, hgb. von S. Bauer und M. L. Hartmann, Ergänzungshefte, IV.

Classics of International Law, The. Edited by James Brown Scott. Publications of the Carnegie Endowment for International Peace. Division of International Law, Washington, D.C. New York, Oxford, 1911-. In progress. Herein abbreviated: C.I.L.

CLEARY, PATRICK. *The Church and Usury.* Dublin, 1914.

CLEMEN, OTTO. "Zwei Gutachten Franz Lamberts von Avignon." *Zeitschrift für Kirchengeschichte,* XXII (1901), 129-44.

CLEMENT OF ALEXANDRIA. *Opera quae exstant omnia.* In Migne, *PG,* VIII-IX.

———. [*Opera*]. Edited by Dr. Otto Stählin. 4 vols. Leipzig, 1905-1936. *Im Auftrage der Kirchenväter-Commission der Königlichen Preussischen Akademie der Wissenschaften: Die griechischen christlichen Schriftsteller der ersten drei Jahrhunderte,* XII, XV, XVII, XXXIX.

———. *Works.* Greek text with English translation by G. W. Butterworth. London, 1919. "Loeb Classical Library."

Clementis Papae quinti constitutiones una cum profundu apparatu domini Johannis Andreae. Lyons, 1507. I have also used the edition of Venice, 1604.

COBBAN, ALFRED. "Paley, William." *Encyclopedia of the Social Sciences,* XII (1933), 535-36.

[178]

*COBBETT, WILLIAM. *A History of the Protestant Reformation in England and Ireland.* 2 vols., London, 1829.

Codex iuris canonici Pii X pontificis maximi iussu digestus Benedicti Papae XV auctoritate promulgatus . . . Edited by P. Card. Gasparri. Rome, 1917.

Codicis iuris canonici fontes. Edited by P. Card. Gasparri. 8 vols., Rome, 1926-1938.

COHN, EMIL. *Der Wucher (Ribâ) in Qor'ân, Châdith und Fiqh: Ein Beitrag zur Entstehungsgeschichte der muhammedanischen Rechtes.* Berlin, 1903.

COKE, SIR EDWARD. *The First Part of the Institutes of the Laws of England; Or, A Commentary upon Littleton.* . . . 2 vols., Philadelphia, 1853.

———. *The Third Part of the Institutes of the Laws of England concerning High Treason and other Pleas of the Crown and Criminal Causes.* London, 1797.

*COLE, ARTHUR H. *The Kress Library of Business and Economics. Catalogue through 1776.* Cambridge, Mass., 1940.

COLLET, PHILIBERT. *Traité des usures, ou explication des prêts et des intérêts par les lois qui ont été faites en toutes les siècles.* s.l., 1690. Original publication without author's name, place, or date.

COLLIER, J. P. *Shakespeare's Library.* 2nd edition, revised and greatly enlarged by W. C. Hazlitt. 6 vols., London, 1875.

*COLORNI, V. "Prestito ebraico e comunità ebraiche nell'Italia centrale e settentrionale con particolare riguardo alla comunità di Mantovà." *Rivista di storia del diritto italiano,* VIII (1935), 406-58.

COMESTOR, PETER. *Historia scholastica.* In Migne, *PL,* CXCVIII.

CONCINA, DANIEL, O.P. *Theologia christiana dogmatico-moralis.* 10 vols., Rome, 1749-1751.

Conference on Christian Politics, Economics and Citizenship, 1924: C.O.P.E.C. Commission Reports. 12 vols., London, 1924.

Consiliorum theologicorum decas I. See Bidembach, F.

Corpus iuris canonici. 3 vols., Venice, 1604.

Corpus iuris canonici Gregorii XIII pontif. max. auctoritate post emendationem absolutam . . . et appendice nova auctum. Edited by Justus Henning Boehmer. 2 vols. in one, Halle, 1747.

Corpus iuris canonici. Edited by E. Friedberg. 2 vols., Leipzig, 1879-1881. Reprinted 1922.

Corpus iuris civilis (Justinian). Edited by Th. Mommsen, W. Kroll, P. Krueger and R. Schoell. 3 vols., Berlin, 1928-1929.

Corpus Reformatorum. Edited by C. G. Bretschneider, H. E. Bindseil, *et al.* 98 vols., Brunswick, Berlin, Leipzig, 1834-1935.

Corpus scriptorum ecclesiasticorum latinorum. 69 vols., Vienna, 1866-1939. In progress.

*CORRELL, ERNST H. *Das schweizerische Täufermennonitentum: Ein soziologischer Bericht.* Tübingen, 1925.

COVARRUVIAS DE LEYVA, DIDACUS. *Opera omnia.* 2 vols., Antwerp, 1638.

———. *Opusculum variarum resolutionum, necnon practicarum quaestionum.* In *Opera omnia,* II.

CREBERT, HEINRICH. *Künstliche Preissteigerung durch Für- und Aufkauf: Ein Beitrag zur Geschichte des Handelsrecht.* Heidelberg, 1916. Deutschrechtliche Beiträge, Band XI, Heft 2.

CULPEPER, THOMAS *(the Elder). A Tract against Usurie.* London, 1621. Reprinted in Josiah Child, *A New Discourse of Trade.* London, 1690.

CURZON, ROBERT DE. *Le traité "De Usura," de Robert de Courçon.* Edited and translated into French by G. Lefèvre. Lille, 1902. Travaux et Mémoires de l'Université de Lille, x, no. 30.

DAMIANI, PETER, ST. *Testimonia libri Deuteronomii.* In Migne, *PL,* CXLIV.

DEDEKENNUS, GEORG, ed. *Thesaurus consiliorum et decisionum theologicarum et juridicarum.* 2 vols., Jena, 1671.

DELIUS, NICOLAUS. "Die Freundschaft in Shakespeare's Dramen." *Sh.J.,* XIX (1884), 19-41.

DEMPSEY, BERNARD W., S.J. *Interest and Usury.* With an introduction by Joseph A. Schumpeter. Washington, D.C., 1943.

DENZINGER, HEINRICH, ed. *Enchiridion symbolorum definitionum et declarationum de rebus fidei et morum.* 11th edition, by C. Bannwart, Freiburg, 1911. Often reprinted.

*DE ROOVER, RAYMOND. *Money, Banking, and Credit in Mediaeval Bruges: Italian Merchant-Bankers, Lombards, and Money-Changers.* Cambridge, 1948. Mediaeval Academy of America. Publication, no. 51.

DESMARETS, SAMUEL. See Maresius, Samuel.

DETMER, HEINRICH. *Bilder aus den religiösen und sozialen Un-*

ruhen in Münster während des 16. Jahrhunderts. 3 vols., Münster, 1903-1904.

———. *Bernhard Rothmann. Kirchliche und soziale Wirren in Münster 1525-1535: Der täuferische Kommunismus.* Münster, 1904. *Bilder* . . . , Vol. II.

——— and R. KRUMBHOLTZ, eds. See Rotman (Rothmann), Bernhard.

D'EWES, SIR SIMONDS. *A Compleat Journal of the Votes, Speeches and Debates, Both of the House of Lords and House of Commons throughout the Whole Reign of Queen Elizabeth.* London, 1693.

DICKSON, ARTHUR. *Valentine and Orson: A Study in Late Medieval Romance.* New York, 1929.

———, ed. *Valentine and Orson.* Translated from the French by Henry Watson. London, 1937 (for 1936). E.E.T.S., original series, no. 204.

DICKSON, MARCEL and CHRISTINE. "Le Cardinal Robert de Courçon: Sa vie." *Archives d'histoire doctrinale et littéraire du moyen-âge,* IX (1934), 53-142.

DIESTEL, L. *Geschichte des alten Testamentes in der christlichen Kirche.* Jena, 1869.

DIGEON, A. "Le jeu de l'amour et de l'amitié dans *Le Marchand de Venise.*" *Revue anglo-américaine,* XIII (1936), 219-31.

DITTRICH, OTTMAR. *Luthers Ethik in ihren Grundzügen dargestellt.* Leipzig, 1930.

DODSLEY, R., ed. *A Select Collection of Old Plays.* New edition with additional notes and corrections by the late I. Reed, O. Gilchrist, and the editor. 12 vols., London, 1825-1827.

DONELLUS (DONEAU), HUGO. *De usuris.* Paris, 1556.

DORMER, JOHN (*pseud.*). *Usury Explain'd; or Conscience Quieted in the Case of Putting out Mony(!) at Interest.* By Philopenes (*pseud.*). London, 1695/6. ("John Dormer" proves to be a pseudonym for John Huddleston, S.J.)

DOUMERGUE, ÉMILE. *Jean Calvin, les hommes et les choses de son temps.* 7 vols., Lausanne, 1899-1927.

DRAPER, JOHN W. "Usury in *The Merchant of Venice.*" *Modern Philology,* XXXIII (1935), 37-47.

DRIVER, SAMUEL R. *A Critical and Exegetical Commentary on Deuteronomy.* New York, 1895. "International Critical Commentary."

DUBNOW, SIMON N. *Weltgeschichte des jüdischen Volkes.* Translated from the Russian by A. Steinberg. 10 vols., Berlin, 1925-1929.

DUBOIS, PIERRE. *De recuperatione terrae sanctae.* Edited by C. V. Langlois. Paris, 1891. Collection de textes pour servir à l'étude et à l'enseignment de l'histoire, IX.

DUGAS, L. *L'amitié antique.* 2nd edition, Paris, 1914.

DUHR, BERNHARD, S.J. "Die deutschen Jesuiten im 5%-Streit des 16. Jahrhunderts: Nach ungedruckten Quellen." *Zeitschrift für katholische Theologie,* XXIV (1900), 209-48.

———. "Noch einige Aktenstücke zum 5% Streite im 16. Jahrhundert." *Zeitschrift für katholische Theologie,* XXIX (1905), 178-90.

———. "Der 5% Streit im protestantische Regensburg: Ausweisung vom 5 Predigern." *Zeitschrift für katholische Theologie,* XXXII (1908), 608-10.

DU MOULIN, CHARLES. *Omnia quae extant opera.* Edited by François Pinsson. 5 vols., Paris, 1581.

———. *Tractatus commerciorum et usurarum redituumque pecunia constitutorum, et monetarum.* Cologne, 1584. The title page carries the legend: *Omnia denuò diligentissimè recognita, & quibusdam à Romana Ecclesia improbatis rebus repurgata.* The following subtitle appears on page 2: . . . *Cum nova & analytica explicatione 1. eos. C. de usur.* . . . *Compilatore Gaspare Gaballino I.C.* The name "Gaspare" also appears in the *Epigramma ad Auctorem* (p. *4, l. 6).

DURANDUS DE SANCTO PORCIANO. *In sententias theologicas Petri Lombardi.* Lyons, 1563.

DURANTIS, GUILLELMUS *(the Speculator). Les instructions et constitutions de Guillaume Durand le Spéculateur.* Edited by J. Berthelé and M. Valmary. Montpellier, 1900. Extrait des Mémoires de l'Académie des Sciences et Lettres de Montpellier. Section des Lettres, 2e sér., III.

EDWARDS, RICHARD. *Damon and Pithias; A Comedy.* Earliest edition, 1571. Also found in Dodsley, *A Select Collection of Old Plays,* I, 175-262, and in Adams, *Chief Pre-Shakespearean Dramas,* 571-608.

EELLS, H. "Bucer's Plan for the Jews." *Church History,* VI (1937), 127-35.

EGENTER, R. *Gottesfreundschaft: Die Lehre von der Gottesfreundschaft in der Scholastik und Mystik des 12. und 13. Jahrhunderts.* Augsburg, 1928.

EGLI, EMIL. *Schweizerische Reformationsgeschichte.* Band I: *Umfassend die Jahre 1519-1525.* Zurich, 1910. No more published.

EGLINGER, RUTH. *Der Begriff der Freundschaft in der Philosophie: Eine historische Untersuchung.* Basel, 1916.

EITNER, THEODOR. *Erfurt und die Bauernaufstände im 16. Jahrhundert.* Halle, 1903.

*ELERT, WERNER. *Morphologie des Luthertums.* 2 vols., Munich, 1931-1932.

EMERSON, RALPH WALDO. *Complete Works.* With a biographical introduction and notes by E. W. Emerson. Centenary edition. 12 vols., Boston and New York, 1903-1932.

Encyclopaedia Judaica: Das Judentum in Geschichte und Gegenwart. Edited by Jacob Klatzkin, *et al.* Vols. I-X, Berlin, 1927-1934. Incomplete.

Encyclopedia of the Social Sciences. Editor-in-Chief: Edwin R. A. Seligman; Associate Editor: Alvin Johnson. 15 vols., New York, 1930-1935.

*ENDEMANN, WILHELM. *Studien in der romanisch-kanonistischen Wirthschafts- und Rechtslehre bis gegen Ende des siebenzehnten Jahrhunderts.* 2 vols., Berlin, 1874-1883.

ENDERS, LUDWIG, ed. *Aus dem Kampf der Schwärmer gegen Luther. Drei Flugschriften.* Halle, 1893. Neudrucke deutscher Litteraturwerke, no. 118. Flugschriften aus der Reformationszeit, x.

ENGELS, FRIEDRICH. *The Peasant War in Germany.* Translated by M. J. Olgin, with an introduction by D. Riazanov. New York, 1926.

English Studies: A Journal of English Letters and Philology. Vols. I-XXI, Amsterdam, 1920-1947. In progress.

ERHARDT, P. "Die nationalökonomischen Ansichten der Reformatoren." *Theologische Studien und Kritiken,* LIII (1880), 666-719; LIV (1881), 106-41.

ESMEIN, A. "Sur quelques lettres de Sidoine Apollinaire." *Mélanges d'histoire du droit et de critique: Droit romain.* Paris, 1886, 359-92.

Essays and Studies in Memory of Linda R. Miller. Edited by Israel Davidson. New York, 1938.

EVANS, AUSTIN PATTERSON. "Social Aspects of Medieval Heresy." In *Persecution and Liberty: Essays in Honor of George Lincoln Burr.* New York, 1931, 93-116.

*FANFANI, AMINTORE. *Catholicism, Protestantism, and Capitalism.* London, 1935.

*———. *Le origini dello spirito capitalistico in Italia.* Milan,

1933. Pubblicazione della Università Cattolica del Sacro Cuore, serie terza, scienze sociali, XII.

FAUST, AUGUST. "Der Begriff des Nächsten als Grundbegriff einer Sozialphilosophie und Sozialpädogogik. Ein Vortrag." *Logos*, XVI (1927), 287-310.

FAVRE, JULES. *Le prêt à l'intérêt dans l'ancienne France.* Paris, 1900.

FENTON, ROGER. *A Treatise of Usurie, divided into three bookes*: The first defineth what is usurie; The second determineth that to be unlawfull; The third removeth such motives as persuade men in this age that it may be lawfull. London, 1611.

FILMER, ROBERT. *A Discourse whether it may be Lawful to take Use for Money.* Published by Sir Roger Twisden, with his preface to it. London, 1678.

FIORENTINO, GIOVANNI. *Il pecorone.* 2 vols., Milan, 1815. *Classici italiani*, Vols. XXV-XXVI.

————. *The Pecorone of Ser Giovanni.* Translated by W. G. Waters. 3 vols., London, 1898. Privately printed for the Society of Bibliophiles. Appears as Vols. V-VII of the same author's *The Italian Novelists Now First Translated into English.*

FISCHOFF, EPHRAIM. *Max Weber's Sociology of Religion.* New York, 1942. Unpublished doctoral dissertation in the Library of the New School for Social Research in New York City.

*————. "The Protestant Ethic and the Spirit of Capitalism: The History of a Controversy." *Social Research*, XI (1944), 53-77.

FLACH, J. "Le compagnonnage dans les chansons de geste." *Études romanes dédiées à Gaston Paris le 29 décembre 1890.* Paris, 1891, 141-80.

FRANCISCUS DE MAYRONIS. *Scriptum super quattuor libros sententiarum.* Venice, 1520.

FRANZ, GÜNTHER. *Der deutsche Bauernkrieg.* 2 vols., Munich and Berlin, 1933-1935.

FREUND, MICHAEL, ed. *Thomas Müntzer: Revolution als Glaube.* Eine Auswahl aus den Schriften Thomas Müntzers und Martin Luthers zur religiösen Revolution und zum deutschen Bauernkrieg. Potsdam, 1936.

FRIEDMANN, M., ed. See *Sifre.*

FRIEDMANN, ROBERT. "Conception of the Anabaptists." *Church History*, IX (1940), 341-65.

FUNK, FRANZ X. "Scipio Maffei und das kirchliche Zinsverbot." *Theologische Quartalschrift,* LXI (Tübingen, 1879), 1-55.

GALLUS, NIKOLAUS. *Zwo Predigten wider den Wucher aus dem XV. Psalm* ... (Regensburg, 1569). Jena, 1572.

GENTILI, ALBERICO. *De iure belli libri tres.* 2 vols., Oxford, 1933. C.I.L., no. 16. Vol. II: A Translation of the Text, by John C. Rolfe.

GERARD ZERBOLT of ZUTPHEN. "Het traktaat 'Super modo vivendi devotorum hominum simul commorantium' door Gerard Zerbolt van Zutphen." Edited by A. Hyma. *Archief voor de geschiedenis van het Aartsbisdom Utrecht,* LII (1926), 1-100.

GERHARD, JOHANN. *Loci theologici.* Edited by E. Preuss. 9 vols. in 5, Berlin, 1863-1875.

GERSON, JOHANNES. *Opera omnia.* 4 vols., Cologne, Johann Koelhoff *(the Elder),* 1483-1484. Another edition by Ellies du Pin. 5 vols., Antwerp, 1706. The latter edition does not reprint the works (mentioned below) by Henricus de Hassia and Henricus de Oyta.

GESENIUS, WILLIAM. *A Hebrew and English Lexicon of the Old Testament.* Edited by Francis Brown . . . with the cooperation of S. R. Driver . . . and Charles A. Briggs. Boston and New York, 1906.

GIBALINUS, JOSEPH, S.J. *De usuris, commerciis deque aequitate et usu fori lugdunensis tractatio bipartita.* 2 vols. in one, Lyons, 1657.

GILBERTUS UNIVERSALIS. See *Glossa ordinaria.*

GILLET, J. F. A. *Crato von Crafftheim und seine Freunde*: Ein Beitrag zur Kirchengeschichte nach handschriftlichen Quellen. 2 parts in one vol., Frankfurt, 1860.

GIOVANNI DA CAPISTRANO, ST. *De usuris seu cupiditate.* In *Tr. univ. juris,* VII, 91-113.

Glossa ordinaria. In *PL,* CXIII-CXIV. No longer ascribed solely to Walafrid Strabo. For recent discussions of the authorship and date, see above, p. 9, n. 11.

GLUNZ, H. H. *History of the Vulgate in England from Alcuin to Roger Bacon.* Cambridge, 1933.

GOLLANCZ, I. *Allegory and Mysticism: A Medievalist on The Merchant of Venice.* London, 1931. Printed for Private Circulation by George W. Jones.

*——. "Bits of Timber: Some Observations on Shakespearian Names—'Shylock,' 'Polonius,' 'Malvolio.' " *A Book of Hom-*

age to Shakespeare, edited by I. Gollancz. London, 1916, 170-78.

GOTTLOB, ADOLF. *Kreuzablass und Almosenablass: Eine Studie über die Frühzeit des Ablasswesens.* Stuttgart, 1906. Kirchenrechtliche Abhandlungen, hgb. von Dr. Ulrich Stutz, Heft 30/31.

GRATIAN. *Decretum.* Customarily published as Vol. 1 of the *Corpus iuris canonici.*

GRAYZEL, SOLOMON. *The Church and the Jews in the XIIIth Century.* A Study of their Relations During the Years 1198-1254, Based on the Papal Letters and the Conciliar Decrees of the Period. Philadelphia, 1933.

GREGORIUS, PETRUS. *Tractatus de usuris.* In *Tractatus . . . trium clarissimorum iureconsultorum.* Frankfurt, 1598.

GRISAR, HARTMANN. *Luther.* Translated from the German by E. M. Lamond, edited by Luigi Cappadelta. 6 vols., London, 1913-1917.

*GROETHUYSEN, BERNHARD. *Die Entstehung der bürgerlichen Welt- und Lebensanschauung in Frankreich.* 2 vols., Halle, 1927-1930.

GROSS, HEINRICH (Henri). *Gallia Judaica; Dictionnaire géographique de la France d'après les sources rabbiniques.* Translated into French by M. Bloch. Paris, 1897. "Société des études juives."

———. "Meïr b. Simon und seine Schrift Milchemeth Mizwa. Analekten." *MGWJ*, XXX, n.s. XIII (1881), 295-305, 444-52, 554-69.

GROTIUS, HUGO. *Annotationes in libros quatuor Evangeliorum et Acta Apostolorum.* In Vol. 1 of *Opera omnia theologica*, 3 vols. in 4, Amsterdam, 1679.

———. *De jure belli ac pacis libri tres.* 2 vols., Washington, D.C., and Oxford, 1913-1925. C.I.L., no. 3. Vol. II: A Translation of the Text, by Francis W. Kelsey, with the Collaboration of Arthur E. R. Boak, Henry A. Sanders, Jesse S. Reeves, and Herbert F. Wright, with an Introduction by James Brown Scott.

GRUNSKY, KARL. *Luthers Bekenntnisse zur Judenfrage.* Stuttgart, 1933.

GUTSCH, M. R. "A Twelfth Century Preacher." *The Crusades and Other Historical Essays, presented to Dana C. Munro by his former students.* Edited by L. J. Paetow. New York, 1928, 183-206.

HAARHOFF, T. J. *The Stranger at the Gate: Aspects of Exclusiveness and Co-operation in Ancient Greece and Rome, with some Reference to Modern Times.* London, 1938.

HAGEN, KARL. *Deutschlands literarische und religiöse Verhältnisse im Reformationszeitalter.* 2nd edition, 3 vols. in 2, Frankfurt, 1868.

HAINISCH, MICHAEL. *Die Entstehung des Kapitalzinses.* Leipzig and Vienna, 1907.

HALLER, WILLIAM, ed. *Tracts on Liberty in the Puritan Revolution, 1638-1647.* 3 vols., New York, 1934.

HALLIWELL, J. O. *The Remarks of M. Karl Simrock on the Plots of Shakespeare's Plays.* With notes and additions by J. O. H. London, 1850. Printed for the Shakespeare Society.

HARDELAND, AUGUST. *Geschichte der speciellen Seelsorge in der vorreformatorischen Kirche und der Kirche der Reformation.* 2 vols. in one, Berlin, 1897-1898.

HARKNESS, GEORGIA. *John Calvin: The Man and his Ethics.* New York, 1931.

HARRIS, JAMES RENDEL. *Boanerges.* Cambridge, 1913.

———. *The Cult of the Heavenly Twins.* Cambridge, 1906.

HARVEY, A. E. *Martin Bucer in England.* Marburg, 1906.

HASKINS, CHARLES HOMER. *Studies in Medieval Culture.* Oxford, 1929.

HASTINGS, JAMES, ed. *Dictionary of the Bible.* With the assistance of John A. Selbie . . . A. B. Davidson . . . S. R. Driver . . . H. B. Swete . . . 5 vols., New York and Edinburgh, 1898-1909.

———, ed. *Encyclopaedia of Religion and Ethics.* With the assistance of John A. Selbie and others. 13 vols., New York and Edinburgh, 1908-1927.

HAURÉAU, J. B. "Notice sur le no. 3203." *Notices et extraits des manuscrits de la Bibliothèque Nationale,* XXXI, pt. 2 (1886), 261-74.

HAUSER, HENRI. *Les débuts du capitalisme.* Paris, 1927.

———. *La modernité du XVIe siècle.* Paris, 1930.

———. "À propos des idées économiques de Calvin." *Mélanges d'histoire offerts à Henri Pirenne,* I (Brussels, 1926), 211-24.

———. "L'économie calvinienne." *Bulletin de la Société de l'histoire du protestantisme français,* LXXXIV (1935), 227-42.

——— and AUGUSTIN RENAUDET. *Les débuts de l'âge moderne.* Paris, 1929. 2nd edition, revised and enlarged, Paris, 1938.

HAZELTINE, H. D. "William Blackstone." *Encyclopedia of the Social Sciences*, II (1937), 580-81.

HEATON, HERBERT. *Economic History of Europe*. Revised edition, New York, 1948.

*HECKSHER, ELI F. *Mercantilism*. Authorized translation by M. Shapiro. 2 vols., London, 1935.

HEFELE, KARL JOSEPH VON. *Histoire des conciles d'après les documents originaux*. Translated from the 2nd German edition into French by Henri Leclerq. 10 vols. in 19, Paris, 1907-1938.

———. *Der Hl. Bernhardin von Siena, und die franziskanische Wanderpredigt in Italien während des* XV. *Jahrhunderts*. Freiburg, 1912.

HEICHELHEIM, F. M. "Jewish Religious Influences in the Adler Papyri?" *Harvard Theological Review*, XXXV (1942), 25-35. See Tscherikower, V.

*HEJCL, JOHANN. *Das alttestamentliche Zinsverbot im Lichte der ethnologischen Jurisprudenz sowie des altorientalischen Zinswesens*. Freiburg, 1907. Biblische Studien, hgb. von O. Bardenhewer, XII, no. 4.

HELLER, JOSEF. "Butzer (Bucerus), Martin." *Encyclopaedia Judaica*, IV, 1231-32.

HENKE, OSCAR. *Der Sabbatismus: Ein judaistische Reliquie in der christlichen Kirche*. 3rd edition, Barmen, 1892.

HENQUINET, FRANÇOIS-MARIE. "Clair de Florence, O.F.M., canoniste et pénitencier vers le milieu du XIIIe siècle." *Archivum Franciscanum Historicum*, XXXII (1939), 3-48.

HENRICUS DE HASSIA (Heinrich von Langenstein). *Tractatus bipartitus de contractibus emptionis et venditionis*. In Gerson, *Opera omnia*, IV, 185-224. Cologne, 1484.

HENRICUS DE OYTA. *De contractibus*. In Gerson, *Opera omnia*, IV, 224-54. Cologne, 1484.

HENRY OF GHENT. *Quodlibeta*. Paris, 1518.

HERDING, WILHELM. *Die wirtschaftlichen und sozialen Anschauungen Zwinglis*. Erlangen, 1917.

HERTZ, J. H. See *Pentateuch*.

HOBHOUSE, LEONARD T. *Morals in Evolution: A Study in Comparative Ethics*. 5th edition, New York, 1923.

HOBSON, JOHN A. *John Ruskin, Social Reformer*. London, 1899.

HOFERER, MAX, ed. See Johannes Monachus.

HOFFMANN, DAVID. *Das Buch Leviticus übersetzt und erklärt*. 2 vols., Berlin, 1905-1906.

————. *Der Schulchan-Aruch und die Rabbiner über das Verhältniss der Juden zu Andersgläubigen.* Berlin, 1885.

*Hoffmann, Moses. *Der Geldhandel der deutschen Juden während des Mittelalters bis zum Jahre 1350.* Leipzig, 1910. Staats- und sozialwissenschaftliche Forschungen, hgb. von G. Schmoller und Max Sering, Heft 152.

Holl, Karl. "Die Frage des Zinsnehmens und des Wuchers in der reformierten Kirche." *Gesammelte Aufsätze zur Kirchengeschichte,* iii (Tübingen, 1928), 385-403.

Holorenshaw, H. *The Levellers and the English Revolution.* London, 1939. New People's Library, Vol. xxi.

Holzapfel, Heribert. *Die Anfänge der Montes Pietatis (1462-1515).* Munich, 1903. Veröffentlichungen aus dem Kirchenhistorischen Seminar München, hgb. von Alois Knöpfler, xi.

Hopf, Constantin. *Martin Bucer and the English Reformation.* Oxford, 1946.

Horsch, John. *The Hutterian Brethren, 1528-1931: A Story of Martyrdom and Loyalty.* Goshen, Indiana, 1931. Studies in Anabaptist and Mennonite History, edited by Harold S. Bender, Ernst Correll, Silas Hertzler, Edward Yoder, no. 2.

Hostiensis (Henricus de Segusio). *In primum (sextum) decretalium commentaria.* 6 vols., Venice, 1581.

————. *Summa aurea.* Venice, 1586.

Hotman, François. *Operum tomus primus (-tertius).* 3 vols., Geneva, 1595-1600.

————. *De usuris libri duo.* Lyons, 1551.

Hove, Petrus van, ed. *Liber Deuteronomii vulgatae editionis, versione belgica, notis grammaticalibus, literalibus, criticis etc.* Vol. ii, Antwerp, 1780.

Howell, A. G. Ferrers. *S. Bernardino of Siena.* London, 1913.

Huber, Marie. *The World Unmasked: Or, the Philosopher the Greatest Cheat; in Twenty-Four Dialogues. . . . Translated from the French.* London, 1736.

Huddleston, John, S.J. See Dormer, John (*pseud.*)

Hudson, Cyril E. and Maurice B. Reckitt. *The Church and the World.* Being Materials for the Historical Study of Christian Sociology. 3 vols., London, 1938-1940.

Huet, Gédéon. "Ami et Amile. Les origines de la légende." *Le moyen âge,* xxx (1919), 162-86.

————. *Les contes populaires.* Paris. 1923.

Hume, David. *A Treatise of Human Nature.* 3 vols., London, 1739-1740.

————. "Of Interest." In *The Philosophical Works of David Hume*. 4 vols., Edinburgh, 1826. Vol. III, 333-47.

————. *The Philosophical Works*. Edited by T. H. Green and T. H. Grose, 4 vols., London, 1878.

HUNNIUS, AEGIDIUS. *Operum latinorum*. 5 tomes in 3 vols., Wittenberg, 1606-1609.

————. *Commentarius, in posteriorem epistolam D. Pauli apostoli ad Corinthios, posthumus*. In *Opera*, tome 4, Vol. II, 279-381.

————. *Epistola divi Pauli apostoli ad Titum expositio plana et perspicua*. Marburg, 1592. Bound with Luke Osiander, *Institutio christianae religionis*.

HUNT, R. N. CAREW. "Thomas Müntzer." *Church Quarterly Review*, CXXVI (1938), 213-44; CXXVII (1939), 227-67.

HURTER, HUGO. *Nomenclator literarius theologiae catholicae, theologos exhibens aetate, natione, disciplinis distinctos*. 3rd ed., 5 vols. in 6, Innsbruck, 1903-1913.

HUTCHESON, FRANCIS. *A Short Introduction to Moral Philosophy, in three Books; containing the Elements of Ethicks and the Law of Nature*. Translated from the Latin. 2nd edition. Glasgow, 1743.

*HYMA, ALBERT. *Christianity, Capitalism, and Communism: A Historical Analysis*. Ann Arbor, Michigan, 1937.

————, ed. "Het traktaat 'Super modo vivendi devotorum hominum simul commorantium' door Gerard Zerbolt van Zutphen." *Archief voor de geschiedenis van het Aartsbisdom Utrecht*, LII (1926), 1-100.

————. "Is Gerard Zerbolt of Zutphen the Author of the Super modo vivendi?" *Nederlandsch Archief voor kerkgeschiedenis*, XVI (1922), 107-28.

————. *The Life of John Calvin*. Grand Rapids, Michigan, 1943.

*ILGNER, CARL. *Die volkswirtschaftlichen Anschauungen Antonins von Florenz (1389-1459)*. Paderborn, 1904. Jahrbuch für Philosophie und spekulative Theologie, Ergänzungshefte, 8.

INNOCENT III (Pope). *Regesta sive epistolae*. In Migne, *PL*, CCXIV-CCXVII. 4 vols., Paris, 1855, reprinted 1889-1891.

INNOCENT IV (Pope). *In quinque libros decretalium commentaria*. Lyons, 1562.

IRMEN, FRIEDRICH. *Liebe und Freundschaft in der französischen Literatur des 17. Jahrhunderts*. Speyer, 1937.

JACOBS, JOSEPH. *The Jews of Angevin England*. Documents and Records, from Latin and Hebrew Sources, printed and manuscript, for the first time collected and translated. London, 1893.

JASON DE MAYNO. *Consiliorum sive responsorum*. 4 vols., Venice, 1581.

JAUERNIG, R. "D. Jakob Strauss, Eisenachs erster evangelischer Geistlicher und der Zinswucherstreit in Eisenach." *Mitteilungen des Eisenacher Geschichtsvereins*, Heft 4 (1928), 30-48. Not available to me.

JEHIEL NISSIM OF PISA, RABBI. *Eternal Life* (Hebrew). Translated excerpts in Marx, *Studies in Jewish History and Booklore*, 167-73.

JEROME, SAINT. *Commentariorum in Ezechielem prophetam libri quatuordecim*. In Migne, *PL*, XXV.

———. *Biblia sacra . . . iussu Pii PP XI*. Vols. I-IV, Rome, 1926-. In progress.

JEWEL, BISHOP JOHN. *Works*. Edited for the Parker Society by the Rev. J. Ayre. 4 vols., Cambridge, 1845-1850.

———. *De usura*. In *Works*, IV.

JOACHIMSEN, PAUL. *Sozialethik des Luthertums*. Munich, 1927.

JOHANNES MONACHUS. *Liber de miraculis*. Edited by Max Hoferer, Würzburg, 1884. Edited by M. Huber, Heidelberg, 1913. Sammlung mittellateinischer Texte, VII.

*JOHNSON, E. A. J. *American Economic Thought in the 17th Century*. London, 1932.

———. *Predecessors of Adam Smith*. New York, 1937.

JOSEPHUS, FLAVIUS. *Works*. Greek text with English translation by H. St. J. Thackeray and Ralph Marcus. Vols. I-VII, London and Cambridge, Mass., 1926-1943. Vols. VIII-IX to be issued. "Loeb Classical Library."

JUNKER, HUBERT, ed. *Das Buch Deuteronomium übersetzt und erklärt*. Bonn, 1933. Die heilige Schrift des Alten Testamentes, Band II, Abteilung 2.

KAHN, ZADOC. "Étude sur le livre de Joseph le Zélateur." *Revue des études juives*, III (1881), 1-38.

KARLSTADT, ANDREAS RUDOLF BODENSTEIN VON. *Von Abtuhung der Bylder und das keyn Betdler unther den Christen seyn sollen*. Wittenberg, 1522. Modern reprint. Edited by Hans Lietzmann. Bonn, 1911. *Kleine Texte für theologische und philologische Vorlesungen und Übungen*, hgb. von Hans Lietzmann, LXXIV.

KASER, KURT. *Politische und soziale Bewegungen im deutschen Bürgertum zu Beginn des 16. Jahrhunderts, mit besonderer Rücksicht auf den Speyerer Aufstand im Jahre 1512.* Stuttgart, 1899.

KAUTSKY, KARL. *Communism in Central Europe in the Time of the Reformation.* Translated by J. L. and E. G. Mulliken. London, 1897.

KELLER, FRANZ. *Unternehmung und Mehrwert: Eine sozialethische Studie zur Geschäftsmoral.* Paderborn, 1912. *Görres-Gesellschaft . . . Sektion für Rechts-und Sozialwissenschaft,* Heft 12.

KELLING, K. *Das Bürgschaftsmotiv in der französischen Literatur.* Leisnig, 1914.

KELLY, JAMES BIRCH. *A Summary of the History and Law of Usury.* London, 1835.

KEYNES, JOHN MAYNARD. *The General Theory of Employment, Interest, and Money.* London, 1936.

————. "Saving and Usury," *Economic Journal,* XLII (1932), 135-37. Forms part of a symposium in the *Journal* on the relation of Keynes to the medieval canonists. The participants were: B. P. Adarkar, E. Cannan, Lawrence Dennis, B. K. Sandwell, and H. Sommerville. The latter's articles opened and closed the debate. See Sommerville, H.

KIRK, KENNETH E. *Conscience and its Problems: An Introduction to Casuistry.* London, 1927.

*KLINGENBURG, GEORG. *Das Verhältnis Calvins zu Butzer, untersucht auf Grund der wirtschafts-ethischen Bedeutung beider Reformatoren.* Bonn, 1912.

KLUCKHOHN, PAUL. *Die Auffassung der Liebe in der Literatur des 18. Jahrhunderts und in der deutschen Romantik.* Halle, 1931.

KNAPPEN, MARSHALL M. *Tudor Puritanism: A Chapter in the History of Idealism.* Chicago, 1939.

KNIGHT, FRANK H. "Historical and Theoretical Issues in the Problem of Modern Capitalism." *Journal of Economic and Business History,* I (1928), 119-36.

*————. "Interest." *Encyclopedia of the Social Sciences,* VIII (1932), 131-44.

————. trans. See Max Weber, *General Economic History.*

*KNIGHTS, LIONEL C. *Drama and Society in the Age of Jonson.* London, 1937.

*KNOLL, AUGUST M. *Der Zins in der Scholastik.* Innsbruck, 1933.

[192]

KOBER, ADOLF. "Die rechtliche Lage der Juden im Rheinland während des 14. Jahrhunderts im Hinblick auf das kirchliche Zinsverbot." *Westdeutsche Zeitschrift für Geschichte und Kunst*, XXVIII (1909), 243-69.

KÖHLER, REINHOLD. *Kleinere Schriften*. . . . hgb. von J. Bolte. 3 vols., I: Weimar, 1898; II-III: Berlin, 1900.

———. "L'âme en gage." In *Kleinere Schriften*, II.

KÖHLER, WALTHER. *Bibliographia Brentiana*: Bibliographisches Verzeichnis der gedruckten und ungedruckten Schriften und Briefe des Reformators Johannes Brenz. Nebst einem Verzeichnis der Literatur über Brenz, kurzen Erläuterungen und ungedruckten Akten. Berlin, 1904.

———, ed. *Das Buch der Reformation Huldreich Zwinglis*. Munich, 1926.

KÖNIG, EDUARD, ed. *Das Deuteronomium eingeleitet, übersetzt und erklärt*. Leipzig, 1917. Kommentar zum alten Testament, hgb. von Ernst Sellin, Band III.

KOHLER, MAX J. *Menasseh ben Israel and Some Unpublished Pages of American History*. New York, 1901. Originally printed in *The American Hebrew*, LXIX (1901), 625-31.

KOSTANECKI, ANTON VON. *Der öffentliche Kredit im Mittelalter. Nach Urkunden der Herzogtümer Braunschweig und Lüneburg*. Leipzig, 1889. Staats- und sozialwissenschaftliche Forschungen, hgb. von G. Schmoller, Band IX, Heft I.

KOSTERS, JAN. *Les fondements du droit des gens: Contribution à la théorie générale du droit des gens*. Leyden, 1925. Bibliotheca Visseriana, IV, no. 9.

KRAPPE, A. H. "The Legend of Amicus and Amelius." *Modern Language Review*, XVIII (1923), 152-61.

———. "The Molionides." *Amicitiae Corolla*, edited by H. G. Wood. London, 1932, 133-46.

KUTTNER, STEPHAN. *Repertorium der Kanonistik (1140-1234): Prodromus corporis glossarum*, I. Vatican City, 1937. Studi e testi, LXXI.

LAINEZ, DIEGO. *Disputatio de usuris variisque negotiis mercatorum*. In H. Grisar, *Jacobi Lainez . . . Disputationes Tridentinae*. 2 vols., Innsbruck, 1886. Vol. II.

LANGTON, STEPHEN. *Quaestiones*. Excerpts from manuscripts, in F. M. Powicke, *Stephen Langton*. Oxford, 1928.

LA PIANA, GEORGE. "Joachim of Flora: A Critical Survey." *Speculum*, VII (1932), 257-82.

LA PORTE DU THEIL, F. J. G. DE. "Mémoire sur la vie de Robert de Courçon." *Notices et extraits des manuscrits de la Bibliothèque Nationale*, VI (1800-1801), 130-222, 566-616.

*LARMANN, HANS. *Christliche Wirtschaftsethik in der spatrömischen Antike*. Berlin, 1936.

LARNED, JOSEPHUS N., ed. *A Multitude of Counsellors*: Being a Collection of Codes, Precepts, and Rules of Life from the Wise of All Ages. Boston and New York, 1901.

*LASPEYRES, ETIENNE A. T. *Geschichte der volkswirthschaftlichen Anschauungen der Niederländer und ihrer Litteratur zur Zeit der Republik*. Leipzig, 1863. Preisschriften gekrönt und hgb. von der Fürstlich Jablonowski'schen Gesellschaft zu Leipzig, XI.

LATTES, ALESSANDRO. "Carlo Dumoulin e Gaspare Caballino." *Archivio giuridico 'Filippo Serafini,'* XCV (1926), 7-19.

LAU, FRANZ. *"Äusserliche Ordnung" und "Weltlich Ding" in Luthers Theologie*. Göttingen, 1933. Studien zur systematischen Theologie, hgb. von A. Titius und G. Wobbermin, XII.

LAURENTIUS DE RIDOLFIS. *De usuris*. In *Tr. univ. juris*, VII.

LEA, HENRY CHARLES. *A History of the Inquisition of the Middle Ages*. 3 vols., Philadelphia, reprint of 1922.

LEFÈVRE, G., ed. See Curzon, Robert de.

LE GOFF, MARCEL. *Du Moulin et le prêt à intérêt: le légiste, son influence*. Bordeaux, 1905.

LEIBER, ERWIN. *Das kanonische Zinsverbot in deutschen Städten des Mittelalters*. Ueberlingen, 1927.

*LEJEUNE, J. "Religion, morale et capitalisme dans la société liégeoise du XVIIe siècle." *Revue belge de philologie et d'histoire*, XXII (1943), 109-54.

LENZ, MAX, ed. *Briefwechsel Landgraf Philipp's des Grosmuthigen von Hessen mit Bucer*. Herausgegeben und erläutert von Max Lenz. 3 vols., Leipzig, 1880-1891. Publicationen aus den K. Preussischen Staatsarchiven, V, XXVIII, XLVII.

LEO OF MODENA. *Historia de' riti hebraici: vita e osservanze de gl' Hebrei di questi tempi*. 1st ed., Paris, 1637. Venice, 1669. French translation by Richard Simon, Paris, 1681. Latin translation, Frankfurt, 1693.

————. *The History of the Present Jews throughout the World, Being an Ample though Succinct Account of their Customs, Ceremonies and Manner of Living at this time*. Translated from the French by Simon Ockley. London, 1707.

LEOTARDUS, HONORATUS. *Liber singularis de usuris.* 2 parts in one, Venice, 1761-1762. Appendix contains F. X. Zech, *Dissertationes tres.*

LESSIUS, LEONARDUS, S.J. *De iustitia et iure ceterisque virtutibus cardinalibus libri quatuor ad 2.2. D. Thomae a quaestione 47 usque ad quaestionem 171.* Antwerp, 1621.

Letters on Usury and Interest, Shewing the Advantages of Loans for the Support of Trade and Commerce. London, 1774. These *Letters* seem to have been published previously in the *Edinburgh Weekly Magazine.*

LÉVY, LOUIS G. *La famille dans l'antiquité israélite.* Paris, 1905.

LEWIN, REINHOLD. *Luthers Stellung zu den Juden*: Ein Beitrag zur Geschichte der Juden in Deutschland während des Reformationszeitalters. Berlin, 1911. Neue Studien zur Geschichte der Theologie und Kirche, x.

Lexikon für Theologie und Kirche. 2nd edition. Edited by Dr. M. Buchberger. 10 vols., Freiburg, 1930-1938.

Libri numerorum et Deuteronomii ex interpretatione S. Hieronymi. . . . In *Biblia sacra . . . iussu Pii PP XI,* Vol. III, Rome, 1936.

Liber septimus decretalium constitutionum apostolicarum a Petro Mattheo, icto Lugdunensi, collectus et anno MDXC primum editus. Edited in the appendix to Boehmer, *Corpus iuris canonici,* after col. 1200. Separate pagination.

LILJEGREN, S. B. "Harrington and the Jews." *K. Humanistiska Vetenskapssamfundets I Lund Årberättelse (Bulletin de la Société royale des lettres de Lund),* IV (1931-1932), 65-92.

Litterae monitoriae DD. Bellicensis episcopi ad clerum suae dioecesis directae, circa quoddam opus de mutuo recenter editum. In Migne, *Theologiae cursus completus,* XVI, 1065-90.

LOCKE, JOHN. *Works.* 11th edition, 10 vols., London, 1812.

———. *Some Considerations of the Consequences of Lowering the Interest, and Raising the Value of Money: In a Letter Sent to a Member of Parliament, 1691.* Reprinted in *Works,* V, 3-130.

LOEFFLER, KLEMENS. *Die Wiedertäufer zu Münster 1534/1535*; Berichte, Aussagen und Aktenstücke von Augenzeugen und Zeitgenossen. Jena, 1923.

LOEVINSON, ERMANNO. "La concession de banques de prêts aux juifs par les papes des seizième et dix-septième siècles." *Revue des études juives,* XCII (1932), 1-30; XCIII (1932),

27-52, 157-78; xciv (1933), 57-74, 167-83; xcv (1933), 23-43.

LOEWE, H. "On Usury." In *Starrs and Jewish Charters*, edited by I. Abrahams *et al.*, II (1932), pp. xcv-cviii.

LOHMANN, ANNEMARIE. *Zur geistigen Entwicklung Thomas Müntzers.* Leipzig and Berlin, 1931. Beiträge zur Kulturgeschichte des Mittelalters und der Renaissance, hgb. von W. Goetz, xlvii.

LOMBARD, PETER. *Liber sententiarum.* In Migne, *PL*, cxcii.

LOVEJOY, A. O. *The Great Chain of Being: A Study of the History of an Idea.* Cambridge, Mass., 1936.

LOY, FRIEDRICH. "Der Regensburger Wucherstreit: Ein Beitrag zum Kampf des Luthertums gegen den Kapitalismus." *Beiträge zur bayerischen Kirchengeschichte*, xxxi (1925), 3-28.

LUDOVICUS À PEGUERA, DON. *Quaestiones criminales, in actu practico, frequentiores et maxime conducibiles.* Venice, 1590.

LÜHE, WILHELM. "Die Ablösung der ewigen Zinsen in Frankfurt a. M. in den Jahren 1522-1562: Beitrag zur Wirtschaftsgeschichte in der Reformationszeit." *Westdeutsche Zeitschrift für Geschichte und Kunst*, xxiii (1904), 36-72, 229-72.

LUTHER, MARTIN. *Werke—Kritische Gesammtausgabe.* Edited by J. K. F. Knaake, G. Kawerau, E. Thiele, and others. 57 vols. in 67, Weimar, 1883-1947. In progress. Herein abbreviated: *WA*.

———. *Sämmtliche Werke.* Edited by J. G. Plochmann and J. K. Irmischer. 67 vols., Frankfurt and Erlangen, 1826-1857. Familiarly known and herein cited as the ERLANGEN edition.

———. *Luthers Werke für das christliche Haus.* Edited by G. Buchwald *et al.* 4th edition, 10 vols., Leipzig, 1924.

———. *Briefwechsel.* Edited by Ludwig Enders *et al.* 19 vols. in 12, Frankfurt, 1884-1932.

———. *Briefwechsel, 1501-1542.* 9 vols., Weimar, 1930-1941. In progress.

———. *Tischreden, 1531-1546.* 6 vols., Weimar, 1919-1921.

———. *Luther's Correspondence and other Contemporary Letters.* Translated and edited by Preserved Smith and Ch. M. Jacobs. 2 vols., Philadelphia, 1913-1918. Only to 1530.

———. *Luther's Primary Works.* Together with his Shorter and Larger Catechisms. Translated and edited by Henry Wace and C. A. Buchheim. London, 1896. Also appeared under the title: *First Principles of the Reformation; or the Ninety-*

Five Theses and The Three Primary Works. . . . London, 1883.

———. *Works.* Partial English translation, with an introduction and notes by a committee of Lutheran pastors headed by H. E. Jacobs. Vols. I-VI, Philadelphia, 1915-1932. Additional volumes promised.

———. *An den christlichen Adel deutscher Nation von des christlichen Standes Besserung* (1520). *WA*, VI, 381-469; *Luther's Primary Works,* edited by Wace and Buchheim, 157-244; *Works,* edited by H. E. Jacobs, II, 57-164.

———. *An der Rat zu Erfurt. WA,* XVIII, 531-40.

———. *An die Pfarrherrn wider den Wucher zu predigen Vermahnung* (1540). Edited by G. Buchwald. *WA,* LI, 325-424.

———. *Decem praecepta Wittenbergensi praedicata populo. WA,* I, 394-521.

———. *(Grosser) Sermon von dem Wucher* (1520). *WA,* VI, 31-60; *Works,* IV, 37-69.

———. *In Genesin Mosi librum sanctissimum Declamationes* (1527). *WA,* XXIV.

———. *Kampfschriften gegen das Judentum.* Edited by Walther Linden. Berlin, 1936.

———. *(Kleiner) Sermon von dem Wucher* (1519). *WA,* VI, 1-8.

———. *Matthäus Kapitel 18-24 in Predigten ausgelegt 1537-40.* Edited by G. Buchwald. *WA,* XLVII, 232-627.

———. *Ordnung eines geimeinen Kasten* (1523). *WA,* XII, 11-30; *Works,* IV, 87-98.

———. *Papst Clemens VII. Zwei Bullen zum Jubeljahr, mit Luthers Vorrede und Anmerkungen* (1525). In *WA,* XVIII, 251-69.

———. *Von Kaufshandlung und Wucher* (1524). *WA,* 279-322; *Luthers Werke,* edited by G. Buchwald *et al.,* VII (1924)—contains helpful introduction by S. Eck, 494-513; *Works,* IV, 12-36.

———. *Vorlesungen über das Deuteronomium* (1523/1524); *Deuteronomion Mosi cum annotationibus* (1525). *WA,* XIV, 492-744.

———. *Wider die himmlischen Propheten* (1525). *WA,* XVIII, 36-214.

———. *Wider die räuberischen und mörderischen Rotten der Bauern* (1525). *WA,* XVII, 344-61; *Works,* IV, 247-54.

LUZZATTO, GINO. *I prestiti della repubblica di Venezia (sec. xiii-xv). Introduzione storica e documenti.* Padua, 1929. R. Accademia dei Lincei. Documenti finanziari della repubblica di Venezia editi dalla Commissione per gli atti delle costituzionali assemblee italiane, ser. 3, Vol. I.

LYLY, JOHN. *Complete Works.* Edited by R. W. Bond. 3 vols., Oxford, 1902.

*McCULLOCH, JOHN RAMSAY. *The Literature of Political Economy.* London, 1845. Reprinted by the London School of Economics and Political Science. London, 1938. Series of Reprints of Scarce Works on Political Economy, no. 5.

————. *Treatises and Essays.* 2nd edition, London, 1859.

MACKINNON, JAMES. *Luther and the Reformation.* 4 vols., New York, 1925-1930.

*McLAUGHLIN, T. P. "The Teaching of the Canonists on Usury (XII, XIII, and XIV Centuries)." *Mediaeval Studies,* I (1939), 81-147; II (1940), 1-22. Published for the Pontifical Institute of Mediaeval Studies.

*McNEILL, JOHN T. "Thirty Years of Calvin Study." *Church History,* XVII (1948), 207-40.

MAFFEI, SCIPIONE. *Dell'impiego del danaro libri tre.* Verona, 1744; Rome, 1745; Rome, 1746. The latter printing contains the legend: *Seconda edizione. Accresciuta d'una Lettera Enciclica di Sua Santità ed' altra Lettera dell' Autore alla medesima Santità Sua.*

MAIMONIDES, MOSES. *Mishneh Torah* (Hebrew). 4 vols., Berlin, 1862.

————. *The Code of Maimonides. Book Thirteen: The Book of the Civil Laws.* Translated from the Hebrew by Jacob J. Rabinowitz. New Haven: Yale University Press, 1949. *Yale Judaica Series,* Vol. II.

————. *The Book of Divine Commandments (The Sefer ha-Mitzvoth of Moses Maimonides).* Translated by Rabbi Charles B. Chavel. Vol. I: *The Positive Commandments.* London, 1940.

MAINE, SIR HENRY SUMNER. *Village-Communities in the East and West. . . . To which are added other addresses and essays.* Third enlarged edition, New York, 1876.

MALYNES, GERARD DE. *Consuetudo, vel, Lex mercatoria: or, The ancient law merchant.* 3rd edition, London, 1686.

MANDELKERN, SOLOMON. *Veteris Testamenti concordantiae Hebraicae atque Chaldaicae.* Leipzig, 1896.

MANDEVILLE, BERNARD DE. *The Fable of the Bees: or, Private Vices, Public Benefits. With an Essay on Charity and Char-*

ity-Schools and a Search into the Nature of Society. 2 vols., Edinburgh, 1772.

————. *The Fable of the Bees.* . . . Edited with a commentary critical, historical, and explanatory by F. B. Kaye. 2 vols., Oxford, 1924.

MANSI, JOHANNES D. *Sacrorum conciliorum nova et amplissima collectio.* 31 vols., Florence and Venice, 1759-1796.

MARESIUS, SAMUEL. *Amplissimi, consultissimi, & eruditissimi cuiusdam viri Considerationes Erotematicae circa foenus trapeziticum, cum Samuelis Maresii . . . brevi & sinceri ad eos responsione.* Groningen, 1657.

MARLOWE, CHRISTOPHER. *The Works and Life.* Under the general editorship of R. H. Case. 6 vols., New York, 1930-1933.

————. *The Jew of Malta.* Edited by H. S. Bennett. In *The Works and Life,* III.

————. *Tamburlaine the Great.* Edited by U. M. Ellis-Fermor. In *The Works and Life,* II.

MARQUARDUS DE SUSANNIS. *De iudaeis et aliis infidelibus, et de inimicis crucis Christi, tam visibilibus quam invisibilibus.* Venice, 1568.

MARWICK, BRIAN A. *The Swazi: An Ethnographic Account of the Natives of the Swaziland Protectorate.* Cambridge, 1940.

MARX, ALEXANDER. *Studies in Jewish History and Booklore.* New York, 1944.

————. "A Description of Bills of Exchange, 1559." *American Economic Review,* VI (1916), 609-14. Reprinted in Marx, *Studies in Jewish History and Booklore,* 167-73.

MARX, KARL. *Der historische Materialismus.* Die Frühschriften hgb. von S. Landshut und J. P. Mayer unter Mitwirkung von F. Salomon. 2 vols., Leipzig, 1932. Kröners Taschenausgabe, Bände 91-92.

MATHER, COTTON. *Durable Riches: Two Brief Discourses, Occasioned by the Impoverishing Blast of Heaven, which the Undertakings of Men, Both by Sea and Land, have met withal.* Boston, 1695.

————. *Magnalia Christi Americana; or, The Ecclesiastical History of New-England, from its first planting in . . . 1620 to . . . 1698.* Edited by the Rev. Thomas Robbins. 2 vols., Hartford, Conn., 1855, 1853.

MAULTROT, GABRIEL NICOLAS. *L'usure considérée relativement au droit naturel.* . . . 2 t., Paris, 1787. The Kress Collection. Harvard School of Business.

MAURUS, RABANUS. *Enarratio super Deuteronomium.* In Migne, *PL*, CVIII.

MAYRONIS, FRANCISCUS DE. See Franciscus de Mayronis.

MEDICES, SIXTUS. *De foenore iudaeorum libri tres.* Venice, 1555.

MELANCHTHON, PHILIP. *Opera quae supersunt omnia.* Edited by C. G. Bretschneider and H. E. Bindseil. 28 vols., Halle and Brunswick, 1834-1860. *CR*, Vols. I-XXVIII.

———. *Commentarii in aliquot politicos libros Aristotelis* (1530). *CR*, XVI. Halle, 1850.

———. *Disputatio de iubileo.* Wittenberg, 1549.

———. *Dissertatio de contractibus* (1545). In *CR*, XVI.

———. *Ethicae doctrinae elementorum libri duo* (1550). In *CR*, XVI.

———. *In officia Ciceronis Prolegomena* (1525). In *CR*, XVI.

———. *Philosophiae moralis epitomes libri duo* (1538). In *CR*, XVI.

MÉMIN, M. *Les vices de consentement dans les contrats de notre ancien droit.* Le Mans, 1926.

MENASSEH BEN ISRAEL, RABBI. *To His Highnesse the Lord Protector of the Commonwealth of England, Scotland, and Ireland; The Humble Addresses of Menasseh ben Israel, a Divine and Doctor of Physick, in behalf of the Jewish Nation* (*1655*). Reprinted by H. M. Dwight, Melbourne, 1868. Also in L. Wolf, *Menasseh ben Israel's Mission to Oliver Cromwell.* London, 1901.

MENIUS, JUSTUS. *Von dem Geist der Widerteuffer.* Wittenberg, 1544.

MENTZ, F. *Bibliographische Zusammenstellung der gedruckten Schriften Butzer's.* In *Zur 400 jährigen Geburtsfeier Martin Butzer's.* Strassburg, 1891.

MERX, OTTO. *Thomas Münzer und Heinrich Pfeiffer 1523-1525: Ein Beitrag zur Geschichte des Bauernkrieges in Thüringen.* Theil I: *Thomas Münzer und Heinrich Pfeiffer bis zum Ausbruch Bauernkrieges.* Göttingen, 1889.

MEYER, PAUL. *Zwinglis Soziallehren.* Linz, 1921.

MICHAELIS, JOHANN DAVID. *Commentaries on the Laws of Moses.* Translated from the German by Alexander Smith. 4 vols., London, 1814.

———. *Commentatio de mente ac ratione legis mosaicae usuram prohibentis.* Erfurt, 1746.

MIGNE, JACQUES PAUL, ed. *Patrologiae cursus completus. Series latina,* 221 vols., Paris, 1844-1861. *Series graeca,* 161 vols., Paris, 1857-1866.

———, ed. *Theologiae cursus completus.* 27 vols., Paris, 1839-1840.

———., ed. *Dictionnaire de biographie chrétienne et anti-chrétienne.* 3 vols., Paris, 1851.

MILLS, LAURENS J. *One Soul in Bodies Twain: Friendship in Tudor Literature and Stuart Drama.* Bloomington, Ind., 1937.

———. *Some Aspects of Richard Edwards' Damon and Pithias.* Bloomington, Ind., 1927. Indiana University Studies, XIV, no. 75.

MIRBT, CARL. "Lambert, Franz." *RE,* ed. 3, XI, 321-23.

Mishnah, The. Translated with an introduction and brief explanatory notes by Herbert Danby. Oxford, 1933.

MOFFATT, JAMES. *Love in the New Testament.* London, 1929.

MONALDUS. *Summa perutilis atque aurea . . . in utroque jure tam civilique canonico.* Lyons, 1532.

MONROE, ARTHUR ELI, ed. *Early Economic Thought: Selections from Economic Literature prior to Adam Smith.* Cambridge, Mass., 1924.

MORTET, V. "Hugue de Fouilloi, Pierre le Chantre, Alexandre Neckam et les critiques dirigées au douzième siècle contre le luxe des constructions." *Mélanges d'histoire offerts à M. Charles Bémont.* Paris, 1913, 105-37.

MOSSE, MILES. *The Arraignment and Conviction of Usurie.* London, 1595.

MÜLLER, DAVID HEINRICH. *Die Mehri-und Soqotri Sprache.* 3 vols., Vienna, 1902-1907. In *Kaiserliche Akademie der Wissenschaften: Südarabische Expedition.* 10 vols., Vienna, 1900-1911. Vols. IV, VI, VII.

MÜLLER, KARL. *Luther und Karlstadt: Stücke aus ihrem gegenseitigen Verhältniss untersucht.* Tübingen, 1907.

MÜLLER, LYDIA. *Der Kommunismus der mährischen Wiedertäufer.* Leipzig, 1927. *Schriften des Vereins für Reformationsgeschichte,* Jahrgang 45, Heft I (no. 142).

———, ed. *Glaubenszeugnisse ober deutscher Taufgesinnter.* Vol. I, Leipzig, 1938. *Quellen und Forschungen zur Reformationsgeschichte* (früher *Studien zur Kultur und Geschichte der Reformation*), hgb. von *Verein für Reformationsgeschichte,* Band XX.

MULLINGER, JAMES BASS. *The University of Cambridge.* 3 vols., Cambridge, 1873-1911. Vol. II: *From the Royal Injunctions of 1535 to the Accession of Charles the First.* Cambridge, 1884.

MUNDAY, ANTHONY. *Zelauto; the Fountaine of Fame.* London, 1580. Modern Language Association, Collection of photographic facsimiles, no. 80, s.l., s.a. Also in Brie, "Zur Entstehung des 'Kaufmann von Venedig'." *Sh.J.*, XLIX (1913), 97-121.

MÜNTZER, THOMAS. *Briefwechsel.* Edited by H. Böhmer and P. Kirn. Leipzig and Berlin, 1931. Schriften der Sächsischen Kommission für Geschichte, XXXIV.

————. *Hoch verursachte Schutzrede und Antwwort, wider das Gaistlosse Sanfft lebende fleysch zu Wittenberg. . . .* (1524). Edited by L. Enders, *Aus dem Kampf . . . ,* Halle a. Salle, 1893. Neudrucke deutscher Litteraturwerke, no. 118.

————. See Brandt, Otto, ed.

————. See Freund, Michael, ed.

MURRAY, J. B. C. *The History of Usury from the Earliest Period to the Present Time.* Philadelphia, 1866.

MUSCULUS, WOLFGANG. *In Davidis Psalterium sacrosanctum commentarii, . . . accessere etiam de iuramento et usura.* Basel, 1573.

MUTHER, THEODOR. *Aus dem Universitäts- und Gelehrtenleben im Zeitalter der Reformation.* Erlangen, 1866.

NAPOLÉON (I). *Correspondance, publiée par ordre de l'Empereur Napoléon III.* 32 vols., Paris, 1858-1870.

NATHUSIUS, MARTIN VON. *Die christlich-socialen Ideen der Reformationszeit und ihre Herkunft.* Gütersloh, 1897. Beiträge zur Förderung christlicher Theologie, 1, Heft 2.

*NELSON, BENJAMIN N. "The Usurer and the Merchant Prince: Italian Businessmen and the Ecclesiastical Law of Restitution, 1100-1550." *The Tasks of Economic History* (Supplemental Issue of *The Journal of Economic History*), VII (1947), 104-22.

*————, and JOSHUA STARR. "The Legend of the Divine Surety and the Jewish Moneylender." *Annuaire de l'Institut de philologie et d'histoire orientales et slaves,* VII (1939-1944), 289-338.

NEUBAUER, A. "Rapport sur une mission dans le midi de la France à l'effet de cataloguer les manuscrits hébreux qui s'y trouvent, et en Italie pour recueillir des documents hébreux concernant l'histoire des rabbins français." *Archives des missions scientifiques et littéraires,* ser. 3, 1 (1873), 551-61.

Neudrucke deutscher Litteraturwerke des XVI. und XVII. Jahrhunderts. 314 vols. in 57, Halle, 1876-1939.

NEUMAN, ABRAHAM A. *The Jews in Spain. Their Social, Political and Cultural Life during the Middle Ages*. 2 vols., Philadelphia, 1942.

*NEUMANN, MAXIMILIAN. *Geschichte des Wuchers in Deutschland bis zur Begründung der heutigen Zinsengesetze (1654)*. Halle, 1865.

New Schaff-Herzog Encyclopedia of Religious Knowledge, The. Based on the 3rd edition of the *Realencyklopädie*, and edited by S. M. Jackson. 12 vols., New York, 1908-1912.

NIETZSCHE, FRIEDRICH W. *Complete Works*. First complete and authorized translation, edited by Dr. Oscar Levy. 18 vols., New York, 1910-1927.

NOVARIUS, JOHANNES MARIA. *De privilegiis miserabilium personarum tractatus*. In Vol. II of Alvarez de Velasco, *De privilegiis pauperum et miserabilium personarum*. 3rd edition, 2 vols. in one, Lausanne, 1739.

NYGREN, ANDERS. *Agape and Eros*. Translated by A. G. Hebert. 2 vols. in 3, London, 1932-1939.

O'CALLAGHAN, REV. JEREMIAH. *Usury or Interest proved to be Repugnant to the Divine and Ecclesiastical Laws and Destructive to Civil Society*. London, 1825. There is a 1st edition of New York, 1824.

————. *Usury; Or, Lending at Interest; Also, the Exaction and Payment of Certain Church Fees, such as Pew-Rents, Burial-Fees, and the like, together with Forestalling Traffick; All Proved to be Repugnant to the Divine and Ecclesiastical Law, and Destructive to Civil Society. To Which is Prefixed a Narrative of the Controversy between the Author and Bishop Coppinger, and of the Sufferings of the former in consequence of his adherence to the Truth*. London, 1828.

*————. *Usury, Funds, and Banks; Also Forestalling Traffick, and Monopoly; likewise Pew Rent and Grave Tax; Together with Burking and Dissections; as well as the Gallican Liberties, are All Repugnant to the Divine and Ecclesiastical Laws, and Destructive to Civil Society. . . .* Burlington, 1834.

————. *Usury. Funds and Banking. Monopoly, forestalling Traffick. Gallican Liberties, Graves, Anatomy*. 5th edition, revised and enlarged, New York, 1856.

OREL, ANTON. *Oeconomia Perennis*. 2 vols., Mainz, 1930. Vol. II subtitled: *Das kanonische Zinsverbot*. Vols. I-II of *Re-*

vision der modernen Wirtschaftsauffassung. 5 vols. to be issued, Mainz, 1930-.

OSBORNE, FRANCIS. *Works; divine, moral, historical, political, in four several tracts.* 9th edition, London, 1689.

OSTERMAN, N. "The Controversy over the Proposed Readmission of the Jews to England (1655)." *Jewish Social Studies,* III (1941), 301-28.

PALEY, WILLIAM. *Works.* With additional sermons . . . and a corrected account of the life and writings of the author, by E. Paley. 7 vols., London, 1825.

PANORMITANUS (Nicolaus de Tudeschis). *Commentaria in quinque libros decretalium.* 8 vols., Venice, 1588.

PANZER, GEORG WOLFGANG. *Annalen der ältern deutschen Litteratur; oder Anzeige und Beschreibung derjenigen Bücher welche von Erfindung der Buchdrucker Kunst bis* MDXX [-MDXXVI] *in deutscher Sprache gedruckt worden sind.* 3 vols. in one, Nuremberg, 1788-1805.

PAPA, GUIDO (Guy de la Pape). *De contractibus illicitis qui usurarii dici possunt vel non.* In *Tr. univ. juris,* VII, 71-74.

PARETO, VILFREDO. *The Mind and Society.* Edited by Arthur Livingston; translated by Andrew Bongiorno and Arthur Livingston, with the advice and active cooperation of James Harvey Rogers. 4 vols., New York, 1935.

PARIS, MATTHEW. *Chronica majora.* Edited by H. R. Luard. 7 vols., London, 1872-1883. Rolls Series, no. 57.

PARSONS, TALCOTT. *The Structure of Social Action.* New York, 1937.

——. "H. M. Robertson on Max Weber and His School." *Journal of Political Economy,* XLIII (1935), 688-96.

PASCAL, BLAISE. *Les lettres provinciales.* Edited by H. F. Stewart. Manchester, 1920.

PAUCK, WILHELM. *Das Reich Gottes auf Erden: Utopie und Wirklichkeit. Untersuchung zu Butzers "De regno Christi" und zur englischen Staatskirche des 16. Jahrhunderts.* Berlin and Leipzig, 1928. Arbeiten zur Kirchengeschichte, X.

PAULUS, NIKOLAUS. *Geschichte des Ablasses im Mittelalter vom Ursprunge bis zur Mitte des 14. Jahrhunderts.* 3 vols. in 2, Paderborn, 1922.

PEAKE, ARTHUR S. *Brotherhood in the Old Testament.* New York, 1923.

PEASE, T. C. *The Leveller Movement.* Baltimore, 1916.

Pentateuch and Haftorahs, The. Hebrew Text and English

Translation with Commentary, edited by the Chief Rabbi (Dr. J. H. Hertz) : *Deuteronomy*. Oxford, 1936.

Pentateuch with Targum Onkelos, Haphtaroth, and Prayers for Sabbath and Rashi's Commentary. Translated by Rev. M. Rosenbaum and Dr. A. M. Silberman in collaboration with A. Blashki and L. Joseph: *Deuteronomy*. London, 1934.

PETEGORSKY, DAVID W. *Left-Wing Democracy in the English Civil War: A Study of the Social Philosophy of Gerrard Winstanley*. London, 1940.

PETER CANTOR. See Cantor, Peter.

PETER COMESTOR. See Comestor, Peter.

PETER DAMIANI. See Damiani, Peter.

PETER LOMBARD. See Lombard, Peter.

PETRUS ALFONSI. See Alfonsi, Petrus.

PETRUS DE ANCHARANO. See Ancharano, Petrus de.

PETRUS GREGORIUS. See Gregorius, Petrus.

PFEIFFER, ROBERT H. *Introduction to the Old Testament*. New York and London, 1941.

PHILO JUDAEUS. *Works*. Greek text with English translation by F. H. Colson and G. H. Whitaker, Vols. I-V; and by F. H. Colson, Vols. VI-IX. London and Cambridge, Mass., 1929-1941. "Loeb Classical Library."

PICHLER, VITUS, S.J. *Jus canonicum practice explicatum, seu decisiones casuum selectorum 185 ad singulos decretalium Gregorii IX*. Ingolstadt, 1735.

———. *Summa jurisprudentiae sacrae universae, seu Jus canonicum secundum quinque decretalium Gregorii Papae IX*. Edited by F. A. Zacharia, 2 vols., Pesaro and Venice, 1758. Not available to me. Vol. I contains an appendix to Lib. V, tit. xix, num. 8 entitled: *Adversus Danielis Concinae criminationes Apologetica pro P. Pichleri sententia disquisitio ex Cl. P. Francisci Zech, S.J., dissertatione II inaugurali Ingolstadii edita anno 1749*.

PIROT, G. *L'apologie pour les casuistes contre les calomnies des Jansenistes par un théologien et professeur en droit canon*. Paris, 1659.

PLANHOL, RENÉ DE. *Les utopistes de l'amour*. Paris, 1921.

PLOWDEN, FRANCIS. *A Treatise upon the Law of Usury and Annuities*. London, 1797.

POLLARD, A. F. "Young, John." In *DNB*, LXIII (1900), 379.

POSTAN, M. M. "Credit in Mediaeval Trade." *Economic History Review*, I (1928), 234-61.

*————. "Studies in Bibliography: 1. Mediaeval Capitalism." *Economic History Review*, IV (1933), 212-27.

POTTER, M. A. "Ami et Amile." *PMLA*, XXXIII (1908), 471-85.

POWICKE, F. M. *Stephen Langton.* Oxford, 1928.

Pro monte pietatis: Consilia sacrorum theologorum ac collegiorum Patavii. . . . Venice?, Johannes Tacuinus de Tridino?, 1498?.

PRYNNE, WILLIAM. *A Short Demurrer to the Jewes Long Discontinued Barred Remitter into England.* 2 vols. in one, London, 1656.

PUFENDORF, SAMUEL VON. *De jure naturae et gentium libri octo.* 2 vols., Oxford, 1934. C.I.L., no. 17. Vol. II: A Translation of the Text, by C. H. and W. A. Oldfather.

PURCELL, RICHARD. "Jeremiah O'Callaghan." *Dictionary of American Biography*, XIII (1934), 613-14.

QURESHI, ANWAR IQBAL. *Islam and the Theory of Interest.* With a Foreword by Professor Gyanchand. And an Introduction by Allama Syed Sulaiman Nadvi. Kashmiri Bazar, Lahore, 1946.

RABINOWITZ, JACOB J. "Some Remarks on the Evasions of the Usury Laws in the Middle Ages." *Harvard Theological Review*, XXXVII (1944), 49-59.

————, trans. See Maimonides, Moses.

RADIN, MAX. "A Juster Justice, A More Lawful Law." *Legal Essays in Tribute to Orrin Kip McMurray.* Edited by Max Radin and A. M. Kidd. Berkeley, 1935, 537-64.

RALEIGH, SIR WALTER. *Works political, commercial, and philosophical; together with his letters and poems.* 2 vols., London, 1751.

————. *Instructions to His Son, and to Posterity.* In *Works*, II.

RANKE, LEOPOLD VON. *Deutsche Geschichte im Zeitalter der Reformation.* 7th edition, 6 vols. in 3, Leipzig, 1894.

RASCH, WOLFDIETRICH. *Freundschaftskult und Freundschaftsdichtung im deutschen Schrifttum des 18. Jahrhunderts: Vom Ausgang der Barock bis zu Klopstock.* Halle, 1936. Deutsche Vierteljahrschrift für Literaturwissenschaft und Geistesgeschichte, hgb. von Paul Kluckhohn und Erich Rothacker, XXI.

RASCHEN, J. F. L. "Earlier and Later Versions of the Friendship Theme. I: 'Damon and Pythias.'" *Modern Philology*, XVII (1919-1920), 105-9.

BIBLIOGRAPHY

————. "The Hostage: An Arabian Parallel to Schiller's Ballad 'Die Bürgschaft.'" *Modern Philology*, XVII (1919-1920), 351-60.

RASHI. See *Pentateuch with Targum Onkelos*. . . .

RAUSCHENBUSCH, WALTER. "The Zurich Anabaptists and Thomas Münzer." *American Journal of Theology*, IX (1905), 91-106.

RAYMOND OF PENNAFORTE, ST. *Summa [casuum]*. . . . Verona, 1744.

REA, JOHN D. "Shylock and the Processus Belial." *Philological Quarterly*, VIII (1929), 311-13.

Realencyklopädie für protestantische Theologie und Kirche. Begründet von J. J. Herzog. 3rd enlarged edition, under the direction of A. Hauck, 24 vols., Leipzig, 1896-1913.

REIDER, JOSEPH, trans. *The Holy Scriptures: Deuteronomy with Commentary*. Philadelphia, 1937.

Repertorium biblicum, seu totius Sacrae Scripturae concordantiae. See Bechis, Michael.

REYMANN, HEINZ. *Glaube und Wirtschaft bei Luther*. Gütersloh, 1934.

RHEGIUS, URBANUS. *Von Leibeigenschaft oder Knechtheit, wie sich Herren und Eigenleute christlich halten sollen, Bericht aus göttlichen Rechten*. Augsburg, 1525. Rostock, 1530.

RICHARDS, RICHARD DAVID. *The Early History of Banking*. London, 1929.

RIGG, J. M., ed. and trans. *Select Pleas, Starrs, and Other Records from the Rolls of the Exchequer of the Jews, A.D. 1220-1284*. London, 1902. Publications of the Selden Society, Vol. XV.

RIGORD OF SAINT-DENIS. *Gesta Philippi Augusti*. Edited by H. F. Delaborde in *Oeuvres de Rigord et de Guillaume Le Breton, historiens de Philippe-Auguste*. 2 vols., Paris, 1882-1885. Société de l'histoire de France, Vols. CCX, CCXXIV.

*ROBERTSON, HECTOR M. *Aspects of the Rise of Economic Individualism: A Criticism of Max Weber and His School*. Cambridge, 1933.

ROCKINGER, L. *Briefsteller und Formelbücher des elften bis vierzehnten Jahrhunderts*. 2 pts., Munich, 1863-1864. Quellen und Erörterungen zur bayerischen und deutschen Geschichte, IX.

ROCKWELL, WILLIAM WALKER. *Die Doppelehe des Landgrafen Philipp von Hessen*. Marburg, 1904. (Dritter Teil: "Zur

[207]

Beurteilung der Polygamie im Reformationszeitalter," 202-309.)

ROLANDUS BANDINELLI (Pope Alexander III). *Die Summa magistri Rolandi, nachmals papstes Alexander III, nebst einem Anhange. Incerti auctoris quaestiones.* Edited by Dr. Friedrich Thaner. Innsbruck, 1874.

ROSCHER, WILHELM. *Geschichte der National-Ökonomik in Deutschland.* Munich, 1874. Geschichte der Wissenschaften in Deutschland, Neuere Zeit, Band XIV.

ROTH, CECIL. "The Medieval Conception of the Jew: A New Interpretation." *Essays and Studies in Memory of Linda R. Miller,* 171-90.

ROTHMANN, BERNHARD. *Restitution rechter und gesunder christlicher Lehre: Eine Wiedertäuferschrift ... (Münster, 1534).* Halle, 1888. Neudrucke deutscher Litteraturwerke, no. 77-78.

———. *Zwei Schriften des münsterschen Wiedertäufers Bernhard Rothmann.* Edited by H. Detmer and R. Krumbholtz. Dortmund, 1904.

RUBOW, AXEL. *Renteforhold i Danmark. I Tidsrummet fra Reformationen til Chr. V's Danske Lov.* Copenhagen and Kristiania (Oslo), 1914.

RUFINUS. *Summa decretorum.* Edited by H. Singer, Paderborn, 1902. Edited by J. F. von Schulte, Giessen, 1892.

SAINT-ÉVREMOND. *Oeuvres mêlées.* Edited by Ch. Giraud. 3 vols., Paris, 1865.

SALTER, F. R. "The Jews in Fifteenth Century Florence and Savonarola's Establishment of a Mons Pietatis." *Cambridge Historical Journal,* V (1936), 193-211.

SALVIOLI, GIUSEPPE. *Le capitalisme dans le monde antique: études sur l'histoire de l'économie romaine.* Translated from the Italian by A. Bonnet. Paris, 1906. Bibliothèque internationale d'économie politique, Vol. XXXI.

SANDERS, NICHOLAS. *A Briefe Treatise of Usurie.* Louvain, 1568.

*SAPORI, ARMANDO. *Studi di storia economica medievale.* 2nd edition, Florence, 1947. Biblioteca storica sansoni, nuova serie, V.

Saunderson v. Warner, 2 Rolle, 239. In *English Reports,* Vol. LXXXII: *King's Bench Division,* X, 772-73. Cited in J. B. Kelly, *A Summary of the History and Law of Usury,* p. 7.

SAUMAISE, CLAUDE DE. *De modo usurarum liber.* Leyden, 1639.
———. *De usuris liber.* Leyden, 1638.
———. *Dissertatio de foenore trapezitico, in tres libros divisa.* Leyden, 1640.
SAVIGNY, FRIEDRICH CARL VON. *Geschichte des römischen Rechts im Mittelalter.* 2nd edition, 7 vols., Berlin, 1834-1851.
*SAYOUS, ANDRÉ-E. "Le capitalisme commercial et financier dans les pays chrétiens de la Méditerranée occidentale, depuis la première croisade jusqu'à la fin du moyen âge." *Vierteljahrschrift für Sozial- und Wirtschaftsgeschichte,* XXIX (1936), 270-95.
SCACCIA, SIGISMUNDUS. *Tractatus de commerciis et cambio.* Venice, 1650. First edition, Rome, 1619.
SCHAPIRO, JACOB SALWYN. *Social Reform and the Reformation.* New York, 1909.
*SCHAUB, FRANZ. *Der Kampf gegen den Zinswucher, ungerechten Preis und unlautern Handel im Mittelalter: Von Karl dem Grossen bis papst Alexander III. Ein moralhistorische Untersuchung.* Freiburg, 1905.
SCHELER, MAX. *Vom Umsturz der Werte.* 2nd edition, 2 vols., Leipzig, 1923.
———. *L'homme du ressentiment.* Paris, 1933.
SCHENKL, K. See Ambrose of Milan.
*SCHLATTER, RICHARD B. *The Social and Religious Ideas of Religious Leaders, 1660-1688.* London, 1940.
SCHMIDT, GUSTAV LEBRECHT. *Justus Menius, der Reformator Thüringens, nach archivalischen und andern gleichzeitigen Quellen.* 2 vols. in one, Gotha, 1867.
SCHMIDT, J. "Lambert, Franz." *Lexikon für Theologie und Kirche,* VI (1934), 352.
*SCHMOLLER, GUSTAV. "Zur Geschichte der national-ökonomischen Ansichten in Deutschland während der Reformations-Periode." *Zeitschrift für die gesamte Staatswissenschaft,* XVI (1860), 461-716.
SCHNEID, J. "Dr. Johann Eck und das kirchliche Zinsverbot." *Historisch-politische Blätter für das Catholische Deutschland,* hgb. von Edmund Jörg und Franz Binder, Vol. CVIII (Munich, 1891), 241-59, 321-35, 473-96, 570-89, 659-81, 789-810.
SCHOTTENLOHER, KARL. *Bibliographie zur deutschen Geschichte im Zeitalter der Glaubensspaltung, 1517-1585.* 26 pts. in 6 vols., Leipzig, 1933-1940. Im Auftrag der Kommission zur

Erforschung der Geschichte der Reformation und Gegen-
reformation.

*SCHREIBER, EDMUND. *Die volkswirtschaftlichen Anschauungen
der Scholastik seit Thomas v. Aquin.* Jena, 1913. Beiträge
zur Geschichte der Nationalökonomie, hgb. von Karl Diehl,
I.

SCHUBERT, HANS VON. *Der Kommunismus der Wiedertäufer in
Münster und seine Quellen.* Heidelberg, 1919. Sitzungs-
berichte der Heidelberger Akademie der Wissenschaften.
Philosophisch-historische Klasse, Jahrgang 19, Band X,
Abhandlung eleven.

SCHÜCKING, L. *Die Familie im Puritanismus; Studien über
Familie und Literatur in England im 16., 17. und 18. Jahrhundert.* Leipzig and Berlin, 1929.

SCHULTE, JOHANN FRIEDRICH VON. *Die Geschichte der Quellen
und Literatur des canonischen Rechts von Gratian bis auf die
Gegenwart.* 3 vols. in 4, Stuttgart, 1875-1880.

SCHULZ, FRITZ. *Principles of Roman Law.* Translated from a
text revised and enlarged by the author, by Marguerite
Wolff. Oxford, 1936.

SCHUYLER, ROBERT L. *Josiah Tucker: A Selection from his Economic and Political Writings.* New York, 1931.

SCOTT, WILLIAM ROBERT. *Francis Hutcheson—His Life, Teaching and Position in the History of Philosophy.* Cambridge,
1900.

SEHLING, EMIL. *Die evangelischen Kirchenordnungen des XVI.
Jahrhunderts.* 5 vols., Leipzig, 1902-1913.

SELBIE, J. A. "Foreigner." In Hastings, *Dictionary of the Bible,*
II (1899), 49-51.

SELDEN, JOHN. *Table Talk.* Edited by Samuel Harvey Reynolds.
Oxford, 1892. Newly edited for the Selden Society by . . .
Sir Frederick Pollock. London, 1927.

Seventeenth Century Essays from Bacon to Clarendon. Edited by
Jacob Zeitlin. New York, 1926.

SHAKESPEARE, WILLIAM. *A New Variorum Edition.* Edited by
H. H. Furness. 25 vols., Philadelphia, 1871-1944.

———. *The Merchant of Venice.* Vol. 7 of *A New Variorum
Edition.* 11th edition, Philadelphia, 1916. Edited by C. K.
Pooler. 4th edition, London, 1917. The Arden Series.

Shakespeare Jahrbuch. Herausgegeben im Auftrage der Deutschen Shakespeare-Gesellschaft. 76 vols., Berlin, Weimar,
Jena, Leipzig, 1865-1948.

Shakespeare's Hand in the Play of Sir Thomas More. Papers by

A. W. Pollard, W. W. Greg, E. M. Thompson, J. Dover Wilson and R. W. Chambers. Cambridge, 1923. In *Shakespeare Problems* by A. W. Pollard and J. Dover Wilson, Vol. II of 6 vols., 1920-1941.

SIDGWICK, HENRY. *Outlines of the History of Ethics for English Readers.* 5th edition, London, 1902.

SIDONIUS APOLLINARIS. *Letters.* Translated with introduction and notes by O. M. Dalton. 2 vols., Oxford, 1915.

SIEBENS, A.-R. *L'origine du code deutéronomique.* Paris, 1929.

SIEVEKING, HEINRICH. *Genueser Finanzwesen mit besonderer Berücksichtigung der Casa di S. Giorgio.* 2 vols. in one, Freiburg, Leipzig and Tübingen, 1898-1899.

Sifre on Numbers and Deuteronomy (Hebrew). Edited by Meir Friedmann. Vienna, 1864.

SILVAYN, ALEXANDER. *The Orator.* Translated by Lazarus Pyott. London, 1596.

SLATER, THOMAS, S.J. *Cases of Conscience for English-Speaking Countries.* 2 vols., New York and Cincinnati, 1911-1912.

———. "Liberalism and Usury." *Questions of Moral Theology.* New York, 1915, 78-98.

SMALLEY, BERYL. *The Study of the Bible in the Middle Ages.* Oxford, 1941.

———. "Gilbertus Universalis, Bishop of London (1128-34), and the Problem of the 'Glossa Ordinaria.'" *Recherches de théologie ancienne et médiévale,* VII (1935), 235-62; VIII (1936), 24-60.

SMITH, ADAM. *An Inquiry into the Nature and Causes of the Wealth of Nations.* 1st edition, 2 vols., London, 1776. Edited by Edwin Cannan. 2nd edition, London, 1920.

———. *Lectures on Justice, Police, Revenue and Arms.* Edited by E. Cannan. Oxford, 1896.

SMITH, CHARLES GEORGE. *Spenser's Theory of Friendship.* Baltimore, 1935.

SMITH, HENRY. *Works; including Sermons, Treatises, Prayers, and Poems.* With a life of the author by Thomas Fuller, B.D. 2 vols., Edinburgh, 1866-1867.

———. "The Examination of Usury: The First Sermon." In *Works,* I, 88-100.

SMITH, PRESERVED, ed. See *Luther's Correspondence.*

SMITH, WILLIAM ROBERTSON. *Lectures on the Religion of the Semites.* 1st edition, Edinburgh, 1889. 3rd edition, with introduction and additional notes by S. A. Cook, New York and London, 1927.

SMITS, F., ed. *Liber Levitici vulgatae editionis versione belgica.*
. . . 3 vols., Antwerp and Amsterdam, 1763-1767.
SOCINUS, FAUSTUS. *Opera omnia.* 2 vols., Irenopolis (Amsterdam), 1656.
SOMBART, WERNER. *The Jews and Modern Capitalism.* English translation with notes by M. Epstein. New York and London, 1913.
SOMMERLAD, THEO. "Martin Luther und der deutsche Sozialismus." *Thüringisch-Sächsische Zeitschrift für Geschichte und Kunst,* XXII (Halle, 1933), 1-38.
SOMMERVILLE, H. "Interest and Usury in a New Light." *Economic Journal,* XLI (1931), 646-49. See above under Keynes.
———. "Usury and Standstill." *Economic Journal,* XLII (1932), 318-23.
SORIERI, LOUIS. *Boccaccio's Story of Tito e Gisippo in European Literature.* New York, 1937.
SOTO, DOMINICUS. *De iustitia et iure libri decem.* Venice, 1568, 1584, 1608. Medina del Campo, 1580.
SOUTER, ALEXANDER. *A Study of Ambrosiaster.* Cambridge, England, 1905. Texts and Studies contributed to Biblical and Patristic Literature, edited by J. Armitage Robinson, Vol. VII, no. 4.
SPENER, PHILIPP JAKOB. *Theologische Bedencken.* 4 vols., Halle, 1712-1715.
STÄHELIN, R. *Huldreich Zwingli: Sein Leben und Wirken.* 2 vols., Basel, 1895-1897.
*STARR, JOSHUA and B. N. NELSON. "The Legend of the Divine Surety and the Jewish Moneylender." *Annuaire de l'Institut de philologie et d'histoire orientales et slaves,* VII (1939-1944), 289-338.
Starrs and Jewish Charters Preserved in the British Museum, with Illustrative Documents, Translations and Notes. Edited by Israel Abrahams and H. P. Stokes with Additions by Herbert Loewe. 3 vols., Cambridge, 1930-1932.
STEUART, SIR JAMES. *Works, Political, Metaphysical, and Chronological.* Collected by General Sir James Steuart, Bart., his son, from his father's corrected copies. 6 vols., London, 1805.
STEUER, GÜNTHER. *Studien über die theoretischen Grundlagen der Zinslehre bei Thomas v. Aquin.* Stuttgart, 1936.
STILLINGFLEET, BISHOP EDWARD. *A Letter to a Deist, in answer to several objections against the Truth and Authority of the Scriptures.* London, 1677.
STILLWELL, MARGARET B. *Incunabula in American Libraries: A*

Second Census of Fifteenth-Century Books Owned in the United States, Mexico and Canada. New York, 1940.

STINTZING, R. *Geschichte der populären Literatur des römisch-kanonischen Rechts in Deutschland am Ende des fünfzehnten und im Anfang des sechszehnten Jahrhunderts.* Leipzig, 1867.

STOBBE, OTTO. *Die Juden in Deutschland während des Mittelalters, in politischer, socialer und rechtlicher Beziehung.* 3rd edition, Berlin, 1923.

STOLZE, WILHELM. *Bauernkrieg und Reformation.* Leipzig, 1926. Schriften des Vereins für Reformationsgeschichte, no. 141.

STONEX, A. B. "Money Lending and Money Lenders in England during the 16th and 17th Centuries." *Schelling Anniversary Papers by his former students* (New York, 1923), 263-85.

———. "The Usurer in Elizabethan Drama." *PMLA*, XXXI (1916), 190-210.

STRABO, WALAFRID. See *Glossa ordinaria.*

STRAUSS, JAKOB. *Das Wucher zu nemen und geben unserm christlichem Glauben und bruederlicher Lieb als zu ewiger Verdamnyss reichent entgegen ist, unuberwintlich Leer, und Geschrifft.* 1st ed., Eisenach, 1524. Not available to me.

———. *Hauptstücke und Artikel christlicher Lehre wider den unchristlichen Wucher, darum etliche Pfaffen zu sogar unruhig und bemüht sind* (1523). Edited in G. T. Strobel, *Miscellaneen,* III.1.

———. See Barge, Hermann.

STRIEDER, JAKOB. *Jacob Fugger the Rich Merchant and Banker of Augsburg, 1459-1525.* Translated by M. L. Hartsough and edited by N. S. B. Gras. New York, 1931.

———. *Studien zur Geschichte Kapitalistischer Organisationsformen: Monopole, Kartelle und Aktiengesellschaften im Mittelalter und zu Beginn der Neuzeit.* 2nd enlarged edition, Munich and Leipzig, 1925.

———. *Zur Genesis des modernen Kapitalismus: Forschungen zur Entstehung der grossen bürgerlichen Kapitalvermögen am Ausgange des Mittelalters und zu Beginn der Neuzeit, zunächst in Augsburg.* 2nd enlarged edition, by Dr. Franz Karaise von Karais. Munich, 1935.

STROBEL, GEORG THEODOR. *Miscellaneen literarischen Innhalts: gröstenteils aus ungedruckten Quellen.* 6 vols. in 2, Nuremberg, 1778-1782.

SUMMENHART, CONRADUS. *Opus septipartitum de contractibus.* Hagenau, Henricus Gran, 1500.

SUTCLIFFE, D. "The Financial Condition of the See of Canterbury, 1279-1292." *Speculum*, X (1935), 53-68.

TAEUBER, WALTER. *Molinaeus' Geldschuldlehre*. Jena, 1928.

TANNENBAUM, SAMUEL A. *Shakspere's "The Merchant of Venice": A Concise Bibliography*. New York, 1941. Elizabethan Bibliographies, no. 17.

TARN, WILLIAM WOODTHORPE. *Alexander the Great and the Unity of Mankind*. London, 1935. Also in *Proceedings of the British Academy* (1935), 123-66. The Raleigh Lecture on History.

TAWNEY, JEANNETTE. See Baxter, Richard.

*TAWNEY, R. H. *Religion and the Rise of Capitalism. A Historical Study*. New York and London, 1926. Reprinted by Penguin Books, Inc., New York, 1947. Contains the 1937 preface.

*————. "Studies in Bibliography: II. Modern Capitalism." *Economic History Review*, IV (1933), 336-56.

———— and E. POWER, eds. *Tudor Economic Documents, being Select Documents illustrating the Economic and Social History of Tudor England*. 3 vols., London, 1924. *University of London Historical Series*, no. 4.

————. See Wilson, Thomas.

————. Foreword to Talcott Parsons' translation of Max Weber, *The Protestant Ethic and the Spirit of Capitalism*. London, 1930.

TAYLOR, JEREMY, D.D. *Whole Works*. 3 vols., London, 1836.

TAYLOR, OVERTON H. "Tawney's *Religion and Capitalism* and Eighteenth-Century Liberalism." *Quarterly Journal of Economics*, XLI (1927), 718-31.

THAER, EVA. *Die Freundschaft im deutschen Roman des 18. Jahrhunderts*. Hamburg, 1917.

THAMIN, RAYMOND. *Un problème moral dans l'antiquité; étude sur la casuistique stoïcienne*. Paris, 1884.

THOMAS AQUINAS, ST. *Opera omnia*. Edited by S. E. Fretté and Paul Maré. 34 vols., Paris, 1871-1880.

————. *Opera omnia*. 18 vols. in 20, Rome, 1570.

————. *De regimine Judaeorum ad ducissam Brabantiae*. In *Opera*, edition of 1570, XVII, f. 192v-193v; edition of Fretté and Maré, XXVII. For a more recent edition, see now: *De regimine principum et de regimine Judaeorum: Politica opuscula duo*. 2nd edition revised, by Joseph Mathis. Turin and Rome, Marietti, 1948.

————. *Summa theologica*. Literally translated by the Fathers of the English Dominican Province. 22 vols., London, 1916-1938. 2nd revised edition, Vols. I-IV, VI-VIII, X, XV-XVI, XVIII. London, 1920-1929.

THOMAS DE VIO (Cajetan). *Opuscula omnia*. 3 vols. in one, Venice, 1588.

————. *Scripta philosophica: Opuscula oeconomico-socialia*. Edited by P. Zammit. Rome, 1934.

————. *De monte pietatis* (1498). In: *Opuscula omnia*, II, 154-62; *Scripta philosophica*, ed. P. Zammit, 41-89; *Tr. univ. juris*, VI.1 (1584), 419r-23v.

THOMPSON, J. M., ed. and trans. *Napoleon Self-Revealed in Three Hundred Selected Letters*. Boston and New York, 1934.

TÖNNIES, FERDINAND. *Fundamental Concepts of Sociology (Gemeinschaft und Gesellschaft)*. Translated and supplemented by Charles P. Loomis. New York, 1940.

TOWERSON, GABRIEL. *An Explication of the Decalogue Or Ten Commandments, With Reference to the Catechism of the Church of England; To which are premised by way of Introduction Several General Discourses concerning God's both Natural and Positive Laws*. London, 1676.

TRACHTENBURG, JOSHUA. *The Devil and the Jews: The Medieval Conception of the Jew and its Relation to Modern Antisemitism*. New Haven, 1943.

Tractatus de usuris triplex, trium clarissimorum iureconsultorum. Frankfurt, 1598. [I]: Petrus Gregorius. [II]: Alfonso Villagut. [III]: Laelius Zecchi.

Tractatus universi juris, duce, et auspice Gregorio XIII Pontifice Maximo in unum congesti: additis quamplurimis antea nunquam editis. . . . 18 vols. in 25, Venice, 1584-1586. *Index tractatus*, Vols. XIX-XXII, Venice, 1584-1586. Individual volumes have title-pages reading: *Tractatus illustrium in utraque tum pontificii, tum caesarei iuris facultate iurisconsultorum*.

TRAVER, HOPE. *The Four Daughters of God: A Study of the Versions of this Allegory with especial Reference to those in Latin, French and English*. Philadelphia and Bryn Mawr, 1907. Bryn Mawr College Monographs, Monograph Series, Vol. VI, 1907.

————. "The Four Daughters of God: A Mirror of Changing Doctrine." *PMLA*, XL (1925), 44-92.

TRETIAK, ANDREW. *"The Merchant of Venice* and the 'Alien' Question." *Review of English Studies*, v (1929), 402-9.

*TROELTSCH, ERNST. *The Social Teachings of the Christian Churches.* Translated by O. Wyon. 2 vols., New York, 1931. Reprinted 1949. New York: The Macmillan Co.; Glencoe, Illinois: The Free Press.

————. *Vernunft und Offenbarung bei Johann Gerhard und Melanchthon.* Göttingen, 1891.

————. *Gesammelte Schriften.* 4 vols., Tübingen, 1922-1925.

TSCHERIKOWER, V. "Jewish Religious Influence in the Adler Papyri?" *Harvard Theological Review*, XXXV (1942), 25-35. See Heichelheim.

TUCKER, JOSIAH. *A Second Letter to a Friend Concerning Naturalizations.* London, 1753. See Schuyler, R. L.

TURGOT, ANNE ROBERT JACQUES. *Oeuvres de Turgot et documents le concernant, avec biographie et notes.* Edited by Gustave Schelle. 5 vols., Paris, 1913-1923.

————. *Mémoire sur les prêts d'argent.* In *Oeuvres*, III, 154-202.

————. *Reflections on the Formation and Distribution of Wealth.* Translated from the French. London, 1793. In *A Select Collection of Scarce and Valuable Tracts*, edited by J. R. McCulloch, IV, 241-317.

UGOLINI, BARTHOLOMEUS. *Tractatus de usuris.* Venice, 1604.

UHL, ERNST. *Die Sozialethik Johann Gerhards.* Munich, 1932. Forschungen zur Geschichte und Lehre des Protestantismus, hgb. von Paul Althaus, Karl Barth und Karl Heim. Reihe 5, Band IV.

UHLHORN, GERHARD. *Urbanus Rhegius- Leben und ausgewählte Schriften.* Elberfeld, 1861. Leben und ausgewählte Schriften der Väter und Begründer der lutherischen Kirche, hgb. von J. Hartmann, Dr. Lehnerdt, Dr. C. Schmidt, *et al.*, VII.

VAN HOVE, PETRUS. See Hove, Petrus van.

VATTEL, E. DE. *Le droit des gens.* 3 vols., Washington, D.C., 1916. C.I.L., no. 4. Vol. III: A Translation of the Text, by Charles G. Fenwick.

VIDAL, JEAN. *Bullaire de l'Inquisition française au* XIVe *siècle et jusqu'à la fin du Grand Schisme.* Paris, 1913.

VILLAGUT, ALFONSO. *Tractatus de usuris.* Venice, 1589. Reprinted in *Tractatus . . . trium clarissimorum iureconsultorum.* Frankfurt, 1598.

VOGELSANG, ERICH. *Luthers Kampf gegen die Juden.* Tübingen, 1933. Sammlung gemeinverständlicher Vorträge und Schriften aus dem Gebiet der Theologie und Religionsgeschichte, 168.

VONTOBEL, KLARA. *Das Arbeitsethos des deutschen Protestantismus von der nachreformatorischen Zeit bis zur Aufklärung.* Berne, 1946. Beiträge zur Soziologie und Sozialphilosophie, hgb. von René König, 2.

WACE and BUCHHEIM, eds. See Martin Luther, *Luther's Primary Works.*

WADDING, LUKE. *Annales minorum seu trium ordinum a S. Francisco institutorum.* . . . Edited by J. M. Ribeiro da Fonseca *et al.* 25 vols., Rome, 1731-1886.

WALCH, JOHANN GEORG. *Historische und theologische Einleitung in die Religions-Streitigkeiten der evangelisch-lutherischen Kirchen von der Reformation an bis auf jetzige Zeiten.* 5 vols., Jena, 1733-1739.

WALDNER, FRANZ. "Dr. Jakob Strauss in Hall und seine Predigt vom grünen Donnerstag (17. April) 1522: Ein Beitrag zur Geschichte der Reformation in Tirol." *Zeitschrift des Ferdinandeums für Tirol und Vorarlberg,* ser. 3, XXVI (1882), 1-39.

WALTON, BRIAN, ed. See *Biblia sacra polyglotta.*

WAPPLER, PAUL. *Die Stellung Kursachsens und des Landgrafen Philipp von Hessen zur Täuferbewegung.* Münster, 1910. Reformationsgeschichtliche Studien und Texte, hgb. von Dr. Joseph Greving, Heft 13-14.

WARD, A. W. "Butzer, Martin." *DNB,* VI (1886), 172-77.

WATERS, W. G., ed. and trans. *The Italian Novelists Now First Translated into English.* 7 vols., London, 1901.

————. *The Pecorone of Ser Giovanni.* 3 vols., London, 1898. Privately printed for the Society of Bibliophiles. Appears as Vols. V-VII of *The Italian Novelists Now First Translated into English.*

WEBER, MARIANNE SCHNITGER. *Max Weber, ein Lebensbild.* Tübingen, 1926.

WEBER, MAURICE. *Les origines des monts-de-piété.* Rixheim, 1920.

WEBER, MAX. *Gesammelte Aufsätze zur Religionssoziologie.* 3 vols., Tübingen, 1922-1923.

————. *Gesammelte Aufsätze zur Sozial- und Wirtschaftsgeschichte.* Tübingen, 1924.

————. *Gesammelte Aufsätze zur Soziologie und Sozialpolitik.* Tübingen, 1924.

————. *Gesammelte Aufsätze zur Wissenschaftslehre*. Tübingen, 1922.

————. *Das antike Judentum*. In *Gesammelte Aufsätze zur Religionssoziologie*, III

*————. *Die protestantische Ethik und der Geist des Kapitalismus*. In *Gesammelte Aufsäzte zur Religionssoziologie*, I. Originally appeared in the *Archiv für Sozialwissenschaft und Sozialpolitik*, XX-XXI, 1904-1905. English translation by Talcott Parsons. *The Protestant Ethic and the Spirit of Capitalism*. London, 1930. With a Foreword by R. H. Tawney.

————. *From Max Weber: Essays in Sociology*. Translated and edited by Hans Gerth and C. Wright Mills. New York, 1946.

————. *General Economic History*. Translated by Frank H. Knight. New York and London [1927].

————. *Max Weber on the Methodology of the Social Sciences*. Translated and edited by Edward A. Shils and Henry A. Finch. Glencoe, Illinois, 1949. The Free Press.

————. *The Theory of Social and Economic Organization*. Translated by Talcott Parsons and A. M. Henderson. Editor: Talcott Parsons. New York, 1947.

WEINRICH, MAX. *Max Weber, l'homme et le savant: Études sur ses idées directrices*. Paris, 1938.

WELCH, ADAM C. *The Code of Deuteronomy: A New Theory of its Origin*. London, 1924.

————. *Deuteronomy: The Framework to the Code*. Oxford, 1932.

WENGER, BERTA V. "Shylocks Pfund Fleisch: Eine stoffgeschichtliche Untersuchung." *Sh.J.*, LXV (1929), 92-174.

WHITE, HELEN C. *Social Criticism in Popular Religious Literature of the Sixteenth Century*. New York, 1944.

WIBBELING, WILHELM. *Martin Luther und der Bauernkrieg; Eine urkundliche Darstellung*. Schlüchtern, 1925.

WIEDEMANN, THEODOR. *Dr. Johann Eck, Professor der Theologie an der Universität Ingolstadt*. Regensburg, 1865.

Wiedertäufer zu Münster 1534/35, Die. See Loeffler, Klemens.

WILCKEN, ULRICH. "Urkunden-Referat." *Archiv für Papyrusforschung*, XXX (1939), 218-47.

WILLIAM OF AUXERRE. *Summa aurea in quattuor libros sententiarum*. 1st edition, Paris, P. Pigouchet, 1500.

*WILSON, THOMAS. *A Discourse upon Usury*. Edited with an historical introduction by R. H. Tawney. London, 1925.

WINSTANLEY, GERRARD. *Works, with an Appendix Relating to the Digger Movement.* Edited with an introduction by George H. Sabine. Ithaca, New York, 1941.

―――. *Law of Freedome in a Platform, or True Magistracy Restored.* In *Works,* 501-14.

*WINTER, ERNST KARL. *Rudolph IV von Österreich.* 2 vols., Vienna, 1934-1936.

WINTHROP, JOHN. *The Humble Request of the Massachusetts Puritans* and *A Modell of Christian Charity, 1630.* Edited by S. E. Morison. Boston, 1916. Old South Leaflets, general series, Vol. IX, no. 207.

*WISKEMANN, HEINRICH. *Darstellung der in Deutschland zur Zeit der Reformation herrschenden nationalökonomischen Ansichten.* Leipzig, 1861.

WOLF, GUSTAV. *Quellenkunde der deutschen Reformationsgeschichte.* 3 vols., Stuttgart and Gotha, 1915-1923.

WOLF, LUCIEN. *Menasseh ben Israel's Mission to Oliver Cromwell.* London, 1901. "Jewish Historical Society of England."

WOLFF, CHRISTIAN VON. *Jus gentium methodo scientifica pertractatum.* 2 vols., Oxford and London, 1934. C.I.L., no. 13. Vol. II: A Translation of the Text, by Joseph H. Drake.

WOLFSON, HARRY AUSTRYN. *Philo: Foundations of Religious Philosophy in Judaism, Christianity, and Islam.* 2 vols., Cambridge, Mass., 1947.

WOLKAN, R. *Geschichtsbücher der hutterischen Brüder.* Vienna, 1923.

WOOLF, C. N. S. *Bartolus of Sassoferrato: His Position in the History of Medieval Political Thought.* Cambridge, 1913.

WRIGHT, CELESTE TURNER. "Some Conventions Regarding the Usurer in Elizabethan Literature." *Studies in Philology,* XXXI (1934), 176-97.

―――. "The Usurer's Sin in Elizabethan Literature." *Studies in Philology,* XXXV (1938), 178-94.

WRIGHT, HERBERT GLADSTONE, ed. *Early English Versions of the Tales of Guiscardo and Ghismonda and Titus and Gisippus from the Decameron.* London, 1937. E.E.T.S., original series, no. 205, 1937 (for 1936).

*WUNSCH, GEORG. *Evangelische Wirtschaftsethik.* Tübingen, 1927.

―――. "Calvins Beurteilung der Zinswirtschaft." *Die christliche Welt,* XXIX (1915), 687-89.

―――. "Luthers Beurteilung des Wuchers: Ein Beitrag zur

reformatorischen Ethik." *Die christliche Welt*, XXIX (1915), 26-31, 66-69, 86-91, 127-31.

YEHIEL NISSIM OF PISA. See Jehiel Nissim of Pisa.

ZABARELLA, CARDINAL FRANCISCUS. *Lectura super Clementinas*. Venice, 1579.

*ZECH, FRANZ XAVER, S.J. *Dissertationes tres, in quibus rigor moderatus doctrinae pontificiae circa usuras a sanctissimo D.N. Benedicto XIV per epistolam encyclicam episcopis Italiae traditus exhibetur*. Ingolstadt, 1747-1751. In H. Leotardus, *Liber singularis de usuris*: Appendix; Migne, *Theologiae cursus completus*, XVI, 765-996. Familiarly known and herein cited as *Rigor moderatus*.

*ZEHENTBAUER, FRANZ. *Das Zinsproblem nach Moral und Recht, geschichtlich behandelt unter besonderer Rücksicht auf c. 1543, Cod. jur. can.* Vienna, 1920. *Theologische Studien der Österr. Leo-Gesellschaft*, Heft 24.

ZEITLIN, SOLOMON. "Prosbol: A Study in Tannaitic Jurisprudence." *Jewish Quarterly Review*, XXXVII (1947), 341-62.

ZERBOLT OF ZUTPHEN, GERARD. See Gerard Zerbolt.

ZWINGLI, HULDREICH. *Sämtliche Werke*. Unter Mitwirkung des Zwingli-Vereins in Zürich, hgb. von E. Egli, G. Finsler, W. Köhler, *et al*. 11 vols., Berlin and Leipzig, 1905-1935. *CR*, Vols. LXXXVIII-XCVIII.

———. *Werke*. Edited by M. Schuler and J. Schulthess. 8 vols. in 7, Zurich, 1828-1842.

———. *Das Buch der Reformation Huldrych Zwinglis*. See Köhler, Walther.

———. *The Latin Works and the Correspondence . . . together with Selections from his German Works*. Edited by S. M. Jackson. 3 vols., New York, 1919-1929.

———. *Auslegen und Gründe der Schlussreden* (July 1523). *CR*, LXXXIX, 1-457.

———. *Von göttlicher und menschlicher Gerechtigkeit* (July 1523). *CR*, LXXXIX, 458-525.

———. *Wer Ursache gebe zu Aufruhr* (December 1524). *CR*, XC, 355-469. Introduction by W. Köhler, 355-68.

POSTSCRIPT AND ACKNOWLEDGMENTS

Many months have passed since the foregoing pages were written. Thanks to a characteristic act of indulgence on the part of the Director of the Princeton University Press, I have been afforded the luxury of this Postscript for the purpose of making a "final" reckoning of my accounts.

The tempest still rages over the theses of Weber and Tawney. Fresh evidence of this fact is found in each successive installment of authoritative scholarly reviews. The reader may wish to know where, ultimately, the present author stands on some of the issues under debate. To these questions he has no single answer. In general, it is his conviction that most current ways of formulating the questions pose equally extreme alternatives. These serve more as incitements to endless controversy than as guides to the productive pursuit of undisclosed facts.

This admission may help to clarify certain hitherto unexplained aspects of my procedure in recording the vicissitudes of Deuteronomy. It will be noticed that I have made little effort to discuss the vital problems of causal imputation. I could not even pause long enough to emphasize the changing contexts and functions of the doctrines of usury. These are only two matters of legitimate interest to specialists, about which I have maintained a studied reticence.

The future should doubtless offer occasion for the making of amends. In the meantime, it seems best to adopt the precedent of the two aforementioned masters. The following avowals and disclaimers should help avert misunderstanding as to my intentions:

I nowhere mean to suggest that I take the ideals of brotherhood as conceived among the Hebrews, the medieval Christians, or among our contemporaries to have been the "active forces" or "preponderant agents" in defining the path of economic and social development of our culture. To say this would be simple folly. It is merely being contended that these different versions of brotherhood did to some extent affect the course of the debate over usury. In any case, the converse of this proposition hardly seems open to doubt: The course of the debate over usury surely had a most significant bearing on the character of the ideal of brotherhood. A disinterested student will feel justified in making only this minimum claim.

If it may be permitted to speak after the fashion of Weber: The different notions of men about the ideal of brotherhood

have been one—only one—among a complex variety of inter-
active factors in the development of the modern world. These
factors, indeed, cannot even now be neatly disengaged one from
another. The different ways in which different cultures have
viewed the universe, used tools, educated the young, distributed
desired values—these and many other circumstances, natural and
cultural, have all contributed to influence the role which the ideal
of brotherhood has chanced to play in different times and places.

Ultimately, of course, it will be necessary to trace these inter-
connections, one by one, in order to arrive at a comprehensive
view of the sources, meanings, and roles of the ideal(s) of
brotherhood. Pending the completion of such special investiga-
tions, I leave it to those better versed than I in statistical veri-
fications of metaphysical issues to decide whether and in what
proportion an "initiative" in influencing the course of history
may be attributed to changes in the ideal of brotherhood.

The author has always felt the need to distinguish between the
history and the *genealogy* of ideas. After such avowals as those
offered in the preceding paragraphs, he will not presume to represent this monograph as a documentary *history* of the idea of
usury.

My debts to previous scholars are too considerable to be cata-
logued in this Postscript. Forthcoming publications may be
expected to supplement the meagre schedule of acknowledgments provided in the foregoing footnotes and Bibliography.
Here I restrict myself to naming those whose aid materially
hastened the appearance of the present volume. They include:
the library staffs of numerous institutions—Columbia University, Harvard University, and their respective Law Schools; the
Jewish and Union Theological Seminaries in New York City;
the New York Public Library; the University of Chicago; the
University of Minnesota—, especially Misses Anne McCabe and
Jean Macalister of Columbia University, and Mrs. H. M. Foster
of the Union Theological Seminary; Wilbur Daniels and Edward
Carterette, formerly my students and personal secretaries and
now good friends; Dr. Joshua Starr of New York City, Professors Austin P. Evans, Paul O. Kristeller, and John Herman Randall, Jr. (Columbia); Stephan Kuttner (Catholic University);
Boaz Cohen (Jewish Theological Seminary); Christian Mackauer and Henry A. Finch of the University of Chicago.

I can only hope that all of these will agree to accept this essay
in partial restitution for the courtesies they have extended me.

Professor Solomon F. Bloom of Brooklyn College spent many thankless hours in the reading of earlier drafts of this monograph. The measure of my gratitude to him is difficult to express in these pages.

I am thankful to the John Simon Guggenheim Memorial Foundation and to its Secretary General, Mr. Henry Allen Moe, for enabling me to quicken the pace of my researches into several related fields of inquiry. My obligation to the Foundation will not be fully discharged until I have completed some additional studies on the interplay of Conscience and Casuistry in the Christian West.

The Carnegie Endowment for International Peace of Washington, D. C., and the Oxford University Press of New York City have graciously allowed me to cite several lengthy extracts from the translations of Gentili and Pufendorf in their notable collection, *The Classics of International Law*.

I count it a great honor that the present volume appears in a series introduced to the public by two of the most distinguished representatives of European and American scholarship. The joint sponsors of this undertaking, the *Journal of the History of Ideas* and the Princeton University Press, have my heartfelt thanks. Throughout the long incubation of the present work, Professor Randall never once faltered in his encouragement to me. Miss Harriet Anderson of the Princeton University Press and Mr. Stuart MacClintock of New York City and a little company of devoted intimates, whose names I will ever cherish, eased my last labors with the proofs and index.

Mine alone is the responsibility for the errors and inadequacies which mar this work.

BENJAMIN NELSON

University of Minnesota
Minneapolis, Minnesota
September 26, 1949

ADDITIONS
1969

AFTER TWO DECADES:
NOTICE TO READERS

TIME and again during the two decades which have now elapsed since the first printing of this study, I have been asked the two following questions about myself and this book:

a) What made me set out to do the initial research on the vicissitudes of the Deuteronomic commandment on usury in the Christian West which is recorded in these pages?

b) What explains my apparent public silence about themes associated with *The Idea of Usury* for so many years since its appearance?

Up to this point, my answers have satisfied no one, not even my closest intimates, but I must repeat them nonetheless, for I have no other answers. Even as I do so now, however, I know full well that the only acceptable evidence in matters of this sort is documentary evidence—properly certified papers and the proofs validated by the additions to the original text now in the reader's hands.

I never knowingly planned to write this book at all. Actually the wholly unexpected responses to the Deuteronomic commandment on usury, especially on the part of Luther and Calvin, forced themselves on my attention at a most inopportune time while I was hastening to complete several more pressing projects—my doctoral dissertation, "The Restitution of Usury in Later Medieval Ecclesiastical Law," and some related studies on the backgrounds and meanings of *The Merchant of Venice*. To the surprise of scholars who were expecting the issue of the full text of my work on restitution, *The Idea of Usury,* or "The Brother and the Other"—as my friends and I fondly called it in our private references to the theme—saw the light first. A well-wishing mentor intent on having an episode from the saga of Deuteronomy in a newly projected series under his charge won the day. The two suspended projects have remained on the agenda to the present hour.

This admission may help to explain the marked contrast in the responses of readers and reviewers to the appearance of the first edition of this book, both the excessively warm welcome of some and the puzzlement of others. Some paragraphs are reserved in the New Acknowledgments for the details of these episodes.

As the years passed, unexpected turns of circumstance and apparent shifts in the public aspect of my interests seemed to be leading me ever farther from the technical problems connected with the medieval law of restitution. It is no wonder that a number of scholars, including some professional colleagues who saw me from time to time, supposed that I had put further research into religious traditions and economic ethic behind me. But that is not the way *I lived the story* and now report it.

The key to the puzzle appears plainly in a sentence I had not so innocently placed in the Acknowledgments of 1949, hinting that I already felt committed to going forward to explore the links of my theme to larger frames of spiritual regulation, frames I was soon to be describing as a triangulated system of institutions and ideas associated with *conscience* in its multiple senses, casuistry, and the cure of souls. All appearances notwithstanding, and whether or not the connecting threads are always seen by readers, this concern with what I shall be calling the "moralities and logics of thought and action" has been at the center of all my work and writing since my earliest days as a graduate student.

My decision to make the move just described did not arise, therefore, from a desire to run away from hard-headed economic history in order to find shelter in the cloistered walks of scholastics. Indeed—at least so I thought *and still think*— I was facing more directly than ever before into the winds of circumstance and the conflicts of wills, the sort of atmosphere which had drawn me to the study of usury in the first place.

The act of writing *The Idea of Usury* only served as a renewed reminder of the urgency of the issues of conscience and casuistry for future progress in the history of ideas and the sociology of cultural experience.

In other words, even before the appearance in 1949 of the first edition of the present work, I was already hard at work trying to see my own volume against even wider backgrounds than the problems illustrated by the passage from Hebraic particularism to Christian universalism. I was searching especially for a way of going below the surface of the meanings of the transition from the notions of medieval images of "Universal Brotherhood" to later versions of "Universal Otherhood," promised in the Reformation exegesis of the Deuteronomic commandment.

I had to find a better way of explaining to others my reasons for stressing the unprecedented novelty of the discussion of Luther and Calvin, the Deuteronomic commandment of usury, brotherhood, the Mosaic Law, and the new views of friendship, equity, utility, and so on. This all became possible when, in the course of seeking to plumb the depths of the notion of conscience, I stumbled upon the idea of the *rationales of conscience*. Now I could say why I had stated the case about Luther and Calvin as I did. It was not because I wanted to show either that the two Reformers and their immediate followers were themselves inclined to Mammonism or even, for that matter, that they celebrated the industrious practice of *economic* virtues for the sake of heaping up treasures on earth "where moth and rust doth corrupt." I knew that this was not the truth.

What I had felt necessary to stress, however, was that their ways of relating to the critical issues posed by the Deuteronomic commandment had a vast effect in preparing the way for decisive changes in the axial assumptions and rationales which had governed the minds of Western Christians through the course of more than a millenium.

Having turned full circle, I was back at my original point of departure. Except that now there was something new in the picture. I had long known there was no writing the history of economic development in the West or anywhere else without taking note of what are called "values," "norms," and related ideas. But with the passing of the years the issue had become more strongly delineated. Now it had become unthinkable to write the history of belief and behavior in Christian Europe with respect to the restitution of usury or, indeed, to any other *matter of conscience* without relating to the organized *rationales* of conscience; the codified *casuistries* for accommodating established principles and perplexing circumstance; and the organized *systems* of spiritual direction and *cure of souls.*

The seemingly insoluble confusions over the meanings, origins, and civilization of the "Protestant Ethic" and "the spirit of capitalism" resulted from the disinclination of many superlatively trained historians to admit the contrasts between *expedient concessions* and the formations of a *new conscience.* There was no way of overcoming this reluctance without proving the importance of the mind's machinery, the *symbolic technologies,* the maps of knowledge, the cultural logics, and so on.

The *makings* of cultures, I was now thinking, were the *makings* of minds working with *mechanisms of conscience* in its multiple senses—its formalized canons, arguments, justifications, criteria, and reasons.

Societies with overarching sets of principles had to plod their way to innovations through the devices of a casuistry. *Conscience* was aways confronted by conflicting alternatives; always worked in the here-and-now to decide cases; always needed to establish evidential criteria by which claims and norms might be validated in act as well as thought; always struggled to explore and "orchestrate" rationales for proposed views of the world.

When I sat down to sum up my experience as a historian and sociologist, I was forced to conclude that everywhere I went I had continued to encounter massive reliance on *matrices of decision:* first the *casuistries of contract of the Roman and canon lawyers;* then the new decision-matrices of the medieval theologians of *conscience* and opinion; and, latterly, the aftermath of the assaults on these and related formalisms in the new paradigms of our own time—our new directive programs, our new ways of making our livings, and our new designs for living—and dying.

Was there no escaping Weber? Here I was, once again marching along his road. And once again I found myself going as far in his direction as the evidence allowed. In this latest instance, the extremity of his stress on the raging fevers of what has come to be called the "functional" rationalization of conduct seemed to obscure critical aspects of the growing powers and pervasiveness, in our age, of automation. Fuller details on the phases of my effort to put all the pieces of these puzzles into some plausible relation with my own research on usury are reserved for the New Postscript.

NEW POSTSCRIPT

THIS New Postscript should help to answer some of the questions left unanswered in the immediately preceding statement. Mainly, however, the present Postscript continues the story and further illustrates the argument begun above in the Preface to this new edition.

For evident reasons further notice will need to be given to changes in attitudes of historians and sociologists to the work of Max Weber.

In hardly more than a year we shall be a half-century removed from Weber's death in 1920 and sixty-five years removed from the appearance of his epochal study, *The Protestant Ethic and the Spirit of Capitalism*. Since those days much has been learned—and *even more has happened*.

Elsewhere in this volume, notably in section 11 of the New References, I list my recent efforts to contribute to the ongoing discussions. The very titles of the papers mentioned should show that, in my view, Weber's celebrated work presents an exceptionally wide variety of challenges at the present juncture, carrying us far beyond most current readings. I shall hardly do more than suggest the surfaces of some of these matters here, in the hope that interested readers will look into the papers when they appear.

A comparable reticence applies within the more limited confines of the questions posed in this volume. Over the past two decades we have been favored with a vast outpouring of new work and argument on aspects of the problem of usury and "the spirit of capitalism." As the infrequent annotations in the selected New References suggest, I regard some of the new research very highly, but I will not presume to speak to all the findings they report and the issues they pose at this time. I shall mainly touch upon selected themes which are embraced by the following rubrics:

A) Inherited Stereotypes on Usury and Restitution

B) Weber and Some Current Historians
C) Some Extensions of Weber Proposed by the Author
D) "Counter-Reformation" Catholicism *v.* Weber?
E) A Proposed Moratorium and Weber's Present Relevance
F) A Look Back—A Look Ahead

A. *Inherited Stereotypes on Usury and Restitution*

IF FORTUNE favors, I hope soon to be able to issue some additional installments of my research into the laws and practice of restitution of usury and ill-gotten gains. A need for such studies remains despite the years which have elapsed since the appearance of the first edition of this book. It is a pleasure, however, to be able to report that in the interim a number of valuable contributions to this field have been made by sympathetic economic historians. Particular attention is called to papers by Raymond de Roover and Florence Edler de Roover, which are cited in section 8 of the New References.

Part of the reason for the slowness of the advance in this field has been continuing reluctance of unduly present-minded historians to abandon inherited stereotypes concerning the motives, beliefs, and behavior of the varied sorts of men and institutions of the pre-Reformation era. The difficulties I have continued to experience with these approaches may already be known to some readers through reviews I have written.

Skeptics notwithstanding, I have no recourse but to insist on the following:

1) The ecclesiastical laws of usury did mean what they plainly declared.

2) The medieval canonists and theologians were not deliberately or unconsciously involved in self-contradiction when they forbade usury (pure interest) in a loan (*mutuum*), while allowing (*a*) interest (*interesse*), damages (*damna*), and expenses (*expensas*) in all contracts; (*b*) fair division of profits

[233]

in legitimate contracts of *partnerships* when the risks were shared. Their rationales for these notions were clearly and consistently expressed and, indeed, are largely derived from Roman law.

3) These so-called "exceptions" and often misnamed "extrinsic" titles were not invented by astute theologians and jurists for the purpose of evading the rules against usury in loans.

4) It proves not to be true that corrupt clerics, cynical judges, and level-headed princes more often than not flagrantly or secretly connived to render the ecclesiastical law of restitution irrelevant in the marketplace, the courts, and the lives of businessmen.

None of these stereotypes will be found to stand up under close scrutiny.

The same strictures apply to other often widely circulated claims, such as those listed below. It is not the case that:

1) Medieval theologians taught or intended to teach that *usura* was forbidden only on loans made for the purposes of production, not those made for the purposes of consumption.

2) Interest (*usura*) was forbidden only in transactions involving "consumptibles" and not "fungibles." (This distinction gained wide circulation through a discussion by W. J. Ashley.)

3) The foundations of what was left of the laws of usury in the fourteenth century were sapped by several French theologians of that era—principally Durandus de Sancto Porciano and Franciscus de Mayronis—and by several celebrated theologians of *quattrocento* Italy—notably St. Bernardino of Siena and St. Antonino of Florence.

4) The rules requiring restitution of usury and ill-gotten gains were never, or rarely, executed.

5) The Church meant its rulings against "manifest" usurers to apply only to the "small fry" who traded on the ignorance and need of the peasant and artisan, and not to the international financiers who did business with kings and popes.

6) The Jews were exempted by the canonists from the laws against usury and usurers.

7) The Church enacted these rules with two main purposes: to browbeat enterprisers and to entice money into its coffers.

8) The "spirit of capitalism" long predates the Reformation. Indeed a developed "market mentality" was a hallmark of the teachings on contracts and other economic issues of the medieval canonists and theologians and is operative in the transactions of the urban environment of the medieval era.

9) By the time of the Renaissance, great enterprisers had all the bracing they needed for vigorous and systematic capitalistic accumulation in the congenial writings of Leon Battista Alberti and Niccolò Machiavelli. Nor were they the only Italian moralists to evolve ethical systems which were fully congruent with the "spirit of capitalism."

10) Everywhere in Europe the leading enterprisers and the most substantial members of the "middle classes" were active proponents and partisans of religious dissent. Some even gave support to heresy and heretics. Above all, they were intent on abolishing all restraints upon the freedom of enterprise.

We shall never recapture the lives lived by our ancestors if we insist upon measuring the vitalities of the past by "common-sense" yardsticks which issue in such deceptive results as those just presented.

Weber did not commit any of these errors, primarily for two reasons:

1) A student of the masterly Levin Goldschmidt, the author of *Universalgeschichte des Handelsrechts,* Weber had done his own doctoral dissertation on the commercial laws of the South European trading companies in the Middle Ages.

2) Weber had a deep insight into the institutions and ideas associated with the workings of the forum of conscience which characterized Catholic cultures. He knew also that every overarching "principial" system of spiritual regulation had to work its way to change through the elaborations of a casuistry.

B. *Weber and Some Current Historians*

IT IS hardly possible to exaggerate the excellence of the research in economic history by which we have been favored during the past two decades. Now we have not only Sapori, Luzzatto, Georges Espinas, Roberto Cessi, and Yves Renouard; we have Bergier, Braudel, the de Roovers, J. Heers, Lapeyre, Le Goff, Mandich, Mollat, Poliakov, and others, some of whose names regrettably go without mention in the selected New References which follow this Postscript.

It needs to be admitted that in one respect we have made less progress than is supposed. Even our alert newer historians have yet to come to grips with the subtly inflected propositions of Max Weber. Among the recent historians, Professor Trevor-Roper and Herbert Luethy stand out for the verve with which they present their cases against Weber.

The latest criticisms of Weber on "historical grounds" are often more subtly rendered than are those of the older critics, F. Rachfahl, F. Keller, W. Sombart, L. Brentano, and others, but they are not better grounded in comparative analysis, documentary detail, or social scientific theory. The continuing attacks do, however, indicate the need for a fresh review of the purposes, claims, method, and outcomes of *The Protestant Ethic*.

The case for Weber has rarely been stated clearly. Indeed, his views continue to be badly misrepresented: Weber never argued a "functional equation" between Calvinism and capitalism; was not primarily interested in tracing the "development of the modern *market* and a *competitive economy* in northwest Europe"; did not intend to denigrate "capitalism" to the advantage of any other economic or political arrangement such as socialism and anarchism. He tells us again and again that his *Protestant Ethic* was intended, above all, as an effort to inquire into the ways in which several ill-understood but crucial changes in the theological orientations of Luther and Calvin appear to have affected the patterning of the economic ethics of the Protestant churches and homes and, thereby, cooperated in promoting—largely as unanticipated consequences!—the full crystallization, predominance, and worldwide spread of the industrial-enterprise organization and its associated outlooks.

Many of Weber's fundamental discoveries and insights have been missed or minimized by his critics:

1) Weber had a deep insight, which grew ever stronger as the years passed, into the central importance of the conflict between "Universalism" and "particularism" posed by the Deuteronomic commandment on usury and its odyssey in the Christian West. This is a distinction which continues to be profoundly explored by Talcott Parsons.

2) The more Weber concentrated on the spread of the spirit of *rationalization,* the more attention he paid to the overcoming of invidious dualisms. He sensed that the spread of universalism had both its positive and negative features, as did the original commandment itself. The overcoming of the Deuteronomic dualism was of utmost importance: it was a dualism no less important—indeed, probably more important —than the dualisms to which Weber gave a large part of his life.

3) Weber was profoundly aware of the ways in which the dualistic medieval Christian attitudes to the attainment of the "status of perfection" inhibited the progress of *this worldly asceticism* and reinforced the complex and distinctively Catholic orchestration, still so fateful for Catholic cultures throughout the world, of the ideas and institutions associated with the workings of conscience, casuistry and cure of souls.

4) Weber insisted that the rationalization of conduct in the Protestant culture areas had profoundly religious and moral foundations as well as extremely impressive positive features no less remarkable than its negative features.

5) Weber understood the contrast between the styles of life of medieval and Renaissance merchant-princes—the Acciaiuoli, the Medici, the Fugger—and the systematic and sanc-

tified pursuit of one's calling encouraged by Protestantism, which gave so notable an impulse to the *rational, disciplined, tempered* pursuit of gain.

6) Weber understood the contrast between the accommodations allowable through a traditional casuistry and the positive religious rewards reinforced by ringing affirmations of a new conscience.

7) He emphasized the crucial importance of the Protestant emphasis on *impersonal service on behalf of an impersonal goal,* notably the selfless ministry in the interest of God's mastery of the world by contrast to the *personal* (or, as we would say today, "existential") imitation of Christ's love, friendship, and suffering for mankind in every act oriented to any other person or object.

8) Weber intended to focus on the incentive given by the new discipline to the methodical and conscientious organization of *consecrated action—collective as well as individual—in accordance with universalistic norms of performance.*

In this light, it is hard to accept the continuing criticisms of Weber which have been put forward recently by Kurt Samuelsson and Herbert Luethy. Some comments on the latter's views are reserved for section C below. I shall not repeat here what I have elsewhere written on the works of J. T. Noonan and K. Samuelsson.

One cannot too often insist that casuistic or political concessions are not to be confused with a new conscience. Evidence that the ecclesiastical rules were recurrently violated in municipal ordinances does not suffice as proof of the irrelevance of the Canon Law of usury or restitution.

Weber is not wholly free of blame for the many misinterpretations of his works. The argument and structure both of his *Protestant Ethic* and his later writings in economic ethics of the world religions have not been easy for historians or, for that matter, sociologists to follow. Nor has their task been made less complex by Weber's habit of probing sociocultural realities from different points of view at different times. The reponses of American social scientists and humanists to Weber's theory present an exceedingly complicated picture. There have been very few historians who have felt equally at home in or have cared to work in the different theaters of action upon which Weber touches. Professors Edmund Morgan and Bernard Bailyn are outstanding current exceptions. More frequently, historians have chosen to remain ensconced in their corners, from which they regard Weber as eccentric or irrelevant to their interests. Those who have not been alienated by his posing of the questions seem to prefer to limit themselves to rather strictly defined behavioristic perspectives in the economic and political spheres.

Professor Parsons and his students represent an entirely different outlook. With Weber's help they have moved forward to promote a sort of revolution in the field of comparative analysis. The writings of these scholars have been distinguished by their readiness to grapple with basic theoretical questions and by their unusual appreciation of cultural dimensions which are bracketed by "fact-minded" historians. Not all American sociologists share these interests or outlooks. Some of them—including a few strongly influenced by Parsons—appear to be moving closer to the political-economic behaviorism ascribed above to many historians.

C. *Some Extensions of Weber Proposed by the Author*

ONE DAY, as I was pondering both Weber's attitudes to the linked problems of usury, conscience, and my attitude to Weber, I saw all the issues in a fresh light. Given Weber's overriding interest in uncovering the "spiritual roots of the vocational asceticism of Occidental rationalism," and given his commitment to the conduct of "thought experiments" by the "ideal-type" method, Weber was correct, *from his point of view,* to stress the decisive importance of the notion of *innerweltliche Askese.* He was, above all, interested in exploring the factors which promoted or retarded the development of the modern rationalized organization of labor and conduct in the bureaucratic enterprise order of modern Western society.

My emphasis was bound to be different, I now realized. I had started with a need to press forward to explore the *rationales* proposed by the contending groups locked in struggles over a whole series of theological, social, economic, and other issues. I sought to understand how the norms governing the settlement of disputed questions in all spheres came to be decided; how the bases for political obligation were reared. The more intensively I searched the documentary remains for answers to questions of this nature, the more I appreciated the central position traditionally given to *conscience* by older historians of the last century. The issue of usury implicated the entire fabric of *opinions and actions* rooted in *conscience* and all the forms of the imbeddedness of *conscience*, including casuistry and the cure of souls.

Suddenly, indeed, the historical emphases ascribed to the notion of *conscience* gained fresh meaning. It was not that Luther or Calvin invented this fateful idea—a systematic exploration of that concept had already been started by others in the Middle Ages—but that these leaders of the Reformation gave everything a new axis and a new center by the scope of their attacks on every aspect of the culture of conscience—its structures, its *decision-matrices*, and its very *rationales*.

My own point of departure came to rest on the following perspectives: To understand the *makings* of early modern cultures we need to understand the *makings* of early modern minds and, therefore, need to have a proper sense of the change in the central paradigms as well as the restructuring of axial institutions in the society. If I may use the language of my current research: the makings of early modern cultures are most clearly in evidence when we study them from the special point of view of the revolutions in the rationale-systems in the sphere of conscience in its dual bearings in the spheres of moral action and intellectual opinion.

It will be recalled that during the entire period under discussion the logics were interdependent; in fact they were woven together in a single fabric of propositions centering around the notion of conscience. As continuing Continental usage should serve to recall, the Latin *con-scientia* referred both to the *moral conscience,* or "the proximate rule of right reason in the moral sphere," and opinions and beliefs in the philosophic and scientific spheres. It is, therefore, no wonder that all important cultural and social innovations in our period had to involve attack upon or a reconstruction of the *logics of decision* in the spheres of action and thought, in the scientific and moral domain alike.

For the present purpose, we need say only that the revolution called the "Reformation" was a breakdown and reconstruction of the Court Christian and the received logics of moral decision. All fundamental images and ideals of self, spiritual direction, and group life were reshaped in the ensuing correlations of newer elements and reconstituted older elements released by the dissolution of the older complex. Those who continued to repeat that Luther had the mind of a peasant, not of an economist, therefore were missing the point. The critical fact is that Luther's teachings and acts promised the breakthrough of the decision-matrices of conscience, sapped the power of the inherited casuistries and system of spiritual regulation, and foreshadowed the demise of the older images of "Religion" and "World," Law and Grace. I would ask those who have questioned this finding—above all, Professor Noonan, C. H. George, and Herbert Luethy: Can they cite an important theologian before Luther who adopted the stance ascribed to him above in Chapter II?

I would ask the same question in respect to Calvin: Who before Calvin spoke so directly to the heart of such critical problems as the forms of the different images of fraternity

[241]

and their variant implications for orientation to thought and action; the historical ground of the changing rationales, equities, utilities, and "welfare-functions" of different organizations of political and personal orders.

Evidence, or claims, that the town of Geneva allowed interest to be taken before the time of Calvin, that the ministry of Geneva was conservative after Calvin, and that Puritans were no whit different from Anglicans simply does not constitute decisive proof on the issues of the reconstructions of the horizons and the *rationales of conscience.*

There is nothing in my argument which implies that every Protestant, Lutheran, Evangelical, or Puritan individual should necessarily give expression to the same position in his writings or acts. What matters is that Luther and Calvin cleared the way for a new *conscience,* a conscience beyond the casuistries of the *moral* conscience of the Middle Ages, a conscience which Paul Tillich correctly called a *transmoral* conscience. The result was the advance of a series of new images and institutions of individual and collective responsibility, new perceptions and types of consensual structures.

A few closing remarks may be allowed on some passages in Luethy's aforementioned discussion which seem particularly open to question. Did Weber's thesis really have to wait fifty years "before Andre Biéler set about examining the ensuing polemic in the light of what Calvin himself actually said . . ."? Were there not papers and books on this theme—long before Biéler—by É. Doumergue, Georg Wünsch, Henri Hauser and others? So far as that goes, Biéler's own summary is not nearly so unqualified as Luethy's statement. Biéler writes:

> What then is to be said of the theories of Weber, Tröltsch and Goyau? Can it really be argued that Calvin is the father of modern capitalism? The answer is by no means simple, for a direct "Yes" would be as false as a direct "No." In one sense it may be argued that Calvin played an important part in the development of capitalism, by delivering loans at interest from the moral slur which the Church had im-

posed upon them; and also by spreading through the various classes of a bourgeois society an ethic of hard work and high moral standards based on the Gospel. This twofold emphasis inevitably produced a rise in production along with moderation in consumption. It was bound to lead very soon to an accumulation of savings favourable to new investment. But what we know of the role and function of money in the thought and practice of the early Calvinists would not justify the centrality of the profit motive that is attributed to the Calvinist ethos by Weber and Goyau. Moreover, the system of restrictions and controls, with which Calvin and his successors surrounded money transactions in order to prevent their misuse, hardly fits the freedom claimed by classical capitalism. ["Calvinism and Capitalism," *The Reformed and Presbyterian World,* XXVI (December 4, 1960), 157-58]

Is it necessary to remark that no noted twentieth-century writer, certainly not Weber, made either of the errors on this subject here criticized by Biéler? Weber never—nor have I ever—attributed "the centrality of the profit motive" to Calvin or his immediate followers. And certainly Weber never—as I have never—argued that the "freedom claimed by classical capitalism" was a hallmark of Calvin or the early Calvinists.

It may be noted that American sociologists almost to a man have escaped falling into the traps which appear to have caught Biéler here. Thanks, above all, to careful analysis by Talcott Parsons and Robert Merton, American sociologists—I do not say historians—have not been misled into thinking that Weber sought to prove the priority of *economic motives* in Calvin or the Calvinists.

Nor are we aided by Luethy when we are told that the key to the Reformation lies in the rediscovery by the reformers of the Old Testament view of life. As our foregoing pages show, this statement of the case conceals at least as much as it reveals. Different strata in the Protestant movements adopted sharply contrasting approaches to the question of the continuance of Mosaism. Luther, Calvin, and the Puritans were bitterly opposed to certain constructions placed upon the law of Moses by their radical opponents. Since Luethy refers so frequently and in so familiar a way to the developments of the idea of usury, one wonders how he could have missed the fact that the principal leaders of the Reformation explicitly opposed the Mosaism which extremist groups derived from the medieval traditions of interpretations of the fateful Deuteronomic commandment on usury.

These reflections on Luethy may be allowed to end with a reference to J. F. Bergier's thoughtful review-article of Biéler's book noted in section 7 of the New References. Bergier offers a welcome corrective to the perplexing statements about Weber which I have been criticizing.

The contrast between the model of analysis which I have adopted here and the pragmatic-externalistic view which is generally adopted is illustrated in the relations of Weber and Tawney. Tawney is actually more explicit than Weber on the significance of casuistries of conscience, but in the end Tawney adopts an *ad hoc* behavioristic position on Luther. To speak of him as unreservedly backward on economic matters by contrast to the more sophisticated schoolmen is to miss both the astonishing timeliness of his views on the Sabbatical Release and the unprecented character of his exegesis of the Deuteronomic law of usury.

For these and other reasons, Weber seems to me more on the right side than Tawney and the historians who have followed in his footsteps. Troeltsch, Tawney, and others accepting their lead go too far in insisting that the Reformations of Luther and Calvin were decidedly medieval in cast. The weaknesses of these views appear especially prominent in the highly condensed summary of the position by S. N. Eisenstadt in his MacIver Lecture (*ASR,* October, 1965, pp. 670-73, esp. at p. 671, col. 2). The heart of the difficulty seems to be that Eisenstadt favors current writers who adopt the present-minded assumption that the political institutions are the primary substructure of all action. In doing this they fail to give due place to the decisive and fateful character of the revolutions in the regulative rationale-systems, especially the logics of decision as I have described them above.

In the Reformation, as in other eras of accelerated change, the disestablishment (de-regulation) of the old order was a necessary first step in the development of a *new order*. Older elements left temporarily suspended in a free-floating state were correlated with newer emerging patterns: the essential sociocultural functions were served in dramatic ways in the newer settings. But that is not a story that can be told in these pages.

Penetrating suggestions in this area can now be found in the work of Talcott Parsons, James L. Adams, and a number of younger scholars they have variously influenced, especially Robert Bellah, David Little, and Jan Loubser. I am happy to find that all these men hold views like my own on the critical character of the relations of Protestantism to what I am calling a new "guidance system," new frameworks of regulation and reference for self, society, culture, and the cure of souls.

D. *"Counter-Reformation" Catholicism* v. *Weber?*

IT IS astonishing how slow twentieth-century historians have been to deal seriously with the structures of thought and rule which elaborated in various Catholic lands—especially those south of the Alps—in the period of the so-called Counter-Reformation. Two among the liveliest of the newer historians, H. R. Trevor-Roper and Herbert Luethy, have recently been insisting that the real key to the earlier development of capitalism and industrialism north of the Alps was not the congeniality of the transalpine lands to a new religiously determined economic value but total hostility and even reaction of the Counter-Reformation South to any modernizing influence.

I consider that this approach, also, is overly oriented to a single corner of Weber's views and fails to account for or provide some clue to the complex civilizations that were elaborated in Catholic culture areas in the sixteenth, seventeenth, and eighteenth centuries in Italy, France, Spain, Portugal, Holland, and elsewhere. Neither of these authors accords enough weight to the critical controversies relative to the sociocultural frameworks of definition and control described here.

Adaptations and modernizations did occur in Roman Catholic lands; indeed, some of the adaptations were of an extraordinarily libertarian cast, but their spirit and substance were essentially different from those of the changes undergone by Protestantism. In Catholic culture areas, "liberty of conscience" in the *moral sphere* was expanded, the casuistry of opinion and action incredibly ramified, and the cure of souls and priestly direction retained. The overall process was one of flexible accommodations by the Church and its main organs to the changing structures of society and to the different social interests.

The triangulated structure of representation and regulation compressed in the "Forum of Penance" and the "Court of Conscience" underwent adjustments of varied sorts, but the essential structures, institutional and spiritual alike, persisted. Indeed, immense new authority, scope, and suppleness were given to the Forum of Penance by the reform of the cure of souls by Loyola and the reform of the casuistry and the direction of conscience by the Jesuit spokesmen of the new system of the lesser probability.

In all Catholic lands—Italy, Spain, France, Portugal, Holland, and elsewhere—great struggles raged throughout the sixteenth, seventeenth, and eighteenth centuries over the niceties of the system, of the lesser probability. Galileo, Descartes, Pascal, the Jansenists, and the Jesuits cannot be understood without referring to this background; the importance of these debates for the student of the history of culture cannot be exaggerated.

Even before the bitter conflicts had subsided a new international army had formed about the Pope. Outer and inner missions were underway in all areas of the earth. The older Church of the Middle Ages had given way to a new baroque style of "benevolent autocracy" in which *fictionalist* philosophies of science and lesser *probabilist* theories of opinion were attempted as flexible accommodations to the new needs. Although the world remembers best the dramatic crises in the Church over Galileo and Pascal, the main outcome so far as the organization of the Church was concerned was the preservation of the triangulated structure in a world in which self-made men formed an important new leaven.

The emergence in the midst of all this of a new middle sort of man, the "self-made" Catholic burgher brilliantly described by Bernard Groethuysen, has failed to be noted. This new modern sort of Catholic layman felt at home in the "secular city."

E. *A Proposed Moratorium and Weber's Present Relevance*

FATHER ANDREW GREELEY, author of impressive studies on current social trends among Roman Catholics in contemporary America, has recently called for a moratorium on the use of Weber's thesis. Weber's notions have little or no relevance, he is convinced, for the contemporary American religious scene.

Although Father Greeley's evidence and arguments hardly seem to me to require his extreme conclusion, I am inclined to join him to the extent of renewing my related call for a change in the tenor of work in Weber's spirit.

Whether or not a moratorium is declared, we need to give more of our time to careful investigation of the logic and history of the issues involved. In the process of doing this—and here is the nub of my differences with certain American critics of Weber—I am certain we shall discover many advantages yet to be realized from the properly and adequately conceived approaches of the Weberian type in various fields of interest, including current sociocultural developments in the United States. Indeed, we shall uncover the more critical fact that Weber's relevance is now assuming vastly greater scope and actuality than ever before.

I shall have more to say about this point presently.

The question is not whether the events described by Weber did or did not occur exactly as he set them forth but how and with what changing effects the processes he was tracing occurred under different conditions.

If our work in this field is to advance, we must agree on a "baseline" which includes the following points:

1) We are long past the time when it was allowable to assert that Weber had set out to prove the affinities of Protestantism, Capitalism, and Mammonism.

2) It is no longer helpful to interpret Weber's purpose— as many specialists continue to do—purely in terms of a local historical proposition on the relations of economy and religion in the sixteenth or seventeenth centuries.

3) Weber always intended the notion of the "Protestant Ethic" to refer to the existential and cultural foundations of any society committed to the mastery of this world through intensive discipline and consensual organization of the personal and social orders.

4) In the end, therefore, the proving grounds for Weber's views are not Prussia or even England, but the Soviet Union, the Far East, the Near East, Africa—in short, *the world.*

For these reasons and others, I find myself unready to accept many of the currently popular notions about the worth of Weber's work in the study of the cultural history of Europe and the United States. I cannot agree that we find a matured "Protestant Ethic" or "Spirit of Capitalism" before the Reformation, namely in the Middle Ages or Renaissance, or that Protestantism did not notably alter the churchly or moral regulative patterns of the previous era. And speaking in a more contemporary vein: I do not even believe that we have now in our age of affluent self-indulgence altogether given up the

"Protestant Ethic" in favor of a cult of strenuous spending, other-directedness, spectator sports, and togetherness.

I am just as strongly convinced today as I was two decades ago that the notion of the new sort of "Brotherhood" which I have called "Universal Otherhood," where all become *equally* rather than *differentially* others, was born in the era of the Reformation. Time and ongoing research continue to add evidence that advances in the direction of Universal Otherhood will remain one of the hallmarks of "ecumenical Protestantism." At the present time, indeed, as I have written elsewhere (*ASR*, August 1965, p. 596), the " 'Protestant Ethic' is now being exported to every corner of the earth along with the dynamo, the computer, the bank, the department store, the central office and the Board Room."

We must be careful, however, not to chart these trends in too schematic a way. On the one hand, we are likely to see the further weakening of tribal kinship polities and ethnic religions of heath and hearth—tendencies working in favor of universalistic syncretisms. On the other hand, we must also expect recurring primitivist "backlashes," efforts at the revitalization of traditional orientations now, oddly, given new thrust by the action of volatile elements borrowed from the dynamic world religions. Both these tendencies—the tendency toward and the tendency away from universalist syncretisms —are occurring in the advanced as well as in the developing areas.

Robert Bellah has taken the lead in studying the "Protestant Ethic analogy" in Asia. Evidence of the expanding relevance of Weber on the world stage continues to accumulate.

I find it hard to conclude this section without mentioning essays by Niles Hansen and Philip Siegelman. Hansen correctly, in my opinion, argues that, properly understood, the "Protestant Ethic" recurs in every society at a critical point in its passage to modernity. Philip Siegelman's study of the Chettiars of Madras offers a fascinating instance of the workings of the themes I have developed in the foregoing pages.

F. *A Look Back—A Look Ahead*

As I reread the original edition of this book in the light of my research since 1949, I find myself wishing to add some words about the distinction I proposed in the 1949 Postscript between the *history* and the *genealogy* of ideas. I see now that the adoption of this stance was part of a larger "strategy," one that may have been at work in the odyssey of Weber himself. The bracketing of so-called "metaphysical questions" of the sort I proposed two decades ago (p. 222) was in the service of an opening out toward wider historical horizons and sociological frameworks.

It must by now be evident—as I hope my readers will readily agree—that the *Idea of Usury* was no more a flight from the hard *facts* of economic history than my recent essays are a flight from the *Idea of Usury*. I see a direct line extending through all my writings—from my graduate research and theses to my latest efforts. If I may speak as a witness in my own case, I experience my writings as a series of moves in the direction of what I have elsewhere (*ASR,* XXX, August 1965) called the "depth-historical cultural sociology of experience and expression."

These moves were neither intended—nor fated—to issue exclusively in historical monographs, admirable as I deem that form to be, but to assist in the development of an expanded and improved "language" for a fresh approach to the sociocultural process, an approach which links itself firmly but does not confine itself exclusively to the study of the *historical "phenomenologies" of experience and expression.*

The furtherance of this approach involved a continuing call to focus renewed attention on "sociocultural process" from the point of view of the changes in what I am now calling the symbolic "guidance systems" and the *decision-matrices* of both the logics *and* moralities of belief and behavior in the various spheres of thought and action.

I must no longer delay mention of the fact that this last-mentioned notion which I long ago made my own is my adaptation of a maxim of Jean Piaget's, who himself adapted to his own purpose a notion of Emile Durkheim. It was precisely the increasing awareness of the centrality and imbeddedness of the decision-structures of "conscience" which made me decide to focus on the mighty workings and the historic and institutional associations of the Witness within.

The ideas and ideals whose courses we have been tracing have undergone—are undergoing—myriad changes in phase, form, strength, and milieu. Measurements of changes so many-sided as these are extremely hard to establish at this time. Regularly in our study of the manifestations of such forms we trap ourselves into taking a localized rendering for its "ultimate essence," and, conversely, we regularly suppose that the "spirit" has lost all life at the very hour we are enveloped by one of its manifestations.

To give adequate expression to the subtler transmutations in such "culture-complexes" as the ideas of Usury, Brotherhood, Friendship, the "Protestant Ethic," and the "Spirit of Capitalism," we shall have to greatly expand the available resources of our "spiritual alchemies."

A last bit of truth must be said here to those who are distressed by our alchemical analogies: Our point tells as well in the languages of music and mathematics as in "cultural chemistry." Sir Henry Sumner Maine, whose name I am here again delighted to cite, in the eleventh hour of this new edition, once wrote: "Except the blind forces of Nature, nothing moves in this world which is not Greek in its origin." In the less lyrical language we use today this would mean in the present context that if we wish to understand man's history and the changes in men's institutions and in their forms of awareness we must closely attend to the workings of men's minds, their uses of "symbolic technologies"; we must explore all the influences at work in the history of the logics and dynamics of their guidance systems and their cultural maps, in all the spheres of action and thought.

In an odd way this book offers an instance of Maine's epigram. Having wished to understand the wanderings of a Hebrew theme and its myriad variations, initially in the Christian West and later possibly everywhere, I first had to find my way back to the wisdom of the Hellenes. Now the task is to go forward in the directions in which they pointed in their most inspired moments. The roles of rationales in the "algebras of the Revolutions" in whose early phases we are all now enveloped are no less in need of their historians than the revolutions in the rationales of *conscience* affected by Luther, Calvin, Galileo, Descartes, Pascal, Leibniz, Kant, Bentham, Hegel, and others more recent.

High on the program of our own day is the so-called race between civilization and catastrophe. Among those spirits whose insights will continually have to be recalled if the hopes for a favorable outcome of this race are to have an increased chance are two pioneer scholars with whose names I am proud to associate my own—Max Weber and Sir Henry Maine.

NEW REFERENCES

NEW ABBREVIATIONS

AGA	*Affaires et Gens d'affaires*
CEH	*Cambridge Economic History*
AHA	American Historical Association
ASA	American Sociological Association
ASR	*American Sociological Review*
BRES	*Biblioteca della Rivista "Economia e Storia"*
H. Eg.	*Histoire de l'Eglise*
IESS	*International Encyclopedia of the Social Sciences*
J.	*Journal*
NRS	*Nuova rivista storica*
Proc.	*Proceedings*
SSSR	Society for the Scientific Study of Religion
Zt.	*Zeitschrift*

NEW REFERENCES

The following lists of selected New References are mainly intended for those who wish to pursue the discussion of the issues posed by the present work in the literature which has appeared since its original publication in 1949. Here, as in the original Bibliography, no attempt has been made to be exhaustive. The entries which follow are only a sample of the studies I have found most scholarly, fruitful, or provocative up to the present hour.

To allow easy follow-up of particular subjects, the material has been arranged in twelve sections, with explanatory titles. I have deliberately kept my annotations to a minimum.

I hope to have several added opportunities in the near future to deal at greater length with certain of the issues posed in the new literature. Indications to this end will be found under my name in the items listed as now in press or forthcoming. I should particularly like to call attention to the remarks in section 6 under the name of the late Yves Renouard and to the series of papers to appear presently on the "cultures of *conscience*" and the revolutions of its *rationales* (section 11).

1. THE IDEA OF USURY—SOME REVIEWS AND DISCUSSIONS

AUDEN, W. H. "Brothers and Others." In *The Dyer's Hand and Other Essays*. New York, 1962, 218-37. This essay, largely devoted to *The Merchant of Venice,* forms a part of section entitled "The Shakespearean City."

BAINTON, ROLAND H. *Review of Religion,* March, 1952, 214-15.

BOAS, GEORGE. *Journal of Philosophy,* XLVII (1950), 452.

DAUBE, DAVID. *Journal of Ecclesiastical History,* II (1951), 123-24.

DE ROOVER, RAYMOND. *Revue belge,* XXIX.4 (1951), 1338-41.

GEORGE, C. H. See my citation and comment in section 7 below.

HOSELITZ, BERT F. *Explorations in Entrepreneurial History,*
  ser. 1, IV (1951-1952), 54-56.
KUEHNELT-LEDDIHN, ERIK VON. *Catholic World,* CLXXI
  (1950), 398.
LOPEZ, ROBERT S. *Speculum,* XXVI.2 (1951), 401-4.
LUZZATTO, GINO. *NRS,* XXXIV (1950), 521-23.
MATTINGLY, GARRETT H. *J. of Modern History,* XXIII.1
  (1951), 73.
NOONAN, JOHN T. *The New Scholasticism,* XXVI (1950),
  7-10.
POLANYI, KARL. *Commentary,* X.2 (1950), 192-94.

2. WEBER, TAWNEY, AND BEYOND:
REPRESENTATIVE VIEWS OF HISTORIANS

BARBIERI, G., *et al. L'opera di Werner Sombart nel centenario
  dell'nascità.* Milan, 1963. (*BRES,* VIII.) Includes essays
  by Luzzatto and Melis.
BERGIER, J. F. "La pensée économique et sociale de Calvin."
  Annales, XVII (1962), 348-55.
BIÉLER, ANDRÉ. "Calvinism and Capitalism." *Reformed and
  Presbyterian World,* XXV (1960), 145-59. This paper re-
  veals that this much-mentioned author presents a much
  more qualified position on this question than do most of
  his interpreters, notably Herbert Luethy, whose writings
  are listed below in this section.
BURRELL, SIDNEY A., ed. *The Role of Religion in Modern
  European History.* New York, 1964.
CANTOR, NORMAN F. "A Prolegomenon to Reformation."
  Political Science Quarterly, LXXXI.2 (1966), 63-81.
EISENSTADT, S. N., ed. *The Protestant Ethic and Modernization. A Comparative View.* New York, 1968. For a com-
  ment, see below under section 10.
GEORGE, CHARLES H. and KATHERINE GEORGE. *The Prot-
  estant Mind of the English Reformation, 1570-1640.*
  Princeton, 1961. A discussion of the argument of this

book will be found in the Harvard doctoral thesis of David Little, now being prepared for publication. See below under section 7 for a critique of *The Idea of Usury*, by C. H. George, and my comment.

GREEN, ROBERT W., ed. *Protestantism and Capitalism: The Weber Thesis and Its Critics*. Boston, 1959.

HELLEINER, KARL F. "Moral Conditions of Economic Growth." *J. of Economic History*, XI.2 (1951), 97-116.

HILL, CHRISTOPHER. "Protestantism and the Rise of Capitalism." In *Essays in . . . Honour of Tawney*, edited by F. J. Fisher (1961), 15-39.

———. *Society and Puritanism in Pre-Revolutionary England*. London, 1964.

———. *Reformation to Industrial Revolution: British Economy and Society 1530-1780*. London, 1967.

LUETHY, HERBERT. "Once Again: Calvinism and Capitalism." *Encounter*, no. 124 (January 1964), 26-38.

———. "Max Weber—Luethy's Reply" (to B. Nelson). *Ibid.*, no. 136 (January 1965), 92-94.

LITTLE, DAVID. *Religious Conflict, Law and Order: A Study in Pre-Revolutionary England*. New York, 1969.

MILLER, PERRY. *Nature's Nation*. Cambridge, 1967. Pp. 14-49 are devoted to Miller's striking essay, originally published in 1941, "Declension in a Bible Commonwealth."

MORGAN, EDMUND. Review of K. Samuelsson's *Religion and Economic Action*. *William and Mary Quarterly*, XVIII (1963), 135-40.

NELSON, BENJAMIN. Review of J. T. Noonan's *The Scholastic Analysis of Usury*. In *AHR*, LXIV (1959), 618-19.

———. Review of K. Samuelsson's *Religion and Economic Action*. *ASR*, XXVII (1962), 856.

———. "Über den Wücher." In *Max Weber in Gedächtnis*, pp. 407-47, hgb. von René König und Johannes Winckelmann. Cologne and Opladen, 1963. (Kölner Zt. für Soziologie und Sozialpsychologie 1963, Sonderheft 7.)

Translation of edited sections of *The Idea of Usury.*

———. "Max Weber's *The Protestant Ethic:* 1904-64." *Abstracts of Papers.* 59th Annual Meeting of ASA (1964).

———. "In Defense of Max Weber" (Reply to H. Luethy). *Encounter,* no. 131 (August 1964), 94-95.

———. "Max Weber's *The Sociology of Religion:* A Review-Article." *ASR,* xxx (1965), 595-99.

———. *Usura e cristianesimo: Per una storia della genesi dell'etica moderna.* Translation from the English by S. Moravia. Florence, 1967. (Biblioteca Sansoni no. 19.) This is a translation of the 1949 edition of *The Idea of Usury.* It includes a new Preface by the author.

RIEMERSMA, JELLE C. *Religious Factors in Early Dutch Capitalism, 1550-1650.* (Studies in the Social Science, no. 2, edited by C. A. O. van Niewenhuijze.) The Hague and Paris, 1967.

ROBERTSON, HECTOR M. "Marx, Menger, Mercantilism and Max Weber." *Studi in onore di A. Fanfani,* VI (1962), 442-66.

SAMUELSSON, K. *Religion and Economic Action.* New York, 1961.

SIEGELMAN, PHILIP. "Religion and Economic Activity: The Chettiars of Madras." In *Proc. of the Sixth World Conference of the Society for International Development 1964,* pp. 71-77. Edited by T. Geiger and L. Solomon.

SOMBART, WERNER. *The Jews and Modern Capitalism.* Translated by M. Epstein, with an Introduction to the American edition by B. F. Hoselitz and a Bibliographical Note in association with B. Nelson. Glencoe, Illinois, 1951.

TREVOR-ROPER, H. R. *The Crisis of the Seventeenth Century.* New York, 1968. Ch. 1 reprints his far-reaching essay, "Religion, the Reformation, and Social Change," which offers exceptionally lively, if not equally telling, criticisms of Weber. A full review of the evidence is not possible in the present setting.

TRINKAUS, CHARLES. "The Religious Foundations of Luther's Social Views." In *Essays . . . in Honor of A. P. Evans* (1955), pp. 71-87.

VENARD, MARC. "Catholicisme et usure au XVIe siècle." *Revue de l'histoire de l'église de France,* LII (1966), 59-74. An exceptionally stimulating essay based on thorough knowledge of original sources.

WINCKELMANN, JOHANNES, ed. *Max Weber: Die protestantische Ethik, II: Kritiken und Antikritiken.* Munich, 1968. Includes: the older critiques by H. Karl Fischer and Felix Rachfahl; Weber's replies up to 1910, and essays by E. Troeltsch, E. Fischoff, and Reinhard Bendix; Editorial Introduction and Bibliography.

3. NEW ENCYCLOPEDIAS, JOURNALS, MONOGRAPH SERIES

A. *Encyclopedias*

Cambridge Economic History of Europe (CEH)
Vol. III: *Economic Organization and Policies in the Middle Ages.* Edited by M. M. Postan, E. Miller, and E. E. Rich. Cambridge, 1963.
Vol. IV: *The Economy of Expanding Europe in the 16th and 17th Centuries.* Edited by E. E. Rich and C. H. Wilson. Cambridge, 1967.

International Encyclopedia of the Social Sciences (IESS). Edited by D. L. Sills. 17 vols., New York, 1968.

B. *Journals and Monograph Series*

Annales. Économies—Sociétés—Civilisations. 2nd Series. Comité de Direction: F. Braudel, G. Friedmann, and C. Morazé. Paris, 1949-.

Comparative Studies in Society and History. Edited by S. L. Thrupp. October, 1958-. The Hague: Mouton.

Economia e Storia. Edited by A. Fanfani. I.1, 1954. Milan. Includes a monograph series, *Biblioteca della Rivista,* described below.

Explorations in Entrepreneurial History. Series 1, Harvard University, Research Center in Entrepreneurial History, 1949-59. Series 2, Earlham College, Richmond, Indiana, 1963-.

Biblioteca della Rivista "Economia e Storia" (BRES). Milan.

Ecole Pratique des Hautes Etudes. VIe Section. Centre de recherches historiques. Includes seven series of indispensable monographs. Numerous titles in the celebrated sub-series, *Affaires et Gens d'affaires,* are listed in other sections (see esp. section 4 below).

4. COMMEMORATION VOLUMES, BIBLIOGRAPHIES

Unless otherwise indicated, names given as authors are men to whom the studies are dedicated.

ASTON, TREVOR, ed. *Crisis in Europe: 1560-1660.* London, 1965. (Essays from *Past and Present,* 1952-1962.)

BABEL, ANTONY. *Melanges d'histoire économique et sociale en hommage au professeur Antony Babel.* 2 vols., Geneva, 1963.

CESSI, ROBERTO. *Miscellenea in onore de Roberto Cessi.* 3 vols., Rome, 1958. (Storia e litteratura : Raccolta di testi e studi, LXXI, LXXII, LXXIII.)

EVANS, A. P. *Essays in Medieval Life and Thought: Presented in Honor of A. P. Evans.* Edited by J. H. Mundy, R. W. Emery, and B. Nelson. New York, 1955. Includes several papers relevant to the wider backgrounds of the present work, notably the papers by W. H. May, D. Phillips, P. Riesenberg, and the two first-named editors.

FANFANI, AMINTORE. *Studi in onore di Amintore Fanfani.* 6 vols., Milan, 1962.

FISHER, E. J., ed. See below under Tawney.

LE BRAS, GABRIEL. *Etudes d'histoire du droit canonique dédiées à Gabriel Le Bras.* 2 vols., Paris, 1965.

LUZZATTO, GINO. *Studi in onore di Gino Luzzatto.* 4 vols. Milan, 1949-50.

————. A later tribute to Luzzatto, occasioned by his passing, will be found in Vol. XLIX (1965), Fasc. 1-2 of the *NRS.* For an updated list of Luzzatto's writings, see pp. 185-211.

SAPORI, ARMANDO. *Studi in onore di Armando Sapori.* 2 vols., Milan, 1957.

TAWNEY, R. H. *Essays in the Economic and Social History of Tudor and Stuart England: In Honour of R. H. Tawney.* Edited by F. J. Fisher. Cambridge, 1961.

5. PRIMARY SOURCES AND STUDIES

Affairs et Gens d'affaires. Over thirty volumes have appeared in this celebrated series since its beginning in 1952. Individual titles will be listed below under the names of their authors.

ALEXANDER (LOMBARDUS) OF ALESSANDRIA. (d. 1314.) *Tractatus de usuris.* In *Un Traité de morale économique au XIVe siècle.* Edited by A. M. Hamelin, O. F. M. Louvain, 1962.

BAILYN, BERNARD, ed. *The Apologia of Robert Keayne: The Self-Portrait of a Puritan Merchant.* New York, 1965. Offers a fascinating account of a case of restitution of ill-gotten gains under church injunction. The text does not bear out Professor Bailyn's impression that Keayne made amends for "usury."

BORLANDI, ANTONIA. *Il manuale di mercatura di Saminiato de' Ricci.* Genoa, 1963.

BRUCHEY, STUART, ed. *The Colonial Merchant: Sources and Readings.* New York, 1966.

BRUCKER, GENE, ed. *Two Memoirs of Renaissance Florence: The Diaries of Buonaccorso Pitti and Gregorio Dati.* Translated by J. Martines. New York, 1967.

CARNEGIE, ANDREW. *The Gospel of Wealth and Other Timely*

Essays. Edited by E. C. Kirkland. Cambridge, Massachusetts, 1965.

CASSANDRO, GIOVANNI. *Un trattato inedito e la dottrina dei cambi nel cinquecento.* Naples, 1962.

CIANO, CESARE. *La "Practica di mercatura" datiniana (Secolo XIV).* Preface by F. Melis. Milan, 1964. (*BRES,* IX.)

GRICE-HUTCHINSON, MARJORIE. *The School of Salamanca: Readings in Spanish Monetary Theory.* Oxford, 1952.

JEHIEL NISSIM OF PISA. *[The] Eternal Life. (Haye olam.)* Hebrew text and English translation. Edited with an Introduction and Notes by Gilbert S. Rosenthal under the title *Banking and Finance among Jews in Renaissance Italy.* New York, 1962. See above, p. 199, for the essay by A. Marx.

KINGDON, ROBERT M. and J. F. BERGIER. *Registres de la compagnie des pasteurs de Genèva au temps de Calvin.* 2 vols., Geneva, 1962.

LOPEZ, ROBERT S. and IRVING W. RAYMOND, eds. and trans. *Medieval Trade in the Mediterranean World.* New York, 1955.

MCLAUGHLIN, T. P., ed. *The Summa Parisiensis on the Decretum Gratiani.* Toronto, 1952.

MOLLAT, M., ed. *Les affaires de Jacques Coeur, journal du procureur Dauvet, procès verbaux de séquestre et d'adjudication.* Paris, 1952-53. (*AGA,* II.1-2.)

MORGAN, E. S., ed. *The Diary of Michael Wigglesworth, 1653-1657: The Conscience of a Puritan.* New York, 1956.

NIDER, JOHANNES. *On the Contracts of Merchants.* Edited by Ronald B. Shuman. Translated by Charles H. Reeves. Norman, Oklahoma, 1966.

ORESME, NICHOLAS. *The De moneta of Nicholas Oresme and English Mint Documents.* Edited and translated by Charles Johnson. New York, 1956.

SAPORI, ARMANDO, ed. *I libri degli Alberti del Giudice.* Milan, 1952.

SCHNEIDER, LOUIS, ed. *The Scottish Moralists on Human Nature and Society.* Chicago, 1967. A remarkable foreshadowing of one aspect of the theme of the present work will be found in the excerpt which Professor Schneider has reprinted (pp. 56-62) from Dugald Stewart's *Philosophy of the Active and Moral Powers* (1828).

YEHIEL NISSIM OF PISA. See above under JEHIEL NISSIM OF PISA.

6. ECONOMIC HISTORY

BAILYN, BERNARD. *The New England Merchants of the Seventeenth Century.* New York, 1955.

BERGIER, J. F. *Genève et l'économie européene de la Renaissance.* Paris, 1963.

BRAUDEL, FERNAND. *La Méditerranee et le monde méditerranéen a l'époque de Philippe II.* 2 vols. 2nd ed. revised and enlarged. Paris, 1967.

CESSI, R. *Politica ed economia di Venezia nel Trecento.* Rome, 1951.

COORNAERT, EMILE. *Les Français et le commerce international à Anvers.* 2 vols., Paris, 1961.

DELUMEAU, J. *Vie économique et sociale de Rome dans la seconde moitié du XVIe siècle.* 2 vols., Paris, 1957-59.

DE ROOVER, RAYMOND. *The Rise and Decline of the Medici Bank, 1397-1494.* Cambridge, 1963.

———. "The Organization of Trade." *CEH*, III (1963), ch. 2, 42-105.

———. *The Bruges Money Market around 1400.* With a Statistical Supplement by Hyman Sardy. Brussels, 1968.

DOLLINGER, PHILLIPPE. *La Hanse (XIIe-XVIIe siècles).* Paris, 1964.

EMERY, RICHARD W. *The Jews of Perpignan in the Thirteenth Century.* New York, 1959.

GIOFFRÈ, DOMENICO. *Gênes et les foires de change de Lyon à Besançon.* Paris, 1960. (*AGA*, XXI.)

HEERS, JACQUES. *Genes au XVe siècle: Activité économique et problèmes sociaux.* Paris, 1961. (*AGA,* XXIV.)

JEANNIN, PIERRE. *Les marchands au XVIe siècle.* Paris, 1957.

LANE, FREDERIC C. *Venice and Its History: The Collected Papers of F. C. Lane.* Edited by a committee of colleagues and former students. Foreword by F. Braudel. Baltimore, 1966.

LANE, FREDERIC C. and J. C. RIEMERSMA, eds. *Enterprise and Secular Change.* Homewood, Illinois, 1953.

LAPEYRE, HENRI. *Une famille de marchands: Les Ruiz.* Paris, 1955. (*AGA,* VIII.)

LE GOFF, JACQUES. *Marchands et banquiers du moyen-âge.* Paris, 1956.

LUETHY, HERBERT. *La Banque Protestante en France de la Révocation de l'Édit de Nantes à la Revolution.* 2 vols., Paris, 1959. (*AGA,* XIX, 1-2).

LUZZATTO, GINO. *Studi di storia economica veneziana.* Padua, 1954.

MAURO, FREDERIC. *Le XVIe siècle européen: Aspects économiques.* Paris, 1966.

MOLLAT, MICHEL. "Les affaires de Jacques Coeur à Florence." *Studi in onore di Armando Sapori,* II, 759-72. Milan, 1957.

ORIGO, IRIS. *The Merchant of Prato, Francesco di Marco Datini.* New York, 1957.

POLIAKOV, LÉON. *Les Banchieri juifs et le Saint-Siège du XIIIe au XVIIe siècle.* Paris, 1965. (*AGA,* XXX.)

RENOUARD, YVES. *Les hommes d'affaires italiens du moyen-âge.* Paris, 1949. This genial work is scheduled to appear soon in a specially edited translation under the supervision of the present writer. The new edition will include fresh notes, a survey of literature since 1949, and critical reviews of problems currently under active discussion.

RUDDOCK, ALWYN A. *Italian Merchants and Shipping in Southampton 1270-1600.* Southampton, 1951.

SAPORI, ARMANDO. *Le marchand italien au moyen-âge: Conférences et bibliographie*. Paris, 1952. (*AGA*, I.)

——. *Studi di storia economica (Secoli XIII-XIV-XV)*. 3rd ed., 2 vols., Florence, 1955. Vol. 3, Florence, 1967.

SISTO, ALESSANDRA. *Banchieri-feudatari subalpini nei secoli XII-XIV*. Turin, 1963.

SLESSAREV, VSEVOLOD. "Die sogenannten Orientalen in mittelalterlichen Genua: Einwanderer aus Südfrankreich in der ligurischen Metropole." *Vierteljahrschrift für Sozial- und Wirtschaftsgeschichte*, LI (1964), 22-65.

STONE, LAWRENCE. *The Crisis of the Aristocracy: 1558-1641*. Oxford, 1965.

——. "Social Mobility in England 1500-1700." *Past and Present*, XXXIII (1966), 16-55.

——. Introduction to the Harper Torchbook edition of R. H. Tawney, *The Agrarian Problem in the Sixteenth Century*. New York, 1967.

7. DOCTRINES OF USURY, PRICE, EXCHANGE

BALDWIN, JOHN W. *The Medieval Theories of the Just Price: Romanists, Canonists, and Theologians in the 12th and 13th Centuries*. Philadelphia, 1959.

BARGE, HERMANN. *Luther und der Frühkapitalismus*. Gütersloh, 1951. (*Schriften des Vereins für Reformationsgeschichte*. Nr. 168, Jahrgang 58, Heft 1.)

BERGIER, J. F. "La pensée économique et sociale de Calvin." *Annales*, XVII.2 (1962), 348-55. A critical review of A. Biéler's volume on Calvin's economic thought cited below. A comparison of this discussion with the remarks of H. Luethy in *Encounter*, January, 1964, listed above in section 2 is instructive.

BIÉLER, ANDRÉ. *La Pensée économique et sociale de Calvin*. Geneva, 1959.

CAPITANI, O. "La *venditio ad terminum* nella valutazione

morale di San Tommaso d'Aquino e di Remigio de'Girolami." *Bullettino dell'Istituto storico per il medio evo*, LXX, 229-363. Rome, 1958.

————. "Sulla questione dell'usura nel medio evo. (A proposito del volume di J. T. Noonan.)" *Ibid.*, 537-66.

DALLE MOLLE, LUCIANO. *I contratti di cambio nei moralisti de secolo XIII alla metà del secolo XVII.* Rome, 1954.

DE ROOVER, RAYMOND. "Il trattato di fra Santi Rucellai sul cambio, il monte commune e il monte delle doti." *Archivio storico italiano*, CXI (1953), 3-41.

————. *L'Évolution de la lettre de change, XIVᵉ-XVIIIᵉ sieclès.* Paris, 1953. (*AGA*, IV.) Includes extensive bibliography of original sources.

————. "Scholastic Economics: Survival and Lasting Influence from the 16th Century to Adam Smith." *Quarterly J. of Economics,* LXIX (1955), 161-90.

————. "Les doctrines économiques des scolastiques: À propos du tráité sur l'usure d'Alexandre Lombard." *Revue d'histoire écclesiastique,* LIX (1964), 854-66.

————. *San Bernardino of Siena and Sant'Antonino of Florence: The Two Great Economic Thinkers of the Middle Ages.* Boston, 1967.

————. "Economic Thought: Ancient and Medieval." *IESS,* IV (1968), 430-35.

FABIUNKE, GÜNTER. *Martin Luther als Nationalökonom.* Berlin, 1963. (Deutsche Akademie der Wissenschaften zu Berlin. Schriften des Instituts für Wirtschaftswissenschaften. Nr. 18.) A striking East German view of Luther. Luther's 1540 Treatise against usury is reprinted as an Appendix.

GEORGE, CHARLES H. "English Calvinist Opinion of Usury, 1600-1640." *J. of History of Ideas,* XVIII (1957), 455-74. A critique of *The Idea of Usury.* The critic's remarks about the roots of medieval theory and the situation prevailing up to 1600 seem insubstantial to the present writer. The summing-up of the materials described in the title of the paper needs review by expert historians of English Puritanism. Further discussion of the wider questions underlying the issues in dispute will be found in sections *B-C* of the New Postscript.

GIAMMANCO, R. "La dottrina scolastica dell'usura." *NRS,* XLIII (1959), 122-25. Review of J. T. Noonan's book.

HÖFFNER, JOSEPH. *Statik und Dynamik in der scholastischen Wirtschaftethik.* Cologne, 1955.

IBANÈS, JEAN. *La Doctrine de l'Église et les réalités économiques au XIIIe siècle.* Paris, 1967. Preface by Jean L'Homme.

JOHNSON, HERBERT. "Some Medieval Doctrines on Extrinsic Titles to Interest." In C. T. O'Neil, ed., *An Etienne Gilson Tribute,* 86-100. Milwaukee, 1959.

KLASSEN, PETER J. *The Economics of Anabaptism, 1525-1560.* The Hague, 1964.

LE BRAS, GABRIEL. "Usure." *Dict. de théol. cath.,* XV.2 (1950), 2316-90.

MANDICH, GIULIO. *Le Pacte de "ricorsa" et le marché italien des changes au XVIIe siècle.* Preface by Gino Luzzatto. Paris, 1953.

NOONAN, JOHN T., JR. *The Scholastic Analysis of Usury.* Cambridge, 1957.

PACETTI, P. DIONISIO, O.F.M. "Un trattato sulle usure e le restituzioni di Pietro di Giovanni Olivi falsamente attribuito a Fr. Gerardo da Siena." *Archivum Franciscanum Historicum* XLVI (1953), 448-57.

RAMP, ERNST. *Das Zinsproblem: Eine historische Untersuchung.* Zürich, 1949. Independently confirms (see especially pp. 82-83) the stress on the historic importance of Calvin's discussion of the Deuteronomic Commandment made in the first edition of this book. Similarly there are independent confirmations of other emphases relating to Luther and Zwingli. Unfortunately, the discussion in the sixth chapter on Catholic doctrine since the sixteenth century is relatively weak.

ROGGE, JOACHIM. *Der Beitrag des Predigers Jakob Strauss zur frühen Reformationsgeschichte.* Berlin, 1957.

SCHNAPPER, BERNARD. *Les rentes au XVIe siècle: Histoire d'un instrument de crédit.* Paris, 1957. (*AGA*, XII.)

————. "Les rentes ches les théologiens et les canonistes du XIIIe au XVIe siècle." *Études dédiées à Gabriel Le Bras,* II (1965), 965-95.

SCHUMPETER, JOSEPH A. *History of Economic Analysis.* New York, 1954.

SOUDEK, JOSEF. "Aristotle's Theory of Exchange: An Inquiry into the Origin of Economic Analysis." *Proc. of the American Philosophical Society,* XCVI (1952), 45-75.

STEIN, SIEGFRIED. "The Laws of Interest in the Old Testament." *J. of Theological Studies,* IV (1953), 161-70.

————. "The Development of the Jewish Law on Interest from the Biblical Period to the Expulsion of the Jews in England." *Historia Judaica,* XVII (1955), 3-40.

————. "Interest Taken by Jews from Gentiles: An Evaluation of Source Material (14th to 17th Centuries)." *J. of Semitic Studies,* I (1956), 141-66.

VERAJA, FABIANO. *Le Origini della controversia teologica sul contratto di censo nel XIII secolo.* Rome, 1960.

WEBER, WILHELM. *Geld und Zins in der spanischen Spätscholastik.* Munich, 1962.

8. MANIFEST USURERS AND MERCHANT-PRINCES IN LIFE, LAW, AND LITERATURE

BARBIERI, GINO. "L'usuraio Tomaso Grassi, nel racconti bandelliano e nella documentazione storica." In *Studi . . . Fanfani,* II (1961), 19-89.

BECKER, M. "Three Cases Concerning the Restitution of Usury in Florence." *J. of Economic History,* XVII (1957), 445-50.

BERGIER, JEAN FRANÇOIS. "Taux de l'intérêt et crédit à court

terme à Genève dans la séconde moitié du XVIe siècle."
In *Studi . . . Fanfani,* IV (1962), 89-121.

COHEN, BOAZ. "Antichresis in Jewish and Roman Law." In *Alexander Marx Jubilee Volume,* pp. 179-202. New York, 1950.

COLEMAN, D. C. "Sir John Banks Financier: An Essay on Government Borrowing under the Later Stuarts." In *Essays . . . Tawney.* Edited by F. J. Fisher. Cambridge, 1961, 204-30.

CRISTIANI, EMILIO. "Note sulla legislazione antiusuraria." *Bollettino storico pisano,* XXII (1953), 3-53.

DE ROOVER, FLORENCE EDLER. "Restitution in Renaissance Florence." In *Studi in onore di Armando Sapori,* II (1957), 775-89.

DE ROOVER, RAYMOND. *"Cambium ad Venetias:* Contribution to the History of Foreign Exchange." *Ibid.,* I (1957), 631-48.

———. "The Concept of the Just Price: Theory and Economic Policy." *J. of Economic History,* XVIII (1958), 418-34.

FRYDE, E. B. and M. M. FRYDE. "Public Credit, with Special Reference to Northwestern Europe." *CEH,* III (1963), ch. 7, 430-542.

KUTTNER, STEPHEN. "Conciliar Law in the Making." *Miscellanea Pio Paschini,* II (1949), 39-81.

LANE, F. C. "Gino Luzzatto's Contributions to the History of Venice: An Appraisal and a Tribute." *NRS,* XLIX (1965), 49-80.

LE BRAS, GABRIEL. "Conceptions of Economy and Society." *CEH, III* (1963), ch. 8, 554-70.

LE GOFF, JACQUES. "Temps de l'église et temps du marchand." *Annales,* XV (1960), 417-33.

———. "Métiers licites et métiers illicites dans l'occident médiéval." *Etudes Historiques: Annales de l'école des hautes études de Gand,* V (1963), 41-57.

————. "Métier et profession d'après les manuels de confesseurs au moyen-age." *Miscellanea mediaevalia*, III (1964), 44-60.

LOPEZ, ROBERT. "I primo cento anni di storia documentata della banca a Genova." *Studi in onore di Armando Sapori*, I (1957), 217-53.

LUZZATTO, GINO. "Tasso d'interesse e usura a Venezia, nei secoli XIII-XV." In *Miscellanea in onore di Roberto Cessi*, I (1958), 191-202.

McCLELLAND, E. M. "Sidelights on Universal Benevolence." *Comparative Studies in Society and History*, IX (1967), 349-61.

MOLLAT, MICHEL. "Les affaires de Jacques Coeur à Florence." In *Studi in onore di Armando Sapori*, II (1957), 759-72.

NELSON, BENJAMIN. "Blancardo (the Jew?) of Genoa and the Restitution of Usury in Medieval Italy." In *Studi in onore di Gino Luzzatto*, I (1949), 96-116.

SHARMA, R. S. "Usury in Early Medieval India." *Comparative Studies in Society and History*, VIII (1965), 56-77.

STAUFFENEGGER, R. "Réforme, richesse et pauvreté." *Revue d'histoire de l'église de France*, LII (1966), 47-58.

9. CITIES: MIDDLE AGES, RENAISSANCE, REFORMATION

BECKER, MARVIN B. *Florence in Transition.* Vol. 1: *The Decline of the Commune.* Baltimore, 1967.

BRUCKER, GENE. *Florentine Politics and Society. 1343-1378.* Princeton, 1962.

FANFANI, AMINTORE, ed. *Città, mercanti, dottrine nell'economia europea del IV al XVIII secolo.* Milan, 1964. (Saggi in memoria di Gino Luzzatto. *BRES,* XI.) Includes essays by distinguished specialists on the modes of economic life in major European centers: Venice, Genoa, Florence, Geneva, Milan, Seville, Antwerp, and Amsterdam.

HERLIHY, DAVID. *Pisa in the Early Renaissance: A Study of Urban Growth.* New Haven, 1958.

HYDE, J. K. *Padua in the Age of Dante: A Social History of an Italian City State.* New York, 1966.

MARTINES, LAURO. *The Social World of the Florentine Humanists: 1390-1460.* Princeton, 1964.

―――. *Lawyers and Statecraft in Renaissance Florence.* Princeton, 1968.

MILLER, S. M., ed. *Max Weber: Selections from His Work.* With an Introduction by the editor. New York, 1963. Attention is called to the judicious comments in the section on "Weber and Marx," pp. 7-9.

MONTER, E. W. *Calvin's Geneva.* New York, 1967. (New Dimensions in History, Historical Cities.)

SCHNEIDER, JEAN. *La ville de Metz aux XIIIe et XIVe siècles.* Nancy, 1950.

STRAUSS, GERALD. *Nuremburg in the Sixteenth Century.* New York, 1967.

10. WEBER: REPRESENTATIVE VIEWS OF SOCIOLOGISTS

BAUMGARTEN, EDUARD. *Max Weber: Werk und Person. Dokumente ausgewählt und kommentiert.* Tuebingen, 1964.

BELLAH, ROBERT N. "Reflections on the Protestant Ethic Analogy in Asia." In S. N. Eisenstadt, *The Protestant Ethic and Modernization,* pp. 243-51. NewYork, 1968. A stimulating essay originally printed in 1963.

―――, ed. *Religion and Progress in Modern Asia.* New York, 1965.

BENDIX, REINHARD. "The Cultural and Political Setting of Economic Rationality in Western and Eastern Europe." In R. Bendix, ed. (1968), pp. 335-51. (This essay appeared originally in 1960.)

―――, ed. *State and Society: A Reader in Comparative Political Sociology.* Boston, 1968.

BIRNBAUM, N. "Conflicting Interpretations of the Rise of Capitalism: Marx and Weber." *British J. of Sociology,* IV (1953), 125-41.

CAHNMAN, W. J. and A. BOSKOFF, eds. *Sociology and History: Theory and Research.* New York, 1964.

EISENSTADT, S. N. "Transformation of Social, Political, and Cultural Orders in Modernization." *ASR,* XXX (1965), 659-73. Briefly discussed in section 6 of the New Postscript.

————, ed. *The Protestant Ethic and Modernization: A Comparative View.* New York, 1968. This is the most helpful anthology to date. It may, however, be noted that the editor does not remark that the essays by sociologists seem to differ markedly in spirit from those by the historians.

GREELEY, ANDREW. "The Protestant Ethic: Time for a Moratorium." *Sociological Analysis,* XXV (1964), 20-33.

HANSEN, NILES M. "The Protestant Ethic as a General Precondition for Economic Development." *Canadian J. of Economic and Political Science,* XXIX (1963), 462-74. Recommended to historians who insist on seeing Weber only in local terms.

————. "Weber and Veblen on Economic Development." *Kyklos,* XVII (1964), 447-69.

LENSKI, GERHARD. *The Religious Factor: A Sociological Study of Religion's Impact on Politics, Economics, and Family Life.* Rev. ed., New York, 1963. Originally published in 1961.

LITTLE, DAVID. "Max Weber Revisited: The 'Protestant Ethic' and the Puritan Experience of Order." *Harvard Theological Review,* LIX (1966), 415-28. A thoughtful statement. Includes a critique of M. Walzer's *Revolution of the Saints.*

LOUBSER, JAN. "Puritanism and Liberty: A Study of Normative Change in Massachusetts, 1630-1850." Cambridge, 1963. (Dissertation on deposit in Harvard University Library.)

MARX, KARL. *Pre-capitalist Economic Formations.* Translated by J. Cohn. Edited and with an Introduction by Eric Hobsbawm. This is a translation of a fragment of a manuscript composed by Marx in 1857-58, which only became generally available in 1953 with publication of a German edition under the title *Grundriss der Kritik der Politischen-Ökonomie.*

Hobsbawm's thoughtful sixty-page Introduction includes a statement praising G. Lichtheim's conclusion that Weber's views on religion and capitalism are "either anticipated by Marx or can readily be fitted into his framework."

The matter is too complex to be discussed at any length in these pages. I admit, however, that I incline to the more temperate statements of such authors as K. Löwith, A. Salomon, T. Parsons, and R. Bendix, which are partly reflected in some judicious remarks by S. M. Miller (see the citation in section 9 above).

MAY, HENRY F. *Protestant Churches and Industrial America.* New York, 1964.

MORGAN, EDMUND S. *Visible Saints: The History of a Puritan Idea.* New York, 1963.

NELSON, BENJAMIN. "Religion and Development." *Proc. of the Sixth World Conference, Society for International Development,* pp. 67-68. Edited by T. Geiger and L. Solomon. Washington, D.C., 1964.

———. "Max Weber's *The Sociology of Religion:* A Review-Article." *ASR,* XXX (1965), 595-99.

———. "Max Weber and Talcott Parsons as Interpreters of Western Religious and Social Development." *Abstracts of Papers Presented at the Annual Conference of the SSSR,* p. 4. New York, 1965.

———. Introduction to Bernard Groethuysen's *The Bourgeois: Catholicism vs. Capitalism in Eighteenth-Century France.* Translated by M. Ilford. New York, 1968.

PARSONS, TALCOTT. Preface to new edition, *Max Weber, The*

Protestant Ethic and the Spirit of Capitalism, pp. xiii-xvii. New York, 1958.

———. "Christianity and Modern Industrial Society." In E. A. Tiryakian, ed. (1963), 33-70.

———. "Christianity." *IESS,* 11 (1968), 425-47.

ROSTOW, W. W. *The Stages of Economic Growth: A Non-Communist Manifesto.* Cambridge, 1960.

———, ed. *The Economics of Take-off into Sustained Growth.* New York, 1963.

TIRYAKIAN, E. A., ed. *Sociological Theory, Values and Sociocultural Change: Essays in Honor of Pitirim A. Sorokin.* New York, 1963. Paperbound edition, Harper Torchbooks.

WEBER, MAX. *Max Weber on Law in Economy and Society.* Translated by E. Shils and M. Rheinstein. Cambridge, 1954. (1st edition of Weber's original treatise, 1922.)

———. *The Sociology of Religion.* Translated by E. Fischoff. Introduction by T. Parsons. Boston, 1964. (1st edition of Weber's original treatise, 1922.)

———. *Economy and Society.* Ed. and tr. G. Roth and C. Wittich. 3 vols. Totowa, New Jersey, 1968. This is the long-awaited variorum translation. An extended introduction by Roth will be found at pp. xxvii-civ of the opening volume.

11. CULTURES OF CONSCIENCE AND REVOLUTIONS OF RATIONALES: RECENT ESSAYS BY THE AUTHOR

NELSON, BENJAMIN. "Casuistry." *Encyclopaedia Brittanica,* VI (1963), 51. Reprinted in 1967.

———. "Conscience, Moral and Transmoral: Historic Encounters and Current Perplexities." SSSR *Newsletter,* 11 (1963). *Abstracts.*

———. "Probabilists, Anti-Probabilists, and the Quest for Certitude in the 16th and 17th Centuries." In *Actes du*

Xme congrès internationale d'histoire des sciences [*Proc. of the Xth International Congress for the History of Science*], I, 102-7. Paris, 1965.

————. "Self-Images and Systems of Spiritual Direction in the History of European Civilization." In *The Quest for Self-Control*, pp. 49-103. Edited by S. Z. Klausner. New York, 1965.

————. "*Conscience* and the Makings of Modern Western Cultures: The *Protestant Ethic* beyond Weber." *Abstracts of Papers*, 62nd Annual Meeting, ASA (1967), 138. (In press.)

————. "The Early Modern Revolution in Science and Philosophy: Fictionalism, Probabilism, Fideism, and Catholic 'Prophetism'." *Boston Studies in the Philosophy of Science*, III, 1-40. Edited by R. S. Cohen and M. Wartofsky. Dordrecht, Holland, 1968.

————. "Scholastic *Rationales* of 'Conscience,' Early Modern Crises of Credibility, and the Scientific-Technocultural Revolutions of the 17th and 20th Centuries." *J. for the Scientific Study of Religion*, VII (1968-1969), 155-77.

————. "The Medieval Canon Law of Contracts, Renaissance 'Spirit of Capitalism,' and the Reformation 'Conscience': A Vote *for* Max Weber." In ποικιλία: *Studies and Essays in the Humanities in Honor of Philip Merlan*. The Hague, 1969. (In press.) An extended summary of research on theologies of *conscience*, juridical casuistries, political *rationales*, and the doctrines of usury from the Schoolmen to Calvin.

12. RELIGION, LAW, SOCIAL INSTITUTIONS AND THOUGHT: GENERAL

AUBENAS, ROGER and ROBERT RICARD. *L'Eglise et la Renaissance (1449-1517)*. Paris, 1951. (*H. Eg.*, xv.)

BEC, CHRISTIAN. *Les marchands écrivains: Affairs et humanisme à Florence, 1375-1434*. Paris, 1967.

BELOW, KARL-HEINZ. *Die Haftung für "lucrum cessans" in römichen Recht.* Munich, 1964.

BELSHAW, CYRIL. *Traditional Exchange and Modern Markets.* Englewood Cliffs, New Jersey, 1965.

BUSHMAN, RICHARD L. *From Puritan to Yankee.* Cambridge, 1967.

COHEN, BOAZ. *Jewish and Roman Law: A Comparative Study.* New York, 1966.

DIAMOND, SIGMUND. *The Reputation of the American Businessman.* New York, 1966.

FIFOOT, C. H. S. *History and Sources of the Common Law: Tort and Contract.* Vol. II. London, 1949.

FOREST, AIMÉ, F. VAN STEENBERGHEN and M. DE GANDIL-LAC. *Le mouvement doctrinal du IXe au XIVe siècle.* Paris, 1951. (*H. Eg.,* XIII.)

HALÉVY, ELIE. *The Growth of Philosophic Radicalism.* Boston, 1955.

HALLER, WILLIAM. *Liberty and Reformation in the Puritan Revolution.* New York, 1955.

HARRIS, ABRAM L. *Economics and Social Reform.* New York, 1958.

HASKINS, GEORGE LEE. *Law and Authority in Early Massachusetts.* New York, 1960.

HOMER, SIDNEY. *A History of Interest Rates: 2000 B.C. to the Present.* New Brunswick, New Jersey, 1963.

JORDAN, WILBUR K. *Philanthropy in England: 1480-1660; A Study of the Changing Pattern of English Social Aspirations.* London, 1959.

KATZ, JACOB. *Exclusiveness and Tolerance: Jewish-Gentile Relations in Medieval and Modern Times.* New York, 1961.

LETWIN, WILLIAM. *The Origins of Scientific Economics: English Economic Thought, 1660-1776.* London, 1963.

LOTTIN, DOM. ODON. *Psychologie et morale au XIIe et XIIIe siècles.* 6 vols., Gembloux and Louvain, 1942-1960.

McCLELLAND, DAVID C. *The Achieving Society*. Princeton, 1961.

MICHAUD-QUANTIN, PIERRE. *Sommes de casuistique et manuels de confession au moyen-âge (XII-XVI siècles)*. Montreal, 1962. (*Analecta medievalia namurcensia*, XIII.)

MILLER, WILLIAM, ed. *Men in Business: Essays on the History of Entrepreneurship*. Cambridge, 1952. For the present context, see, especially, Editor's Introduction and essays by D. Landes, H. Aitken, R. K. Lamb, R. R. Wohl, and A. D. Chandler, Jr.

MOREAU, E. DE, PIERRE JOURDA and PIERRE JANELLE. *La Crise réligieuse du XVIe siècle*. Paris, 1950. (*H. Eg.*, XVI.)

MOSSE, GEORGE L. *The Holy Pretence*. Oxford, 1957.

MOUSNIER, R. *Les XVIe et XVIIe siècles: Les progrès de la civilisation européene et le declin de l'Orient (1492-1711)*. Paris, 1954.

ONG, WALTER J., S. J. "Ramist Method and the Commercial Mind." *Studies in the Renaissance,* VIII (1961), 155-72.

OWEN, DAVID E. *English Philanthropy, 1660-1960*. Cambridge, 1964.

STELZENBERGER, JOHANNES. *Syneidesis, Conscientia, Gewissen*. Paderborn, 1963.

STONE, LAWRENCE. Introduction to R. H. Tawney's *The Agrarian Problem in the Sixteenth Century*, pp. vii-xxii. New York, 1967.

TAYLOR, O. H. *Economics and Liberalism*. Cambridge, 1955.

NEW ACKNOWLEDGMENTS

I BEGIN these lines of the New Acknowledgments with a report I had promised in the Prologue.

As I hint there, the appearance of the first edition of *The Idea of Usury* was a source of surprise to some of my friends and sponsors in the circles of American medievalists. This sense of puzzlement found its way into a few of the amiable reviews which fellow historians wrote of this work in specialized journals here and abroad. The reviewers had been expecting that my first published book would be the summing-up of my studies in the restitution of usury and ill-gotten gains in the Middle Ages and Renaissance, offering the detailed evidence of the issues discussed in my essay on "The Usurer and the Merchant-Prince." Except for a specialized paper on the fascinating case of "Blancardo (The Jew?) of Genoa . . . ," which appeared in the *Studi* in honor of the revered historian of Venice, Gino Luzzatto, I have been slow to publish other specialized papers setting forth my findings on restitution. I have offered part of an explanation for this in my Prologue and New Postscript.

The course of the present year should see the appearance of additional publications broaching themes which were at the center of my graduate research. The New References lists two such projects. The last-mentioned paper in section 11 constitutes an extended discussion, benefiting from the hindsight of later reflection, of a whole series of misunderstandings which have continued to confuse students of the economic life and spirit of the men of the Middle Ages, Renaissance, and Reformation since the beginning of the present century. I have subtitled it "A Vote *for* Max Weber" to suggest the ambience within which the long statement speaks most significantly.

I can only hope that the present edition and these newer studies will help to satisfy the entirely legitimate expectations of colleagues who have been patiently waiting to see more

results of my research into the theories and practices of usury
and restitution in the Middle Ages and early modern era.

On this same score, this seems the appropriate time to clear
up a confusion about this book which has gained some credence
in the absence of the explanation which now follows. Across
the world many scholars and librarians have mistakenly supposed that *The Idea of Usury* was my doctoral dissertation.
Actually, it was not. The story, as it was unofficially reported
to me and as I now recall it, runs as follows: At the instance
of the Graduate Dean and the Dissertation Committee, the
Graduate Faculty of Columbia University agreed to accept
the first edition of this book in lieu of the approved dissertation on Restitution (see above, p. 12) as meeting the printing
requirement which had applied five years earlier at the time
of my successful defense. I am happy to have this chance to
express thanks for the understanding and prudence shown in
this connection by Dean John A. Krout, Professor Joseph
Dorfman, and other friendly spirits of the Columbia Faculty
involved in confirming the decision.

I conclude the theme of the initial reception of this edition
of the book on a few further notes of joyful remembrance:

The most unforgettable—because the least expected—
reward I received on the publication of this book was the great
generosity shown to my book and myself by readers, correspondents, and reviewers who had little or no previous
knowledge of my specialized research. I could not have hoped
for more warmhearted welcomes than those extended by a
number of distinguished authors—poets, humanists, social
scientists—renowned everywhere for their candor and insight.
I owe deep debts of gratitude to W. H. Auden and David
Daube; Reinhard Bendix and Talcott Parsons; the late Garrett Mattingly and Karl Polanyi; and to some others I do not
now mention. In all the years which have passed since I began
to dream of the achievement of this new edition of my book
I have again and again been buoyed up by the memory of their
cordial greetings.

I allow myself a few remarks about the singular inspiration I have derived from the work of Professor Parsons. Every time I have turned to his masterly *The Structure of Social Action* to check a point on Weber, I have come away from his pages with the awareness that I had a long way yet to go before I would know all the reasons for the odd ways in which I have continued to gravitate in Weber's sphere : first retracing Weber's steps and then, before the journey's end, stopping to make my own detours and project my own maps of the terrain.

I must avow that Professor Parsons' example gave me added warrant to persist in my efforts to cross the disciplinary barriers which separated the fields of history, theoretical sociology, dynamic and cognitive psychology, and the philosophy of science. If I allow myself to range freely here across the boundaries of the humanities and the social sciences, it is because I find myself being ever more strongly drawn to take a part in the forging of a comparative depth-historical sociology of sociocultural process in the spirit of Weber, Maine, Durkheim, and Parsons himself. Only I am hopeful of extending these perspectives so as to give due stress to the distinctive senses of cultural existence, experience, and expression exemplified my our most accomplished historians and psychologists of culture, whose pages have continued to sustain me through the passing years.

If I have not followed Professor Parsons into every one of his turnings, the explanation is partly that I needed time to learn to breathe easily in the atmosphere in which he moved so readily; partly that I have continued to be haunted by the spirits of the great historian mentors on whom I was nurtured.

In the last several years, indeed, my obligations to Professor Parsons have been growing rather than declining. The heritage he has happily been handing on to his students is proving a fresh source of pleasure and profit to me. I am always especially moved when I find an echo of my own interest in the work of the younger men who have variously been influenced by both Professor Parsons and the now retired Professor

Emeritus of the Harvard Divinity School, James Luther Adams, who is about to begin new service as Distinguished Professor of Social Ethics at the Andover Newton Theological School in Newton Center.

Once again, as in the last hours of the preparation of the first edition, I feel impelled to call the names of associates and friends who have afforded me aid, counsel, and spiritual sustenance in recent years:

First I would mention four "old regulars" of the Columbia University Faculty Seminar on the Renaissance: John Herman Randall, Paul Kristeller, Edward Rosen, and Charles Trinkaus. They and other newer members of the Columbia University Seminars have served as a continuing reminder that the life of learning is a demanding pilgrimage no less than a high adventure. My commitment to both the pilgrimage and the adventure has recently had to be renewed, regrettably, by too infrequent contacts with the Seminars and Seminarians.

In the same spirit I would mention four friends who have never faltered in their faith in me even when I may have seemed to them to have strayed from the true way: Saul Bellow, Paul Goodman, Meyer and Diana Liben have again and again proved to me that the one direction in which to fare is—*forward*.

Behind every endeavor such as this one, one must always expect to find a lucky arrangement of a domestic economy. My secretaries—Mrs. Rose Ripel, Mrs. Elsie Winkler, and Mrs. Lea Rissner—rendered services beyond the ordinary in an exemplary spirit. I must also thank individual members of their families for their patience and "back-up" support. During the course of the preparation of this edition, Donald Nielsen passed from the role of eager student to that of trusted aide. And how shall I speak of my wife's contribution? The memorable words used by the abbé Sièyes when asked to sum up his own contribution to the French Revolution tell only part of the story: My wife "survived." In truth, she did more than that.

An author in her own right, she benefited from my professorial "absences of mind" to publish a book of her own!

My debts to members of the publishing profession must be mentioned now. Three men deserve special notice for the patience they have shown through many trials and delays: Melvin L. Arnold and Hugh Van Dusen of Harper & Row, and Morris Philipson, director of the distinguished Press under whose imprint this augmented edition now appears. I truly hope that these associates of many years will be able to derive a portion of the pleasure from the reading of this new edition that I found in the preparation of it. I also thank the members of the Press staff for the tact they exercised in the execution of their intricate tasks.

I leave for last the names of two too soon departed old friends who were mentioned in my earlier statement of acknowledgments: Solomon F. Bloom, formerly of Brooklyn College, and Henry A. Finch, latterly professor of philosophy at the State University of Pennsylvania. I can scarcely recall Henry Finch's name without being reminded vividly of our first meeting in the middle 1940's on the campus of the College of the University of Chicago, to which we had just come as eager new assistant professors to take part in a great educational experiment which has now become legend. We had come to teach, but we stayed to learn.

The new perspectives I was to encounter at the University of Chicago and later at the University of Minnesota understandably play a much larger part in the enlarged edition than they did in the original. Indeed, it has apparently taken me two decades to integrate my experiences in the East Coast and the cultural environments of the Middle West. I can only hope that sympathetic readers will judge that I have here succeeded in achieving a tolerable fusion of my identities as historian, sociologist, and "social scientist."

In these perplexing times, everyone has a charge to state his faith plainly. In this spirit I allow myself to extend the dedication given on the reverse of the title page. Since so much doubt has lately been cast on the scholarly work which goes on at universities, I tender these pages anew to the great institutions which have offered me opportunities to serve; the great scholars who inspired me to become a lifelong member of the community of learners; and to the honor roll of incredulous students who demanded that I go to the roots of questions by which, thanks in part to their insistence, I had become possessed.

I permit myself a last word on some unspecified sources of the present work. In some of the pages added in this edition, I have allowed myself to draw freely on essays of mine which have recently been issued or are on point of being issued in various scholarly reviews here and abroad.

The Graduate Faculty   BENJAMIN NELSON
New School for Social Research
November 11, 1968

INDEXES

This Index falls into three parts:
Names, Selected Subjects, Scriptural Passages

The present Index of Selected Subjects replaces the copious Index of Subjects which appeared in the original printing. Our decision to undertake a simplified consolidated arrangement of the topical entries was partly prompted by the reports of scholarly colleagues that they had found the annotated Table of Contents a substantial aid in tracing the locations of essential names and subjects. Materials newly added in this enlarged edition are represented in the following alphabets at appropriate points.

INDEX OF NAMES

[287]

INDEX OF SCRIPTURAL PASSAGES